THE COMPLETE ENCYCLOPEDIA OF

FOUR-WHEEL DRIVE VEHICLES

THE COMPLETE ENCYCLOPEDIA OF

FOUR-WHEEL DRIVE VEHICLES

JIŘÍ FIALA

REBO
PUBLISHERS

© 2004 Rebo International b.v., Lisse, The Netherlands

This 2nd edition reprinted in 2006.

Text and photographs: Jiří Fiala
Photograph on p. 300: Petr Zajíček, RNDr.
Translation: Lea Hamrlíková
Graphic design: Granit, Prague, The Czech Republic
Editing and production: Granit, Prague, The Czech Republic
Typesetting: Artedit, Prague, The Czech Republic
Cover design: Minkowsky Graphics, Enkhuizen, The Netherlands
Reproduction of photographs: Artedit, Prague, The Czech Republic
Proofreading: Eva Munk, Emily Sands

ISBN 90 366 1698 0

Table of Contents

Foreword

The book you are holding is an overview, the first of its kind, of civilian off-road vehicles, SUV's, beach vehicles, as well as light-duty work and utility vehicles made in Europe (including branches) and Asia following WWII, vehicles that generally can be operated by driver license holders for passenger vehicles.

Writing a book about four wheel drive civilian vehicles produced mainly on the European market means, in some cases, going back to the beginning or even the time before the beginning of WWII. Many projects were instigated by the military. Directly or indirectly, the armed forces left their mark on most European and Asian cars from the 1950s through the 1980s. The size of this book makes it impossible to include American vehicles. The North American market and concept of 4WD/off-road vehicles is completely different. The same goes for clones of American and Japanese makes of cars produced in America, Australia, Japan (for the home market), Africa and the Far East, although the opportunity to become familiar with these attractive cars was hard to resist. On the other hand, classic off-road vehicles described here are complemented by vehicles used for off-road driving, entertainment and work—namely beach vehicles, pick-up trucks and light-duty utility vehi-

cles, for they are designed to be driven specifically over uneven off-road terrain, or at least roads with occasionally reduced capacity, such as forest paths, fields, beaches, harsh climate areas, or bumpy crooked rugged streets in the inner cities. A whole separate category contains floating cars. Nevertheless, it is still true that a skillful driver is worth more than a heap of wondrous technological contrivances.

History

In the 1960s, four wheel drive vehicles (mainly military) aroused the curiosity of mining, prospector and construction companies, foresters and farmers. Soon after that, the first individual motorists expressed their interest. As this trend intensified, off-road vehicles designed exclusively for work use became more comfortable, easier to control, and began to feature basic equipment and a softer suspension system. The "forefather" for most of them (including the Toyota Land Cruiser, the GAZ and the Land Rover—the other three pinnacles of the world's off-road icons) was the American Jeep. The young generation of the 1970s took a fancy to the California-born buggies—open cars on the VW beetle platform—and later also small off-road vehicles (Daihatsu and Suzuki), designed for driving over rough terrain and for road trips taken by young people for fun, rather than for any ma-

Left: the ARO 244 LUX (2003) in the forefront
Left: the ARO M 461 (1968) in the background

The Peugeot Hoggar—a study from 2003

The Rickman Co. (1987–92) produced car kits of the Ranger based on the Ford Escort Mk I and II

jor working purposes. An alternative to off-road vehicles, mainly around the Mediterranean, were light, simple, undemanding and open beach vehicles featuring an emergency canvas roof and usually a plastic 2- or 4-seat convertible or a pick-up-type body. Most of them were based on compact Citroëns or Renaults. They were produced both by the car factories themselves and by bodywork specialists (mainly in Italy, on a Fiat chassis). Large sales centers in the 1960s through 1980s were located in Italy, Greece, Monte Carlo, Marseille, Nice, Lyon, Paris and Barcelona. The

Iberian Peninsula—a region with less advanced infrastructure—as well as mountainous areas in the Pyrenees, Alps and Scandinavia, have possessed wonderful conditions for off-road vehicles. Apart from people who buy them for purely practical reasons, they increasingly attract buyers who simply consider them a safer alternative to road vehicles, pseudo-romantics and fashion freaks. Often, the greatest adventure such owners expose their "pets" to is driving down a dirt road on the way to a recreational facility. A growing number of people long to escape from the om-

The Czech ARO 328 MT expedition vehicle (the Maxi Taxi or the Mountain Taxi)—2003, for use around alpine chalets

nipresent pressure of their social, working and information environments, created by modern civilization. They hope that their off-road vehicles will give them a sense of freedom, adventure and independence. Potential buyers come with requirements for comfort, equipment, safety, and driving and handling properties comparable to those of road cars. These requirements have, among other things, necessitated the development and installation of a large number of electronically controlled systems. The cars have thus become complex and often cannot be repaired without a well-equipped repair service of the particular car make. Long gone are the times when a piece of lash wire or a local blacksmith were all you needed to fix your "ride" if it broke down in the wild.

Off-road vehicles, usually with canvas roofs, later gave way to 4WD station wagons that protected their users from bad weather. First, full-value SUV's (Sport Utility Vehicles) were imported from the U.S.A., followed by middle-class SUV's—off-road station wagons with sporty styling. The latest fashion trend that has also found its way to Europe is represented by 2-d or 4-d LUV pick-up trucks (Light Utility Vehicles), designed to transport various sports equipment such as mountain bikes, surfboards or ski, as well as the most luxurious SUV's including the Range Rover, Porsche,

VW, Audi, BMW, Mercedes and Lexus. The construction of the Maserati Buran and the smaller Alfa Romeo Kamal is under way. Kit cars, such as the Rickman Ranger or the amphibious S2 Dutton Mariner, are also available. Possible future trends are suggested by various prototypes, such as the Italdesign Colon expedition vehicle, the Fioravanti YAK, the Coggiola (based on the Hummer H1) or the Peugeot Hoggar. The 4WD vehicle has even ventured off of the planet Earth. In October 1969, under a contract from NASA, Boeing constructed 10 examples of the LRV (Lunar Roving Vehicle, nicknamed Lunar Rover). The resulting vehicle had the following parameters: wheelbase—90 in, length—122 in, height—82.74 in, curb weight—462 lbs, payload—540 lbs including two astronauts. The LRV, transported in a folded form, was made up of a platform carrying wheels with tires constructed of woven piano wire reinforced with titanium chevrons. Each wheel was powered by an electric engine with a 0.18 kW power input. The axles could be steered. The astronauts sat on seats and drove the Rover by means of a hand controller. Three LRVs made it to the Moon in three consecutive Apollo modules (1971 and 1972). The astronauts handled the first one with great care, but they let loose with the other two. Each LRV cost 3.8 million USD.

Dutton distributed the Portuguese-made Moke California, produced kits of the Sierra Estate 3-d station wagon (4x2, based on the Escort), and the amphibious Mariner. The photo shows the S2 model (1998, based on the Ford Fiesta Mk 3)

The potential of off-road vehicles on Earth has been proved by expeditions to remote areas, as well as the ever more popular long-distance races in rough terrain such as the raid rally or the Baja rally, the best-known of them being the annual Paris-Dakar Rally (the name varies every year depending on the origin and destination cities), hereafter "Dakar."

Mechanics

One of the most crucial characteristics is the four-wheel drive (4WD, 4x4), also known as all-wheel drive (AWD), a feature which distinguishes these vehicles from those with a classic drive layout—namely those with an engine in the front and rear-wheel drive (4x2), or the latest type with an

The Coggiola Studio presented a study of an SUV, based on the Hummer H1, in Geneva in 2001

engine in the front and front-wheel drive (2x4). The origin of AWD goes as far back as 1904 to the Spyker! Rough terrain off-road vehicles have the engine (usually longitudinally mounted) in the front, permanent 4WD with or without inter-axle differential, which may be further equipped with a differential lock that is activated at a standstill, or a limited slip differential. A more common alternative is permanent RWD (rear-wheel drive) with optional FWD (front-wheel drive). This is now usually activated when the vehicle is in motion, before reaching a speed of 50 mph. The transmis-

A little Czech adventure: the Mitsubishi Pajero, sunken "belly-deep" (1997), and a little tractor that has come to the rescue

sions in genuine off-road vehicles feature a manual gear-reduction transmission for driving slowly off road, when performance is required even at a very low speed. The reduction regime is designed to be activated by the driver at a standstill. Many cars also have differential locks on both the front and the rear axle. Freewheel hubs on the unpowered wheels (controlled manually or automatically) or a central freewheel are installed to disconnect the power or the wheel hubs from the wheel shafts and the differential, thereby reducing the number of rotating parts—and thus also the wear, noise and gas mileage. Many electronically controlled systems are described below, in the individual sub-sections.

Off-road vehicles are characterized by a robust ladder chassis, onto which the body was until recently bolted. The axles were usually rigid with leaf springs or, in exceptional cases (and also later), with a torsion-bar or a coil-spring suspension. The SUV station wagons usually have a spacious and high, comfortable and well-equipped body. They are designed for active pastimes and will perform well only in a less rugged terrain. The engine is in the front, sometimes mounted transversally and usually with FWD and the option to add RWD. This used to be the driver's decision, but some recently produced vehicles come with an automatic activation of the rear axle. The function of the inter-axle differential lock tends to be replaced (although not fully) by a viscous coupling. The transmission may be automatic. Electronic features are fully employed, turning the once me-

chanic systems into electro-mechanic, electro-hydraulic and hydraulic ones. Some components of off-road vehicles were taken from passenger cars. The body is usually self-supporting, the axles—at least the front one—tend to be fitted independently, with coil-spring suspension or torsion-bar suspension systems. The latest hit of the most luxurious SUVs consists of an aluminum underbody, an air suspension technology and an adjustable ground clearance. A vehicle's performance in the off-road depends on the quality of its tires.

The 4x4 types of passenger cars and station wagons are based on their road "siblings." The engine is mounted transversely in the front and it delivers power to the front wheels. The rear-axle wheels are usually engaged automatically without the driver's input. The wheels tend to be suspended independently; the bodies are self-supporting, made of steel, and feature above-average ground clearance. The vehicles aspire to nothing more than providing a safer ride on rain-swept or snow-covered mountain roads and gravel paths.

4x4 pick-up trucks are mechanically identical to the off-road vehicles, or they feature a simplified 4x2 drive layout. Many light pick-up trucks are derived directly from road cars with 4x2 or 2x4 drive.

Abbreviations and explanatory notes

The vehicles in this book are described in a standardized manner using uniform criteria, so as to allow (where possible) for an easy comparison between all the models. Due to space constraints, I have made use of numerous abbreviations. For easier time orientation, I specify the cities in which the specific motor shows were held at which the cars made their debut. An advantage is that the shows tend to be held at the same time every year—Los Angeles, Detroit, Brussels (January), Geneva (March), Turin (April), Leipzig (April), Brno (CR, The Brno International Trade Fair, September; since 1991 known as Brno Motor Show, June), Moscow (summer), Frankfurt (IAA-International Motor Show, September), Paris (Mondial), London and Birmingham (The National Exhibition Centre, October), Tokyo (November). The horse power is listed according to "DIN" regulations, or—where indicated—according to "SAE" regulations (England, the U.S.A.), "JIS" regulations (Japan), or "ECE" regulations (the EU). Revolutions per minute are indicated by "@". "D" stands for a diesel engine, "TD" for a turbo-diesel engine. If a transmission has a direct manual shift, it is described simply as a "transmission." The telescopic shock absorbers are normally not mentioned. The "d" abbreviation stands for the number of doors. It won't come as a surprise that designers of Anglo-Saxon and some other makes do not use the metric system. The length of the wheelbase given in inches—e.g., 88"—has in some cases been used in the name of a particular model. In an effort to provide the greatest possible amount of information, some simplifications were used that may have caused inaccuracies. Accurate information on many marginally interesting vehicles can be obtained only with great difficulty.

Silent Santana vehicles at the end of their journey, Spain 1999

An overview of makes

A.C.L. / Teilhol (France)

The Teilhol Auto Works was active between 1970 and 1993, during which time it underwent five reorganizations. The sixth shake-up proved fatal but other small French companies took over the production of the TXA micro-vehicles. In the 1980s, the company took up an extensive production program involving recreational, utility and pick-up-truck reconstructions of the Citroën C 15 (2x4). In 1989, the company introduced the Theva—a beach fiberglass hard-top pick-up truck with Citroën AX (2x4) mechanics. The capacity of the assembly plant in the 1980s was 10,000 units per year but reality fell short of expectations.

Left: the Mitsubishi Pajero— winner of the 2002 Dakar Rallye

The Teilhol Tangara, 1989

The Renault R6 Rodéo, Annecy, France 2003

Renault Rodéo ❷ ❹

Possibly in the first year of its existence, the A.C.L. (Atelier de Construction de la Loire) produced for Renault the Rodéo beach vehicles, some of which were bought by the French army. The last specimens of the Rodéo were manufactured sometime in 1986–1988. The number of units of the Renault Rodéo, R4 Pick-up, Rodéo 6 and (since 1982) Rodéo 5 exceeded 50,000, with an output of over 30 units per day.

Teihol Tangara, Tangara 1100 ❹

In 1987, Teilhol came up with a successor to the Citroën Méhari. The Teilhol Tangara was equipped with a Citroën 2CV platform (2x4) or, at a premium, 4x4 drive made by Voisin. The popularity of this model is shown by the number—800—of units produced. It was powered by a Citroën 602cc (29hp @ 5750, 71 mph) 2-V engine or a CNG power unit, and had a four-speed transmission. Its two-seat fiberglass body was protected by robust plastic bumpers and side skirt. The fiberglass roof part between the windshield frame and the targa arch was detachable and could be stored under the hood. A model with a canvas tilt on a light structure, a fiberglass hard-top with large side windows, and a pick-up truck were also available. The dimensions: weight— 2,932 lbs, payload—1,301 lbs (including the crew), length—137.9 in, width—60.7 in, ground clearance—7.9 in. The 4x4 version was able to negotiate a 70% slope, a 40% side tilt and had a 40° overhang angle. The Geneva motor show featured a 2-/4-seat Tangara 1100, with a Citroën AX 11 TRS 1124cc (55hp, 99 mph) 4-V engine, a five-speed transmission, and a payload of 893 lbs.

ACM
(Italy)

ACM

Ali Ciemme S.p.A. was an importer of AROs. Between November 1988 and March 1991, it assembled the ARO 10 with a D engine, which was followed by a short-lived TD. Investing in new assembly halls was intended to eliminate the ARO's poor quality and an engine that did not pass regulations. But, the miserable reputation of the original prevailed and the project ended in a debacle. In Turin in 1991, a beach prototype named Scorpion was presented, featuring top-hinged "wing" doors, an elegantly curved bodywork and an ARO 10 chassis. ACM also sold the ARO Ischa (=ARO 10).

ACM Enduro x4 ❷

The color of the grille of the ACM Enduro x4 matched the color of its body. The model featured matt black plastic fender flares and many more improvements, some more obvious than others. This model was derived from the ARO 10.4 (3-d station wagon) or the ARO 10.1 (2-d soft top) with a 4-cylinder VW diesel 1595cc (75 hp @ 5,000) engine. It had a 4- or 5-speed transmission with a reduction gear. Another version was also powered by a D VW engine, but with different parameters—1588cc (53hp @ 4,800)—and a 4-speed transmission. The last innovation, introduced in March 1991, was a TD VW 1.6–1 (69 hp @ 4,500) engine. All the other characteristics correspond to those of the ARO.

The ACM Enduro x4, 1990

The AIL L-240 Storm, 2000

AIL
(Israel)

AIL Storm ❷

Since 1966, the Israeli "Automotive Industries Limited" company based in Nazareth produced 2-d, 4-seat, 4x4, convertible or soft-top off-roaders. They resembled Land Rovers, but with Jeep components. They were powered by a 4.0-L (182hp) engine. A total of 1,250 units were produced in 2000; most were bought up by the Israeli army, and some were exported to Africa and Central America. In 2002, a new model was made, bearing the name of Storm. It was conceptually identical but it resembled (both in name and appearance) the Wrangler Jeep. This model is available either as a 4x2 or a 4x4. The installation of engines made by various producers has been advertised, an example being the 2.5-L (107hp @ 4,000, 81 mph) engine. The Storm has a 5-speed transmission, a 163.5-in wheelbase, a 66-in width, and a 75.6-in height.

The AIL M-240 Storm

The AIL Storm-Jeep, 2003

Aixam-Mega
(France)

Aixam of Aix Lex Bains in Savoy rose from the ashes of Arola in 1983, taking over Arola's typically French Aixam micro-vehicles. Their biggest European producer presented the Mega Club and Ranch versions for recreational use in Paris in 1992.

Mega Club / Ranch ❹

Its front wheels were powered by a gasoline 4-V OHC engine, either 1124cc (60hp), 1361cc (75hp), or—since 1996—also a D 1527cc (58hp) engine. The vehicles were also available in a 4WD version, featuring 1.4L and D engines. The model has a 5-speed transmission, including a "slower first gear" for the 4x4 version. An option of adding RWD is available. The front wheels are suspended independently on McPherson struts and the rear suspension is also independent, with trailing arms and transversal torsion bars. The Citroën AX platform serves as a base. A modular-design body made of crash-resistant, heat-shaped plastic is available as a 4-seat beach convertible, a travel van or a utility van, as well as a station wagon (pick-up) with a removable roof. Its models include the Club (a 4-passenger tourer) and the Ranch (a 2-passenger utility version). The 4x4 (2x4) version has the following characteristics: wheelbase—91 (90) in, length—138 in, width—64 in, height—59 (59) in, ground clearance—7.5 (5.5) in, curb weight—between 1,797 and 2,028 lbs, payload—between 860 and 959 lbs, top speed—86 (90) mph, overhang angles—32° /46°. The sales of the Mega Club reached a total of 1,000 in 1993. The Mega specials with supercharged 4V 2.0-L Ford Cosworth engines and all-wheel steering, driven by star-drivers such as

Bernard Darniche or Paul Belmondo, were victorious in many events of the polar Andros Tropheé. A prototype of the Mega Concept (2x4), which was intended to replace them, was introduced in Paris in 1998. The vehicle featured a 94-in wheelbase. Its plastic body was again designed as a multi-functional module including a pick-up truck, a convertible and a station wagon. Power was supplied by a PSA 1360cc (75hp, 104 mph) gasoline engine. An LPG power unit was also advertised by the producer.

The Mega Ranch, 1995

Mega Track ➍

The giant luxury four wheel drive "supersport" 4-seat Mega Track made its debut in Paris in 1992, with the following features: a V12 Mercedes 5987cc (394hp @ 5200) engine mounted in front of the rear axle, permanent AWD, with a 34:66 front / rear axle power ratio, a center planetary differential with a viscous brake and a 5-speed transmission. The coupe version of the Mega Track was not able to accelerate beyond 155.3 mph because of an electronic speed limiter. The frame consists of steel sections and pipes and bears a Kevlar body. The wheels, featuring coil springs and stabilizers, are suspended independently. Dimensions: length—200 in, width—88.6 in, height—55.1 in, ground clearance—8.7 in, curb weight—5,027 lbs. For driving on rugged terrain, the ground clearance can be increased by 3.9 in by means of suspension-optimizing hydraulics. Growing pains in transmitting the enormous power hindered mass production, although it was possible to order the vehicle individually.

The Mega Concept, 1998

Alfa Romeo (Italy)

The first part of the company's logo, A.L.F.A., is short for "Anonima Lombarda Fabbrica Automobili"—a firm founded in 1910. When it fell into his hands in 1933, engineer Nicola Romeo "provided" the second part of the name. Cars and engines produced by this company won a great deal of renown for their performance both on the road and on the racetrack. In 1933, Alfa Romeo was bought by IRI (Instituto Riconstruzione Industriale, a state organization), which, however, let the company maintain its autonomy. In November 1986, Fiat bought Alfa Romeo from IRI (from the state, that is). Alfa Romeo also produced aircraft engines, buses and utility vehicles—such as the franchised French "Saviem A15" through "A40" after WWII, while simultaneously producing the F 12 series of vans with gasoline engines (60hp). The AR8, F8 and F12 minivan, microbus and pick-up series were gradually improved and standardized with Fiats. The AR8 4x4 with D or gasoline Fiat en-

The Alfa Romeo 1900 M in Egypt

The Alfa Romeo Matta

The Alfa Romeo Matta

The Alfa Romeo 1900 M station wagon

gines were presented in Turin in 1989. In 1997, Bertone came up with a prototype of the off-road Alfa Romeo Sportut with a sporty styling. Rumor has it that the company plans to launch its own SUV by the end of 2004.

Alfa Romeo 1900 M – "Matta" ❷

In 1950, the factory got a contract from the ministry of defense to develop a prototype of the 1900 R "La Folle," following the ministry's specifications. In 1952-54, it produced a light-duty off-road vehicle Alfa Romeo 1900 M, Tipo 51 (for the army) and 52 (for the air force). Gradually, the vehicle earned the nickname Matta—Italian for "crazy"—for its incredible ability to climb up steep hills. The ministry wanted to replace the worn-out army and police Jeeps with home-made technology. The code number is reminiscent of the legendary pre-war sedans and coupes, whose spark-igni-

tion 4-V DOHC engine was inherited by the Matta. The 1884cc (65hp @4400, CUNA standard, 65 mph) series engine was complemented by a 1995cc power unit. The vehicle featured drum brakes, a 4-speed transmission and two clutches that were used to engage either the rear or all four wheels. A ladder frame carried a steel "Torpedo"-style, hard- or soft-top body with an emergency cover over the crew and cargo. The front axle featured an independent control-arm suspension with longitudinal torsion bars; the rear axle was rigid with longitudinal leaf springs. In addition to the driver and the front passenger, the vehicle carried up to four more passengers on the backbenches. The army sometimes used the vehicle with a trailer in tow. Specifications: length—143 in, length of the wheelbase—86.7 in, width—62 in, height—71.7 in, curb weight—2,756 lbs, payload—1,433 lbs. A total of 2,050 units of the Matta were produced (2,075 according to some sources), 50 of which got into civilian hands. There were a total of 1,921 units of the A.R.51 and 154 units of the A.R.52. 120 cars had the privilege of serving the Carabinieri troops. Matta expeditions around Northern Africa have enjoyed great popularity.

In Geneva in 2003, Alfa Romeo showcased a study of the SUV Kamal, closely-related to the forthcoming series-model

This Romanian ARO 243 (2001) was used as the basis for the Czech-made ARO 324 XT "transitional model"

ARO
(Romania)

The city of Câmpulung-Muscel had a paper-mill and workshops where the IAR Brasov company manufactured aircraft parts and weapons during the war. In 1953, after WWII had ended, a team of employees embarked on developing the first Romanian motorcycle. In 1966, they established "Uzina Mecanica Muscel," a company also known as MICM. In 1970, the name changed to Intreprinderea Mecanica Muscel (IMM), only to become ARO SA, Câmpulung, in the 1990s. The company has been a specialist in off-road vehicles since the 1960s and gained its initial experience with off-roaders in producing spare parts for GAZs and UAZs. This state-owned company continued to produce cars even in the dire 1990s. In 1999, the total number of cars sold by ARO was only 279, with a steady increase ever since. The company has had a hard time settling the debts inherited from its former COMECON (Council For Mutual Economic Aid) partners. If it manages to secure enough funds, it may develop further and update one of the prototypes of the late 1980s or a combo version of a station wagon/pick-up truck with the working name of ARO 266. In 1999, ARO began to assemble cars in Namibia. In 2003, the company was bought by the South American Crosslander.

The ARO IMS-57

An exquisitely restored ARO 461 from 1968

IMS-57

The first car made on Romanian soil was the "IMS-57." It was based on the Soviet "UAZ 69." Series production was launched in 1957 (hence a part of its name), and some gradually improved Russian parts and Romanian components were used. The chassis was completed in an old military factory in Câmpulung. The functionality of the vehicle was tested on a transport route connecting Câmpulung with Colibasi. Sheet metal body parts were manually shaped on wooden lasts; the bodies including paintwork were made in the Motorcar factory in Pitesti, Romania. The chassis bore a 2-d body with a canvas tilt. The single windshield wiper was hand-operated. A gasoline 4-V 3260cc (50hp @ 2800, 50 mph) engine had a gas mileage of 9.8 mpg. Production ran for two years, during which time 914 cars were made.

M-59 and M-461 ❷

ARO is short for Automobil Romanescu (Romanian Car). The "M-59" (1959) represented a significant step forward in the company's production. The Romanian designers altered the straight frame, fiddled with the chassis, improved the engine and modernized the body. They cut the Bucegi truck 8-V engine (an old franchised 5024cc engine of the Fiat bus)

in half to get a D127 unit with the capacity of 2512cc (56hp, 56 mph). The supply was extended to include a 2-/4-d vehicle and a pick-up truck, each featuring a single electric windshield wiper. The bodies were spray painted and finished in Câmpulung, after the idea of transporting unfinished cars on the open road had been abandoned. Annual output rose from 803 cars in 1959 to 3,222 cars in 1963, which is when production of the M-59s came to an end. They were replaced by the vastly superior M-461. An improved gasoline 4-V 2512cc (70hp, 62 mph) engine achieved a gas mileage of 13.83 mpg at 50 mph. The gasoline power unit served as a model for a L27 diesel engine— 1660cc (68hp @ 3800). The 4-speed transmission had the 3rd and 4th gears synchronized, and all four or only the rear wheels could be engaged. Export of the improved cars began in 1965. China and Columbia bought 2,000 cars. This robust automobile won the 1970 Forest Rally (Belgium), and the 1973 Sons of Beaches (Oregon). A total of 80,233 improved units were produced by 1975, out of which 46,549 went for export, and most of the rest were taken by the Romanian army.

The ARO 324 XT "transitional model" made in Hradec Králové, Czech Republic, featuring a Romanian chassis; Brno 2002

The final version of a new Czech off-roader—the "Projekt XT" 4x4—made by Auto Max with an original chassis, an ARO 324 body and an Andoria E110 Di EURO 4 engine. Production is scheduled for 2005.

ARO 24 ❷

The development of a much more modern 4x4 ARO of purely Romanian provenance was launched in 1966. The ARO 24, presented in 1972, was distinguished by its angular appearance. The driver's and passenger's compartment became safer, more comfortable and spacious. Generation 1 had angular headlights copied from the Dacia; the newer vehicles had round headlights. The engines used were either a licensed gasoline 4-V Renault L25 2495cc engine (83 hp, 75 mph, with a 17 mpg gas mileage), or a 3119cc power unit (68hp, 71 mph) D unit made by Tractorul Brasov, a Romanian tractor company. It turns out that this model with a 1,764-lb payload is great offroad, negotiates a 70% slope and has a 24-in fording depth. Coil springs in the front make the car well maneuverable. The rear axle remained rigid, with coil springs. A reduction gear was another novelty. In 1972, Ford Europe organized a test in which Range Rover came first, followed by ARO, Jeep, Ford Bronco and Land Rover. At first, 2-d, 8-seat (240) and 4-d, 5-seat station wagons (244) were made, serving as models for pick-up trucks in the long (242) and short versions, as well as a 3-d, 8-seat hard-top (243) and a 5-seat, 4-d soft-top (241). The ARO shared some parts with the "TV" minivan made by a Bucharest producer of 4x2 and 4x4 buses. (They had a cab over the engine, modernized in 1969, and a 2,756-lb payload. They were sold in England as "Tudors.") The ARO's wheelbase was 92.6 in / 94.6 in, the short version was 155.6 in long, 69.9 in wide, 73.2 in high, it had 43° /36° overhang angles and a 23.6-in fording depth. In 1978, the ARO 320 pick-up truck was developed. It was as-sembled by a Bucharest-based bus company. The car underwent many modifications. The dictator Ceausescu himself ordered a special customized stretched station wagon version. In some countries, importers spruced up the model by adding Perkins or Indénor Diesel engines. The 1980s brought about some modernization, characterized by two pairs of round-shaped headlights and, for some markets, Peugeot D engines. By 1985, as many as 125,000 units of the ARO 24 were made, out of which 93,000 were exported. Its good price and driving properties made it possible for the car to be exported to many countries including Canada, the U.S.A. and Australia. ARO won the Pharaos Rally, and in 1997–1999 it became the champion of the H-group of the Romanian Carpathian Trophy rally series. The car indirectly penetrated the more sophisticated markets by way of

The ARO 328 TD fire engine, 2001

with a Ford Cosworth and Cross Lander engine. The 320 pick-up truck featured a wheelbase of 126 in, it was 199 in long, 70 in wide, 75 in high, and it had a 10.2-in ground clearance, a 4,189-lb curb weight, a 2,646-lb payload, 41°/35° overhang angles, a 45° side tilt, a 70° slope and a 19.7-in fording depth. The ARO pick-up truck has four doors, five seats and is 1.8 in longer and 165 lb heavier. There are many factory and local variants known to exist. The Czech and Polish importers equip the cars with TD Detroit Diesel 2.5 VM (105 hp) engines or with Polish Andoria 2.5-L (92 hp) engines. The Czech importer—Automax Ltd.— has had to implement over 150 modifications and technological revisions in order to homologate the car and meet customer requirements. (It sells models of the 24 series —Klasik (240), Pickup (242), Standard (243), Sport (244) and a 7-seat Safari (246), as well as Series 32— Rodeo (324), a 324 action pick-up truck and a 5- to 6-seat Maxi model (328) and the 33 model designed for special-purpose vehicle bodies. Its specialty is the 7-d ARO 328 MT station wagon with an extended wheelbase, 3 rows of seats and an elevated roof of the rear body.)

Portaro—a Portuguese-based company—after being assembled by Hisparo in Spain. The reputation of the cars was spoilt by their poor quality, low corrosion-resistance and unsuitable engines. After 1989, the company tried to remedy this deficiency by an mounting Ford, Peugeot, Daewoo and Chrysler 2.5-L engines, which were installed on the spot by the importers to replace their Romanian counterparts. These were accompanied by five-speed transmissions, two-speed gear-reduction transmissions and the 4x2 drive was complemented by an optional front-axle drive. A big French importer negotiated an exception and had a Toyota 2446cc (90hp @ 3500) TD engine mounted directly in the factory. The L25 and L27 engines remained in use for the home market. In the 1990s, the company's production included 3-d cars (243), the Forester station wagon (244), a stretched version of a station wagon (246 and 323), a pick-up truck (320), a chassis with a cab (324), and the luxurious ARO Hunter

ARO 10 ❷

It took five years to develop the ARO 10—a smallish off-roader coined the "Dacia 10" by Romanians, produced by the Arges factory. It was characterized by an angular shape and a 2-d hard or soft top. Its front wheels had an independent suspension with trailing arms and coil springs; the rear axle was rigid, with four longitudinal half-elliptic springs. The ARO 10

A racing modification of the ARO 10.2, 2001

The ARO Spartana (4x2), 1998

shared components with the franchised R 12 (Dacia 1300 sedan), including a 4-V 1.3L unit originally from the R5. The models included: 10.0, 10.1, 10.3 and 10.4. Since 1984, it featured an OHV 1397cc (65hp, 73 mph) engine from the R5 model. The transmission had four speeds. In 1985, the 10.8 pick-up truck with a normal and shortened wheelbase and a double cab were introduced. Round headlights were replaced with double round headlights, which later gave way to rectangular ones. The bumpers underwent a revision and side protective strips were added. From the very start, many cars were exported: within five years, the share of exported cars rose to 90%, to countries such as Italy (ARO Ischia), France (ARO Trappeur), Germany, Greece, Spain (Dacia) and Great Britain (1982–1993, after 1989 also the "Dacia Duster" ver-

sion with a D 1596cc, 57hp @ 4800 engine), and the following special models: the Roadster Plus, the Showman. The exported cars were powered with a D VW or Pegaso engine. In Italy, the vehicle was manufactured under the ACM mark. ARO is currently available with RWD or AWD and an old ex-Renault 1.3- and 1.6-L (73hp) engine or a 1.6-L (105hp) Daewoo engine. The bodywork is one of the following: a 3-/5-d station wagon, a 2-d soft-top pick-up truck and a short pick-up truck. The ARO 10 Spartana is powered by a Renault D 1870cc (TD version, 92hp) engine. The cars have a 5-speed transmission, two-speed reduction, and permanent RWD with optional FWD. The basic specifications (the older version dimensions are in parentheses) are as follows: wheelbase—95 in, length—(149 in) 152 in, width—(63 in) 65 in, height—(69 in) 71 in, ground clearance—(8.9 in) 8.1 in, curb weight—3,175 lbs, payload—904 lbs, slope—60°, side tilt—35°, approach / departure angles—55°/50°, fording depth—15.7 in. A new model known as ARO 10 Super was presented in 1999, featuring a modified shape and an ARO 244 chassis, but large-scale production did not occur. French models of the early 1990s included the Spartana—a 4x2 beach vehicle powered by a Renault Twingo 1239cc (54hp @ 5300) engine, the Stream Gulf—another beach vehicle, the Chasse—a green hard-top for hunters, and another hard-top named Green City. Stretched pick-up / soft-top, double- / single cabs are called Pancho, and there are also the Chasse and the Tolé 3-d station wagons, a 2-d soft-tops known as Baché and Baroudeur. In addition to these models, the company also produces hard-top, ambulance and fire engine versions.

The ARO 10.9 Double Cabine, 2000

Asia Motors
(South Korea)

Asia Motors had an assembly plant in Kwangju, Korea. Since 1976, 28.3 % of the company's stocks have been bought by Kia (part of Kia was later acquired by Mazda), and in 1999 the Hyundai concern became a 51% owner of Asia and Kia, which in practical terms brought about the end of Asia Motors, a make of cars active between 1965–2000. Besides off-road vehicles, this name was borne by vans, trucks and buses.

Asia Rocsta ❷

In 1994, the first Asia Rocsta—a copy of the Jeep—rolled off the assembly line (the name perhaps sounds like "rock star" to a Korean ear), with 4x2 or 4x4 drive. A version with optional FWD was successfully imported to England. The car was in fact a civilian version of the military $^1/_4$ ton derivation of the Jeep CJ-5. Power was provided by 4-V engines—a lightweight, high-performance diesel R2 (MAGMA) 2184cc (72 hp @ 4250, 86 mph), or a 1789cc (85hp @ 5600, 87 mph) Mazda gasoline engine taken from the former 626, whose production finished in 1992. The model featured a 5-speed manual transmission and hand-operated freewheel locks on the front wheel hubs. The rigid axles were equipped with leaf springs and a torsion bar in the front. The 5+1-seat, hard- or soft-top had the following specifications: wheelbase—84 in, length—141 in, width—67 in, height—72 in,

ground clearance—8.1 in, curb weight—2,822–2,932 lbs, payload—up to 1,058 lbs, a 97% slope, and a 46° side tilt. A version featuring a longer wheelbase (165 in) and a height of 73 inches was available in Korea. Besides Italy (Rocsta Telonato/Hard Top), the cars were exported to Germany, Great Britain and other countries. Unfortunately, the model lacked sufficient support from its producer. This high-quality vehicle was an attractive and affordable alternative to a compact off-road vehicle for the young generation. In the early 1990s, Rocsta participated in Dakar. In 1994, a slightly modified version—the Rocsta R2—was launched onto the market. Customized lightweight off-road vehicles named $^1/_4$ t Utility Truck and $^5/_4$ t Shop Van (its heavier and larger sibling) were employed by the Korean army.

Asia Retona ❷

The Retona, made in the spring of 1997, of a similar, only curvier, appearance, was distinguished by a longer wheelbase and a more powerful DOHC 16V (139 hp, 96 mph) gasoline engine, or an optional TD of the same capacity—1998cc. Alternatively, a D 2.2-L was provided, same as in the Rocsta. The Retona was 157 in long, 69 in wide, 72 in high, and it weighed 3,219 lbs. Its production was terminated less than 12 months after its debut. It had to give way to the Kia Retona—a similar but more modern "concert-type" vehicle bearing a name borrowed from the Asia company.

Audi
(Germany)

The Audi Allroad Quattro 4.2, 2002

Audi was established in 1910 by August Horch in Zwickau after he had left his original company of Horch Motorwagenwerke, fed up with the other managers. Audi manufactured quality cars. In 1928, a majority of the company was bought by Jurgen Skafte Rasmussen, a Danish-born producer of motorcycles and DKW lightweight automobiles. The early 1930s saw tough times in Germany, and many auto works were on the brink of bankruptcy. In 1932, Audi, DKW, Horch and Wanderer formed a joint venture that became known as Auto Union. Most assembly plants of the original makes ended up in the Soviet zone and it was not until 1965 that Auto Union GmbH was established in Ingolstadt. The company merged with Audi AG in 1969 as part of the VW group. As far as 4WD was concerned, VW had experience with the off-road DKW Munga and the VW Iltis models. In 1977, Audi performed trials beyond the Arctic Circle. Besides sedans, the technicians had the VW Iltis at their disposal, powered by an Audi 80 engine. On snow-covered tracks, the Iltis surpassed the much more powerful sedans. Development engineer Jorg Bessinger decided to test the 4x4 drive in passenger cars as well. He designed several groups of the Audi 80 with a VW Iltis steering mechanism. Next came a 2-d racing coupe with an Audi 80 platform. It was powered by a supercharged 5V (170 hp) engine taken from the Audi 100. The torque was transmitted from the engine to the rear axle wheels through an integrated differential and a 2-part cardan shaft. The Audi Quattro series coupe with permanent 4x4 drive first appeared in Geneva in 1980, equipped with a turbo 2144cc (200hp @ 5500) engine and an intercooler. In the same year, the Quattro (285 hp) was introduced in the rally, scoring a victory 21 times in the World Cup competitions and winning the World Cup overall in 1982 and 1984. In 1984, it gave

way to the extremely expensive Audi Quattro Sport featuring a 12.5-in-lower wheelbase and a supercharged four-valve engine (up to 500 hp). It only came first in two World Cup competitions. Star drivers including Hannu Mikkola, Stig Blomquist, Michelle Mounton and Röhrl Quattro have been seen at the wheel of Audi. Most of the following Audi series included 4x4 models: Coupe Quattro, 80, 90, 200, A3, A4, A6, A8, S2, S4, S6, S8, RS4, RS6, TT in both the sedan version and the Avant station wagon version, which initially bore the cognomen of Quattro.

Audi Steppenwolf ⑩

In 2000 in Paris, the Steppenwolf made its first appearance. This was not a road vehicle with 4x4 drive but a 3-door coupe designed for driving over extremely rough terrains, as well as for high-speed driving on the freeway. With its 6V, 3.2L (225hp, 143 mph) engine, the vehicle goes from 0 to 62 mph in 8 seconds. An electronically-powered Haldex clutch distributes the power between the front and rear wheels. If the front wheels begin to slip, part of their power is automatically transferred to the rear axle wheels. Additionally, an EDL (electronic differential lock) lends torque to the wheels of one axle and the ESP helps the driver control the vehicle if a critical situation occurs. One of the mo-

The Audi S 4 Avant, 2002

del's special features was the "air" suspension of the wheels, adjustable to 4 levels with a 23.6-in interval, allowing it up to 8.8 in of ground clearance in an uneven terrain. A new powerful electro-hydraulic parking brake employed on the rear wheels' brake discs was also provided. The carbon fiber body comes in two versions—hard-top and soft-top. A prototype of a 4-d, 4+2-seat SUV called the Audi Pikes Peak Quattro made in Detroit in 2003 was inspired by this feat. This model featured an 8V turbo engine from the RS6 (500hp) powering all four wheels, and adjustable shock absorbers.

Audi Allroad Quattro ❸

In Geneva 2000, high expectations were fulfilled when Audi showcased the Allroad Quattro—a dynamic luxury 5-door SUV derived from the A6 Avant—thus setting a high standard. The factory chose time-tested engines—a 6V 2671cc engine (250hp @ 5800, 2x2 OHC, 30v, 2 x turbo, 2 x intercooler, 145 mph, acceleration from 0 to 62 mph in 7.7s), an 8V 4200cc engine (300hp @ 6200, 2x2 OHC, 30v, 149 mph, acceleration from 0 to 62 mph in 7.2s) and, last but not least, a 2496-cc, 6V TD power unit with direct fuel injection (179hp @ 4000, 24v, intercooler, 127 mph, accelera-

tion from 0 to 62 mph within 10.2s). This super powerful Audi has permanent 4WD, a torsen inter-axle self-locking differential and the ESP (Electronic Stability Program), a 6-speed manual transmission, or a 5-speed automatic transmission with the DSP (Dynamic Shift Program). At a premium, the manual transmission can be equipped with a practical "Low Range" reduction. The self-supporting steel body is comfortable and safe. The axles support subframes with independently suspended wheels equipped with a stabilizer and adjustable gas shock absorbers. This allows, depending on the driving speed or the driver's actions, one of the four levels of ground clearance (between 5.6 and 8.2 in). The vehicle carries 5 persons or 1,433 lbs of cargo. It has a 109-in wheelbase; it is 190 in long, 73 in wide, 61 in high, has a curb weight of 3,957 lbs plus, a 15.7-in fording depth, and 27° / 25° overhang angles.

The Audi Steppenwolf, 2000

The Audi Pikes Peak, 2003

Austin
(Great Britain)

When Mr. Herbert Austin, with work experience from Wolseley, founded Austin Motor Co. in 1906, he had no idea of the somersaults the company bearing his name would turn in the years to come. After the war ended, it became part of the Austin-Morris division of the BLMC concern, and later British Leyland, BL Cars and Austin-Rover Group, respectively.

Morris Gutty   ❷

The Morris Gutty 4x4 prototype is considered the ancestor of the artificially terminated life of Austin off-roaders. WWII showed the indispensability of lightweight 4WD vehicles. In 1947, the British administration held a tender for a $^1/_4$ ton army vehicle, known as the FV 1800. The Nuffield Organization, which also embraced both Austin and Morris, tried to meet the requirements with a 1947 prototype of the Morris Gutty. Only one specimen out of a total of two or three has been preserved. Its unattractive open rectangular steel self-supporting body is covered with a canvas roof. The Gutty was powered by a Morris Minor flat-four. The engine drove through a 5-speed transmission and a two-speed auxiliary transmission, and featured independently suspended wheels.

Wolseley Mudlark,
Austin Champ   ❷

The designers of the off-road Austin Champ tried to use their experience with the Gutty and meet the requirements with their FV1800. Its immediate ancestor was the Wolseley Mudlark made in 1948. The model was approved for production and a small group of specimens was born. The Mudlark was tested in 1951 by the American army and almost undoubtedly inspired Ford's American M-151 MUTT off-road vehicle program. The team of designers was even joined by Alec Issigonis, the "Father of the Mini." In 1952, Austin signed a contract to make 15,000 Champs and production was launched immediately. The army gave the $^1/_4$ t vehicle the code name WN1, FV1801. It was characterized by a simple steel body with front door cutouts. A four-

The Austin Gipsy fire engine, 1963

30

The Austin Gipsy featuring the Flexitor rubber suspension

The Austin Gipsy Mk II Soft Top

designed to engage the rear axle drive and also to change the direction of rotation. As a result, the Austin had five gears even for reversing! A propeller shaft transmitted the power to the transmission and the rear differential connected to it. From there, another shaft led to the clutch in the front axle differential. When running, the gears made a lot of noise. As far as power is concerned, the Champ can be compared to the Land Rover. The repair and service costs of this complicated machine were an absolute nightmare. The production of the Champ was terminated before the contract ran out in 1956. By that time, approximately 11,700 units of the model had been produced, only a few of which made it into private hands and were exported to countries such as the Netherlands and the USA. The Champ featured an 84-in-long wheelbase, a 145-in length, a 62-in width, a 73-in height, a curb weight of 3,668 lbs and a payload of 811 lbs.

member crew was protected by a simple canvas tilt. An independent suspension of wheels made use of trailing arms and torsion bars. Power was supplied by an aluminum 4V Rolls-Royce B-40 OHV 2803cc (71hp @ 3750) engine. The engine was encased and sealed, with the induction outlet run out on the roof to enable the vehicle to operate in extreme conditions and water. A number of the vehicles were equipped with Austin A-40 sedan engines. The transmission was connected to a special one-speed transmission that was

The Austin Gipsy, 1963

Austin Gipsy ❷

The Gipsy was built in order to satisfy, alongside the Land Rover, the growing demand of both the military and civilians for lightweight off-road vehicles. The model inherited many of the qualities of its predecessor Champ, but it assumed even more from the LR Series I. Series II was available from 1958, while the Gipsy, featuring a 90" wheelbase, a year later. The two competitors did not differ much in appearance but the Austin's management hoped that the vehicle's more advanced technological concept would boost sales. The Gipsy featured independently suspended wheels with trailing arms equipped with "Flexitor" rubber springs consisting of large-diameter tubes attached to the chassis and torsioned as the trailing arms moved. The differentials were mounted on the bottom of the chassis. The rubber springs gave the vehicle less ground clearance when heavily laden, which could cause a reckless driver to break the differential off when driving over boulders. The vehicle acted unpredictably and therefore the 1960 Gipsy with a 111" wheelbase was fitted with a standard rigid axle with leaf springs. The Flexitor suspension was not available until 1965. Austin engines with a higher torque were used—a gasoline OHV 2196cc (62hp @ 4100) power unit from the A70, and an alternative D 2180cc (55hp @ 3000) engine from the A90. The Gipsy featured a four-speed transmission and a 2-speed auxiliary gear-reduction transmission. Dimensions: wheelbase—90 / 111 in, length—139 / 160 in, width—67 in, height—74 in, curb weight—3,380 lbs (90"). A propensity for the body to corrode quickly blemished the Gipsy's reputation

and as a result only a few examples of the Gipsy have survived to this day. The visual resemblance of the Gipsy with the Land Rover did not help matters. The car was also sold in the civilian sector and exported to countries such as Canada and the USA. This quality vehicle could have been saved by a contract from the army; unfortunately, just as the negotiations were drawing to a close, the year 1968—an unfavorable one in the history of the British industry—put an end to the efforts. Many weak assembly plants were nationalized at that time. Austin ended up being "swallowed up" by Land Rover, which put the Gipsy project on ice. A total of 21,208 units of the Gipsy were produced.

The Austin Mini Moke, St Tropez 2001

Austin / Morris Mini-Moke ❹

In the 1960s, England was seized by the Mini mania. BMC, pampered by the contract for the Citroën 2 CV, which the army had employed in paratrooper operations, and hoping for more army contracts, decided to develop a few new versions. The Mini's low weight enabled it to get virtually anywhere. However, the army soon discovered the flaws of the prototype—its small wheels, low ground clearance and 2x4 drive did not exactly perform miracles in rough terrains. Admittedly, Alec Issigonis came to the rescue in 1962, shortening the Mini's wheelbase to 72 inches, changing the wheel suspension and adjusting the ground clearance, but it was already too late. Incidentally, his work at the drawing board was not completely futile as it gave rise to the Moke (orig. a slang term for a donkey). The assembly plant did not give up hope and Issigonis designed a prototype of the Twin Moke with two engines—one powering the front wheels and the other one powering the rear wheels. Coordination of both units did not prove an easy task and the board of directors turned the project down. The only alternative left was to market the Mini Moke as a leisure-time vehicle. Today, these tiny things can be seen (sometimes "under full canvas") cruising around the Mediterranean. Their doorless, self-supporting steel bodies seated four persons with no trunk. The wheels were suspended independently on rubber cones, with trapezoids in the front and wishbones in the rear. The platform was different from that on the Mini. A BMC A-Series 848cc (34hp @ 5500, 65 mph) engine was mounted transversally in the front, coupled to a 4-speed transmission with unsynchronized first gear. The front wheels were powered. Basic dimensions: wheelbase—80 in, length—120 in, width—52 in, height—56 in, curb weight—1,175 lbs. In the late 1960s, the Moke became a symbol of the British Golden Youth. In 1968, the Longbridge assembly plant was closed down and the machines were transported to Australia and a few years later to Portugal. The Moke, which was resurrected in the early 1980s, continued to be manufactured in Italy, South Africa, Spain and—a copy of it—in Germany (although that model was already quite different). The Portuguese did not terminate the production until 1993. In total, 14,518 Mini Mokes were made in Britain in 1964–68.

Austin Ant ❿

In 1968, Alec Issigonis designed a prototype of the Austin Ant, a pick-up truck the size of a Mini, with a canvas roof covering the cab and the loading space. It had a 1275cc engine mounted in the front and 2x4 drive with optional RWD. However, the manufacturing costs were too high—comparable to those of the larger Land Rover.

The original Austin Champ, Nottingham 2004

Autoland (France)

The Autoland company existed between 1983 and 1985. In 1983, it took over the production of Cournil vehicles. In 1985, the firm was renamed Auverland. It continued to be based in Saint Germain Laval but its headquarters were now located in Boulogne. By 1985, a total of 1,000 heavy-duty rustic vehicles were produced. They found their way into civilian and military hands in France and elsewhere.

Autoland Cournil II ❷

In the 2nd series, the designers did their best to "civilize" the vehicle. Its body retained the typical beveled edges, but the main headlights were moved to the front fenders on both sides of the grille. The body was mounted on a ladder frame with box-type steel crossmembers. Both axles were rigid, with longitudinal leaf springs. The Cournill II was powered by 4V engines: a gasoline Renault (83hp), a D (67.4hp), and a D Peugeot (85hp, maximum speed of 68 mph). According to the information provided by the company, the stretched version had 4x2 or 4x4 drive, whereas the short version only came as a 4x4. The vehicle featured a standard rear differential lock and a four-speed transmission with a cross-country reduction. The company distributed the following versions: a pick-up truck, a Bâché (a convertible with a canvas tilt), and a Tôlé (a hard-top with a polyester glassed-in superstructure). The models differed in the length of their wheelbase — SC 200 (80 in) / SC 250 (100 in). Other characteristics: length — 142 / 167 in, width — 63 in, height — 75 in, ground clearance — 9.1 in, curb weight — 3,153 / 3,682 lbs, payload — 1,984 / 2,138 lbs (3,968 lbs for the heavyweight version). Auverland featured this car only as model SC II.

Autoland Series 220 / 275 ❷

Although derived from a model bearing the confusing name of Cournil (produced by Simi towards the close of the era after selling a franchise of the first model of Cournil), it betrays a relation to the first generation of off-roaders. This feature is further enhanced not only by the slanted front hood and the front wheel fenders, but also the location of the headlights in the front bumper. The 220 / 275 series inherited the basic design features. The numbers in the name are equivalent to the wheelbase length measured in centimeters. Other dimensions: length — 151 / 169 in, width — 75 in, ground clearance — 9.1 in, curb weight — 4,365 / 4,486 lbs, payload — 1,918 / 2,282 lbs, payload of the stretched reinforced version — 3,064 lbs. Also available was a pick-up truck version with a canvas tilt or with a detachable polyester hard-top roof. Power was provided by one of the following Renault engines: a gasoline engine (115 hp), a D engine (70 hp), or a TD engine (90 hp). The model featured a 5-speed transmission and included a reduction transmission and a rear differential lock.

The Autoland Series 220 / 275

The Autoland Series 220 / 275

Autozávod Český Dub (Czech Republic)

The T5D Alena trim of the Land Rover Defender in service with the Czech Army, 2000

Autozávod Český Dub was established in Czechoslovakia in the late 1960s as a service garage for the GAZ-69, UAZ-469 and UAZ-452 military vehicles. In 1992, the company began importing UAZ-469 vehicles, improving their quality and at the same time converting them to meet the local standards. The main aim of this enterprise was to supply the Czech army with transport vehicles. Autozávod tendered for the contract in the late 1990s in partnership with Land Rover, competing with models including Hummer-Tatra, Ross-Honker, Avia-Auverland and Tatra-Sipox-Mahindra. As there was no modern Czech lightweight off-road vehicle available, the participants sought to join forces with a renowned make, offering in turn Czech production capacities and a familiarity with the environment. Autozávod won this demanding competition.

UAZ Český Dub ❷ ❾

Autozávod used various accessories to tweak the UAZs, while also paying attention to the special wishes of its customers. The revisions included: AVM, a steering booster, front disc brakes, a fiberglass hard-top, new seats and upholstering, guard frames and a heater. Besides the original UMZ (2445cc, 71hp @ 4000) Russian version, an Italian D VM (2498cc, 90hp @ 3200) engine was also available. A specialty was the installation of a D Peugeot XD3P (2498cc, 67hp @ 4000) engine, or alternatively a TD VM. The 4-d UAZ 4x4 2.5 Maraton soft-top vehicles were used by UN troops. The UAZ 4x4 2.5 D Tuareg model was distinguished by white accessories, wheels, a canvas tilt and a Peugeot engine. The stretched 2-d UAZ 4x4 2.5 TD featured a VM engine. Later, a UAZ 4x4 Tornado 2.5 TD with a VM engine (2498cc, 114hp @ 4200) was added. None of the model's excellent AWD or RWD driving qualities over rough terrains were affected by the conversion. Both axles remained rigid, with half-elliptic springs. About 150 units were made between 1993 and 1996.

Land Rover Defender (England, Czech Republic) ❾

Seeking to replace the archaic Russian UAZ's, the Czech Ministry of Defense invited bids for a contract to manufacture small four wheel drive vehicles. Autozávod Český Dub won the competition (outmatching the other bidders in 6 out of 7 criteria) and the first specimens—the Defender 90 TDi and 110 TDi—rolled off the company's assembly line in 1995. The decisive factors were the vehicle's quality, reliability and compatibility with NATO vehicles. Autozávod followed the army's specifications in equipping the Defenders, including the front grille. The army took up the first cars in February 1996. The contract obliged Autozávod to supply the first 150 in a ready-to-use state—141 for the Rapid Deployment Brigade and 9 for the Military Police. There was a plan to begin, in the 2nd half of 1996, to assemble the vehicles from both imported and Czech-made components and, based on the army's financial situation, a complete rearmament was scheduled to take place within the following few years. The Czech army is the first army in the former Warsaw pact to use Defenders.

The Autozávod Český Dub UAZ 4x4, 1993

Auverland (Sovamag) (France)

Auverland of Saint Germain Laval has borne its name since August 20, 1984. Before then (in 1983–84/85), it was known as Autoland. For the 20 years that ensued, it became a safe haven for the followers of Bernard Cournil's Cournil off-roader from the turn of the 1950s and 1960s. Cournil featured an 80-or-100-in wheelbase. In 1970, the founder sold a franchise of the car to another company and only the third new model—S.I.M.I., later spelled as Simi—became a success. In 1978, the Cournil franchise was bought by UMM, which certainly did not discredit the brand. The production over recent years, however, hasn't taken anyone's breath away. In 2000, it amounted to 140 units, including the A5 microcar. By 1996, a total of 10,000 Auverlands had been made. At present, Auverland, a specialist in producing four wheel drive and military vehicles with a 1,102-to-5,512-lb payload rating, is part of the Groupe Servanin industrial group. In addition to assembly lines in Saint Germain Laval, the company owns a testing track in Boën.

Auverland SC II ❷

In 1982, the era of the Simi, the 2nd generation of the car—Cournil II—was presented. Autoland had taken it over as Cournil II with models named after their wheelbase length in cm: SC 200 (80 in) and SC 250 (100 in). The original Renault gasoline and Peugeot D engines, as well as the bodyworks, were maintained. In the second half of the 1980s, they were joined by a D 3.6-L (85hp) engine. The production had most likely been terminated before 1990.

Auverland Type A, A2 ❷

At the close of the Simi era, a second—more civilized—model appeared, featuring a softer suspension and several plastic body parts. Its construction was supervised by Engineer Benoit Contreau. Simi gave it the simple name of Cournil, since the model that originally bore the name was no longer produced, anyway. The wheelbase was 87 or

The Auverland A 275, 1986

The Auverland SC II, around 1986

108 in long. The only version available was a 4WD convertible with a canvas tilt. Autoland made some minor visual touch-ups and gave the model the new name of "Series 220 / 275" matching its wheelbase. A 4-speed transmission was replaced by a 5-speed one. The Auverland (87 / 109 in) continued to be produced. This series was also known as the A-Series, or more precisely, A 220 / 275. At that time, the vehicles carried various engines, including atmospheric or TD SOFIM and gasoline Fiat engines. After 1988, the car was renamed A2, but its production was already almost over.

Auverland A3, A3 SL, A4 ❷

The Auverland A3, which debuted in 1988, was an updated version of the then-ending A2 series. Its short and stretched versions, in contrast to their predecessors, had the same wheelbase length (89 in), and their difference in total length was achieved by two different lengths of the rear overhang (26 / 33 in). Other characteristics: width—61 in, height—67 in, ground clearance—9.8 in. The model featured a ladder frame and rigid axles with half-elliptic leaf springs that differed from their older "siblings" only in small details. Initially, the body was a 3-door, 2- or 4-seat steel station wagon. The A3 featured a curb weight of 2,612 / 2,635 lbs and was able to carry a 1,157 / 1,135-lb load of passengers or cargo. It had 50° /45° overhang angles, a 100% slope, a 40° side tilt, a 23-in fording depth, and a top speed of 71 mph. Originally, it was sold with a 4V D Peugeot XUD 91905cc (64hp @ 4600) engine and a 4-speed Peugeot transmission that was later replaced with a 5-speed Peugeot transmission. In both cases, a reduction gear was provided. Gradually, in addition to the stretched version (payload of 1,058 lbs, wheelbase of 89 in and length of 152 in), the company began manufacturing a variant with the payload enhanced to 1,940 lbs and a super-stretched model with a 104-in wheelbase (that later became known as the A4), a length of 171 in and a payload of 1,874 lbs.

In the mid-90s, some minor revisions were made. While maintaining the length of the wheelbase, the front overhang was shortened by 2 inches and the rear one to 41 inches. The weight of the vehicle rose to 2,932 / 2,998 lbs, and the payload to 1,257 / 1,190 lbs. The 2- or 4-seat bodyworks were either of the soft-top or the fiberglass type and featured heightened superstructures. In addition to civilian models, specially built police and firefighter vehicles (and others) were available. Another step forward was represented by a TD version of the 1.9-L (90hp @4000) engine. Later still, more powerful Peugeot D 2.1-L and gasoline 1.6-L engines were installed. All of the cars had permanent AWD but after 1991, a 4x2 version featuring a 2-speed transfer case and optional FWD was introduced. The 4x2 version had a differential with an automatic limited slip differential. Extra accessories were available, including underbody treatment, sway bar, oil cooler, guardrails, and "half-doors."

An updated A3 was showcased in Paris in 1998, in the following versions: Bâché (a canvas-covered soft-top), Hard Top, Pick Up truck, as well as the Pare Brise Panoramique—a beach pick-up truck with a window in the hard-top roof of the cab. This choice was further extended to include a model A4 with the same mechanics but an extended wheelbase. The maximum output of its TD 1.5-L engine (in all versions) was now 92hp, @ 4000. The A4 came in as a 5-seat, 4-d station wagon or a 5-seat minivan and a double cab with an open-type body. In the new millennium, the choice was extended even further, while the mechanics remained the

The Auverland A3, around 1989

same, although the car became faster. The departure angle is 25° for the A3 SL, and 35° for the A4. The A3 series with a wheelbase of 89 inches included: a 2-door, 2/4-seat soft-top (the Canvas Top), the Bâché (length x width x height: 152 x 61 x 67 in, a 3,208-lb curb weight, a 2,326-lb payload), the Hard Top and the Compétition—a lightweight open terrain-trial vehicle. A whole separate category includes the "Police" Hard Top and the "Sécurité Autoroute" model for the police and highway assistance. The A4 series (wheelbase—104 in, length—175 in) came as a 4-d passenger and utility station wagon with a polyester body and a 2,006-lb payload capacity. Its departure angle has been

The Auverland A3—assembled in Prague as "Avia A11 Trend" (chassis # 006 for a 1995 army tender); Třebíč, CR, 2004

decreased to 35°. The A3 SL series (wheelbase—118 in, length—191 in) represents—paradoxically so, considering the name of A3—the longest car (SL= super long). The chassis carries a body with the payload of up to 3,307 lbs and usually comes as a pick-up truck, a 4-d Double Cabine, Tri-Benne (a 3-way dump truck), and serves as a base for special-purpose such as fire engines, rescue squads' vehicles and 4WD ambulances. Since 1990, the company has been competing in trial rallies. Auverland became the French trial champion in 1989–98, the absolute champion of France in 1995, 1997 and 1998, the European champion in 1994 and 1998, and the European champion in the category of prototypes in 1999.

The Auverland A4 utility station wagon, 1998

Auverland "Administration" ❷

The company has recently divided its production into three categories according to the utility purposes of the vehicles: Auverland "Civil" for personal and commercial purposes; Auverland "Administration" for state service purposes, with components or chassis of the Auverland A3, A3 SL; and A4, including a station wagon version, as well as the above-mentioned versions for the police, firefighters, rescue squads and highway assistance.

Auverland "Militaire" ❾

Since 1988, the army vehicles produced by Auverland have borne the name Sovamag, while only the smallest version based on the A3/A3 SL continues to bear the name Auverland. The A3 Baché for the air force and navy looks a lot like the civilian version. The same cannot be said about the lightweight paratrooper A3 V LA for the army and A3 SL VRI transported by planes and helicopters respectively, or the A3 SL Blindé Niveau 3 model with armor-plating. A franchised production of the A3 was carried out in 1993–1996 in the Czech Republic (see Avia), and in 1997 by Holba and co. also in the CR. The model is still made under the name of JPX in Brazil, and—as Magirus—in Hungary since 2002 (with one prototype so far). Most components of the French cars are manufactured in the Czech Republic.

Avia – Aeronautica Industrial (Spain)

Jeep-Avia

In 1923, Jorge Loring Martinez, Eng., founded an aviation assembly plant in Madrid. After the war, it produced three-wheelers, and later vans. The model series including a pick-up truck, a double cab ("camion"), a minivan and a mini-bus was known as Granjero. Later, the selection increased to include trucks and buses bearing the name of Avia. In 1970, Motor Ibérica entered the company, to gain full control of it in 1975. The original production of Avia was maintained under the name Ebro-Avia. The Avia platform trucks and mini-vans can still be seen in use in the Spanish countryside. Avia distributed the off-road Jeep-Viasa SV (bearing the name of Jeep-Avia), featuring a cab-over-engine cab, 4WD and the body of a mini-bus or one of the utility versions (see Willys-Viasa).

The Jeep-Avia Campeador

The Avia-Ebro 3500-Alcocebre, Spain 2002

Avia
(Czech Republic)

This company based in the Prague quarter of Letňany produced airplanes after 1919, quality sports and military weapons between the two world wars, Škoda buses and trucks in 1946-51, and Praga and Tatra trucks after 1961 (including the invincible Praga V3S four wheel drive truck). In 1967, Avia obtained a franchise to manufacture the lightweight Renault-Saviem, and the first Avias were produced in October 1968. Lighter-duty A15 series and heavier-duty A30 series were produced, featuring a payload of 3,307 lbs and 6,614 lbs respectively, and a 3.3-L D engine—72hp (A15) and 80hp (A30). In the mid-1990s, the factory was bought by Daewoo.

The Avia A11 Trend—a short hard-top, around 1994

There were over 20 body versions. The modernization program carried out in 1994 resulted in the production of modified versions: the A21 with a D engine, and the A31 with a TD engine. Besides the standard 4x2, this generation also featured 4x4 drive, assembled by specialized finalists, mainly service personnel and producers of military technology. The production of the 4x4 Avias ended with the production of a short minivan. A total of about 80 vehicles were made. In

The Avia A11 Trend paratrooper vehicle, IDET Brno 1994

1998–2001, a further-updated series of A60 / A80 was scheduled for production, but without a 4x4 alternative. The production of a new model series of Daewoo-Avia 2000 was launched
in 2000, with a plan to introduce to the market an A 4x4 model
after 2003, in affiliation with VOP Přelouč Company.

Avia A11 Trend ❷

In 1995, the Czech Army, whose UAZs had reached a retirement age, called a tender for the contract to manufacture
a lightweight 4WD vehicle. The traditional Czech manufac-

The stretched Avia A11 Trend with an elevated laminated roof superstructure, around 1994

turers leapt at the opportunity, but having no suitable vehicle of their own to offer, they looked for foreign partners. Avia bought a franchise for the A3 / A4 from the French company Auverland. The vehicle's show-room debut took place at the COMA exhibition in Prague, CR in April 1994, and a month later at the 1994 IDET (International Defense Industry Trade Fair) in Brno, CR. The vehicles, featuring an 89-in wheelbase (length: 144 and 152 in) and a 104-in wheelbase (length—171 in), were assembled in Prague. They were powered by a Peugeot XUD 9 D 1.9-L power unit (64hp @ 4600 or 70hp

The 40 Avia A60 / A80

@ 4600), or an optional Peugeot XU52C (94hp @ 6000) gasoline engine. The transmission had 5 speeds and was complemented with a 2-speed Auverland A80 transfer case, giving the option of disconnecting the FWD. The rear axle was equipped with a limited slip differential. In addition to 4WD, a 4x2 version was available. The axles were rigid, with coil springs and hydraulic shock absorbers. The body versions with short, normal or stretched lengths for 2 crew members and a load, or for a 2-to-6 member crew—be it 4WD convertibles, soft- and hard-tops with both normal and elevated roof / canvas tilt, an ambulance, a military paratrooper version with a targa arch, or the A11 Trend Military SL (= super long) special—all corresponded with the original. There were two versions of accessories—"Komfort" and "Standard"—differing in price (up to USD 780). The price (not including VAT) ranged between USD 18,00 and USD 21,100 in 1995. The versions available for purchase included a 4WD passenger version and a truck. After 1993, the cars were assembled in Prague, at first from the French CKD assembly kits, but Czech subcontractors were gradually invited to participate. But because the contract was won by the Defenders from Autozávod Český Dub, and the sales did not reach sufficient numbers, the production was terminated in 1996. As for the total number of vehicles produced, the company itself claims to have made about 250 units of the Avia A11 Trend, while other sources mention 72 units. The French were eminently interested in entering the Czech market, hoping to make it a springboard for their activities in Central and Eastern Europe. As a result of their negotiations, they sold a franchise for the A3 / A4 to HOLBA and co., JSc.—a Czech company based in Vsetín, CR. The firm prepared an ambitious production and expansion plan that it managed to execute for some time. However, shortly after the manufacturing of the first batch of cars started in 1997, catastrophic floods hit the region, destroying the firm physically, as well as financially.

AZLK - Moskvich (USSR and Russia)

AZLK—"Avtomobilnyi Zavod Imeni Leninskogo Komso-mola" (=The Lenin Komsomol Auto Works) with the Kremlin in its logo is better known by the name of Mosk-vich. Established in 1930, it only produced cars for the general population, relatively many of which were exported in the 1960s. Moskviches had an obsolete design and a significant breakdown rate. Throughout its existence, the plant suffered from insufficient financial and human resources necessary for further development and progress. AZLK is, along with GAZ, the oldest active Russian car make. It started as KIM, a subsidiary of GAZ, by assembling the American A and AA Fords. In 1939, it showcased the Tudor KIM 10—its first automobile. Stalin interfered in both the design and appearance of the car. After the war, the company re-emerged as MZMA (Small Car Moscow Factory). The 400 / 420 model already bore the name Moskvich. It was a copy of the pre-war Opel Kadett. AZLK bade its last farewell to this 1930s design in 1956 by designing the 402 model, albeit with the original 1.2-L (35hp) engine and a 3-speed transmission. This handicap was eliminated in the 407 model featuring an engine with an aluminum cylinder head (45hp, 4 gears), which fed on low-quality gasoline (octane rating: 72). In addition to a sedan, the 423N station wagon and the 403 model with an elegant two-color finish were also available. The front axle with an independent suspension of the wheels was equipped with coil springs and a stabilizer, the rear axle was rigid with reinforced, longitudinal, half-elliptic springs. The vehicle featured drum brakes and a 7.9-in-high ground clearance. The cars were made until the mid 1960s and they even featured AWD. In the late 1980s, Moskvich hovered on the brink of bankruptcy. Since 1997, the Moscow municipal government has held a 59% share in A. O. Moskvich. At the moment, the car works are facing a crisis. The cars have been assembled in Moscow and, since 1999, 2335 pick-up trucks have also been assembled by the

The Moskvich 411N with a 423N body—in a Soviet pamphlet from 1958

KPP company based in Omsk, Russia and the KARZ-5 company in Kiev, Ukraine.

Moskvich 410N a 411 ❷

The 402 model became a basis for the new 410 generation, out of which a robust off-road 4x4 sedan emerged. The Moskvich 410 was fitted with an old engine (35hp), while the 410N 4x4 (or 410H in Cyrillic) with features from the 407 got a more modern engine (45 hp, 56 mph). However, an advertisement pamphlet issued in 1958 shows a combination of the 45 engine with only a 3-speed transmission. For driving over rough terrains, a two-speed reduction gear was of great help. The body remained the same, except for the ground clearance, which was 8.7 inches high thanks to an off-road GAZ chassis and bigger tires with widely spaced knobs. The Moskvich could ford 21.6 inches of water mass and a road covered with up to 12 inches of snow. Model 411 was represented by a station wagon with a body taken from the 423N (4x2). Each of the 12,000 units produced worked like magic in the rugged terrain. Model 410N was made between 1958 and 1960. (The names of the models originating in the USSR, among other places, are greatly confused due to an incorrect transcription of the Cyrillic into the Latin alphabet).

The Moskvich 410N—in a Soviet pamphlet from 1958

The Moskvich 410N had an air of gracefulness, not only in a pamphlet from 1958

The Moskvich 410N

Moskvich – 4x4 prototypes ❷ ❿

Designer Igor Aleksandrovich Gladilin gained recognition for drafting promising prototypes of the 415 (an off-road convertible with a canvas roof) and the 416 (a hard-top). The engine (1360cc, 40hp, 65 mph) was taken from the 407 and there was a 4-speed transmission with a 2-speed reduction. Mass production did not occur, partly due to a lack of capacity, which did not even suffice to cover the demand for sedans, and partly to a lack of financial resources for the production. In the early 1980s, an attempt was made to resurrect the project. The 2150 model represented a more elegant body and a 1.5-L engine taken from the 412. Other prototypes emerged in the late 1980s, including the Ivan Susanin off-road fastback (probably based on the Kalita sedan), and the 2141-KR (2.0L engine) competition car from 1989, built according to the parameters of the B Series specials. The X1 project launched in the late 1990s represented a prototype of a luxury MPV derived from the Alexander Nevsky—an expensive model of Moskvich—and featuring a V6 3.0-L (185hp), or a V8, or 4 or 5-V diesel units, a ten-year corrosion guarantee and 4WD.

Moskvich Pick-up Truck ❻

The year 1989 saw the debut of the 233500 / 233522 / 23523 series of pick-up trucks derived from the 2141 sedan. AZLK has been making them since 1992 with different VAZ and UZAM engines with a capacity ranging from 1.6 to 2.0 liters. The cars weigh over 3,527 lbs and are able to carry loads of 1,102–1,543 lbs. In December 2000, the 233521 pick-up truck (based on the 2141) made its first appearance, featuring a stretched cab seating 5 persons; the launch date for mass-production was set as 2001. It has 4x2 drive and a UZAM 2.0-L engine, and it carries 882 lbs of load. In contrast to the 2335 Pick-up (4x2), both the 2335-21 Pick-up and the 2444-21 Pick-up Double Cab feature 4x4 drive, as does the 2901 pick-up truck. The latter has been made since 1994. It has a plastic removable roof, a minivan superstructure, 4x2 drive, and is able to carry 882 lbs of cargo and 5 persons. Its engine and origin are equivalent to those of the previous models.

The Moskvich 2150

Bajaj Tempo (India)

Bajaj Tempo's advertising slogan goes like this "Today's Tempo giving wheels to India." The Bachraj Trading Corporation was established in 1945, and in the early months of 1948 it imported (and later also produced) Italian three-wheelers and Piaggio scooters. Simultaneously, it co-operated with the Hamburg-based Vidal & Sohn Tempo Werke, whose Tempo Hanseat three-wheeler had been franchise-produced by them since 1951. Seven years later, the Germans gained 26% of the stock in the company, which changed its name to Bajaj Tempo. It has continued to produce Minidor three-wheelers to this day. In 1976, the Indians established a partnership with Mercedes. At the outset of the new millennium, DaimlerChrysler owned 16.8 % of the stock, while the rest—83.2%—was held by the Bajaj Group. In 1964, the company obtained a franchise to produce the Tempo Viking four-wheeler. In 1986, the Trax—an off-road model—was presented. Further development of an older version of the OM-616 Mercedes (equipped with a G1-18 transmission) is under way, which is beginning to find its customers around Europe. Approximately 5,500 off-road cars, 4,000 utility vehicles and 16,500 three-wheelers were produced yearly at the turn of the century. The company has also been trying to export its cars to Europe.

Tempo Trax

The multifarious Tempo Trax is a rustic off-roader from 1986. Its resemblance to the Mercedes G is not purely coincidental. The Indians used and modified a large number of German components. In addition to the latest model—Judo/Gama (a stretched 5-door station wagon)—older models are also available, including the open or closed Town & Country, the Challenger (a doorless convertible of the late 1990s), as well as the Roughroad Master—the latest road hard-top with a short or long wheelbase—and a pick-up truck version with a single or dual cab (the Dual Cabin). The vehicles usually feature 4x2 drive, but 4x4 versions are also

The Bajaj Tempo Trax Roughroad Master Pickup, 2001

available, including pick-up trucks produced between 1986 and 1998. Until 1998, the offer included the curious 6-door Trax Limo with a super-long wheelbase, 3 rows of seats and a canvas roof. Some of the parts of its (hard-top) body were made of fiberglass; the rest was molded from steel sheets. The best-equipped model—Judo—features an AC, a steering booster and a metallic finish. It's powered by a franchise-produced DOM 616 engine with the capacity of a 2.4 or 2.6-L engine. The transmissions are manual and have four speeds. The central member frame of the station wagon with an extended wheelbase is reinforced with an aluminum plate. The front wheels are suspended independently, while the rear axle is rigid. The total weight of the station wagon is (+)5,512 lbs. In 1998/99, a major modernization of the front and rear resulted in the tough Ghurkha 4x4 model series named after the tribe of respected and feared warriors characterized by courage, perseverance and fighting spirit. The vehicle is designed for the roughest conditions, and is strictly utilitarian. The car has more power—a 4-speed transmission, a cross-country reduction, and optional FWD. The total weight of the vehicle is 5,181–6,195 lbs. The 4x4 model has an 8.7-in ground clearance, while the Gama and Roughroad Master Pick-ups have 8.3 inches and the station wagon of the same model features a 7.5-in ground clearance. In the Himalayas, the Ghurkha 4x4 undertook test drives up to an altitude of 5,500 m.

The Bajaj Tempo Trax Judo, 2001

The Bajaj Tempo Trax Ghurkha 4x4, 2001

Barkas (GDR)

P2M ❷

The name of Barkas does not correspond precisely with the contents of this sub-section. It belongs to the producer of Barkas vans, minibuses, platform trucks and off-road P2Ms. A BMW assembly plant used to be located in Eisenach, GDR. Following the war documentation and using the parts spared from transportation to the USSR, they assembled an 4WD vehicle—the first one in the GDR. It bore the name H1. 161 units were made in 1952. As the H1 was large and expensive, the company soon focused its efforts on of the P1—a smaller car featuring a 6-V gasoline engine (1971cc, 50hp). The P1 was 142 in long, 66 in wide and 76 in high. It was a copy of the pre-war BMW 325/3. The umbilical cord with the pre-war design was cut by the 4-seat P2M with various body types including a limousine, an off-roader and an amphibious P2S. The sedan did not come out well, while the other two versions were manufactured until 1954. The cars had a 2-d body and a 6-V Horch engine (2407cc, 65hp @ 3500, 59 mph). Other characteristics: length—148 in, width—67 in, height—

72 in, clearance—11.8 in, curb weight—3,902 lbs, payload—882 lbs. They had permanent AWD, four-speed transmission, reduction, rear differential lock and rigid axles with longitudinal leaf springs. Only about 2,000 were made between 1954 and 1958, of which only 17 were amphibious. The P2M was good off road but its production had to give way to the Trabant. This caused resistance in the GDR, and in the early 1960s the robust 6-seat P3 was designed, featuring the same engine but with different power—75 hp @ 3750, 59 mph; length—146 in, width—69 in, height—79 in, ground clearance—13 in, curb weight—4,101 lbs and payload—1,543 lbs. In 1962–66, nearly 3,000 units were produced. Unfortunately, the decision of COMECON to concentrate the production of 4WD vehicles in the USSR put an end to any further efforts. The GDR producers were obliged to resign themselves to making only an open version of the plastic Trabant (P 601 A) for the border patrol, troop commanders, and a few vehicles for farmers and foresters. In the early 1990s, a lucky few got their hands on this car in the form of the Trabant Tramp, with an air-cooled two-stroke 2-V engine 600cc (26hp). The amphibious, 4-d, convertible Wartburg 353/400 was set for a higher level of quality. It featured an air-cooled two-stroke 3V 992cc (55hp) engine and the following dimensions: length—152 in, height—61 in.

The Barkas P3 at the Broken Half-axle 4x4 veteran cars reunion in Třebíč, Czech Republic

The Barkas P3

Bedford (Great Britain)

Bedford debuted in 1931 as part of Vauxhall, a British car-maker, which was then already firmly anchored in the General Motors combine. The Americans had been assembling their 6V Chevrolet trucks in the Hendon factory in Britain since 1929. The millionth Bedford was manufactured as early as in 1958, and a two-millionth one ten years later. In the 1980s and 1990s, the make of Bedford was also borne by the Japanese Isuzu lightweight four wheel drive vehicles and pick-up trucks, sold mainly on the British Isles.

Bedford Brava

The Bedford Brava from the late 1980s is equipped with

a 3-seat body borne by a ladder frame. The 4x4 pick-up trucks feature a mud pan protecting the cooler, transmission and gas tank. The front axle has an independent trapezoid suspension with a stabilizer and torsion bars, while the rear axle is rigid with half-elliptic springs. Power is provided by 4V engines—either a gasoline 2254cc (89hp @ 4600) or a D 2238cc (53hp @ 4000)—through a 5-speed transmission to the rear wheels. The 4x4 version has the option of "fast" and "slow" gears. (Driving in the off-road mode automatically locks the front wheel hubs.) The Brava features a 119-in wheelbase, a 194-in length, a 67-in width, a 67-in height, an 8.3-in ground clearance, (8.7 inches for the 4x4 version), a curb weight between 2,758 lbs (the 4x2 version powered by gasoline) and 3,219 lbs (the 4x4 version powered by a D engine), and a payload rating between 2,646 lbs and 2,183 lbs.

The Bedford Brava 4x4

The Bertone 127 Villager, around 1974

Bertone
(Italy)

It's been a long time since Bertone was a mere design studio founded by the divinely gifted Nuccio Bertone. Now it also includes developer workshops and an assembly plant specializing in smaller series of special purpose vehicles—mostly convertibles—for big auto works. One of them was

a Bertone off-roader. Occasionally, Nuccio set about developing a prototype of a beach vehicle (e.g., the 2x4-powered Fiat 127 Villager with a doorless 4-seat body) or an off-roader (such as the Shake—a buggy introduced in Paris 1980 and based on the Simca 1200 S, due to be replaced by the Fiat 128 mechanics). In 1996, he designed the SUV Enduro based on the 4x4 Opel Calibra coupe and a prototype of the Alfa Romeo Sportut SUV.

The Bertone Freeclimber 1ˢᵗ generation

Bertone Freeclimber ❷

In 1989, Bertone surprised everybody with the updated 2- or 5-seat Daihatsu Rugger / Rocky. He altered the appearance, front panel and interior of the original 3-d hard-top. The casual sporty spirit of the car was enhanced by in-line 6V BMW engines of the following types: a 1990cc gasoline (129hp @ 6000, 99 mph) or a 2693cc gasoline (129hp @ 4800) engines, and a 2443cc TD engine (116hp @ 4800, 94 mph). The car featured a 5-speed transmission with a reduction. Both axles were rigid with leaf springs, Panhard rods, anti-roll bars and shock absorbers with 3 alternative levels of hardness. Later, following Daihatsu's example, it was equipped with independently suspended wheels with torsion bars in the front. The model had the following characteristics: wheelbase — 100 in, length — 157 in, width — 65 in, height — 65 in, ground clearance — 7 in, weight of soft-top — 3,423 lbs, weight of hard-top — 3,488 lbs, payload rating — between 959 and 1,087 lbs, climbing ability — 100 %, overhang angles — 42°/32°, side tilt — 43°, and fording depth — 23.6 in.

Bertone Freeclimber 2 ❷

The 1994 Geneva motor show saw the debut of the (not yet roadworthy) Freeclimber 2; a full-value model was not produced until the end of the spring. Even though interest in 4x4 cars has risen among European customers, only few cars will actually have the chance to drive over truly rough terrain. It isn't necessary to bounce along in an uncomfortable work vehicle. People are looking for a more comfortable car to drive around the city jungle. And that is the kind of vehicle that Freeclimber 2 is. Its length was sized down (149 in) but it is wider, which makes it more spacious inside and easier to park. The grille is new, as are the plastic bumpers and plastic fender flares. The mechanics are still Daihatsu, except for the

The Bertone Enduro, 1996

The Bertone Freeclimber 1ˢᵗ generation, 1989

engine, which is by BMW. Bertone assembles them, like the 1ˢᵗ version, in Grugliasco — a suburb of Turin — from components supplied by Daihatsu, BMW and others. The bold original goal of manufacturing 10,000 units a year has fallen through owing to a fluctuating economy.

The Bertone Freeclimber 2

BMW
(Germany)

The Bayerische Motoren Werke AG (BMW) company was founded in 1917. Initially, it produced aircraft engines, later (since 1923) motorcycles and, in 1928, it took Dixi under its wing—a producer of Wartburgs since 1898. BMW swallowed up many marques over the years including Glas, Mini and Rolls-Royce. It shunned four wheel drive vehicles, unless one includes: the Touring BMW 325 iX / iX KAT (1985–91)—2-d and 4-d sedans, 2-d convertibles and 5-d station wagons; the Touring station wagon / sedan 325 iX / 330 iX / 330 dX (spring 2000; facelifted since the fall of 2001), or a temporary acquisition of Rover including its Land Rover Division (1984–2000). The German engineers had their fingerprints on the Range Rover III.

The interior of the BMW X5, NEC 2000

BMW X5 (USA) ❸

The star of the 1999 Detroit motor show was the BMW X5 luxury SUV with features of the Series 5 sedans. The vehicle took America by storm, but Europeans had to wait until the spring of 2000. Their appetite was whetted by a single specimen of the no-nonsense BMW X5 Le Mans showcased at the 2000 Geneva motor show. The car is powered by a V12, 6-L, 700hp, 172 mph engine originally mounted in the winning car of the 24-hour Le Mans 1995, and features spoilers and anatomically-shaped seats. This series-produced BMW fares well on the road but less so in the off-road. It is produced in Spartanburg, SC. Its self-supporting 4-d steel body carries up to 5 people but its payload rating— 1,345 lbs—is far from astonishing. The "locals" prefer a gasoline in-line fuel-injection 6V engine (24v, 2979cc, 231hp @ 5900, 126 mph, acceleration from a standstill to 62 mph in 8.5s), or a "thirsty" V8 4398cc 32v engine (286hp @ 5400, 128 mph, from 0 to 62 mph in 7.5s), or a power unit with the following parameters: 4619 cc, 32v (347hp @ 5700, 149 mph, from 0 to 62 mph in 6.5s).

Europeans prefer the "Common Rail" engine—a direct-fuel injection TD with six in-line cylinders and the following specifications: 2926cc, 24v, 184 hp @4000, 124 mph, from 0 to 62 mph in 10.5s. Theoretically, the producer should be supplying a 5-speed manual transmission to go with the 3.0i engine, but since mid-2002, the cars have been fitted exclusively with 5-speed automatic transmissions. The BMW has permanent AWD (38:62), an inter-axle differential and electronic slip control by stepping lightly on the brake. The electronic crinkum-crankum of controlling the car's behavior and an optimization of the chassis adjustment is made up of the DSC III advanced driving stability control system including the HDC, DBC, ASC, ABS, CBC, DSC, ASC-X and ADB-X subsystems. The car is equipped with discs brakes and a parking drum brake on the rear auxiliary drums. The wheels are suspended independently, with coil springs and stabilizers. At a premium, the rear part of the body is available with adjustable height, as is the "Sport Package" chassis kit. The hot new plan is to leave out the electronic speed limiter and to install rear head airbags and GPS with a DVD-player. Specifications: wheelbase—111 in, length—184 in, width—74 in, height—68 in, ground clearance—7 in, curb weight (+)4,828 lbs, fording depth—20 in, and overhang angles—30° /31°. The 2001 IAA saw the debut of the experimental X5 fitted with a X5 Connect Drive telematic system. AC Schnitzer, Alpina and Hamman were the companies that took charge of the tuning.

BMW xActivity (X3) (Germany, Austria) ❸

The X3 has been planned as an equivalent of the Series 3. Its forerunner is the xActivity 4-d SUV concept car presented in Detroit in 2003—a 4x4 with an electronic sports chassis, a new wheel slip control system and an in-line fuel-injection 6V 3.0L engine (231hp), and later also a 3.6L engine in the M-specification. Curious but practical are the large windows in the middle and rear part of the roof without the B-pillars, giving the option of turning the car almost into a convertible and/or of transporting bulky equipment such as mountain bikes or surfboards. The X3 is supposed to be produced by Steyr. It has been derived from the platform of the Series 3

The BMW X5 Le Mans, 2000

4WD station wagon, using a modified front axle and steering taken from the X5. The X3 was launched at the 2003 IAA motor show.

The BMW x Activity, Geneva 2003

The Bremach Transporto Squadra, 2003

The Bremach Cabina Dopla, 2003

The Bremach Trek Furgonato 9 posti, 2003

Bremach
(Italy)   BREMACH

In 1956, a company was established in Varese, which since 1971 has made orthodox boxy "Italian Unimogs" with frontal D / TD Iveco engines and rectangular grilles. To date, the company has made 10,000 cars, including 2,500 units of the first GR series and 2,800 units of the NGR and TGR series. Since about 2000 the newer and curvier Brio has been complemented by the variable 4x4 Brick, the off-road Extreme and the Job road car featuring modern cabs; about 240 variants include chassis, platform trucks, minibuses, as well as 4x4 or 4x2 heavy duty box bodies. Their payload is between 1.4 and 2.8 t. (See also SCAM).

The Bremach Trek Camper, Africa 2002

The Bremach Guado, 2002

Bronto
(Russia)

In the late 1980s, a team of specialists from the VAZ car works gained the status of "Experimental Production Division," affiliated with the development center. They were joined by another team developing special modifications. With the approval of VAZ's top management, the new Bronto marque was backed up by the concern Lada Banka. Within one year, they had designed the Lada Niva – the VAZ 2121B - resistant to bullets from a Kalashnikov—a weapon popular with terrorists. Since 1993, a separate production line has been producing limited-series special-purpose vehicles. Simultaneously, the VAZ 2121 B was fine-tuned by weapon experts. The team presented their products for the first time

in Moscow in 1995, where visitors were invited to admire the Fors, the Marsh, the Gnom and the Elf prototypes, financed by the AVTOVAZ group. The manager of AVTOVAZ strives for the greatest possible quality. As the company's slogan has it: "We would buy the cars we make." By the end of 2002, this assembly plant had produced over 2,500 cars.

VAZ 2121 B / Bronto Fors (VAZ-212182)

During the first two years of its production run, the firm made 500 units of the VAZ 2121 B. They were immediately sold out in restless Russia. The Bronto Fors is a facelifted VAZ 2121 B designed for transporting valuables, based on the Lada Niva. The wheelbase of the Niva 4x4 was extended by 12 inches (the side doors were also extended). The car was equipped with an automatic fire extinguisher, the right

The Bronto VAZ 212182 Fors, 2002

door interlocking system, armor-plating, light alloy wheels, concealed portholes, and AC; at a premium, the engine can be equipped with an exhaust recycling system and a hole in the rear partition to crawl through. There is only a driver's seat in the front, two seats behind it, and a separate transport space in the back. What makes the Bronto conspicuous is an elevated roof and a distinctive finish. A flat windshield is divided by a cross-piece, and the size of the front side windows has been diminished. The glass is bulletproof and opaque when looking from the outside. The car carries up to 882 lbs of cargo including the crew. Its top speed is 78 mph. Over 1,000 units of the Bronto Fors are in use in Russia, the former USSR countries and perhaps even outside of the former USSR borders. 50% of them cruise around Moscow and the Moscow district. The author of this book came across a Bronto Fors (with an UAZ mark) in service in

a security agency in Košice, Slovakia, in 2002. His request to take a photo was categorically refused.

Fors Niva 212180 "VIP" / (Bronto) ❷

This vehicle is designed for the safe travel of VIPs over rugged tracks. It is distinguished from a classical Niva by its security features, the Fors wheelbase length and roof; on the other hand, its windows are proportionally equivalent to those of the Niva. The mechanics and most of the equipment is identical with those of the Fors.

Bronto Marsh (VAZ-1922)   ❷ ❺

The Marsh is one of the few mass-produced vehicles featuring massive balloon tires. It is built and designet for driving around marshland, sands, swamps, snowdrifts and other off-road terrains. The UAZ-469 frame carries a Lada Niva body, complemented by extended fenders and a guard frame. The vehicle has a markedly high ground clearance. Rear seats and hydraulic boosters are available at an extra cost. The pressure of the special TREKOL tires on the roadbed is 1.4-5.7 lb/in^2. It is thanks to them that the Marsh can float. When afloat, the vehicle is emergency-powered by the gripping power of the tire tread. The Marsh carries 882 lbs including the crew and has a top speed of 43 mph.

Bronto Landole (VAZ-212183) ❷ ❹

The two-seat open Landole was presented in 1998 as a vehicle designed for touring southern countries and on safari. It is based on the VAZ 21213 Niva. The Niva's wheelbase was extended by 11.8 inches, its original doors were replaced by reinforced plastic doors with large cutouts in place of the glass, and guard frames were added.

Bronto Inkas (Lada 2120)   ❼ ❾

The first Russian minivan—the VAZ 2120 Nadyezhda—made its debut in Moscow in 1997. Three years later, it received a styling. It carries up to 7 passengers. It is derived from the VAZ 2131 Niva. Its Bronto version is called the Inkas. It features armor-plating and has enough space for 3 people and over 21 cu ft of cargo space designed for transport of up to 882 lbs of valuables.

The Bronto VAZ 212183 Landole, 2002

The Bronto VAZ 212090 Inkas, 2002

An early spring idyll with a Citroën, the Savoy Alps, mid-1930s

Citroën
(France)

In Paris in 1919, Engineer André Citroën founded a company which—after several makeovers—became part of the Peugeot industrial empire. A double arrow in its logo repre-

sents a stylized arrow-like tooth system made by Citroën's factory since 1901. Apart from his technical talent, André Citroën gained renown as a great businessman and organizer. He realized that the quality and the price of a product are the key to success. In Ford's factory in the U.S.A., he acquainted himself with the effective system of the conveyor belt; he had the courage to buy a franchise for making all-steel bodies welded from pressed panels; he was

The Citroën ZX Rallye Raid, 1997

the first to address female customers as part of his marketing strategy; and in 1925, he lit up the Eiffel Tower with a Citroën sign. But it was not roses all the way. A liquidation of the factory after it went bankrupt in 1934 was only prevented by the Michelin "tire" family, which took Citroën under its wing. In 1934, the Traction was introduced, featuring 2x4 drive. From 1955, the DS boasted a hydro-pneumatic suspension system and hydraulic high pressure brakes. Out-of-the-ordinary design was almost the rule. As regards the off-road factor, the factory had got a taste of it during the production of tractors, including the J-Type testing vehicle (4x4 with all-wheel steering), manufactured right after the war. In the early 1920s, Citroën signed a contract with the firm of Engineer Adolph Kégress—a pioneer in the field of

The Citroën Berlingo Coupé de Plage, 1997

rubber caterpillar belts. In Mont Revard in 1920–21, cars derived from the Citroën 10 HP were tested. The company prepared specimens for the ministry of defense. In 1921, it launched the sales of the B2 Autoneige—a half-track vehicle for farming purposes. This open vehicle with 4–8 seats was equipped with a new transmission, rear wheel suspension and a Citroën-Kégresse-Hinstin drivetrain. It came in three modifications: for snowy tracks (with skis in the front), rugged terrain, and long-distance rides. Power came from a 4V 1452cc engine (20hp @ 2000). The transmission had 5 speeds. Later models made before the outbreak of WWII included the C4, the C6 and the AC6-F from 1931, featuring a 6V SV 2442cc engine (42hp @ 3000), a 4-speed transmission and a 2-speed reduction. The car from 1934 was powered by a 4V 1767cc engine. The C4 and C6 gained fame in several expeditions around Africa (10 HP–1922/23, 1924/25) and Asia (1930/31/32, 1934). In modern times, 4x4 drive has been used in sports related vehicles, such as the Visa, the 1000 Pistes (1982), the BX (since 1988 also with 4x4), a top-notch rally derivative of the BX 4 TC (1985), and recently also the Xsara Kit Car WRC. The ZX Rally in various modifications was crowned with laurels in almost all raid rallies in 1990–97: it came first 5 times in the Dakar, 3 times in the Paris-Moscow-Bejing type of rallies, 5 times in the Rally of Tunisia, 3 times in the Rally Atlas. In total, it celebrated 36 victories in the World Cup races before the rules changed in 1997 and the factory opted out. Currently, remodeling of the nifty Berlingo (2x4), the C15 utility vehicle, the Jumpy and the C25 (4x2; later replaced with the Jumper), into the 4x4 Dangel is under way. The compact MPV Xsara Picasso (2x4) was showcased in Paris 2002—only as a concept—with AWD. This fate has been destined neither for the MPV Evasion (4x2, 1994), nor for its successor—the C8 (2x4, 2002). In Geneva in 1997, the company presented a concept of the Berlingo Coupé de Plage beach pick-up truck, and in Paris 2002 it came up with the little C3 Pluriel (2x4). At the IAA 2001, their concept of the SUV

C-Crosser with a 2.0 Hpi engine first appeared. This 6-seat single-space vehicle is marked by a transparent removable roof part. Thanks to a "drive-by-wire" system, all the mechanical connections of the components such as the engine, steering and brakes were taken over by electronics. The car features electronically-controlled viscous couplings, steering and AWD, an independent wheel suspension and a chassis with a hydro-active suspension of the 3rd generation with both ESP and ABS, which lends the car a ground clearance of 5.5–7.9 in.

Citroën 2 CV 4x4 Sahara

The "Duck" 2 CV (2x4) made between 1949–90 (3,868,634 units in France, a total of 5,114,961 units worldwide) came in many modifications. The bizarre 2 CV 4x4 Bimoteur made its debut on the sandy banks of the Lake of Ermenonville near Paris in March 1958. The series-produced 2 CV 4x4 Sahara, designed for driving through the desert, was produced between December 1960 and 1966. A total of 694 units were made. The Sahara negotiated a slope of 1:2.5. It was distinguished by a spare wheel on the front hood. It boasted a unique feature—two standard flat 2V air-cooled 425cc engines (24hp @ 3500, 62 mph). The front—"normal"—engine powered the front wheels, while the rear one fitted in the trunk powered the rear wheels. Each had its own 4-speed transmission. The transmissions' control lever linkages were joined and the driver changed gears by a lever sticking out from the floor by the seat. When in motion, the driver had the option of disabling the RWD by means of the rear transmission. All wheels were suspended independently, with friction shock absorbers and drum brakes. In Paris 1950, the 2 CV Fourgonnette delivery van was presented, which later became the basis for an ultra-light pick-up truck. Sixty-five specimens of the pick-up truck were bought by the British Navy, which used them (in a doorless form) as the first cars in history in helicopter paratrooper operations in 1960 in Suez, Cambodia and Borneo. The 2x4 cars proved useful in transporting water, ammunition and supplies, and for the Signal Corps. They served until 1966, when they gave way to the Land Rovers.

Citroën Méhari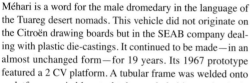

Méhari is a word for the male dromedary in the language of the Tuareg desert nomads. This vehicle did not originate on the Citroën drawing boards but in the SEAB company dealing with plastic die-castings. It continued to be made—in an almost unchanged form—for 19 years. Its 1967 prototype featured a 2 CV platform. A tubular frame was welded onto a platform carried by steel tubes and clad in an airy body made of ABS plastic (Cycolac). The result—a lightweight utility vehicle—was presented to the management of Citroën in late 1967 and the car went into production. It made its debut in Deauville in March 1968 but it was not until the 1968 Paris motor show that its proper "premiere" took place. Power was provided by a 6.2-V 602cc engine (26hp @ 5400, or 29hp @ 5750—after 1987), connected to a 4-speed transmission. The wheels were suspended independently, and there were drum brakes. Other characteristics: wheelbase—95 in, length—138 in, width—60 in, curb weight—1,157 lbs and payload—882 lbs. A year later, a 4-seat version was added. A new front was made in 1978, followed by an LM dashboard and disc brakes a year later. The vehicles were used by the Gendarmes as well as the army, which took up 11,457 Méharis in 1972–87. They transported 4-member crews, casualties, paratroopers and radio operators. In May 1979, the time came for a 4x4 (29hp) version with a low gravity center and a reduction. It had a spare wheel on the front hood, independent wheel suspension, coil springs and hydraulic shock absorbers. Specifications: wheelbase—93 in, length—145 in, width—60 in, ground clearance—9.4 in (empty car) / 7.9 in (loaded

A later model Citroën Méhari; Alcocebre, Spain 2002

car), weight—1,576 lbs and payload—882 lbs. The body was the same as that of the 2x4 with a light canvas tilt and had either 2 or 4 seats. The Méhari 4x4 proved its vitality as a medical assistance vehicle in the 1980 Paris-Dakar Rally. It was produced, including the limited-series Méhari Azur, until 1987 in Nanterre and Rennes. Later the assembly was transferred to Forest, Belgium, and later still to Vigo, Spain, and Manguade, Portugal (the Méhari 4x4). As many as 1,213 units of the 4x4 version (1979–83) out of the total output of 144,953 units produced are collectors' items today.

Citroën A 4x4

The A 4x4, first presented in April 1981, was in fact an improved version of the Méhari. It featured a Dyane 6 platform, an engine taken from the LN and the Visa (2V 652cc 34hp @ 5250, 68 mph), a 4-speed transmission, an auxiliary 2-speed reduction and a rear axle differential lock. It bore a strong resemblance to the FAF. Its 2-d soft-top body carried up to 4 persons. Its wheels were suspended independently, with stabilizers, coil springs and disc brakes. Other characteristics included: wheelbase—93 in, length—147 in, width—60 in, height—66 in, ground clearance—7.9 in, curb weight—1,852 lbs, payload—882 lbs, slope—60%. The A 4x4 was intended to replace the Méhari used by the French army. In 1981, the army ordered 5,000 vehicles, after testing 10 prototypes in 1979–80. The first 1,000 units arrived shortly afterwards. After the contract ran out, the army switched over to the P4 Peugeots.

The Citroën 2 CV / Méhari clones (Worldwide)

The first to come up with the idea of remodeling the Citroën 2 CV to a lightweight transporter with an Ami 6 engine was Maurice Delignon from Abidjan, Ivory Coast. In 1963, he built the open "la Baby-brousse" (the Baby-Bush). Delington in fact envisioned the shape, concept and design of the future Méhari. The only aspect to set it apart was the materials used on the body—steel, aluminum and plywood. The car was series-produced by the Axion workshops and iron works. (He had toyed with the idea of making his own pro-

The company showcased a wide range of automobiles in Paris in 1986. Between 1985 and 1987, the British company CVC manufactured the Bedouin—a 3-d off-road station wagon on a 2 CV / Dyane platform. The Éole, featuring a beach fiberglass 2- or 4-seat body, was powered by a Peugeot 1360cc (50hp, 90 mph) engine, it weighed 1,609 lbs and its producer—the GPM company—made no secret of it having been inspired by the Méhari. For information on other marques including Dallas, Teilhol, Axiam-Mega, MX Cooperation, Namco, Poncin, and Fiberfab, see the individual sub-sections.

Citroën FAF (Portugal)

In 1973, Citroën tested a few specimens of the Dalat and decided to manufacture a similar vehicle on a Dyane 6 chassis. Citroën's subsidiary based in Mangualde, Portugal, which had already supplied the 2 CVs, was put in charge of the development. Production of the FAF with a Méhari platform was launched in 1977 and the model made its debut at the Dakar Trade Fair in November 1978. The version range included a sedan, a station wagon, a fourgonette, a pick-up truck, a beach vehicle with a tilt and a 4x4 beach vehicle. The latter was powered by a Méhari 4x4 engine. A 2V 602cc engine (29hp @ 5750, 62 mph) was mounted in the car, coupled to a 4-speed transmission with a reduction. Specifications: wheelbase—95 in, length—141 in, width—61 in, ground clearance—7.9 in. When empty, it (the Torpedo) weighed 1,587 lbs; a hard-top weighed 1,653 lbs. The payload rating reached 915 lbs and the car negotiated a 60% incline. Barely a year later, the company signed major contracts with companies in Equatorial Africa, Ivory Coast and Indonesia. It was in Ivory Coast that the FAF 2x4 and 4x4 were assembled. 200 units were taken up by the Portuguese army and the last few specimens of the total of 2,295 were exported to Indonesia in 1990.

totype based on the Renault 4L financed by Renault, but eventually he gave the idea up.) In 1969, Citroën bought a franchise for the Baby-Bush and an assembly line a year later. The new factory struggled financially and the local subsidiary was bound to step in. Between 1976 and 1979, it produced 31,305 undemanding helpers tailored to the needs of Africans. Several thousand units were made in Iran between 1970 and the Islamic Revolution in 1979, and 651 Baby-Bushes Yagan were manufactured in Chile between 1972 and 76. In the period between 1969 and 1975, similar models featuring 602cc engines were "born" in Vietnam. In 1936, as part of a third world aid program, Citroën installed a production line in Dalat—a town about 185 miles north of Saigon—in a former cigarette-making factory. A vehicle of the Dalat marque, partly assembled from French parts, featured several body types, including a 5-d station wagon and a military version exported to Indonesia and Laos. A company named Vancle tried to break through in Belgium with the Emmet—a Méhari-type of creation; the Emmet was a polyester hard-top with a 602cc engine (75 mph). In 1987, the French company SIFTT came up with the Katar (652cc, 71 mph, 1,389 lbs)—a beach 4x4 pick-up truck featuring a targa arch. A later version of the Katar was powered by a D 4V 1769cc Citroën / Peugeot engine and a 4x4 version derived from the Citroën C15 by a 1124cc power unit. A prototype of Katar was sent to Dakar 1987, but a trivial accident eliminated it 93 miles before the finish. In 1972, the Dyane served as a base for a prototype of the Morvan with a polyester body made by the Rocaboy Kirchner company. In 1976, the open Lohr FL 500 was born, designed chiefly for military purposes. In 1985, the Ponticelli-Gretz company—a specialist in communal technology—came up with the Vux 600. This vehicle, featuring either a long or a short wheelbase and 4x2 or 4x4 was powered by BX-type engines: a gasoline 1.6L or a D 1.9L. Besides the army, these vehicles went down well with the police, firefighter squads, postal services, beach patrols and civilian protection troops.

The Citroën FAF, 1981

Cournil, S.I.M.I. (France)

Simi

After the war, Bernard Cournil opened a branch of Hotchkiss. As he was not happy with their Jeeps, he decided to reinforce the chassis, modify the body and mount French-made Hotchkiss or Ferguson D engines. However, the authorities and Hotchkiss kept their eyes open and noticed the modifications. The bureaucrats insisted on a new homologation, and that is how the Tracteur Cournil marque was born. Bernard designed the vehicle as an alternative to a farming tractor. The newcomer soon aroused interest. A prototype was made in 1957 and a year later a few units rolled off the assembly line. In 1970, Bernard Cournil sold the rights. Once in new hands, the model underwent two rather unlucky production launches. The time came to look for a new engine, but Ferguson had terminated production of diesels in 1965. Cournil gave a try to Indénor, Leyland and Saviem, only to go back to a Peugeot diesel and Renault gasoline and diesel engines in the early 1980s. In the 1970s, around 1,000 cars were made. Between 1977 and 1981, the company was renamed Sté Gevarma and was based in Saint-Germain, Laval. In 1981–84, the S.I.M.I. SA company from the same town obtained a franchise and took things in the right direction. In 1983, Autoland (which soon changed its name to Auverland) picked up the threads. The Portuguese-based UMM bought a franchise in 1978.

The Cournil, Central France, 2003

Cournil, Simi Cournil ❷

Bernard Cournil constructed this car as a robust off-road 4x4 with a ladder steel chassis and a body welded onto it. The Cournil featured rigid axles and clusters of half-elliptic springs. The customers had a choice between liquid-cooled 4V (D 2304cc, 67.4 hp) Peugeot engines, Saviem (gasoline 2600cc, 69hp) engines, Renault (gasoline, 1995cc, 83hp) engines and Saviem (D, 3595cc, 85hp) engines. A 4-speed transmission was connected to a gear-reduction transmission. The rear axle differential was equipped with a lock. The cars sported the following bodies: a Pick-up truck, a Bache (a convertible with a canvas roof, with/out plastic rear side windows), a Pick-up Bache (with a solid cab roof and a canvas-covered rear with/out plastic rear side windows), a Hard Top (a metal roof with/out rear side windows)

The SIMI Cournil II

and the Mines (a doorless convertible with a tubular guard frame). All the body types were available for cars with the following specifications: wheelbase—80 in or 100 in, length of short/long version—142 / 167 in, width—63 in, height—75 in, ground clearance—8.5 in, curb weight—(+)3,285 / max 3,968 lbs. Depending on their design, the vehicles carried between 1,433 lbs and 1,698 lbs of payload.

Simi Cournil II ❷

Benoit Contreau designed a modernized version of the Cournil II and introduced it in 1982. The changes consist in flexible polyester bumpers with inbuilt headlights. The car came either as a 4x2 or 4x4. Production later continued under the Autoland make.

The Cournil

Simi Cournil, later Autoland Series 220 / 275 ❷

Towards the end of the "Simi" episode, the producer (Simi) came up with a whole new series of off-roaders, calling it simply Cournil. In actuality, this was the first generation of vehicles as described in the Autoland - Serie 220 / 275 subsection. The car had an 87-in or 108-in wheelbase. Characteristically, it featured a pliant plastic bumper and its grille was made of strong wire mesh, as opposed to the four horizontal ribs typical of the later Autoland. The only body version on offer was an open car with a tilt. Other features included a ladder chassis and rigid axles with half-elliptic springs. The basic specifications of both generations differed somewhat: length—143 in (short version) / 169 in (long version), width—63 in, height—75 in, ground clearance—9 in, curb weight—3,968 lbs / 441 lbs (4,850 lbs for the heavyweight version), payload—1,874 lbs / 1,984 lbs (3,858 lbs for the heavyweight version). Engines included 4V Peugeot engines—a 2498cc (D, 76hp @ 4500) and a 2304cc (TD, 80hp @ 4150), a Renault 1995cc gasoline engine (80hp, @ 5000), and a Renault V.I. (ex-Saviem) 3595cc engine (D, 85hp @ 3000). The vehicle was equipped with a 4-speed transmission, a gear-reduction transmission and a rear limited slip differential.

Dacia
(Romania)

The Dacia company based in Pitesti-Colibasi was established as ARO from the IAR armory. In 1952–68, it produced car and tractor parts. Then it obtained a franchise from Renault and in 1968, the first Dacia 1100 sedan (R8 with a rear engine, 4x2) left the company's gateway, followed by its larger sister—the Dacia 1300 (R12 with a front engine, 2x4) a year later. In 1975, Dacia introduced the Dacia 1302 Pick-up, followed by an updated version—the 1304 Pick-up—as well as the Drop-side featuring metal sidewalls. The following models were included: in 1986 the Dacia 1304 King Cab double-cab and, in 1992, the Dacia 1307 and the Dacia 1309 Double-Cab (all 2x4). In some markets, the company sold the 4WD AROs as Dacias. Output in 1999 amounted to 85,851 vehicles including 16,326 pick-up trucks. In the same year, Renault got hold of 51% of the company's stocks and went on to own 92.71% of them in 2001.

Dacia 1304 / 1305 / 1307   ❻

In 1988, the company modernized its pick-up trucks and extended the range of drive layout choice (4x2 and 2x4) to include 4x4. The following models were manufactured: the 2-seat 1304 Pick-Up, the 2-d 5-seat 1304 King-Cab, the 2-seat 1304 Drop-Side and the 4-d 5-seat 1307 Double-Cab. Power was provided by a 1397cc engine (69hp, 87 mph), alternatively a D 1870cc (47hp @ 4500, 84 mph). The 5-speed transmission was manual. Specifications: wheelbase—105 /

110 in (for the Double-Cab), length—184 / 189 in, width—64 in, height—60 in, clearance—6.5 in, curb weight—3,307 lbs, payload (for the 4x4)—2,425 lbs. The cars are exported to many countries.

A Spanish pamphlet displaying the Dacia (ARO), 1991

The Dacia 1304 Pick-up; Brno, Czech Republic, 2002

Daewoo
(South Korea)

The Daewoo Korando 2.3, 2000

In 1967, Woo-Choong Kim founded a company known to-day as Daewoo Motor Co. He ran the business for 31 years. However, the roots of the company reach as far back as 1937, when the National Motor Co. began assembling Japanese trucks. It changed its name to Saenara Motor Co. in 1962, and two years later it became part of the concern of Shinjin Industrial Co., a producer of buses and four wheel drive Willyses since the 1950s. In 1962, they introduced a proto-type of a passenger car and in 1965–72, the Shinjin Motor Co. assembled Toyotas. General Motors obtained half the company's stocks in 1972 and a period of Opel and Chev-rolet derivatives was launched. Four years later, the cars were renamed from Opel to Sachean and in 1978, Shinjin sold 50% of its stocks to the Daewoo Industrial Co. The name of the company changed to Daewoo Motor Co. GM in 1983. In 1992, GM withdrew from the now technologically more independent auto works. Daewoo proceeded to de-velop a new generation of vehicles which was often based on Suzuki and expanded to the Czech Republic (Avia), Poland (FSO), Romania, Uzbekistan and the Ukraine. In

The Daewoo Korando 2.3, 1999

The Daewoo Musso 2.9 TD, 1999

1998–2000, Daewoo got 51.7 % of the stock of the South-Korean company SsangYong. The late-1990s chill in the Korean economy proved lethal for Daewoo. The company went bankrupt in November 1999 and was placed in the hands of the Korean Bank for Development. The offer of the car division was solicited by Fiat and GM, who eventually won it. A concept car of the SUV DMS-I mini was showcased at the 1999 IAA, followed two years later (also at the IAA) by the Daewoo VADA, which suggested the possibilities of a potential SUV with a 103-in wheelbase and the following dimensions: 169 x 71 x 66 in. The car featured an "intelligent" 4x4 drive layout and an electronic stability control. Ground clearance was adjusted pneumatically depending on the type of terrain. The engine was a 1998cc (140hp @ 5300, 127 mph). All the wheels were suspended on McPherson struts. The MPV Tacuma and the Rezzo are both 2x4.

The Daewoo DMS-I, IAA 1999

Daewoo Korando ❷

Since about mid-1998, the SsangYong Korando has been available (at some places) as Daewoo Korando.

Daewoo Musso ❷

The SsangYong Musso suffered the same fate as the previous model in 1998. The Daewoo Musso differs from its predecessor in having a characteristic grille, as well as in other details.

Daewoo Rexton ❸

The latest model—the luxury SsangYong Rexton—was not spared a change of name either. It was presented in Paris 2002 under the Daewoo make.

A study of the Daewoo Tacuma Sport 2.0, IAA 1999

Daihatsu
(Japan)

On March 1st, 1907, Yoshiaki Yasunaga (Principal of Osaka Technical College) and Masahiro Tsurumi (a manufacturer of machinery who taught at the same school) were joined by several businessmen—Hiroyasu Oko, Masashi Kuwabarra and Zenjiro Takeuchi—to establish a business together. Their Hatsudoki Seizo Co. then produced internal combustion engines. Their first wheeled vehicle—the HA three-wheeler—rolled off the assembly line in 1930. The first car named FA followed 7 years later. In 1951, this Hiroshima-based company changed its name to Daihatsu Kogyo Co. and at the same time launched another three-wheeler—the Bee—onto the market. In 1967, Daihatsu became part of the Toyota auto works empire. At first, Toyota acquired 20% of the Daihatsu stocks and later its shares increased to to-day's 51%. The company changed its name again in 1974 to Daihatsu Motor Co. Each of the two makes operates independently, although Daihatsu shares many components of the bigger Toyota. A wide range of AWD road vehicles is available: the compact Mira 4WD and the Mira Turbo 4WD (1984), the Charade (a bigger version), the Applause, the Sirion, or the HiJet (a compact utility series) exported as "Atrai," as well as the Delta mini bus / van / platform truck. Production has also been going on since 1984 in China, and a European branch was opened in Belgium in 1979. The company has collaborated with the South-Korean Asia Motors Co. since 1990 and with the Italian Piaggio since 1991.

The Daihatsu F 10, 1977

Daihatsu Taft / Rocky 4WD / Wildcat GL ❷

The first Daihatsu off-roader appeared in 1974. Its construction was based on the only legitimate "recipe" dictated by Jeep. The Daihatsu Taft (F10) was created at a time when off-road vehicles were used exclusively on farms and in inaccessible areas. The first F10 made in the fall of 1974 was fitted with a 4V Toyota Publica 958cc engine (45hp @ 5400), RWD and optional FWD. The transmission had 4 speeds and a cross-country reduction. The model was

The Daihatsu F 50 JK, 1981

The Daihatsu F 50 V, 1982

The Daihatsu F 60, a Michelotti modification; Geneva, 1983

made in 1975–85 either as a station wagon or a soft-top. Further specifications included: wheelbase—80 in, length—132 or 137 in, width—58 in, height—72 in and curb weight—(+)2,249 lbs. Besides the nickname, the model was also known as the F10 and the F60. The German distributor decided that a term for a textile material was unsuitable for an off-roader and chose a more fitting name—Wildcat. In Great Britain, the vehicle appeared in 1976 under the name "F10 Taft." The Taft ranks among the smallest off-road vehicles in history. A year after the Taft, the F 20 model made its debut (produced in 1975–84), featuring a 1587cc engine (66hp @ 4800). The F10 L and F20 L were stretched versions; the F25 featured 10 seats, similarly to the F55 and F65. The F50 model (1978–84) was powered by a 2V 2530cc engine (62hp @ 3600), and the F60—a fall-of-1982 debutant—featured a Toyota D 2765cc (69hp @ 3600) power unit. Most of the first batch of cars with a rectangular grille, as well as of the later version with a flatter grille, were

available with open bodies (with an emergency canvas tilt for protection of the passengers and cargo), as opposed to the steel station wagon version. The axles were rigid with longitudinal leaf springs. The model was RWD with optional FWD and it featured a 4-speed transmission with a reduction.

Daihatsu Rocky / Rugger / Fourtrak

In March 1984, the 4WD / Wildcat GL made its debut. The Rocky was a more civilized, better and more universal version of the rustic and uncouth Taft. On the home market, it was sold as "Rugger," while in some other countries such as England (since June 1984), it was known as the Fourtrack. In addition to the SWB convertible and station wagon versions, it also featured a rarer LWB pick-up truck or a SWB van. The first generation Rocky (F80: 1984–94 / 93–2001) was a twin-brother of the Toyota Blizzard—a model less well known around Europe. It was powered by a single gaso-

The Daihatsu F 60 P, 1984

line 1998cc engine (88 hp @ 4800). With only one standard length of wheelbase, the car was longer (146 and 162 in / 151 in), and wider (62 in / 67 and 70 in). It featured an 8.3-in ground clearance, a 100 % slope, a 100 % side tilt and a 60° fording depth. The Bertone company based in Italy derived their Freeclimber from the Rocky, giving it a facelift and placing BMW engines under the hood. In 1989, the development department of the factory built a prototype of the Rugger EV—perhaps one of the first four wheel drive vehicles featuring an electric drive. At the same time, in 1984, the 2nd generation—the Rocky 4WD (F70 / F75)—was launched. Its dimensions—a wheelbase of 87 / 100 in, a length of 150 / 164 in and an unchanged width and height—enabled the Rocky to fit on the platform of middle-

class vehicles. It was equipped with a Toyota D engine, known from the F60, in an atmospheric (73hp) or super-charged (102hp) version. It had a steel ladder frame. Initially, both axles remained rigid with leaf springs, with an added stabilizer in the front. In 1993, a (softer) independent suspension was installed in the front, and coil springs with a Panhard rod in the rear. Thanks to a more luxurious interior, the Rocky became more useful for everyday road transport. A higher level of equipment and a two-color finish were the features of the Rocky El I (blue-and-silver in 1987, black in 1987, black-and-gray in 1990), and the green-and-gray Timberline (1995). Owners of the hard-tops enjoyed their practical feature—an elevated roof. The following specifications are based on information from the producer: ground clearance—8.3 in, slope—100 %, side tilt—45°, fording depth—23.6 in.

The Daihatsu Cab Pick-Up 1000 4WD, 1985

The Daihatsu Rocky Pick-up, 1991

The Daihatsu Rocky SX Longbody, 1996

Daihatsu Feroza ❷

In the fall of 1988, Feroza widened the choice of its compact off-roaders with a ladder frame. They were updated in March 1991 and produced until 1999. Its front wheels were suspended independently with torsion bars and a stabilizer, while the rear axle was rigid with half-elliptic leaf springs and shock absorbers, adjustable—except in the case of the Exi models—to 3 degrees of hardness. Before March 1991, the front wheels sported freewheels and hand-operated locks; after this date, automatic locks were used. The Feroza estranged itself from the die-hard fans of off-roaders by being included in the segment of leisure time vehicles. The car had a good-quality construction to speak for it. It was derived from the Rocky Series. It was sold as "Rocky" in the U.S.A., as "Rocky SX" in Japan, and as "Sportrak" in Great Britain. It was designed for less rough terrains (95hp @ 5700, 93 mph) and it featured a 1589cc engine (95hp @ 5700) and a 5-speed transmission and the following dimensions: wheelbase—86 in, length—150 in, width—62 in, height—68 in, and curb weight—(+) 2,610 lbs. The body types included a 3-d hard- or soft-top. In addition to optional FWD, a version with permanent 4x4 without a reduction was available on some markets (Italy, Switzerland). The

marque of Feroza EL II represents a model featuring two colors of finish and more expensive equipment, for example: 1990 black, 1990—Efi—black, white or blue, 1995—Timberline—green-and-gray. A modified version of the Feroza came first in the third class of the 1991 Rally Pharao, and a year later it won the first place T1 class and the fifth overall in the Australian Safari.

Daihatsu - minivans and LUV 4WD ❼ ❽ ❶

The category of compact vehicles contains 4x4 city and cross-country vans. They are used mainly by younger generation customers for fun rides on the asphalt city roads. Typically, they feature a self-supporting body, an independent front-wheel suspension of the McPherson type with a transversal stabilizer, a rigid rear axle with a Panhard rod and coil springs and, last but not least, strong smaller-capacity engines. The Torios introduced in Geneva 1997 is a compact mini-SUV. In the mid-1988, the smashing black-and-silver Terios Black Magic was launched on the market, followed by the smaller Terios Kid, the Atrai—the "Best Minivan of the Fall 1999"—and the 7-seat Delta Wagon from the end of 1999. The Hijet Truck—a series of ultra-light trucks—has been produced ever since 1999. These small platform trucks or box-type minivans weighing 1.2–1.3 tons carry up to 772 lbs of load. They are available as 4x2 or 4x4 drives. The heavier-weight Hijet Cargo series, and the heaviest Delat Van (a twin of the Toyota Liteace Noah) bear similar features.

The Daihatsu Feroza Soft Top El, 1991

Dallas
(France)

Dallas   ❷ ❹

In 1981, the Automobiles Dallas auto works was established
in Neuilly-sur-Seine. The designer Jean-Claude Hrubon put
forth the Dallas leisure-time vehicle. It was based on the
platform of the R4 GTL with a 4V 1108cc engine, and was
sold either as a 2x4 (same as the R4) or in a 4x4 version featuring Sinpar mechanics. Its curb weight ranged between
1,433 and 1,587 lbs. It featured a self-supporting body the
color of khaki, with the following body-type range: a pick-
up truck with a hard-top or a soft-top, a beach vehicle, a soft-
top and a hard-top. Dimensions: 117 in (short) or 133 in
(long), wheelbase—54 in, ground clearance—8.3 in. Production was terminated in 1986.

Dallas II   ❷ ❹

In 1984, the company was bought by the singer Franck
Alamo and its name was changed to Automobiles Grandin
S.A. The technical director Patrick Müller was responsible
for the Dallas II (see Fargo). The company took over the
Peugeot 205 mechanics, including its gasoline (1360cc,
75hp @ 6200) and diesel (1769cc, 59hp @ 4600—after
1995) engines. The transmission has 5 speeds. The vehicle is
supported by a chassis of steel box sections. Its fiberglass
bodies, including a beach version, a hard- or soft-top and
a pick-up truck, are all of identical length. They seat four
and have 3 plastic or canvas doors. Length x width x height:
122 x 63 x 64 in, wheelbase—79 in. The beach "Funtastic"
features a 1,676-lb curb weight and a 683-lb payload. In the
early 1990s, a 2-/4-seat 2x4 version and a 2-seat 4x4 version
(in France, the number of seats influenced the VAT rating)
appeared, both equipped with an engine featuring 85hp

The Dallas, 1982

The Dallas Pick-up Vescovato, 1996

@ 6400. When empty, the car weighed 1,389 lbs (2x4) or
1,455 lbs (4x4) and had a payload (including the crew) of
1,323 lbs and 1,455 lbs respectively. The 1996 Geneva motor show saw the debut of the Vescovat pick-up truck featuring a hard-top over a 2-seat cab and a canvas-covered cargo
area. An updated version named Dallas Phase 3 was built by
Francois Quirin in 1996/97. Later, he went over to the Fargo
company.

The Dallas II, 1996

Dangel
(France)

The Dangel Peugeot 504 Break, 1983

In 1978, Henri Dangel started work on a 4x4 version of the Peugeot 504. (He had also tried to modify the Citroën DS and the Renault 16, but the Peugeot proved the most suitable.) The complex construction of the permanent 4x4 for cars with an engine mounted transversally in the front (Peugeot 305) was finished in 1984. The main focus of the project was the Dangel P07 transmission. In 1988 and 1989 the company presented experimental versions of the 4x4 Peugeot 205 S and the 309 GTI 16 sedans featuring an integrated transmission from which the torque was transmitted to all the wheels. Before the end of 1992, the total output of Dangels by the factory in Senthiem amounted to 7,500 units. They won their spurs in raid rallies and races including the Tunisia Rally, the Atlas Rally and the Dakar. In Paris 1998, a prototype of the Peugeot 306 Break 4x4 Dangel was put on display. Dangel has been building cars with permission from their producers and provides a factory warranty. Its existence is perhaps one of the reasons why the PSA hasn't yet been directly involved in the production of 4x4s. The total number of Dangels has been rising. As many as 6,200 units were made between 1994 and March 30, 2002.

Dangel Peugeot 504 4x4 ❷ ❻

The Dangel Peugeot 504 4x4 station wagon was showcased in Paris 1980, followed by a pick-up version two years later. Their large dimensions and good quality production made these cars attractive for the armed forces, private companies, and they also made good leisure-time vehicles and carriers of camping expedition superstructures. The 3-seat pick-up version caught on as well, while the station wagon soon gave way to the Peugeot 505. Besides the Entrepreneur and Comfort equipment packages, a chassis with a cab was also on offer. Both models were powered by gasoline 4V, 1971cc engines (96hp @ 5200); the cheaper versions also came with a D 2304cc (70 hp @ 4500) engine, while the more expensive Comfort featured a D 2498cc (76hp @ 4500) power unit. The original Peugeots had a 4x2 and a 5-speed manual

transmission. Dangel added an interaxle limited-slip differential and a Dangel P03 pneumatically shifted gear-reduction transmission. Another limited-slip differential was installed under the engine in the front. The reinforced rear axle is rigid, with longitudinal leaf springs. The front reinforced McPherson axle has strengthened wishbones. Clearance has been enhanced to 8.5 in. Other specifications: length—187 in, width—70 in, wheelbase—119 in, weight of an empty car—(+) 3,097 lbs; maximum payload including the crew reached 2,447 lbs, slope—75%, overhang angles—45° / 33°. The production of this useful car was terminated in the mid-1990s, after manufacturing a total of 5,533 units of the Peugeot 504 Pick-up / Break and the 505 Break Dangel.

Dangel Peugeot 505 4x4 ❷

In 1985, the following versions of the 5-d 5-seat 504 Dangel 4x4 were presented: the Familial / the Break—a passenger / utility station wagon, the Break Entreprise—a 2-seat utility vehicle, and an ambulance. The latter was also available with a fiberglass superstructure. A year after its premiere, it was replaced by the 505 Dangel 4x4 station wagon. The modified drivetrain was identical with that of the 504, except for the 2,0L gasoline engine (108hp @ 5250), which replaced the less powerful 2.3L diesel. The car was 193 in long, 71 in wide and featured a 115-in wheelbase and an 8.7-in ground clearance. The lightest model weighed 3,439 lbs and had a payload of 1,433 lbs inclusive. In 1986, a prototype of the V6 PRV was built for a trans-African expedition led by Nicolas Hulot. The Peugeot 505 4x4 Dangel CKDs were dis-

The Dangel Peugeot 504 Pick-up

The Dangel Citroën C25, 1988

patched to China to be assembled by the Guangzhou Peugeot Automobiles Company—Dangel's Canton-based subsidiary.

Dangel Peugeot J5 / Citroën C25 4x4 ❽

Dangel Peugeot Boxer / Citroën Jumper / Fiat Ducato; all 4x4 ❽ ❾

In 1987, a conversion of delivery Peugeots and Citroëns J5 / C 25 was introduced. Dangel kept the existing 2x4 drive,

and provided the option of adding the RWD pneumatically through the Dangel P08 transmission. A simpler remodeling was opted for, as only up to 5% of the cars were expected to be used in the off-road. Later, a gear-reduction transmission was available to order. By 1995 inclusive, a total of 3,020 units of the J5 / C25 4x4 Dangel had been made, out of which 1,800 were taken up by the French army, and 800 went to other government organizations. After 1995, Dangel contributed to the new generation of the Peugeot Boxer / Citroën Jumper / Fiat Ducato. The 4x4 drive features an auxiliary two-speed transmission and a connected inter-axle

The Dangel Citroën C25 and C15 4x4, 1993

The Dangel Peugeot Boxer HM3, 1998

The Dangel Peugeot Boxer HM3, 1998

The Dangel Citroën Berlingo, 1998

viscous coupling. The rear differential is equipped with an electro-pneumatically controlled locking system. The Gendarmes, the army and the state administration all favor the Peugeot Boxer HM3, distinguished by a reinforced chassis on a ladder frame. It is based on the Boxer 350 with a D / TD 2.5L engine. Power is transmitted from the engine through a 5-speed transmission into an inter-axle differential placed in the center of the vehicle, and gear-reduction transmissions. The vehicle can venture into really rough terrains by virtue of its 15.7-in-high ground clearance, 38° / 35° overhang angles and off-road tires.

Dangel Citroën C15 4x4 ❽

The lightweight Citroën C15 4x4 Dangel was showcased in Paris in 1990. It was available under the marques of 600 or 765, as a 4-seat station wagon, van or pick-up truck (with a canvas tilt) and a 1769cc (60hp @ 4600) diesel engine. The original version was a 2x4 but came with the option of adding the RWD through the Dangel P012 transmission. The rear differential could be locked. The vehicle featured an 8.3-in ground clearance and 40° / 50° overhang angles. The National Gendarmerie purchased 700 units between 1991 and 1994. A total of 2,013 units were produced.

Dangel Peugeot Partner 4x4 / Citroën Berlingo 4x4 ❽

In Paris 1998, the Peugeot Dangel Partner 4x4 was presented, followed two years later by its sister-car—the Citroën Dangel Berlingo 4x4. The 4x4 drive had undergone further improvements, involving mainly the ground clearance (8.1 in after adding 1.2 in), a reinforced rear suspension, and a transversally positioned rear-axle differential with an electro-pneumatically controlled locking system. The transmission is connected to an inter-axle differential. At a premium, an electro-pneumatic gear-reduction transmission is available, installed in the axis of the connecting shaft. The Partner 4x4 will negotiate a 43° slope and 29°/ 28° overhang angles. Dangel has nicknamed this model "the first French SUV." The Berlingo 4x4 utility vehicle features the same mechanics. The 2nd generation of the Partner / Ber-

The Dangel Citroën Berlingo II; a debut in Paris, 2002

lingo was shown in Paris 2002. Dangel had improved the 4x4 by making it more suitable for driving on asphalt roads and reducing its weight. A viscous coupling replaced the heavy inter-axle differential of the previous generation. The wheel-slip during acceleration is also electronically controlled. The DGL type of a limited slip differential is mounted in the front. The rear (DGLV type) limited slip differential has been equipped with a manually controlled lock. Since July 2002, a special "slow" speed gear has been available on request. The overhang angles of the vehicle are 29° /31°.

The Dangel Berlingo II / Partner II—"slow 1ˢᵗ gear," 2002

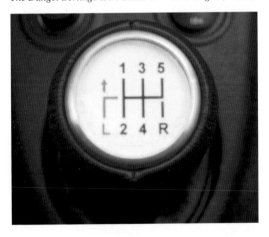

A chassis of the Peugeot Dangel Boxer HM3, 1998

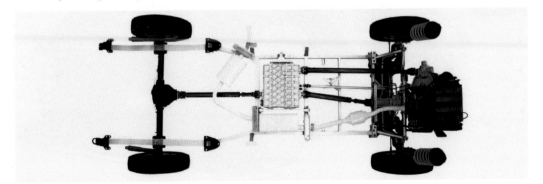

Delahaye
(France)

The Delahaye Type 182, 1951

The make of Delahaye managed to launch its first motor vehicle in the same year as it was established — 1895 — at the automobile section of the Paris bicycle exhibition show. In 1897, Engineer Emile Delahaye sold the firm to two Parisians. The factory produced one graceful model after another. Then post-war poverty and the unfavorable tax system decimated the pride of France — the makers of luxury vehicles. Delahaye, said to have supplied artillery tractors to the German army, strove to weather the storm. In 1954, it made an agreement with Hotchkiss to become part of the company. It proceeded to produce vehicles bearing the Hotchkiss brand but was closed down eventually before the end of 1954.

Delahaye V.L.R. – Type 182

The company pinned its hopes on a lightweight military off-roader code-named Type 182, better known as the V.L.R. (Véhicule Léger de Reconnaissance). The first drafts were created in the late 1940s and in the summer of 1950, and the result was presented to a military committee at a test bed in Saumur, following 2.5 years of development. The soldiers were basically happy with it but requested a simpler design. In order to help the company out, the minister of defense ordered 4,000 V.L.R.'s. The public was first introduced to the model at the Rally Méditerranée-Le Cap at the turn of 1950/1951. But the V.L.R. made no grand impression and later it found only a few buyers in the civil sector. Power was

supplied by a 4V OHV Delahaye 1995cc (63hp @ 3800) engine with an aluminum block. The vehicle featured a 4-speed transmission and a 2-speed auxiliary gear-reduction transmission, differential locks, RWD or AWD and drum brakes. Not many off-roaders of the time boasted an independent suspension of the wheels and transversal torsion bars. Its open steel Spartan soft-top bodies were supplied by the Facel car body works. The model had an 85-in wheelbase, a 136-in length, a 64-in width, a 73-in height, and it weighed 3,219 lbs. Its production was terminated in 1953 because the vehicle had proven inappropriate for the assignment, and for the 14 years that ensued, the French army clung to the franchised Hotchkiss M201 Jeeps. Delahaye made a total of 9,630 units of the V.L.R.

The Delahaye Type 182, 1951

The DKW Munga 6

DKW, Auto Union (Germany)

German four wheel drive vehicles of the 1940s and 1950s
In the 1940s, the Stoewer company based in Germany produced nearly 13,000 units of the R200 Spezial 4x4 in a number of different versions. The cars were powered by a Stoewer 1997cc engine (50hp @ 3600) and featured a 5-speed transmission, a 1-speed auxiliary transmission and an inter-axle differential. A sisterly series of "light-duty universal 4WD vehicles" with a 95-in wheelbase were made by BMW with 6V engines and by Hanomag. The light-duty off-road Tempo G1200 featured a pair of two-stroke 2V air-cooled 598cc engines (19hp) with a 4-speed transmission. Each one provided power for the wheels of one axle. Either one or both engines could be engaged. The wheels were suspended independently. The "middle-class 4WD universal automobile" (4x4) was produced by Auto Union and Horch and distributed as the 901 Typ 40, and by Wanderer and Opel. These vehicles differing only in small details featured 3-speed transmissions with a 2-speed reduction and an inter-axle differential with a locking system. They were powered by 6V Opel or V8 Horch 3.5L and 3.8L engines. They had independently suspended wheels with coil springs. The wheelbase was 122 in long. Several above-mentioned makers later merged to form Auto Union. In 1948–1950, Autowerke Salzgitter launched their Jeeps developed in a process of repairs and civilian modifications. Their 3-d station wagons were distributed under the name AWS.

The DKW Munga

DKW F91 / M-Wagen / Munga (Germany, Brazil)

The DKW was founded in 1928 by Jürgen Skafte Rasmussen. Before 1939, the company only produced 2x4 popular vehicles. The main part of the firm after the war was in the Soviet zone. Production was resumed in the GDR under the name IFA, while in the BRD, the production of DKW was launched in 1950 in Düsseldorf. It was part of the Ingolstadt-based Auto Union, which later gave rise to Audi. DKW supplied the Bundeswehr with the $^1/_4$ ton DKW M-Wagen (Mehrzweckwagen = a multi-purpose vehicle), or the DKW / Auto Union F91/4. In March 1957, a civilian version was introduced at last. The vehicle's open body had at first 4 seats (the Munga 4), later 6 seats (the Munga 6—after 1960), and later still also 8 seats (the Munga 8—after 1962). The vehicle got the name Munga (Mehrzweck-Universal Geländefahrzeug mit allradAntrieb). The last specimen was taken up by the army in December 1968. A total of 46,750 units of the DKW M-Wagen / Munga were made. They were replaced by the VW Iltis. The DKWs featured a 3V two-stroke 896cc engine (38hp @ 4200, in 1957 40hp @ 4250). In 1958, the capacity was raised to 980cc (44hp @ 4500, 60 mph). It provided power to all the wheels through a 4-speed transmission and a 2-speed reduction. Specimens made before 1956 came with an option to disengage the RWD. A steel frame chassis bore an open all-metal body. The wheels were suspended independently with transversal leaf springs. Other specifications included: wheelbase—79 in, length—136 in, width—59 in, height—53 in, ground clearance—9.5 in, curb weight—2,447 lbs, payload—750 lbs, fording depth—19.7 in. In 1956, DKW established partnership with the Brazilian company Vemag. In addition to the DKW passenger cars, the company also produced the Candango—an open off-road vehicle. In 1958, DKW-Vemag introduced their 0.9L off-road vehicle, which was nothing other than the F91/4. In 1960, this 4x4 car got the name Candango and a 1,0L engine (50hp). It was followed by the Candango-2 with a 4x2 drive. Eventually, the Brazilians got into financial difficulties and terminated the production in 1963, having sold nearly 8,000 Candangos.

The Stoewer AVZ in the Czech Army Vehicles Museum, Lešany, Czech Republic

The Dong A Jeep 4x4 Family Wagon, 1981

Dong A
(South Korea)

Dong A emerged in 1977, picking up the baton from Ha Dong-Hwan—a manufacturer of utility vehicles founded in 1954. In 1984, Dong A was swallowed by Keohwa Co. Ltd.—a producer of a Korean mutation of the Jeep. In 1986, Dong A was bought by the SsangYong Business Group, which turned it into an automobile division, naming it SsangYong Motor Company. After the war, the Willys Jeep CJ was also made in Korea under the name Shival.

The Dong A Jeep 4x4 SR-7, 1981

Keohwa Jeep 4x4 ❷

The Koreans produced the Willys Jeep CJ with a wheelbase length of 94 and 114 in. The length of the soft-top version was 157 in, as opposed to the station wagon (150 in and 183 in). The width of the vehicle was 67 in. It was 72 inches high, except the "Family Wagon"—a long, 3-d station wagon—which was (+)5 inches higher. The short soft-top version (SR-7) carried 3 people and weighed 4,200 lbs, the short 3-d station wagon ("Patrol") seated 6 persons and weighed 4,189 lbs and the long station wagon seated 12 people and featured 5,005 lbs of curb weight. Without exception, the cars were all powered by 2775cc gasoline engines (85hp @ 4000, 79 mph). They were exported and distributed in some countries under the name of Stampede.

Eagle
(Great Britain)

In 1981, Eagle Cars—another producer of kit cars—entered the market.

Eagle Rhino, Eagle 4x4 and RV, Milan RV   ❷ ❹

In 1981–83, the Rhino Jeeps based on the VW Beetle were breathing their last. Eagle bought their rights and after modification it launched them as "RV's." Several models were made over the years, although the main concept and shape remained the same. The RV sports a ladder chassis and an open laminated body similar to that of the CJ / Wrangler

Jeep. A hard-top version is likewise available. The vehicles cannot be approved for sale in all European countries because they don't have the chance of acquiring a homologation. The Eagle 4x4 uses components of the Range Rover including a V8 engine. Its production ended in 1986. The Eagle RV Series makes use of some components of the Ford Cortina Mk III and IV, or the VW Beetle. The latest model—the Eagle DB50—features components of the Daihatsu F20 or F50. In the mid-1980s, the production and distribution of the cars in Germany was taken up by the Milan Automobile company based in Lennep. The Jeep Milan RV made in 1987 relied on Ford components, including the gasoline and diesel 4V or 6V engines. Specifications: wheelbase—95 in, length—145 in, width—69 in, height—67 in, weight—1,984 lbs. This "copycat" kit car featured RWD and a plastic body borne by a tubular frame with an optional canvas tilt.

The Eagle RV 4x4

The Milan RV

The Fadisa Romeo—Ebro F 100

Ebro, Motor Ibérica (Spain)

EBRO

Between 1920 and 1936, the Ford Motor Ibérica company assembled, and later in that period also produced, passenger vehicles and trucks. In 1954, it withdrew from Spain. In 1956, Motor Ibérica SA, Barcelona, rose from its ashes, to produce the franchised Ford trucks (of the Thames model) under the make of Ebro. The name derives from a major river that flows into the Mediterranean. In 1966, the firm joined forces with Perkins Hispania—a producer of diesel engines, which it mounted in their trucks—and Massey-

Ferguson—a manufacturer of agricultural machinery. In 1970, Motor Ibérica bought a share of the stocks of Aeronautica Industrial SA—an aircraft factory from Madrid. Since then, it has distributed its trucks under the name Avia Ebro. The process of acquisition of the Madrid-based company was completed in 1975, but the make remained the same. In 1967 they began selling Alfa Romeo vans, followed by their own generation of Romeo-Ebro F100 in 1072–75 and the steadily-growing F Series, respectively. A gradually modernized production of the latter was kept up until the early 1990s (the F 275, the F 350, featuring D Perkins engines with a prechamber, where the numbers indicate the vehicles' total weight). They were replaced by vehicles constructed in co-operation with Nissan. In the same period, they also made the Ebro-Siata minibuses and vans (Siata had produced passenger and delivery vehicles since 1960 before being swallowed up by Motor Ibérica in 1973.) In 1980, 36% of the Barcelona-based company was bought by Nissan, which increased its share to 95% in 1985. The Japanese made Spain their European outpost for light off-road and utility vehicles.

Jeep Ebro ❷

In 1974, Motor Ibérica took under its wing the distribution of the Zaragoza-made Willyses. The cars known as Jeep Ebro remained on offer long into the 1980s when they were replaced by the franchise-made Nissan Patrol.

The Jeep Ebro Commando

Ebro Patrol ❷

The first visible fruits of the company's partnership with Nissan came in 1983 in the form of the franchise-made Nissan Patrol. This hard worker suitable for rough terrains was produced until 2001. The Ebro Patrol 4WD was not remarkably comfortable, but it made easy meat of hard labor. In the early 1990s, it was popular with farmers, owners of suburban family houses, power companies, as well as all military and police armed forces. The basic — heavier — version bore the name TH, the more luxurious version featuring a steering booster was known as the TB. Its body was welded from sheet steel. The vehicle featured a Spanish gasoline in-line 4V Perkins MD-27 engine with the following parameters: 2,710cc, 70hp, @ 3600, 68 mph (TH) and 75 mph (TB). It featured a 5-speed transmission. The engine

powered either the rear or all wheels and there was an optional cross-country reduction for the 4x4 mode. The Patrol's axles were rigid. Further characteristics: wheelbase — 93 in, total length — 160 in, width — 67 in, height — 72 in or 5 in more (for the elevated-roof version), ground clearance — 7.5 in. The car got safely through a mass of water as deep as 23.6 in and negotiated a 90% (TB) or an 85% slope (TH). The version with a standard roof height weighed 4,079 lbs. The 2-d station wagon version carried 2 passengers and up to 948 lbs of cargo, or alternatively up to 7 people and 948 lbs of cargo; the payload rating was 3,306 and 3,748 lbs. In the late 1980s, "Ebro" disappeared from the vehicles name.

The Ebro Patrol

The Ebro F 275

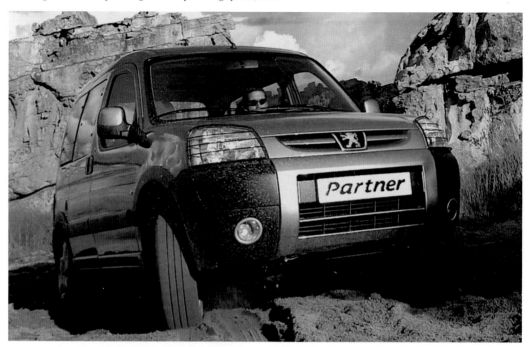

FAM Automobiles (France)

The FAM Automobiles motor works of Exincourt in the Doubs region of France was established in 1986. The FAM assists major car works, develops and refines car parts, builds special versions and supplies small-series components. In 1986–90, it assembled 80 units of the Peugeot P4 per year for the government. Its "Peugeot Sport" department took care of the logistics of the sharp P4s in long-distance and off-road raid rallies. In 1993–95, following its own documentation, it converted the 4700 Lada Niva (+ the 3000 Samar and the 150 Pontiac Transport) to diesel-powered machines, and another 20,000 cars of other makes to LPGs and CNGs. It has also had its fingers in the pie of the Indian Mahindra 4WD, and on the 3000 Expert and 300 Partner models from 2001–2003, designed to transport the dogs serving in the French police force. The company supplies parts for the Peugeot Sport factory team. In 2000, it started selling relatively cheap modifications designed for occasional off-road use where there is no need of 4x4 drive. The concept consists in the installation of a limited slip differential, for if a car equipped with a normal differential runs one of its powered wheels on a slippery surface and the wheel begins to slip, 100% of torque is transmitted on it and the car is trapped. The FAM limited-slip differential will ensure that at least 25% of torque continues to be transmitted to a wheel running on a firmer or rougher surface and the car avoids getting trapped. The modifications also involve increasing the ground clearance, reinforcement of the protection of the engine underpan and floor of the vehicle, and the provision of off-road tires. FAM focused on the make of Peugeot. The modifications concern the following models: the 260 3- and 5-d sedan/ "driving school" (1.9 D and 2.0 HDI); the 307 3- and 5-d sedan/station wagon (2.0 ES, 2.0 HDI), the Partner 3-d station wagon/utility vehicle (ditto and a gasoline 1.6 ES), the Expert 3- and 5-d station wagon/van (ditto) and a van/chassis/minibus featuring engines ranging between 2.0 ES and 2.8 HDI. The latter three models are available with wheelbases of different lengths.

The Peugeot FAM 206 Break, 2002

The Fargo DF

Fargo (France)

The make of Fargo of the Automobiles De Fremond company from Béhoust was presented in 1999. Arnaud de Frémond and Patrick Müller (producer of the Dallas) met through an advertisement in Le Parisien issued two years before. They took on Engineer Francois Quirin, who had developed the Dallas Phase 3. They drew inspiration from the Citroën Méhari. Since 2000, the company has been making the Fargo DF. A prototype of this model was born in March 2000 and first presented at a local motor show in Plongeé; its international debut took place shortly afterward in Paris in 2000. The mechanics of the vehicle are derived from the Peugeot 106/ Citroën Saxo. It is powered by a 1,124cc engine (60hp @ 6200, 87 mph). Its simple steel chassis bears a 2- or 4-d beach polyester body. The front axle sports McPherson struts, while the rear axle features wishbones and transversal torsion bars. This 2x4 car carries 4 people, or the driver plus 794 lbs of load. The rear part of the floor is flat. When empty, it weighs 1,642 lbs. Dimensions (length x height x width): 142 x 62 x 66 in.

The Fargo DF

Felber (Switzerland)

The Felber Oasis, 1981

This small Swiss company based in Morges and owned by W. H. Felber used to be a concessioner of luxury makes including Rolls-Royce, Bentley, Ferrari and Lotus. In the late 1970s and in the early 1980s, it was also engaged in car remodeling.The small Roberta hatchback and the Pacha (a big sedan or coupé) were all geared toward the requirements of their wealthiest customers. Mr. Felber liked to base his activities on Lancias. Unlike Monteverdi, for instance, the designer also paid attention to a new grille and side profiles, in the hope of giving them an aristocratic touch.

Felber Oasis

In March 1979, the company showcased the Felber Oasis—a luxury AT station wagon—for the first time in Geneva. This model, too, was derived from the 3-d American all-steel AT station wagon of International Scout (see Monteverdi). Its American V8 5.7L engine (165hp), as well as the overall technological design are identical with the original or the Monteverdi Safari. Noteworthy is the option to choose from a range of transmissions: a manual 3-speed transmission, two manual 4-speed transmissions with a different range of gears, and a 3-speed automatic planetary transmission made by Chrysler. At a premium, Felber offered an alternative

pedigree Rolls-Royce engine. Other features: wheelbase—100 in, length—166 in, width—70 in, height—66 in, and ground clearance—7.7 in. The top speed as described in a pamphlet provided by the company was 106 mph, and the car had a curb weight of 3,693 lbs. The list of accessories is very long but smoke-collored windows were part of the standard equipment sold at 46,000 Swiss Francs. The likelihood of coming across one of the few specimens of this model that were produced is close to zero.

The Felber stall at the 1981 Geneva Motor Show

The Fiat Panda SUV, Leipzig, Germany, 2004. (A study showcased in the previous year was named Fiat Simba.)

Fiat
(Italy)

Fiat is short for "S.A. Fabbrica Italiana di Automobili, Tori-no," founded in 1899 by Giovanni Angelli, aged 33. He began making the history of this Italian giant which penetrated many domains. After the war it showed how to mass-produce economical cars which had a reputation of being bigger on the inside than the outside. Fiat manufactured a wide range of utility vehicles, including the 900E van, several generations of the Ducato series and the smaller Scudo series, all with a 4x4 alternative. The same cannot be said about the original MPV Multipla from the fall of 1998. The car of the fall of 2000—the Dobló 5-d minivan with engines—a 1.2L (65hp /80hp-16v), a 1.6-L (103hp / 106hp), or a D 1.9L (63hp and 101hp for the TD common rail)—positioned transversally in the front, lived to see its 4x4 variant. In Bologna 2002, Fiat introduced its concept of the Sandstorm-Dobló 4x4 featuring a self-locking differential and plastic fender flares. Next to it stood a concept of the Fiat Simba—a compact SUV with a 5-d AT body of the future Panda and a 4x4 drive distributed through a viscous coupling. As far back as Turin 1976, Fiat presented a prototype of the 126 Cavalletta—a beach vehicle with a torpedo or hard-top body mounted on a Fiat chassis and with a 594cc engine (21.5hp) fitted in the rear. Large-scale production did not occur. In 1992, a similar vehicle named Panda Destriero was shown, featuring a targa arch. The 2003 Geneva motor show visitors feasted their eyes on a concept of the Fiat MorraTech beach vehicle.

Fiat Campagnola ❷

Fiat Campagnola with permanent 4x4 made its debut at the Bari Trade Fair in 1951. Fiat has made no secret of being inspired by Jeep. In Italian, the word "Fiat" is used to describe a jolly and slightly noisy Italian countrywoman. In addition to a civilian version, a military version—the AR51 (Auto-vettura da Ricognizione)—was also designed. Its simple open 2-d steel body was placed on a ladder frame. A frontally-mounted 4V 1901cc OHV engine (53hp @ 3700, 62 mph) was connected to a transmission with synchro-gears 2,3 and 4. Power was distributed either to all or only the rear wheels. The rear differential was equipped with a lock. The rear axle was derived from the Fiat 1100 one-ton truck, while the front one came from the Fiat 1100B sedan.

The Fiat Dobló Sandstorm, Bologna, Italy 2002

The Fiat Campagnola

The Fiat Campagnola, 1971

The front wheels were suspended independently with trapezoid arms and coil springs, while the rear axle was rigid with half-elliptic springs. The brakes were of the drum-type. After 1953, the vehicle was also available with a D engine of the same capacity (40hp, @ 3200, 53 mph). Further characteristics of the AR51 included an 85% slope, a 2,758-lb curb weight, a capacity to transport 2 passengers and 728 lbs of cargo or 6 passengers and 110 lbs of luggage, wheelbase—89 in, length—143 in, width—58 in, height—71 in, ground clearance—7.9 in, payload—1,102 lbs. This novelty won its spurs by pulling off the distance from Cape Town to Algeria in 11 days, 4 hours and 54 minutes, setting thus a world record. Many units were bought by the army, 358 by the Carabinieri. The AR51 generation was made until 1955, when it was replaced by the Campagnola A (AR55-military). It differed in terms of performance (63hp @ 4000, 72 mph). In addition to better wiring, it also differed in dimensions and weight: length—143 in, width—61 in, height—77 in, curb weight—2,844 lbs, payload—1,058 lbs, slope—over 90 %. Its Campagnola A diesel engine had been made between 1953 (1955) and 1960 (43hp @ 3200); this type was later replaced by the Campagnola B diesel engine (51hp @ 3800, 59 mph). The AR55 B military vehicle was equipped with a 56hp-engine. In 1959, the AR 59 model got a mild facelift (wiring of 24 V and the engines). The vehicle was adapted to the standard AT $^1/_4$-ton used by NATO. This vehicle was also used for transporting Venezuelan and Mexican soldiers. The last stage was the Campagnola C (1968) with a 1968cc engine (47hp). Over 3,000 units of

The Fiat Campagnola

The Fiat Nuova Campagnola carabinieri

the "B" and "C" models served with the Carabinieri. The production of AR 59 stopped in 1973. Fiat made a total of 31,293 units with gasoline engines and 7,783 units of the 1st generation of the D Campagnola. The vehicle was assembled by the Zastava company in Yugoslavia.

Fiat Nuova Campagnola

In Belgrade 1975 (the home debut took place in June 1974), the Nuova Campagnola (2nd generation) was presented. This model was characterized by the markedly more civilian appearance of its self-supporting body with an integrated frame made of I-profiles; major changes also involved the independent suspension of all wheels (the rear axle now featured trapezoids, torsion bars and double telescopic shock absorbers). The 4V OHV 1995cc engine (80hp @ 4600, DIN, 71 mph) was taken from the Fiat 132/125 sedan. The transmission had four speeds but was already fully synchronized. A central cross-country reduction had been added, enabling the car to negotiate a slope of up to 150%. The design gave the option of disengaging the FWD. Other characteristics: wheelbase—92 in, length—149 in, width—62 in, height—77 in, ground clearance—10.7 in, curb weight—3,461 lbs, payload—1,257 lbs. The vehicle was able to carry the driver plus 1,102 lbs of cargo, or up to 7 people and 176 lbs of luggage. In 1976, the choice was extended by models with a 7.9-in longer rear overhang, and a station wagon. These vehicles were produced until 1979.

Fiat Nuova Campagnola Diesel 2000–2500 ❷

In the middle of November 1979, the new Campagnolas finally appeared, fitted with D Sofim Italian engines and purpose-built for work in the off-road. Typical for them was a bulging hood. Gasoline 4V 2.0L (60hp, DIN) and 2.5L (72hp, DIN) power units were mounted. The increase in total weight by 220 lbs (the short Torpedo soft top) to 463 lbs (the long Hard Top) were partly due to the engines, accessories and in the latter case also a standard steering booster. Short and long Torpedos and hard-tops had their speed limited to 71 mph and negotiated a slope of over

100%. The overhang angles of the short versions were 37°/28°. A breakthrough in mechanics (a 5-speed transmission, a differential lock — even in the front, at a premium), interior (up to 7 seats) and exterior (adjustable headlights), mainly for the civilian sector, won this vehicle the name Nuova Campagnola 2nd Series. A total of 1,910 Torpedos and 214 units of the Hard Top Nuova Campagnola served with the Carabinieri. With a total of 30,000 units made, production ended in 1987, unfortunately without a "successor". Mechanically, the Campagnola could not compete with Japanese cars and the management had missed the trend toward increased interest in 4x4 vehicles.

The Fiat Nuova Campagnola Torpedo, 1974

The Fiat Campagnola carabinieri

The Fiat Panda 4x4

Fiat Panda 4x4

In 1980, the Fiat 127 was followed by an even smaller car—the Fiat Panda—bearing the name of a cute Chinese bear. It was fitted with 2V or 4V engines with the capacities of 652, 843 and 903cc. A 4x4 version of the Panda appeared in late 1983. It scored a bull's eye. Steyr contributed to the conversion of its chassis and drivetrain. This vehicle was powered exclusively by a transversally-positioned 965cc engine (48hp @ 5600) from the Lancia A 112. For easier hill-descent, the 5-speed transmission was equipped with heavier gears. The front axle retained its independent suspension with crossarms and coil springs; the rear axle was rigid with two clusters of three leaf springs. The Panda was able to reach a top speed of 84 mph and negotiate a 42% slope.

Other characteristics included: wheelbase—85 in, length—134 in, width—58.5 in, height—57 in. When empty, it weighed 1,631 lbs, while its payload capacity was 882 lbs. It carried up to 5 passengers and 110 lbs of cargo. It was available only with a two-space 2-d reinforced and strengthened body. The New Panda 4x4 special Series 5000 was prepared in September 1985. Fiat made it until 1986, when the New Panda equipped with the new Fire engines and a new "Omega" rigid rear axle with coil springs was showcased in Turin. Some of these features were also used in the 4x4 version with a gasoline 999cc (50hp) engine; the alternative diesel and the rest of the models in 1986 were not fitted with the Omega axle. As many as 1,283 units found their way to the garages of the Italian police.

Fiat New Panda 4x4

In the spring of 1992, the Panda 4x4 underwent a facelift including a new engine—the Fire 1108cc (50hp @ 5250 or 54hp @ 5500, injection and catalytic converter, 81 mph). From now on, 4x2 drive could be used for driving on a road, and 4x4 drive for the off-road. The front axle sported McPherson struts. The car had a 24° approach angle and managed to go up a 45% slope. In 1992–95, a standard model—the Trekking—was manufactured, followed by a limited series of the Country Club after 1995, a replacement for the original Sisley. Although this car, assembled by Steyr, is rarely found in Fiat's line-up, it continues to be made steadily and in an almost unchanged form. Alpine mountain resorts or Andorra provide sufficient proof that the Panda 4x4 plays the part of an inconspicuous but efficient helper—a mountain "shopping bag."

The Fiat Panda 4x4, Andorra 2002

Fiberfab
(Germany)

The Fiberfab Sherpa

Fiberfab Sherpa ❹

The Fiberfab company active in 1966–73 and 1974-about 83 specialized in laminated bodies. In the first phase of its existence, it was affiliated to its American namesake and was based in Stuttgart; in the 2ⁿᵈ phase it moved to Heilbronn. In the Mediterranean countries such as Greece, it was known for its Sherpa pick-up truck, introduced in 1975, whose 2-seat laminated soft-top body with solid doors carried 2 passengers. It featured a 1,378-lb payload and a curb weight of 2,458 lbs. The Citroën 2 CV was the source of its 2V 602cc engine (32hp) and 4-speed transmission and independent wheel suspension. Other features: wheelbase— 95 in, length—139 in, wheel track—49.6 in, height—60 in, and overhang angles—33° / 45°.

The Fissore Scout 127 first generation

Fissore, Rayton Fissore, Magnum Automobili (Italy)

The origins of this Turin-based body workshop go back to 1920. It was founded by the Fissore brothers—Antonio, Bermando, Costanzo and Giovanni. From the initial horse-driven carriages they moved on to passenger cars and trucks. They designed and built bodies for other companies, such as Monteverdi, for which they produced bodies for sports and representation cars and the Safari off-roaders. The army model of Military was made after the firm was reorganized and established under the new name of Rayton Fissore by the children of the founders and one of its former managers in 1984. The firm experienced constant changes of staff, rivalry and mixing of the several generations of family clans, and the shock caused by the crises in 1973 and 1984 proved fatal. The vehicles, however, lived to see the end of the century. Although Rayton Fissore officially ended in 1988, it continued to exist in 1988–92 under the same name, and

The Fissore Monteverdi 230 M

from 1998 until about 2000, it was known as Magnum Automobili. Since about 1988, Laforza Automobiles Inc. from California has assembled the vehicles from Italian parts. Fissore's interesting projects included special off-road ambulances, which the factory built for Italian as well as foreign customers (Africa, Asia), on the Fiat Campagnola, Range Rover and Toyota chassis.

Fissore Gipsy and Scout 127 ❹

The Fissore Gipsy with 4 or 5 seats made its debut in Turin in 1971. It was designed for minor work purposes and recreational driving. It was soon renamed the Fissore Scout 127. This successful vehicle was sold in many countries, mainly in the Mediterranean. Its open plastic body (with a tilt) was mounted on a steel tubular frame. It had a frontal 4V 127903cc Fiat engine (47hp @ 6200, 87 mph). The engine powered the front wheels via a 4-speed transmission. Both axles were independent, with McPherson struts in the front and trailing arms and coil springs in the back. The Scout 127 featured an 88-in wheelbase and a 5.1-in ground clearance. It was 137 in long, 58 in wide, 54 in high and it weighed 1,444 lbs. It was built by Franco Maina and the planned monthly output was 180. It underwent several changes of styling. Its originally laminated body was later reinforced with steel panels. The last specimens rolled off the assembly line in 1982. They were franchise-built as "Samba" by Emelba in Spain, and as "Amico" in Greece.

Rayton Fissore Magnum ❷

The Rayton Fissore Magnum station wagon was nicknamed "off-road Rolls-Royce." A sneak preview was scheduled for late 1984, and an official debut took place in Geneva 1985, followed there by the Magnum VIP a year later. It had a luxurious 5-d 5-seat body made of steel and laminate. Its slightly bulging hood originally concealed the following engines: a 4V Fiat 1995cc (135hp @ 5500, 96 mph) 2.0 VX; a V6 Alfa Romeo 2492cc (156hp @ 5600 L/min, 106 mph) 2.5i V6; and a VIP (since November 1986, and October 1986 respectively). After 1988, a 6V BMW engine was briefly used, as well as (since November 1989) a TD intercooler VM 2393cc (110hp @ 4200, 93 mph)—2.4 TD, and a 2498cc (120hp @ 4200, 99 mph)—2.5 TD VIP. The engine powered the rear wheels via a 5-speed transmission with

The Fissore Scout 127

The Fissore Scout Hard Top

The Fissore Scout Hard Top

The Magnum American Limited, 1998

a reduction. In the off-road, FWD would be added, the free-wheel hubs locked and use would be made of ZF self-locking differentials in both axles. Both were rigid with stabilizers and aligned shock absorbers, with coil springs in the front and leaf springs in the back. Other features included: a 106-in wheelbase, a 180-in length, a 79-in width, a 74-in height, and a 7.5-in ground clearance. When empty, the vehicle weighed +4,916 lbs, and had a payload of 1,433 lbs, a 20-in fording depth, and managed a 100 % slope. Forest management companies and, above all, the police force sang the praises of the Spartan-equipped Magnum. They were also the target customers of a 3-seat pick-up truck with a hard-top over the cargo area. In 1991, the front face of the luxurious models underwent a few touch-ups.

The Magnum American Limited, 1998

The Magnum, 1998

The Magnum Van, 1998

The Magnum, 1990

Laforza (U.S.A.)

In the U.S.A, the Magnum was assembled by Laforza between 1988 and 92. Most of the parts they used were Turin-made, but they fitted the cars with American Ford V8 4642cc engines (185hp @3800, 101 mph)—5.0 V8. The luxurious Magnum or Laforza were exported to many countries, including the United Arab Emirates.

Magnum Classic

The year 1988 saw the resurrection of a group of companies (Magnum Automobili, Magnum Industriale), as well as the start of production of a revamped version of the Magnum in Cheracso—30 miles from Turin. It included a range of civilian and commercial vehicles (police, army and rescue-squad specials). The luxurious SUV Classic Limited and—since 1999—America Limited became even more bounteous, and the military Classic VAV even more rustic. The more than 1,000 units of the 1st generation provided for the police and the local authorities gained a good reputation. The models included: the Classic Limited—an off-road 5-d station wagon; the Classic Armored—an armored station wagon; the Classic VAV—a 4-d convertible; the VAV (=Veicolo Attacco Veloce)—a fast attack vehicle; the Classic Pick-up, and the Classic Furgone. They were presented in Turin in 1998. The front axle got independent wheel suspension with torsion bars, while the rear axle remained rigid, with half-elliptic longitudinal springs and a stabilizer. A 4-speed automatic transmission was available at a premium, instead of the standard 5-speed manual one. The rear wheels were always engaged, and there was optional FWD for the off-road terrain. The rear self-locking differential was a standard feature. The customer had to pay extra to have it installed on the front axle as well; the same was true about the lockable freewheel of the front wheels. The ABS was likewise available at a premium. The vehicle had disc brakes. The factory relied on economical TD engines with an intercooler—a 4V 2.8L (122hp) or a 5V 2.8L (150hp), or on gasoline power units—a V6 2.8L (185hp) and a V8 5.0L (225hp). Only the height changed (68 in). The late-1990s economic chill froze this initiative, too.

The Magnum Classic VAV, Turin 1998

Foers
(Great Britain)   FOERS

In 1977, John A. Foers founded a company in Rotherham, which in 1990 changed its name to Del Tech Ltd. It faded away around 1995, but it seems to have renewed its activity towards the end of the 1990s.

Foers Nomad, Triton   ❹

The first vehicle made by Foers was the Nomad (2x4) recreational vehicle. The company produced an aluminum body kit which was fastened to a Mini platform. It featured a 4V Leyland 998cc engine (40hp @ 5200, 75 mph) and a 4-speed transmission. This 4-seat vehicle had an 80-in wheelbase, and a 5.9-in ground clearance. Potential buyers had a choice between a convertible, a pick-up truck, a station wagon and a van version. About 200 units of the Nomad were made before 1985, when it was replaced by the Triton—a 4-s 3-d station wagon with the Mini Metro mechanics. After presenting the Ibex, a franchise was sold to Del Tech Ltd—a manufacturer of small vehicles.

Foers Ibex   ❷ ❽

The Ibex off-roader was designed by John Foers, who equipped it with time-tested Land Rover engines and a new ladder chassis. The Ibex did not only become popular with farmers who were the target customers. Its rectangular body made of galvanized sheet and light alloy did not pretend to be beautiful. The vehicle had permanent 4x4, a 5-speed

transmission with a reduction and coil spring suspension. The company made not only 4x4 vehicle, but also 6x6 specials for paramedics, firefighters, rescue squads and repairmen. The 4x4 version was available in the following range of wheelbase: 240" / 260" / 280" (93 / 100 / 110 in), and length 127 / 142 / 163 in. The cars were 71.7 in wide, 79.9 in high, featured a 10-in ground clearance, a carrying capacity of 7/9/11 persons, and the following overhang angles: 85° (approach), 85°/58°/40° (departure). The shortest versions in particular were unbeatable on tough tracks, thanks to their special floor plan with wheels in the corners. The Firefly Ibex 6x6—a fire engine presented in 1999—featured a Land Rover V 8 4.6L engine (220hp), a 144-in wheelbase and a 39-in distance between the rear axles. It was 244 in long, 71 wide and 83 high. It had a ZF 4-speed auto transmission, a 2-speed reduction, a differential lock fo the rear axles, 6x6 or 6x4 and disc brakes.

The Foers Nomad

The Rau Transit Sira 4x4

Ford (Europe)

In 1896, Henry Ford built the Quadricycle, and in 1903 he founded his own factory. His corporation spread around the world and became one of the leading car manufacturers. In 1911, the first Fords were assembled in Great Britain, and a production line was opened in Germany in 1926. In 1967, the branches in England and Germany (including their subdivisions in Spain, Portugal and Belgium) were brought together under the Ford of Europe umbrella company. The Ford empire contains, among others, Land Rover (since

2000), Mazda and Volvo. In addition to those makes, European markets have welcomed off-road vehicles from Thailand, Turkey and a limited number from the U.S.A. The models distributed by Ford included the road vehicle Escort / Orion, the Sierra and the Scorpio with AWD, but they had nothing to do with the off-road terrain. The Ford Transit delivery vehicle of the 1st (1961), the 2nd (1965), the 3rd (1985) and the 4th generations (2000) first featured 4x2 drive, and 4x2 or 2x4 (4th generation). The German-based Rau GmbH company rebuilt the 2nd generation to 4x4 drive—the Ford Sira 4x4 mini bus with 9–15 seats and 2.0L (78hp) or 2.4L D (62hp) engines.

Ford Maverick (Spain)   ❷

Ford, which controls a big part of the off-road-vehicle, pick-up-truck and SUV market in America, neglected these vehicles in Europe. The Maverick off-roader shown in Geneva 1993 had, apart from the name, nothing in common with its American cousin, let alone the Australian Ford Maverick, which was in fact nothing other than the Nissan Patrol GR. The Maverick was born on the drawing boards of the construction and development department of the Nissan European Technology Centre in Cranfield, GB. Its look-alike was the Nissan Terrano II, made by a branch of Nissan in Barcelona. Ford's designers in Brighton designed the interior. The production of Fords was terminated in 1998/99, while Nissan carried on in its own way. In LA 2000, the Mazda Tribute was launched; in Europe, it was available as "Ford Maverick" (= Escape, USA).

The Ford Maverick, 2002

The Ford Ranger, 2000

Ford Galaxy (Portugal) ❼

In June 1995, Ford and VW agreed to jointly produce the MPV Ford Galaxy / VW Sharan (5-doors, 5–8 seats), and later also the Seat Alhambra (2x4). These vehicles, made in a co-managed assembly plant in Setubal, Portugal, shared the same body types, engines and transmissions. A year later, the Sharan Syncro was launched, echoed a year later by the Ford Galaxy 4x4, which featured a gasoline engine V6 2792cc (174hp @ 5800, 120 mph). The 4WD model had a 5-speed manual or a 4-speed automatic transmission and an inter-axle differential with a viscous coupling. The vehicles had independently suspended wheels with coil springs, stabilizers and disc brakes on all wheels. The 2000 Geneva motor show saw the debut of their 2nd generation, without a 4x4 option.

Ford Explorer (U.S.A.) ❷

In Detroit 1990, the Ford Explorer off-roader was showcased—a short 3-d or a long 5-d station wagon with permanent RWD and optional FWD, or as a 4x2. These gradually refined cars are rarely available in Europe. The version with a V6 3996cc engine (162hp @ 4200, SAE, 106 mph) comes either with a 5-speed manual or a 4-speed automatic trans-

mission. The versions with 208hp, @ 5250 (106 mph) and V8 4942cc engines (213hp @ 4500, SAE, 115 mph) have only automatic transmissions. The Explorer 4x4 features an electrically-controlled multi-disc clutch of the inter-axle differential, a rear limited-slip differential and a gear-reduction transmission. A steel body is screwed down to a ladder frame. The front wheels have a double-wishbone suspension with torsion bars and stabilizers, while the rear axle is rigid, with leaf springs and stabilizers (the 4x2 version features coil springs). Dimensions: wheelbase— 102 / 111.5 in, length— 178 / 189 in, width—70.5 / 74 in, height—71 in, ground clearance—7.9 in. When empty, the vehicle weighs +3,682 / 4,189 lbs. In Detroit in 2001, a new generation with a modified appearance and a 4.0L V6 engine with 213hp @ 5250, SAE, later a 4601cc engine (242hp @ 4750, SAE, 115 mph) was introduced.

Ford Ranger (Thailand) ❷ ❻

The Auto Alliance based in Thailand, established in 1995 and managed by Ford and Mazda, has since 1999 been producing the Ford Ranger and Mazda Fighter / B Series commercial pick-ups, with perhaps the only difference being their grilles—see Mazda.

The Ford Explorer, NEC 2000

The Ford Ranger, NEC 2000

The Fiat 125p station wagon

The Polonez Analog

FSO
(Poland)

The construction of the FSO (Fabryka Samochodów Osobowych) assembly plant began in 1945. At first, it produced franchised models of Fiat—the 508 and 1100—and after January 1950, owing to political pressures, the Soviet GAZ M-20 sedans. On December 12, 1965, they went back to their traditional partner and obtained a franchise for the Fiat 125p. In early 1968, the first units of the Fiat 125p, different from the original, rolled off the assembly line. In 1978, they launched the production of the Polonez "national" hatchback. The FSO Nysa company makes utility versions of the Polonez-FSO-Truck. Its origins date back to 1947, when a decision was made to build a metallurgical factory in Nysa, Poland. In 1986, the factory was incorporated within the Warsaw-based FSO. In the 1990s, they assembled units of the Citroën C-15 and Berlingo. Their versions of the FSO-Truck include: a standard version, a long bed version (=a pick-up truck with an extended cargo area) and the 4-d Double Cab. In 2000, the company was renamed the Nysa Sp. and its 100% owner is Daewoo Motor Polska. Recently, an economic crisis broke out, whose impact was aggravated when the maternal Daewoo filed for bankruptcy. In spring 2002, the factory was stricken by a sit-in strike of Solidarnosc trade unions.

Fiat 125p Kombi 4x4   ⑩

A Warsaw Museum exhibit displays the prototype of a 4x4 off-road station wagon featuring some parts of the drivetrain that probably originated from the Lada Niva. Several 4x4 station wagons were manufactured after 1975.

Polonez 4x4   ❻

The Polonez pick-up (4x2), aka the Truck, was intended to replace the obsolete 125p pick-up trucks. A prototype of the Polonez 4x4 pick-up truck was designed and built in 1987–89. Its front axle, now also powered, was in fact a modified rear axle from the Polonez with drive shafts of the Lada Niva-2121. The rear axle was equipped with a transverse stabilizer. In 1984, a prototype with the working name of "Analog 1" (2x4, parts from the Lada Samara) was built, followed by "Analog 2" (axles from the Polonez, 4x2), and "Analog 3" (the Polonez drivetrain, 4x4). After evaluation of the test results they proceeded to build the 3rd version. The military research institute stepped in the development process of a multi-purpose vehicle, the result being a prototype of the Analog 4. It featured a Subaru axle drive and a differential locking system, but its FSO engine was too weak. Further development of the vehicle was frustrated after Daewoo had entered the company.

The Polonez Analog

A prototype of the Polonez 4x4

GAZ
(USSR and Russia)

In the 1930s, the Soviet automobile industry stood on two pillars—the AMO car works (later known as ZIS) in Moscow, and the GAZ factory based in Gorki, (before 1932 and after 1990 known as Nizhnyi Novgorod). The Bolshevik country needed huge numbers of cars, and a franchise wouldn't do: a complete high-capacity assembly plant was required. GM offered a factory with a yearly output of 12,500 Chevrolets, while Henry Ford suggested a full-blooded giant for 100,000 cars per year. The Russians signed a contract which yielded the Ford Motor Company 30 million USD. A complete production base had to be built from scratch. On March 4th, 1929, the papers published a decree of V. Kuybyshev, Chairman of the Supreme Soviet for National Economy (SSNE) concerning the construction of a car factory with a capacity of 100,000 units. On April 6th, it was confirmed that the factory would be built in the vicinity of a village called Monastyrka near Nizhnyi Novgorod. On May 31st, the SSNE USSR and FMC signed a contract about technological aid and cooperation in a large-scale production of the Ford A (model 1927) passenger car and the Ford AA truck. The project was prepared by Austin&K, an American office. The foundation stone was laid on May 2nd, 1930. While the technicians were being trained in the U.S.A., a giant factory rose within 18 months on the fields between the Volga and Oka rivers, built with herculean exertions, hardly any mechanization, in inhuman conditions, chaos and endless waste of building material. The American engineers present at the construction never quite understood the chaos, red tape stupidity and indifference that reigned in the atmosphere. The objective was achieved only thanks to the meticulous efforts of thousands of workers and drill. Partial failures were considered to be the work of saboteurs and "enemies of the nation." Such "malefactors" got the bullet or, if they were lucky, the GULAG. In 1930 alone, as many as 300 "inner enemies" were exposed. S. S. Dybets, the first manager of the NAZ (Nizhnyegorodskiy avtomobilniy zavod) was promoted to Head of the Automobile and Tractor Production of the Ministry of Industry in 1932. His former position was filled by Sergei S. Diakonov. Dybets was exposed as an "inner enemy" and shot in 1937, followed by his successor a year later... The branches of the NAZ factory in Nizhnyi Novgorod (called "The October Siren") began assembling Fords AA from American parts in February 1930, in Moscow (the KIM) from November 1930. Production was frequently suspended for lack of parts. The car works were officially opened on January 1st, 1932 and the first whistle was blown on January 29th, 1932. The first NAZ-AA rolled off the assembly line. But the whistle had hardly been blown before the line was stopped again for lack of parts. After December 1932, the factory also produced the GAZ-A passenger cars. The events of 1990 took the company through a deep crisis. It was transformed into a joint stock company. In 1995, the tables started turning. In 1996, the factory launched a franchised production of Steyr M-1 diesel engines with direct fuel injection. In 1995–97, the GAZ-3102 Volga sedan became a base for at least two pick-up trucks, which differed in superstructure and appearance. The GAZ-2304 Burlak (a toiler which was used to pull ships upstream on the Volga using a towrope from the shore), with a grille featuring vertical ribs, carried 2–3 people and 1,433 lbs of cargo covered by a tilt. The other vehicle had

a horizontally-ribbed grille and a laminated roof superstructure. In 1997, GAZ signed a contract with Fiat for production of 4 models bearing the name Fiat-GAZ. A new joint stock company—ZAO Nizhgorod Motors—was established in Nizhnyi Novgorod to implement this project. The GAZ giant consists of 5 companies, 10 independent factories, and hundreds of assembly lines. The main factory covers an area of 597.5 ha and employs 108,000 people. In 2000, 25% of the stocks were obtained by the Siberian Aluminum concern. The current capacity is fully occupied in the production of the hard-to-come-by Sobol and Gazela models. The first Soviet AWD was the GAZ 61-40, an offspring of the GAZ 11-40 1st series convertible with 4x2 drive and a member of the GAZ M-1 series. It was a robust pre-war convertible with a ladder frame and longitudinally mounted leaf springs, made from 1938. It featured a 6V SV 3485cc (85hp @ 3600) engine and a 4-speed transmission. In 1941, its footsteps were followed (via the GAZ R1=a prototype with a 37-mm canon in place of the back seats) by the GAZ 64-416—a genuine off-roader with a Jeep-like body. In 1941 came the GAZ 61–73, based on the GAZ 11-73 with the same power unit and a one-speed transmission, powering either the rear or all wheels suspended by leaf springs, and an enclosed body. In 1941, a convertible (181) was manufactured for the army. There were two versions: the GAZ 61-40—a convertible, (comfortable) service car of the Soviet marshals, and the GAZ 61-415—a pick-up, of which several hundred units were made. The GAZ 61-417 from 1940 was a follow-up to the GAZ 11-415 pick-up truck, but it featured AWD. It served in the army and was a forerunner of the GAZ 64. One remarkable model was the GAZ 21 pick-up truck featuring 6x4, a follow-up to the GAZ M-415 pick-up

truck. The GAZ 21 was equipped with a 4V SV 3285cc engine (50hp @ 2800, 56 mph, 13.44 mpg) and a 3-speed transmission.

GAZ 64

The Soviet attack on Finland in 1939–1940 showed in the raw all the problems presented by rough terrain coupled with severe winter. The generals needed to provide their commanders and reconnaissance patrols with a simple lightweight vehicle. They'd obtained some information about the American Bantam (Jeep). General-major I. P. Tyagunov, supported by the Commissar for light industry V. A. Malyshev, commissioned GAZ and the NATI designer office to build a simple military vehicle-tractor featuring 4x4 drive, open body, short wheelbase, an 882-lb carrying capacity and a minimum working life of 5,000 working hours. The wheel track and the length had to equal those of the Bantam. The chassis of the GAZ 61-40 was unsuitable. The axle drive, cardans, driving mechanism, brakes and wheels came from the GAZ 61-xx, while the 4V engine, the clutch, the "truck" transmission and the main gear were taken from the GAZ MM. The wheel track of the GAZ 61's axles was shortened, which was a big mistake, as the manufacturing process and above all experience of using the vehicle were to show. (The vehicle did not fit into the deep ruts left by the wider trucks, and it had poor stability when circling a hill: a 17° side tilt was already considered "dangerous".) A 75° approach angle was needed to negotiate a wall 1.6 ft high. The ladder frame was new, the front axle had 4 quarter-elliptic springs and 4 hydraulic shock absorbers. The GAZ 64-416 project was launched on February 3rd, 1941, and the first specimen was put through a trial on March 25th, 1941, driven by Gratchev. The first Soviet Jeep-like vehicle known as "Pigmy" was born. It went up a 38° slope (or 20° with a 1,764-lb trailer), it had a 31.5-in fording depth, and managed to get through a 15.7-in high mass of snow. The chassis, although not very rigid, proved to be first-quality. Problems were caused by the frame members, leaf springs, seats, brakes, occasionally low quality of processing, and a high consumption of fuel and oil. The biggest troublemaker—the narrow wheel track (49 and 50.3 in)—was eliminated in late 1942 (GAZ 64) by being enhanced to 50.9 in. This flaw was more acutely felt in the case of the GAZ 64-125—a related armored vehicle. Owing to the side tilt and stability problems, the Red Army in 1942 took up only 67 units of the GAZ 64-416 and 2,486 armored vehicles. A total of 686 units of the GAZ 64 and the GAZ 64-125 were produced. It was clear that both models needed modernization. A plan to implement it was accepted on September 26th, 1942.

GAZ 67 a GAZ 67B ❷

This updated version was designed to have a wider wheel track (56.9 in, later 57 in); the fenders, side steps and rear leaf springs were moved outside of the axle frame, which lent the vehicle a higher ground clearance. The chassis was reinforced and got rid of the rear stabilizer. The vehicle became longer and wider. It featured a 25° side tilt and was able to drive through 1.5-ft-deep muddy riverbeds. Its 4V SV engine 3285cc (54hp @ 2800) with 4.6:1 compression rate (gasoline with an octane rating between 55 and 60), featured higher performance. As with the GAZ 64, the wheelbase was 83 in. The car was 132 in (130 in) long, 66 in (60 in) wide and 67 in high. The name of the main designer of this car was Vasserman., Eng. The first test units of the GAZ 67 passed the army's requirements in a trial session in April 1943 and it did not take long before large-scale production was launched (September 13th). (NB: some sources give 1942 as the year of construction.) A total of 6,068 units of the GAZ 67 were produced by the end of 1945. The grilles of the wartime cars were welded from steel rods; after the war, they were made of pressed steel sheets. The vehicle was powered by low-quality gasoline, but on the whole it was relatively reliable and came in handy both during and after the war. In October 1943, a prototype of the GAZ 67-420 was built, featuring a wooden body; however, a decision was made not to start production. Since January 1944, the factory supplied and tested a modernized version—the GAZ 67B; it was nicknamed "Chapaev," also available in a simpler 4x2 form for the rear echelon. The vehicle's relative reliability was counterbalanced by its "unquenchable thirst": in rough terrains, it would "ask for" a gallon of gas per 4.7 miles. Its brakes had a high breakdown rate and were hard to fix. It found its niche in the agricultural domain, as a vehicle used by foremen of sovkhozes. A number of uits went for export. In 1950, GAZ 67B made its first "jump" from a Tu-2 plane, and a year later it was thus transported to the North Pole where it assisted in building the SP-2 ice station. In 1950, a light-weight GAZ 67B climbed up the Elbrus mountain to the "Camp of Eleven." Its chassis was used as a base for the NAMI-011 floating vehicles, renamed GAZ-011 after a modification. In 1948, Vasserman outlined a modernized version, but it was never implemented. A successor was being prepared: the GAZ 69. During 10 years of production, 92,843 units of the GAZ 67 and 67B were made. The last specimen was born in September 1953. A total of 62,843 units had been supplied to the Red Army and its allies by 1953. Their chassis was also used by the BA-64B armored vehicles.

Part of the cover of a pamphlet featuring the GAZ-67

GAZ 69 a GAZ 69A ❾ ❷

The GAZ 69, known as "Kozlov," was a post-war child. The team of technicians around Grigoriy Moyseyevich Vasserman finished the first prototypes of the new vehicle sometime in 1948. (At that time, it was nicknamed "Truzhenik".) Its time-tested ladder frame carried a canvas-covered metal body. The GAZ 69 had 2 doors and a drop tailgate. It carried 8 men or only 2 plus 1,102 lbs of cargo. The GAZ 69A had a specific feature—4 doors (interchangeable on one side); it carried 5 people plus 110 lbs of cargo. The two models shared a vast majority of components, and they shared many parts with other GAZs; for example, the engine, hydraulic brakes, driving mechanism, clutch and transmission were originally used in the GAZM-20 "Pobieda" sedan. The engine—a 4V GAZ SV 2 120cc (55hp @ 3600, compression ratio: 6.2–6.5:1) powered either the rear or all wheels via a 3-speed transmission or a 2-speed auxiliary transmission. Transversal or longitudinal benches for soldiers, or various extensions, were placed in the back. Other features: wheelbase—91 in, length—152 in, width—69 in, height—80 in, curb weight—3,362 lbs. A curiosity was the appearance of the "Snyegobolotokhod" with broad balloon tires, whose purpose—driving through snow—is given away by its Russian name. A prototype of an 8x8 vehicle with an enclosed body was designed for similar purposes. Average gas mileage, as stated by the company, was 16.8 mpg with 4x2 drive. The first series-made GAZ 69's rolled off the assembly line in 1952, followed by the 69A model four years later. The army took up 634,256 units and a number of vehicles were distributed in the civilian sector. Specimens for export were distinguished by the letter "M" in their names. The GAZ 19 had only RWD and featured a glassed-in rear superstructure. There was also a tractor for semi-trailers (of the UAZ-456 type) tested in 1960, and the GAZ 69B "Bukhanka"— a test sample for the future UAZ 469. The modernized GAZ 69–68 from 1970 had a canvas roof. In 1954, their production was transferred to Ulyanovsk, where they were manufactured until 1972. An UAZ name-plate was quite a rarity. In Gorki, production finished in 1956. The GAZs were part of the arsenal of many armies in Africa, Mongolia, Cuba, and they also appeared in some recent TV news reports from

The GAZ-69 Snyegobolotokhod

Afghanistan. To make the picture complete, mention ought to be made of the GAZ 69 MAV—a military amphibious vehicle built on a 69 chassis, with an auxiliary transmission. In contrast to the off-roader, it also featured an axle drive used for powering a three-blade propeller for driving on water and a pump for draining water that leaked into the body pan. When afloat, the vehicle was driven by a rudder connected to the steering wheel. This amphibian was a copy of the wartime Ford GPA, 9,500 units of which were sent by Americans to the USSR. The total production of GAZs was probably higher by a few hundred.

GAZ M72 – Pobieda ❷

At the end of WWII, an interesting "crossbreed" vehicle was created from a GAZ 69 chassis and the GAZ M20 Pobieda (=Victory); its author was the chief designer Vasserman's assistant. The body was reinforced in the places where it was bolted onto the chassis, floor reinforcements were added and the A- and B-pillars were strengthened. In addition to the complex pull rod system of the gear lever, traditionally placed under the steering wheel in the Pobiedas, levers for adding the FWD and reduction were added. The vehicle's ground clearance rose by about 8 inches. The GAZ M21 model was made in the USSR in 1956–70 in three series: the GAZ M22 station wagon/ambulance, the GAZ M23 "super-version"—mostly for the KGB, and the GAZ M21—an experimental pick-up truck. A bizarre arctic prototype of the Pobieda featuring skis instead of wheels had an aircraft propeller in the rear. In 1955, the GAZ M73 appeared—a 2-seat

The GAZ M72 Pobieda

The GAZ M73 with 4x4 drive, 1955

The GAZ M73 Pick-up, 1953

prototype of a 4x4 pick-up truck (52hp), with a shorter wheelbase and a more ascetic front panel than those of the road Pobieda. In 1955, Vasserman used the GAZ 72 as the basis for a prototype of the 2-seat Tudor 4x4. It was designed to be used by managers of kolkhozes and sovkhozes. The model passed the tests but the ministry of industry decided not to produce it because the job it was intended for was done just as well by the GAZ 69's.

GAZ 24-95 Volga ❹

GAZ made only 5 units of the GAZ 24 4x4 sedans with leaf springs. It was powered by a 4V ZMZ 24D 2445cc engine (55hp @ 3600, 81 mph). The Volga carried 5–6 persons. Another 4x4 experiment of the Volga, this time the GAZ 3106M model, was a 5-seat sedan featuring an in-line 4V 2.3L (150hp) engine with electronic injection made in 1986.

GAZ 2308 Ataman ❷ ❻ ❾

Fifty years later, GAZ went back to lightweight 4x4 vehicles. The first one was the GAZ 2308 Ataman pick-up truck. A prototype of the 2307 / 2309 Asket was introduced in 1995, followed by the 2106 Ataman in 1996. Its shortened or extended chassis became the basis for other 4x4s. In 1996, a small test series was manufactured. The Ataman has been made since 1999 (or since 2001, according to other sources). Power is provided by a gasoline 4V ZMZ 2890cc engine (105hp, 75 mph). The car has a 5-speed transmission, an inter-axle differential with a lock and a 2-speed gear-reduction

The GAZ 2308 Ataman Pick-up 4x4, 2000

The GAZ 2308 Ataman, 1997

transmission. In addition to 3 people it can carry up to 1,764 lbs of cargo. A pick-up-truck version with a station-wagon body borne by a chassis with an extended wheelbase is advertised by GAZ as the GAZ 230810 (Ataman) Yermak; mass-production is scheduled to start in 2003. Another newcomer shown in Moscow in 2000 was the GAZ 230812 Ataman double-cab, fitted with a ZMZ engine (160hp). There is also a 4x2 variant—the GAZ 2307. The IDAX-2001 exhibition of military technology held in the United Arab Emirates in 2001 saw the debut of an armored vehicle by the name "GAZ 2975 Tiger 4x4," featuring a D Cummins engine (181hp) and a length of 193 in. This "Russian Hummer" was the star of the 2002 Moscow motor show. Its was the result of a joint effort of GAZ technicians, the PKT company (Promyshlennyie Komputernyie Technologiyi / Industrial Computer Technologies) and the King Abdullah II

Design & Development Bureau construction company from the United Arab Emirates. A version of the GAZ 29751 with an enclosed armored body and a GAZ 29752 double-cab version with a canvas-covered rear part were showcased in Moscow. In addition to the presented cars, the photographs show some others in a cheaper military specification. In 2003, the Russian army was supposed to take up 15 units. The "New Russians" are in for an even more luxurious variant. A forgotten prototype was the GAZ 3907 (2.45L, 72hp), which was passed over to UAZ (Jaguar).

The GAZ 2975 Tiger 4x4, 2001

The GAZ 230810 Jermak 4x4, 2002

GAZ 3106 Ataman II ❸

The Ataman gave rise to the "Dzheep"—a luxury 5- to 10-seat SUV shown in Moscow in 1999. It resembles the BMW X5 for 7 persons and 1,323 lbs of luggage. It should have been available since 2003. The car features an 8.5-in ground clearance and a GAZ 3111 chassis with a franchised 5V D STEYR 2.67L engine with an intercooler (141hp, 93 mph). It has permanent AWD.

GAZ 2752 Sobol, Gazelle (aka GAZelle in Russian) ❽

GAZ became the biggest Russian manufacturer of light-weight utility vehicles 4x2 bearing the name of a Siberian beast of prey known as "sobol." A test series was made in 1997 and production was launched in 1998, followed by modernization in 2000. In addition to mini buses, station wagons, vans and box vans with 4x2 drive, there have also been 4x4. The Pick-up 23109 Sobol (4x2) and the "Dopel Cab" 23107 Sobol (4x4) were shown in Moscow 2000. The 27527 4x4 minivan for 7 passengers carried 672 lbs on top of that. The 2752 Sobol 4x4, also known as the Barguzin, is a hybrid of a chassis from the GAZ 2308 Ataman and a body from the GAZ 2752 Sobol. It made its debut in 1999 and has been manufactured since 2000. The vehicle carries 6 persons in 3 rows of seats, and 772 lbs of luggage. Another model of the double-cab series is the 23109 (4x4). It came before the GAZ 330279 Tandem—a 6-seat pick-up truck (+1,764 lbs), 4x4, featuring a gear-reduction transmission, a differential lock, a TD IVECO engine; it generates a top speed of 75 mph and has a ground clearance of 8.3 in—and the GAZ 27527 Sobol-Trophy, which was an updated station wagon 4x4. The

The GAZ 3106 Ataman II 4x4, 2002

The GAZ 330279 Tandem 4x4, 2002

Gazelle, with a carrying capacity of ca 1,102 lbs more than that of the Sobol, has been available in bulk since 1994. At the outset of the new millennium, the plant manufactured all the versions with 4x4 and 4x2 drive. The "new kids on the block" include: the 330279 Tandem—a 6-seat double cab

The GAZ 2217 Sobol, 1997

The GAZ 3308 Eger I 4x4, 2002

carrying +1,764 lbs of cargo; the 2705 / 27057 (4x4) — minivans for 3 persons and 2,535 / 2,425 lbs of cargo; the 2705/ 27057 — a 7-seat station wagon / van (4x4), with an additional 2,094 / 1,653 lbs of carrying capacity. The minibuses seat 7–13 persons. The three different models of them, differing in the arrangement of seats, have the following marques: the 3221 / 32217 (4x4), the 32212 / 322172 (4x4) and the 32213 / 322173 (4x4). The Gazelle are available with D ZMZ engines, or with franchised GAZ Steyr 2.1L power units.

GAZ 3120 Kombat ❷

In Moscow 2000, a rustic off-roader was presented under the

name GAZ 3120 Kombat; in terms of functions and shape it deliberately evoked the legendary GAZ 69. Its main designer, Ogor Soldatov, did a fantastic job. He used the GAZ 2308 Ataman chassis as a base, adding to it leaf springs from the Volga station wagon and mounting on it a TD GAZ 5601 engine (Steyr franchise) with an intercooler (4V 2130cc, 110hp, 81 mph), or a gasoline V8 engine. Other features: wheelbase—87 in, length—169 in, width—74 in, height—75 in, weight—3,638 lbs, ground clearance—8.5 in. The vehicle carries 1,213 lbs of cargo and 5 persons. A hardtop version, the Kombat 3120 Hardtop, was first shown in Moscow in 2001.

GAZ 3308 Eger, GAZ 3325 Eger II ❷ ❾

In cooperation with the NPP Technospas-NN (a manufacturer of superstructures), GAZ prepared a large vehicle known as the Eger, featuring a dual cab and a V8 4.7L gasoline engine (59 mph). It is likely to appeal to a handful of New Russians who like to venture to the backwoods, or military and paramilitary organizations. Another heavyweight off-roader from the same batch is the Eger II. The "Turist" version is designed for expeditions in the wild, the Sport— a pick-up double cab—is purpose-built for long-distance motor races. The canvas-covered soft-top or platform truck versions, both of the double cab type, are meant for the military. The ministry for emergencies ordered a number of units of the "MCS" emergency vehicles. Power is supplied by various ZMZ engines with about 130hp, or the Japanese Hino (138hp).

The GAZ 3120 Kombat

The Giannini CMG 1, 1967

Giannini
(Italy)

From about 1920, Attilio Giannini was known as a virtuoso in tuning Fiat engines. In 1963, following several episodes, he founded a company in Rome bearing his name. In the second part of the 1960s, the Giannini Fiats and their sport modifications, as well as the Fiat 500 Giardinetta (4x2) pick-up truck, enjoyed a great reputation. The company caught a whiff of the Panda 4x4 in the early 1990s—the Giannini Panda Look 4x4 (1987) and the Giannini Panda Prestige 4x4 (1990); they also worked on a Panda 4x4 featuring a super-charged engine. One interesting prototype was the Fiat Tempra 4x4. Its transmission had been used in a prototype from Turin 1993, and it could be found in the bowels of the Giannini Punto 4x4 T.L. (Tempo Libero, 75hp, front frame, plastic fender flares).

Giannini CMG 1

In 1967, Giannini came up with the CMG 1 off-road vehicle, designed by Folgo Lugarini. He developed it in subdivision workshops specialized in engine construction and modification—Costruzioni Meccaniche Giannini spa (C.M.G.)—or building prototypes for the company itself or external customers including Citroën Mehari, Savio Jungla 600, Moretti Mini and Midimaxi, VW. This simple vehicle was powered by a 4V 1025cc engine (65hp @ 5500). It had a 4-speed transmission, and RWD; a 4x4 version is said to be forthcoming. The front wheels were suspended independently, while the rear axle was rigid. The CMG 1 featured an 87-in wheelbase, 130-in length, 65-in width, and 50-in height

The Giannini Punto 4x4 T.L., 1993

without a roof and with a rigid window frame. The ground clearance was 8.7 in. The vehicle seated 4 people and up to 1,323 lbs of cargo, or another 4 people. The car was supposed to be manufactured by a new branch of the company.

The Giannini Panda Prestige 4x4, 1990

Greppi
(Italy)

Greppi Savana / Alpina

Greppi, based in the mountainous province of Como, was active in around 1973–83. After the Drag and Smash buggies mounted on a VW-Beetle platform, the firm came up with the Safari—a small VW-based work vehicle. In 1979, Greppi introduced its new compact 4WD vehicles with mechanics from the Ford Transit. The Savana D—a 3-d, 4-seat hard- or soft-top—was fitted with a 4V 2360cc engine (70hp

@ 3600, 78 mph), and a 4-speed transmission with optional FWD. The vehicle was characterized by a classic design, including a ladder frame and rigid axles with half-elliptic springs. Drum brakes were installed. Other features: wheelbase—87 in, length—142 in, width—68 in, height—78 in, ground clearance—15.8 in, curb weight—3,352 lbs, slope—85 %. The smaller Alpina featured a similar design and a gasoline 4V Ford Taunus engine 1297cc (74hp @ 5500, 84 mph). This vehicle had a cross-country reduction and a 4-seat, 3-d hard-top body. It had the same specifications, except for the width (59 in), height (67 in), ground clearance (9.8 in), weight (2,205 lbs) and slope (80%).

The Greppi Alpina 4x4

The Greppi Alpina 4x4

Hindustan
(India)

The Hindustan Trekker 1.5

Hindustan Motors were founded by the Birla brothers in Calcutta in 1942. It was not until after the war, that they made their first car—the Ten (=Morris) sedan. Later, they embarked on BMCs and Vauxhalls. In 1976, they came up with a 5-d station wagon with off-road features and named it Hindustan Trekker 1.5. It was fitted with a 4V gasoline 1489cc engine (56hp @ 4400, SAE, 62 mph), powering the rear wheels via a 4-speed transmission. In 1977, the Trekker 1.5 Diesel (57 mph) came out. It had the following characteristics: wheelbase—91 in, length—151 in, width—65 in, height—71 in, curb weight—2,566 lbs and payload—1,433 lbs.

Honda (Japan)

In 1922, Soichiro Honda established a car repair service in Tokyo. In 1948, he launched the production of motorcycles, and in time became their biggest world producer. The reputation of progressive cars, especially so far as their engines are concerned, has stuck to Honda to this day. Honda did not make its own off-roaders; it produced vehicles taken over from other manufacturers. In the mid-1990s, the company manufactured—mainly for the home market—the following cars: the Crossroad (=Land Rover Discovery) with a Honda V8 3.9L engine (190hp) and an automatic transmission; the Jazz / Passport—an SUV taken over from Isuzu, where it was known as Amigo / Rodeo (a 4V TD 3.1L engine, 120hp, JIS; or a 3.2L V6 engine for the U.S. market). Isuzu is the source of the Honda Horizon, originally the "Isuzu Trooper" (made in Europe as the "Opel Monterey"). The Horizon from February 1994 was fitted with gasoline 3.2L V6 or TD 3.1L engines; in the U.S., a gasoline 4V 2.6L engine was used. In October 1994, the Honda Shuttle minivan (aka Odyssey on the home market) made its first appearance, featuring 2x4 drive and independently suspended wheels. Along with a facelifted version thereof, a 4x4 version was presented in 2002. The Stream minivan based on the Civic sedan was shown in 2000 in

Japan, and in spring of the following year in Europe. This version, too, features an independent wheel suspension. The front wheels are permanently engaged, while RWD is automatically added in case of loss of adhesion. The MPVs are designed for road use.

Honda CR-V ❸

The CR-V with a 5-d, 5-seat station wagon body became Honda's first SUV. The vehicles made for the European market are manufactured in Swindon, GB. The model was showcased in October 1995. Originally, it was powered by a 4V 1973cc engine (131hp @ 5500, 100 mph), and since 1998 in Europe also by a 1997cc (147hp @ 6300, 110 mph) power unit. The CR-V had an automatic 4-speed transmission with a 2-speed reduction, mechanical Real Time 4WD, a viscous coupling of the interaxle differential and a rear axle differential. (Later they switched to a design known from the 2nd generation of the model.) The body was self-supporting; the wheels had independent suspensions, in the front on the McPherson struts. Further specifications: wheelbase—102 in, length—176 in, width—69 in, height—67 in, ground clearance—7.9 in, curb weight—2,954 lbs. The CR-V isn't wonderful in the off-road but offers good opportunities for standard road use.

The 2nd generation was launched in the fall of 2002. A sneak preview of the new Honda CR-V Study Model took place in Geneva in 2002, alongside of the CR-V Open Air concept

The Honda CR-V, 2002

The Honda CR-V, 2001

car. The originally fairly rigid body was given a curvier appearance. Electronics provided several extra horsepower and lower emissions. The vehicle has FWD, with RWD automatically added when necessary. Apart from a 5-speed manual transmission, a 4-speed automatic one is also available. Other features: wheelbase—103 in, length—177 in and 172 in, width—70 in, height—67 in, ground clearance—8.1 in, curb weight—3,109 lbs, payload—1,257 lbs.

Honda HR-V ❸

The Tokyo 1998 motor show saw the debut of the Honda HR-V—a rectangular leisure-time vehicle. A 3-d version was followed in 1999 by a 5-d version. A 4V 1590cc engine (105hp @ 6200, 94 mph, or 125hp @ 6600, 106 mph) positioned in the front powers the front wheels. If necessary, the

rear wheels can be automatically engaged by means of the Time 4WD system. The model comes with a 5-speed manual transmission or a CVT (centrifugal transmission). Its body is self-supporting. The vehicle's front axle resembles that of the CR-V, while in the rear there is a rigid de Dion axle with two pairs of longitudinal control arms and a Panhard rod. Specifications: wheelbase—93 in, length—158 in, width—67 in, height—62 in (or 66 in with a roof spoiler), ground clearance—6.7 in, curb weight of the 3/5-d (4/5-seat) vehicle—2,480 / 2,635 lbs, payload—893 / 937 lbs, fording depth—11.8 in, overhang angles—29º / 29º. This model is much happier on the road than off of it.

The Honda HR-V 5-d, the 2000 Geneva Motor Show

Hope Motor Company (Japan)

HopeStar ON 360 ❷

The Hope Jidosha company of Tokyo, sometimes called HopeStar, was founded in 1952. It produced delivery tree-wheelers. In 1960, it showcased the Unicar—a small station wagon. Between 1965 and 1967, the company developed a model known as the 4x4 HopeStar ON 360. Its rustic open canvas-covered body did not have a single curvature. The chassis consisted of a ladder frame and rigid axles with lon-

The HopeStar ON 360

The Hotchkiss-Jeep on a French pamphlet

The Hotchkiss M201

The HopeStar ON 360

gitudinal leaf springs. The rear wheels were powered by an air-cooled 2V Mitsubishi ME24 359cc engine (21hp), and there was an option of manually adding the FWD. The vehicle was homologated in 1967 and launched onto the market a year later. Only 15 units were manufactured, before the company dissolved. (According to a history published in Japan, 50 units were made in 1967 and 1968, including 20 for the home market and 30 for export into East Asia.) The company managed to sell production rights of the off-roader to Suzuki before it was too late. The ON 360, known as Jimny, became the forefather of Suzuki's successful off-road production program.

Hotchkiss (France)

Hotchkiss emerged in 1903 and was based in Saint-Denis. The Hotchkiss family had American roots with English and French blood. They were involved mainly in the production of weapons for the military. In time, various investors took over the reins. The beginnings of their production of combustion engines go as far back as 1903, followed by cars a year later. In 1942, a majority of the company was obtained by the Peugeot family, who got rid of it in 1950. In 1954-55, Hotchkiss became known as S. A. Hotchkiss-Delahaye. But not even this association with a famous name was to save the firm. In 1956, on the verge of bankruptcy, the company was bought by Brandt—a producer of home electrical appliances. In 1966, Hotchkiss-Brandt was bought by the giant Thomson-Houston armory and steel works. In 1967–71, it manufactured trucks for the army, bearing the name Hotchkiss.

Laffly / Hotchkiss V15R ❷ ❾

In 1939–40, Hotchkiss made 63 units of 5-seat reconnaissance off-road convertibles called the V15R (a Laffly design with cutouts instead of doors and a canvas roof). It featured an independent suspension with coil springs in the front and a rigid axle with leaf springs in the back. The R15R model had a rigid front axle with leaf springs. A 6x6 version is also known to have existed. A Hotchkiss OHV 2312cc engine (52hp) powered the rear or all wheels via a 4-speed transmission and a cross-country reduction. Basic dimensions: length x width x height—167 x 71 x 51 in, wheelbase—85 in, curb weight—5,732 lbs. A similar mechanical system was used in the Laffly / Hotchkiss S15R—a passenger transporter and semi-trailer tractor with the following dimensions: 183 x 73 x 79.5 in, wheelbase between the front and first pair of rear wheels—92 in, and wheelbase between the rear axles—39 in. The vehicle weighed over 8,818 lbs.

Jeep Willys - Hotchkiss M201   ❷

Since the 1950s, Hotchkiss-Delahaye tried to obtain a franchise of the Willys-Overland, model JH 101. Although Hotchkiss had to terminate the production of its own passenger cars in 1955, it managed to launch the production of Jeeps. The army was disappointed with the Delahaye Type 182 and leant towards the clone of the Jeep, a vehicle older in concept but wonderfully simple. After the first series—identical with the American—was finished, the second version (M201) followed, featuring small modifications and some French components. The last units were taken up by the army in 1967. A total of 27,628 units of the M201 were made. The vast majority were bought by the French military, replacing thus the old wartime Jeeps. The model was powered by an in-line gasoline 4V Hotchkiss / Willys SV 2199cc engine (52hp, later 60hp @ 3500, 62 mph). It featured a 3-speed transmission and a 2-speed auxiliary gear-reduction transmission and a choice between 4x2 and 4x4 drive.

The Hotchkiss-Jeep in the service of a French fire department, Normandy, 1997

A robust steel frame bore a 4-seat open steel doorless body (with a canvas tilt). The interior did not have the slightest indication of comfort and safety features. The axles were rigid with longitudinal half-elliptic leaf springs. Length x width x height—132 x 70 x 62 in; wheelbase—80 in, curb weight—2,315 lbs. It negotiated a 60% slope and featured a 30% side tilt capacity. The Hotchkiss served long into the 1970s.

The Hotchkiss-Jeep first series, Paris, 1996

Hummer,
EBLE hu. 4x4 modification

This German company emerged in 1992 as a specialist in repairing and remodeling 4WD vehicles. It soon specialized in old veteran vehicles of the American army in Germany and their conversions for standard road use fitted with gasoline 3.5L or V8 diesel 6.2L (135hp) engines. First came the EBLE Pick-Up M 1008, based on an army version of the Chevrolet made in 1986; it was followed by the EBLE Blazer M 1009 (ditto, with a 3-d station wagon body) and in 1997 a replica— called the HUMMLET—of the HMMWV based on the Chevrolet Pick-Up K3. As of February 2000, the Army Hummer has been available—a modified version of the 1985 military HMMWV M 998 model and later versions. After about 12,500 miles of army service, the vehicles receive with the above-mentioned diesel engines and other necessary accessories. What remains is a 3-speed automatic transmission, differential locks and permanent 4x4 drive. The body is an all-steel 4-d pick-up with a hard-top or a soft-top.

In 1979, the U.S. administration invited bids for a contract to produce the High Mobility Purpose Wheel Vehicle (HMMWV)—a vehicle that was intended to replace the Jeep. Among the bidders were Chrysler Defense (with a prototype of the Saluki) and Teledyne (with the Cheetah). AM General tested the first prototype of the Hummer in the Nevada Desert in July 1980. In February 1981, the American Army started organizing the purchase of new vehicles. Testing samples from three companies were ordered: AM General, General Dynamics and Teledyne. The first one to supply the vehicle was AM General. Strict military trials ensued and in March 1983, AM General obtained a five-year contract for a total of 55,000 units of the HMMWV. The vehicles performed very well in the Gulf War. Later, they starred in a lot of movies, including some with Arnold Schwarzenegger at the wheel. Schwarzenegger also helped push through a more civilized version known as the

Hummer H1 and became one of its first owners. Towards the end of the last century, GM bought both the make and the franchise. It sells the model with a TD V8 6.5L engine (198hp, 84 mph), a 4-speed automatic transmission and AWD. The model features a 130-in-long wheelbase and the following dimensions: 185 x 87 x 75 in. The bodies have either 2 or 4 seats, and come as both a soft- and a hard-top, station wagon, 2- and 4-d pick-up truck. With independent wheel suspension, overhang angles of 72°/37.5°, a 22° side tilt, a 31° slope and a 30-in fording depth, this 2-ton H1 will negotiate an incredibly rough terrain, including 20-in high thresholds and snowdrifts as high as 35 in. In the fall of 2002, the slightly more civilized Hummer H2 made its debut. It featured the same floor plan and had its expenses completely covered by GM. It features a V8 6L engine (320hp, up to 112 mph), a 4-speed automatic transmission and permanent 4x4 drive. As of 2005, the H2 SUT 4-d pick-up is scheduled to be launched (also in Europe). The 2004 Geneva motor show hosted a concept version of the more subtle Hummer H3 pick-up truck.

The Hummer H2 SUT

Hyundai (South Korea)

Between 1968 and 1985 in Ulsan, Hyundai assembled Ford passenger cars and trucks from British components, and in the early 1970s it started to manufacture them. Hyundai's first homegrown car was the Pony sedan showcased in Turin in 1974. Mitsubishi obtained 9.3% of the company's stocks after selling the Koreans a franchise for engines as well as for older versions or off-road MPVs (The Mitsubishi Space Wagon–Hyundai M-2, The Mitsubishi Space Gear–Hyundai Shuttle). In 1998, Hyundai swallowed up the Korean car manufacturers of Asia Motors and Kia. In 2000, 10% of the corporation was bought by DaimlerChrysler.

The Matrix / Lavita minivans, launched in Europe in 2001, and the Trajet shown at the IAA 1999, all feature 2x4 drive. The Hyundai Santamo is a franchise of the Mitsubishi Space Runner from 1991–98, and it has been available since 1996. The Santamo Plus corresponds to the Mitsubishi Space Wagon from the same period. Both 5-d 5-and 7-seat MPVs have either 2x4 or 4x4 drive. These vehicles are better fit for road use than rough terrains and are sold in Spain and several other European states.

The Hyundai Galloper, Spain 2002

The Hyundai Galloper—a chassis, 2001

The Hyundai Galloper, 1998

Hyundai Galloper ❷

The Hyundai Galloper appeared in 1991. It was in fact the Mitsubishi Pajero of the 1st generation from 1982–91. The Galloper was sold in some countries until 1998, seven years after the production of the original model had been terminated. In Germany, the Galloper was sold with the marque and in the network of Mitsubishi. Its more than good price compensated for its imperfections. In Italy alone, 1,100 units were sold in 1998. The Galloper only comes as a 3/5-d 5-seat station wagon on a ladder chassis. Its independently-suspended front wheels were led by trapezoid control arms and a torsion bar. The rear axle was rigid with a Panhard rod and coil springs. Torsion stabilizers were fitted both in the front and the rear. The basic (European) engines—a 2972cc gasoline V6 engine with multipoint injection (141hp @ 5000, 104 mph, automatic transmission—98 mph) and a D 4L 2776cc (99hp @ 3900, 87 mph), which was replaced by a TD 2477cc (106hp @ 3900, 87 mph)—delivered torque via the clutch to a 5-speed manual transmission or, in the case of the gasoline engine, to a 4-speed

The Hyundai Terracan—a chassis, 2001

automatic one. The driver could choose between 4x2 and 4x4 drive. An inter-axle differential equipped with a viscous coupling distributed the torque between the axles in a 50:50 ratio. The vehicle had a 2-speed reduction transmission. It's distinguished from the Pajero by its length (158 / 183 in), height (72.4 / 73.6 in), ground clearance (8.5 in), curb weight (3,825 / 4,332 lbs), and payload (1,709 / 1,290 lbs). Other features included: a 23.6-in fording depth, a 70% slope, a side tilt of 28° (or 25° for the long Wagon) and overhang angles of 41° / 38° (or 37° / 27° for the Wagon). Its slightly retouched version was temporarily, for clarity's sake, also known as the Galloper II. Since the beginning of 1999, a mildly modified short 3-d version has been available in some places, bearing the name Galloper Innovation and one of these engines: V6 3.0L (141hp) and D 2.5L (105hp).

Hyundai Terracan

The Hyundai Terracan is a more modern successor of the Galloper, with some of its (albeit reconstructed) mechanics. Its premiere took place in Seoul in 1999; Europe had to wait until Geneva 2001. Its well-equipped body and softer suspension makes it suitable for rough tracks rather than smooth road. The more expensive Elegance has heated seats and other delights. Besides a gasoline V6 24v 3497cc engine (195hp @ 5500, 115 mph) with injection, a TD CRDi Common Rail has been used—a 16v with an inter-cooler from the Kia Carnival 2902cc (150hp @ 3800, 103 mph). The transmission is either manual with 5 speeds, or automatic with 4 speeds. 4x2 drive is sufficient for the road, but RWD can be added electro-pneumatically before reaching a speed of 50 mph. The Terracan is fitted with a reduction gear, automatic freewheels on the front wheels and a rear limited slip differential. Disc brakes with the ABS cooperate with the EBD. The vehicle has a ladder frame. The wheels of the

The Hyundai Terracan, 2002

front axle are suspended independently with torsion bars and a stabilizer; the rear axle is rigid, with a Panhard rod, stabilizer and coil springs. Specifications: wheelbase—108 in, length—185.5 in, width—73 in, height—72.4 in, ground clearance—8.1 in, curb weight—+4,387 lbs, payload—1,206 lbs, fording depth—19.7 in, overhang angles—30° / 25°.

Interior of the Hyundai Terracan, 2002

Hyundai Santa Fe ❸

The 2000 Detroit motor show hosted the premiere of a luxurious 5-d 5-seat SUV able to overcome the pitfalls of nature on the way to recreational facilities. At first it carried a gasoline 1997cc engine (136hp @ 5800, 16v, 108 mph). In Spring 2001, the OHC CRDi economical car kits were launched onto the market, designed in partnership with Detroit Diesel. From a choice of 3, 4 and 6V engines, they opted for the 4V 1991cc engine (113hp @ 4000, 16v, 108 mph), while in America, a gasoline 4VSirius 2351cc engine (150hp @ 5500, SAE, 108 mph) or a V6 Delta 2657cc (170hp @ 6000, 24v, SAE, 170hp) have been used. The transmission is either manual with 5 speeds, or automatic with 4 speeds; with some engines, the option of choosing either of the two is given. The Santa Fe has permanent AWD. On the road, it uses the 2x4 mode, while the RWD is automatically added in the off-road, up to a 60:40 ratio. It has an interaxle differential with a viscous coupling and a limited slip control. All wheels are suspended independently with transversal arms (McPherson in the front), a stabilizer and coil springs. Disc brakes work with the ABS. The car has a ladder chassis. Other features: wheelbase—103 in, length—177 in, width—71.7 in, height—68 in, ground clearance—8.1 in, curb weight—(+)3,693 lbs, payload—1,285 lbs, fording depth—11.8 in, and overhang angles—28° / 26°. When production started, the planned output was 100,000 units per year.

The Hyundai Satellite, 2000

Hyundai H1 / Starex / Satellite ❽

The Koreans make the Mitsubishi Space Star as Hyundai H1 / Starex / Satellite 4x2 and 4x4 vans and minibuses. Power is supplied either by a gasoline 2351cc engine (110hp @ 4500, 96 mph), or a TD 2477cc (80hp @ 4000, 90 mph).

Customers have had a choice between a 5-speed manual and 4-speed automatic transmission, and between a 4x2 and 4x4 drives. The 4x4 has also featured a 2-speed reduction. The series is designed more for work use, except the Starex 4x4—a well-equipped minibus and van.

The Hyundai Starex 4x4

IATO
(Italy)

IATO ❷

In the mid-1980s, Francesco Cavallini was leader of a team of designers of off-roaders. As they were from Tuscany, they named their firm Industria Automobilistica Toscana (IATO). The vehicle made its debut at the Expofuoristrada in Turin in October 1988. A ladder frame supports a body made of laminate, carbon fibers and resins. This 2-seat AWD pick-up truck came either with a canvas roof and a targa arch, or as a hard-top. Fiat 4V engines provided power: a 1.6 LS – 1585cc (100hp @ 5900, 87 mph), a 2.0 CHT LS – 1995cc (90hp @ 5400, 90 mph), and a 1.9 TD S – 1929cc (90hp @ 4100, 89 mph). The transmissions had 5 speeds and a reduction. The driver had the option of disengaging the front wheels, while a rear axle torsen differential assisted in the off-road. Other characteristics of the IATO included: a 91-in wheelbase, a 160-in length, a 68-in width, a 75-in height, a 9-in ground clearance, a minimum curb weight of 3,408 lbs, a payload of 992 lbs, a fording depth of 30 in. It negotiated a threshold as high as 15 in, a 53° slope, and it had 41° / 34° overhang angles.

The IATO Hard Top

Isuzu
(Japan)

The origins of Isuzu, the oldest Japanese car manufacturer, date back to 1916. The Tokyo Ishikawajima Ship Building and Engineering Company merged with the Tokyo Gas and Electric Industrial Company, with the intention of manufacturing automobiles. After four years of experiments, a franchised vehicle named the Wolseley (A9) was launched in December 1922. The company underwent further transformations and sold cars under different brand names. The name Isuzu, after a Japanese river, prevailed. In April 1937, the Tokyo Automobile Industries Company was established,

which in 1949 gave rise to Isuzu Motor Ltd. During the war, it produced the PK10. Since 1937, it also produced a 7-seat 4x4 vehicle with a 6V SV 4390cc engine (70hp), later with a 4V D 3400cc (55hp), a 4-speed transmission, 2-speed auxiliary transmission, RWD and an option to engage the front wheels. Its axles were rigid, with leaf springs. Other features: wheelbase — 130 in, length — 195 in, width — 71.7 in, height — 75 in, curb weight — 5,071 lbs. The bigger, 6x4 Isuzu / Sumida K10 military staff vehicle from 1933 was derived from the TU10 truck. The rear wheels were powered via a worm gear. The axles were rigid, with coil springs. Power came from a 4.4L (70hp) engine. The model had a 113-in wheelbase, it was 204 in long, 73 in wide, 79 in high, and weighed 5,732 lbs. Since the mid-1960s, this relatively small firm looked for a partner for technical coopera-

The Isuzu KAI concept car, NEC 2000

tion in the development area. Neither of the brief alliances with Fuji Heavy Industries (Subaru), Mitsubishi or Nissan worked out. Production decreased. In September 1971, 34% of the company's stock was obtained by General Motors. Since then, the firm began to specialize in the production of lightweight utility vehicles. Isuzu became a supplier of diesels for many manufacturers in America, Asia and Australia. In 1999, GM's share was 49%. Isuzu develops cars for sister makes of GM. Besides the marque of Isuzu, they bear the marques of Chevrolet, Opel / Vauxhall, Holden, Honda, Jiangling and Qingling. At the turn of the century, Isuzu made a comeback in Europe with its Trooper series. At the Paris show and the NEC 2000, it presented concept cars of the Isuzu KAI, named after a revolutionary style of Japanese architecture.

Isuzu pick-up trucks KB / TFR / TFS (Japan, Thailand) ❷ ❻ ❽

The Isuzu KB represents a series of typical work pick-up trucks with a classic drive layout and 4WD. The KB became popular not only in Japan; it was exported to the U.S.A. and, until the 1990s, also to Europe. The original pick-up trucks—the Elfin (1961), the Wasp (1963), the Faster and the Faster Rodeo 4x4 (1967) with a classic design were complemented in 1967 by the first export models— the KB(D)20, the KB(D)25 including a 4-d crew-cab, and the KB(D)40 4x4. As of 1971, the series was only known under

The Isuzu Campo Sports-Cab 4x4, 1989

the model name of KB. The vehicles were powered by the following engines: a gasoline 4V 1584cc (80hp @ 5200) and 1949cc, and a D 1951cc (55hp @ 4400) or 2238cc (86hp @ 5000). They had a ladder frame, a 4-speed transmission, and the 4x4 versions also featured a reduction. The carrying capacity of these useful vehicles was up to 1 ton. They were gradually updated. The wheelbase of the 4x2 pick-up trucks was 90 / 104 / 118 in long, while the Spacecabs—4-seat 2-d pick-up trucks—had a 118-in wheelbase. The wheelbase of the 4x4 versions was 104 / 118 in, or 118 / 84 in for the 4x4, 4-seat, 2-d Spacecab pick-up trucks; the 4x2 platform trucks and the hard-tops with elevated roofs all featured a 73-in wheelbase. There were also 4x4, station wagons with elevated roofs 4x4, 4x4 soft-tops, and the Crew Cab 4x2 and 4x4 5-or-6-seat 4-d pick-up trucks. Another series of pick-up trucks—the TFR 4x2 / TFS 4x4—was launched in 1988 and got a facelift in 1996/97. In addition to three variants of pick-up cabs, the company manufactured the Flat Deck—a 2-seat minivan.

Isuzu has been making passenger cars since 1963 and, since the 1980s in Thailand, also 4WD station wagons. 1999 output reached 46,401 units. In Europe, the Pick-Up TFS / Rodeo, the Pick-Up TFR / the Dragon / the Spark, and the Econovan minivan are also known as the Honda Tourmaster and the Opel Campo. In the early 1990s, the Isuzu TFR 4x2 / TFS 4x4 was sold in Europe as "Isuzu Campo," featuring a D 2254cc (89hp @ 4600) engine or a 2.5L (76hp) engine, a 5-speed transmission and a 2-speed reduction. It came with the following body types: a 2-d pick-up truck, a 4-seat 2-d Sports-Cab, and a 4-d double-cab. The model had a 119-in wheelbase, a 194-in length, a 67-in width, a 67-in height, a ground clearance of 8.7 in, a curb weight of +3,307 lbs, and payload rating of up to 2,094 lbs.

Isuzu Trooper / Rodeo Bighorn ❷

In September 1981, the Isuzu Rodeo Bighorn (a 3-d station wagon) was introduced in Japan, followed by a 5-d variant 11 months later. At the same time, the first specimens left the Japanese islands, bearing the export name of Isuzu Trooper. The car was made by Holden as the Jackaroo / Kangaroo (1981), and by GM Venezuela as the Caribe 442 (1981) and

the Subaru Bighorn (1988). A range of variants is available: gasoline 4V 1949cc engines (88hp @ 4600), 2254cc (92hp @ 4600, or 108hp—since 1987), 2559cc (111hp @ 5000), a D 2238cc with direct injection (atmospheric 61hp @ 4000, 72hp after 1987, a TD 75hp) and a TD 2771cc (95hp @ 3800) with a 5-speed manual transmission or, at a premium, a 4-speed automatic transmission for the gasoline engines. In late 1987, more powerful and environmentally-friendlier engines appeared: a gasoline 2559cc (115hp @ 5000, or 122hp, SAE for the U.S.A.) and a TD 2752cc (97hp or 100hp @ 3700, 110hp JIS), coupled to a 5-speed transmission and a 2-speed reduction of permanent AWD. After 1987, a rear limited slip differential was available on demand, and all vehicles came with an option of disengaging the FWD with automatic freewheels. Another innovation consisted in the option of electro-hydraulic adjustment of the hardness of the shock absorbers. Also, a 4-speed automatic transmission was available. There was a ladder frame and the body types included: convertible, soft- or hard-top, short 3-d and stretched 3-d (or 5-d, after Geneva 1985) station wagon. The suspension of the front wheels was independent, trapezoid with torsion bars, while the rear axle was rigid with longitudinal half-elliptic springs. Dimensions: wheelbase—

91 / 104 in, length—160.5 / 172.5 in, width—65 in, height—72 / 71 in, ground clearance—8.9 in, curb weight—(+) 2,844 lbs, payload—1,455 lbs. The vehicle negotiated a 61° slope, a 45° side tilt, and its overhang angles were 43° / 32°. In time, a more comfortable interior and a wider variety of accessories were added. Japanese customers have a liking for models with higher performance and extra equipment, such as the Bighorn Special Edition by Lotus or the Irmscher S and R.

Isuzu Trooper ❷

The Isuzu Trooper, generation II, presented in Europe in 1992, has since 1994 borne the logo of Opel / Vauxhall Monterey. The vehicle was fitted with a gasoline 6V 3165cc engine (174hp @ 5200), or a TD 3059cc with indirect injection (113hp @ 3400) with a 5-speed transmission, or with a 4-speed automatic transmission for the gasoline engines. FWD could be added; the front axle featured automatically disengageable freewheels. The rear axle of the "Duty" models was equipped with a limited slip differential. The Isuzu has the following characteristics: wheelbase—92 / 108 in, length—162 / 179 in, width—69 in, height—72 in, ground clearance—8.5 / 8.3 in, weight—(+)3,956 lbs. In May 1998,

The Isuzu Rodeo Bighorn, 1981

The Isuzu Trooper SWB, 1987

Isuzu MU / Amigo ❷

The Isuzu MU (MU=Mysterious Utility) featuring a targa arch made its debut in May 1989. In the same year, it was launched in the U.S. under the name Amigo (4x4) and, in 1993, Honda began manufacturing it as the Jazz, Holden and Opel / Vauxhall as the Frontera Sport. The vehicle was derived from Isuzu pick-up trucks. The next generation premiered in April 1998 in Japan as the Isuzu MU, in the U.S. as the Isuzu Rodeo (4x4, 4x2), in Australia as the Holden Frontera, and in Europe as the Opel–Vauxhall Frontera Sport.

Isuzu Mu Wizard ❷

In October 1990, the Isuzu Mu Wizard, a stretched 5 (3)-d station wagon appeared in Japan. Outside Japan, it was launched as the Isuzu Rodeo (4x4 and 4x2) as the Honda Passport (4x2) in the U.S.A, as the Opel / Vauxhall Frontera in Europe, as the Chevrolet Rodeo in Latin America, and as the Isuzu Vega in Thailand. This vehicle was derived from Isuzu pick-up trucks. In October 1997, the next generation made its debut, featuring only a 5-d version. In Japan, it was sold as the Isuzu Wizard, in the U.S. as the Isuzu Rodeo (4x4, 4x2) and the Honda Passport, in Australia as the Holden Frontera, in Europe as the Opel Frontera, and in Great Britain as the Vauxhall Frontera Estate.

the model underwent a facelift as well as a return to the Isuzu marque. The design of the Commercial (a 3/5-d station wagon and van) has remained unaltered. Normally, the rear wheels are powered, but FWD can be added before reaching a speed of 62 mph. Engines: a gasoline V6 DOHC 3494cc (158hp @ 5400) or a 4V TD DOHC with direct injection 2999cc (117hp @ 3900). Transmissions: 5-speed manual or 4-speed automatic, plus a 2-speed cross-country reduction. The Duty and the Citation featured a rear limited slip differential as a standard feature. The front wheels were suspended independently with trapezoids and torsion bars and a stabilizer (see above), while the rear axle was rigid with coil springs and a stabilizer. Dimensions: wheelbase—92 / 108 in, length—171 / 186 in, width—72.2 in, height—72.2 / 72.4 in, ground clearance—8.3 in. When empty, the vehicle weighed +4,167 lbs, and it had a payload rating of 1,852 lbs. The Isuzu will climb up a 76 % slope, negotiate a 45° tilted surface, it has a 23.6-in fording depth and 31° / 27° overhang angles. Production of the Trooper was terminated in 2003, without a successor.

The Isuzu Trooper, 1999

Isuzu Bighorn / Trooper ❷

The Isuzu MU Wizard, 1996

In December 1992, the Isuzu Bighorn generation, aka the Trooper (for export) was born. This model was not imported to Europe under the marque of Isuzu. It was again a 3-/5-d station wagon with a short or long wheelbase. After February 1992, the 5-d Bighorn was produced by Subaru, or, as the SLX, by Acura in the USA; it was known as the Chevrolet Trooper (as both a 3- and 5-d) in Latin America, as the Holden Monterey (5-d) in Australia, as the Opel Monterey (3- and 5-d) in Japan (for export), and in Britain as the Vauxhall Monterey (3- and 5-d). After Ferbuary 1994 Honda made a 5-d version known as the Horizon; Holden produced the same car, including a 3-d version, as the Jackaroo.

The Isuzu Trooper

The Izh 27151

The Izh 27171, 2001

Izh
(USSR and Russia)

The Izh 27151

The Izh armory was established in 1807 and continues to make weapons ranging from knives to bazookas to this day. Its most famous product is the Kalashnikov machine gun. The "father" of this gun is Mikhail Kalashnikov, known from portraits as a man wearing a uniform with a chestful of medals and distinctions. During WWII, Izh itself produced 12 million Kalashnikovs—a million more than Germany in the same period. Other commodities made by Izh now include motorcycles, machinery, tools—and cars. The first in line—Ogonok (Little Flame)—was made in 1958. It was powered by a 2V 0.75L boxer engine from the Ural motorcycle. Its prototype was not approved for production. On December 12, 1966, production of the Moskvich 408, 1.4L (50hp), later known as the Izh 412 (1.5L, 75hp) station wagon 2125 (1966), which greatly differed in shape from its Moscow model was launched. In 1972 a prototype of the

Izh-14 1.5L, the first passenger car with 4x4 drive was presented. This vehicle did not make it to the production line either. It featured many components different from the Moskvich. This promising project of an off-roader was passed

The Izh 2126 4x4, 2002

over to VAZ. Because the factory always prioritized its armory program, it was not until 1977 that the millionth Izh car was finally produced. A total of over 2.3 million Izhes are known to exist. Also successful were the Izh-2715 and 27151—compact station wagons and pick-up trucks—which carried 2 people and 882 lbs of cargo, and were typically used by the Soviet postal service. Their production finished in 1998. They were also exported to China. In the late 1970s, development work began on a new model (a Renault engine was tested). A "definitive" prototype was completed in 1984/85. The Izh-2126 Orbita (named after a successful USSR space program) was distinguished by a relatively modern design, a 5-d body and a McPherson independent wheel suspension; on the other hand, it has an obsolete drivetrain of the Moskvich 1.5L generation (ex-BMW 1500 from 1961). Mass production did not start until 1991. In 1999, it was renamed "Oda." Since then, a highly modernized generation—the Oda-2—has been announced. Following in the footsteps of the vans (based on the Izh 2126 and also on the Oda) are the 2717 minivan (ground clearance-6.7 in) and the 27171 pick-up truck. A prototype of the Izh SBCh-4, purpose-built for use in arctic regions, is also interesting; it is able to move through deep and powdery snow by virtue of its balloon tires with widely spaced knobs. It has a 2-seat 2-d cab with components taken from the passenger version of the Oda. It is powered by a motorcycle 2-stroke 2V Izh Jupiter engine. The Izhmash-Avto car manufacturer is a subsidiary of Izhmash, JSc., established in 1996 under the auspices of Dmitri Ustinov—the defense minister and a former pupil of Izh. In 2000, they signed a major contract with VAZ. They moved assembly lines and presses to the Izhevsko region and started producing 6 models of the "Zhiguli" for

The Izh 2126 4x4, 2001

VAZ. In 2001, over 26,000 units of the Izh-2126 were made. The plan for 2002 was to make 120,000 units, including 60 % in the 4x4 version.

Izh 2126 4x4   ❶ ❹ ❻

The Izh 2126, with a classic design, is fitted with a Lada 1.7L engine (75hp). Since 1997, the company has also been making the 2126-060 version with AWD. Different variants of the car are known to have been made in the prototype and production phases; they are marked by two pairs of round frontal headlights. A year later, the 27171 4x4 pick-up truck was launched, followed by the Oda 212614x4 station wagon, reminiscent of the Subaru Forester, a year later. Changes in the appearance of both the front and the rear date back to 2001. The transmission and differential with a lock were originally designed by Izh and inspired by the Niva; the front axle with an auxiliary frame was taken from the Niva, the other components from the VAZ-2108. The 4x4 pick-up truck version was built on the same principle; a pilot series thereof was manufactured in late 2001. The Izh-2126 model has McPherson suspension in the front and a trailing rear axle with coil springs. The ground clearance is 6.1 in, the top speed is 81 mph. Visitors attending the 2001 Moscow motor show got the first look at it. The car is most likely also equipped with new 1.7L and 2.0L Hyundai engines (91hp), in addition to a VAZ 1.6L engine taken from the Niva. The above-mentioned motor show also presented a prototype of the 2126 Pick-up Double Cab.

The Izh 2126 4x4, 2001

The Izh 21261, 2002

Jago
(Great Britain)

In 1965, Geoff Jago was among the first manufacturers of hotrods. He sold hundreds of them. He restored his firm in 1979 and 1994, but a crisis in 1997 drove it under for good.

Jago Jeep / Geep / Sandero ❹

The first kit car ever made was the Jago Jeep in 1971. It was in fact a replica of the Willys. A laminated body taken from the Jeep CJ was mounted on a simple ladder frame and complemented by components from the Ford Anglia 105E. In time, American Motors—the new owner of the Jeep trademark—voiced a protest. The Jeep was renamed to "Geep." In 1976, after a brief episode with parts taken from the Morris Minor, they switched over to the mechanics of the Ford Cortina, Escort Mk I and Mk II. The new owners purchased several hundred of them. In 1984, the interior of both the soft- and the hard-top was altered. In 1987, the outward shape underwent a touch-up. In 1991, Chrysler—the new owner of Jeep—made them rename the model to "Sandero." (This name had originally been given to a prototype of an off-road station wagon/pick-up from 1983, which Jago did not approve for large-scale production.)

The Jago Samuri was a 4-seat off-road buggy with a canvas tilt or a removable laminated roof and Ford engines. It did not go down very well and had to be withdrawn from production in 1990.

The Jago Samuri

Jankel Design (Great Britain)

Robert Jankel is famous for a lot of loony ideas. In the 1970s, he founded the Panther company, well-known for

making quality replicas as well as original vehicles. In the mid-1980s, he established the Robert Jankel Design. Nothing was sacred. He did not hesitate to build crude versions of the most expensive cars including Mercedes Benz, Jaguar, Bentley, Rolls-Royce and Range Rover.

The Jankel Rolls-Royce Val d'Isère

Bentley / Rolls-Royce Val d'Isère and Provence ❹

One of the 12 "large-scale" modifications of the Rolls-Royce and Bentley limousines was the Val d'Isère desert conversion. In the workshop, they cut this multi-million car crosswise in half, shortened the wheelbase to 124 in, and did the same with the rear overhang. They reinforced and welded the body, and reshaped the sedan into a station wagon. They maintained the classic drivetrain and added a high-pressure hydraulic pump driven by a belt to the rear axle drive. At a speed under 30 mph, the driver had the option of adding the hydraulic FWD, regardless of whether the vehicle was going forward or backward. Ground clearance was 12.2 in and could be raised even higher in the off-road. The van's equipment includes sand tires and a spare wheel winch discreetly hidden in the front. The car was designed for use by oil sheiks. Customers for whom this model was not exactly right could choose the Provence—a similarly designed vehicle, featuring a rear overhang.

The military JPX Montez, 2002

The military JPX Montez, 2002

JPX (Brazil)

JPX Montez ❾ ❷

Since 1994, the Brazilian company JPX has been making a short stretched Auverland A3, fitted with a Peugeot 1905cc engine (D, 90.5hp @ 4600), or an "alcohol" power unit. The model features a 5-speed transmission with reduction. Its 2-or 5-d body is either a soft- or a hard-top, or the Pick-Up ST type, and is made mostly of laminate. In 1998, a stretched 4-d Montez Pick-Up Cabine Dupla was launched, equipped with a TD 1.9L (91hp). The model weighs 5,952 lbs and carries a maximum payload of 2,425 lbs.

The military JPX Montez, 2002

Kia
(South Korea)

Kia was founded in 1944 by Chul-Ho Kim. At first, he manufactured bicycle parts, and later became their large-scale producer. It was not until 1961 that he made his first motorcycle, followed by a three-wheeler a year later, a truck of the Titan series in 1971, and finally the first passenger car—the Kia Brisa S100 (franchised Mazda Familia). In 1976, Kia bought 28.3 % of the stocks of Asia Motors, and 7 years later Mazda managed to buy a 7.5% share of Kia. In 1990, a modern assembly plant named Asan Bay was opened, which lent a helping hand to the original Sohari factory. In April 1998, the Korean economic crisis led the firm to bankruptcy. Towards the end of that year, 51% of the stocks of both Kia and Asia were gobbled up by Hyundai. However, it has retained model autonomy within Hyundai. None of its minivans—the Carstar / the Joice (1999), the MPV Carens and the Carnival / the Sedona (U.S.A.), or the Carnival II / the Sedona II (Paris 2002) has 4x4. In Paris 2002, they presented their design of the KCV-II new lifestyle "kamionnetta." This is a crossover between an SUV and a 4x4 pickup truck, with a 3.5L V6 engine (195hp / 5500 1/min, 130 mph). The Besta and the Hi-Besta are vans and minibuses. In addition to a 4x2 version, a 4x4 version was available in the mid-1990s. In 2000, the Besta was replaced by the more modern model series of Pregio 4x2.

Kia Rocsta ❷

The Asia Rocsta was sold in the mid-1990s, in Germany and other countries under the logo of Kia, fitted with a diesel 2184cc engine (70hp @ 4050, 86 mph). The model 1994 had a 90.4-in wheelbase; it was 141 in long, 66.5 in wide and 71.7 in high.

Kia Retona ❾ ❷

In 1997, Asia presented an improved off-roader Rocsta bearing a new name of "Retona." But Kia—now a new owner of Asia—came up with its own vehicle and also named it "Retona." The prototype made its debut in Seoul 1997. It was mechanically very close to the Sportage. Normally, it comes as a station wagon, but hard-tops are available on re-

The Kia Retona, 2001

The Kia Frontier, around 1996

The Kia Sportage, 1999

quest, featuring 1998cc Sportage engines—either a gasoline unit (136hp, 93 mph) or a TD (87hp / 91hp, 77 mph). Other features: wheelbase—93 in, length—157.6 in, width—68.5 in, height—72.4 in, ground clearance—7.6 in, curb weight—3,263 lbs. The Retona will get through a 19.7-in-high mass of water, negotiate an 80 % slope, a 22° side tilt, and its overhang angles are 31° /33°. Also the Retona was available in Europe. In Germany as "Sportage Classic." A plain military version of this model is called "Jeep J7."

Kia Sportage ❷

This model came out in the spring of 1991—its 5-d proto-type was first shown to the public in Tokyo 1991. Its mass-produced version launched in 1996 had at first only a 2.0L engine (139hp @ 6000). The first SUV of the mar-que—the Sportage—was equipped with a chassis platform taken from the Mazda 121 and a single-cam 1998cc engine (95hp @ 5000, 99 mph), and until 1997 also a 16/DOHC version of engine (128hp @ 5300, 103 mph), alternatively

a D 2.2L (see Rocsta, 63hp @ 4050) or TD 1998cc (83hp @ 4000). The vehicle had a 4x2 drive, with optional FWD. It was equipped with an auxiliary 2-speed reduction, a rear limited slip differential and freewheels in the hubs of the front wheels with automatic locks for driving in the 4x4 mode. The transmission had 5 speeds. A comfortable station-wagon or hard-top body with a rigid B-pillar and roof above the front seats is fastened to a ladder chassis. The front inde-pendent suspension has wishbones, a torsion stabilizer and coil springs, while the rear axle is rigid with coil springs and a Panhard rod. In Europe, production of the 3-d Sportage was taken up by the Karmann company in 1994. It won the first prize for "Off-roader of the Year 1996." By 1998, a total of 3,979 units had been made. The Kia Sportage is 148 in long and has a 93-in-long wheelbase, it is 68 in wide and 65 in high. Its ground clearance is 7.9 in, and it weighs +3,131 lbs and has a payload of 1,168 lbs. It has a 13.8-in fording depth, negotiates an 80% slope, has a 38° side tilt and overhang an-gles of 36°/33°. The stretched, 5-d version is 167 in long, has a 104-in long wheelbase and weighs 3,175 lbs.

The Kia Sportage Fresh, Geneva 2000

In 1999, exclusively in Korea, production was resumed of the—slightly modified—Kia Sportage (now 2.4 in longer), both in a 3-d and 5-d form, with single or dual cam 1998cc engines (a TD of the same capacity) and a D 2184cc. The version with a long wheelbase is also known as the "Sportage Grand" and the "Sportage Wagon." In Germany in the late 1990s, the Kia Retona was sold as "Sportage Classic." In Geneva 2000, the Sportage Fresh aroused visitors' interest, featuring an open-air rear part. The 2-d short version is the only one of the lot to be sold only with 4x2 drive. The Sportage team got all the way to the finish in the 2000 and 2001 Paris-Dakar Rally, and in 2000 it came first in the off-road Baha 2000 Rally.

The Kia Sportage, 2000

Kia Frontier ❷ ❻

The platform of the Sportage served as the base for a 4x4 farming and fishing pick-up truck version known as the Frontier. Protection was provided by a reinforced body, plastic bumpers and side protective strips. Its mechanics are derived from the Sportage. Twin trapezoid suspensions of the wheels and coil springs control good performance on an asphalt road; AWD can be activated in the off-road. Power was supplied by a 1998cc engine (70hp @ 4050). The model was 180 in long, 68 in wide and 65 in high. In the mid-1990s, it was sporadically showcased in Europe, but the Frontier was ahead of its time, as it appeared in a period of deepening Korean crisis.

Kia Sorento ❸

The Kia Sorento from Chicago 2002 has a lot in common with the "younger" Hyundai Santa Fe. This SUV has EST (standard electronically activated) front wheel drive, which the driver controls by a switch, and, at a premium, a TOD (Torque On Demand) permanent AWD that automatically distributes power between the front and rear wheels. There is a limited-slip inter-axle differential and a manual 5-speed transmission or, again at a premium, a 4-speed automatic one. All specimens include an electronically-engageable re-

duction. The disc brakes have the ABS and the EBD. The choice of engines includes a D Common Rail 2497cc (140hp @ 3800), a gasoline 2351cc (139hp @ 5500), and a V6 3497cc (195hp @ 5500). A steel body is supported by a ladder frame. The front features a McPherson suspension; the rear has a five-part independent suspension with coil springs. The Sorento has a wheelbase length of 106.7 in, it is 182 in long, 73.4 in wide and 67.7 in high. Its ground clearance is 8 in, it has a curb weight of +4,533 lbs, and a payload rating of 1,199 lbs. The model was named after a quaint, picturesque town of Sorrento in Southern Italy; the word also has a sense of nobility, holiday travel and evokes the name of the Sorrento Valley in San Diego known for innovative technologies. It is produced by a robotized factory called Hwasung along with the Sportage and the Carens models. Test results are flattering and the plant can barely keep up with demand.

The Kia Sorento, 2002

Lamborghini (Italy)

The Lamborghini LM 001

Ferruccio Lamborghini was born near Modena. He went to technical school and, after the war, opened a car repair service. In 1952, he built his first tractors and soon became their 3rd biggest producer in Italy. His production of diesel burners and air conditioning was a success as well. The first sports Lamborghini made its debut in 1963. Each new model made history. The company changed owners a few times. The Geneva 1977 motor show was zapped by their concept car, the monstrous Cheetah. They hoped to get a big order from the army. Nowadays, Lamborghini is owned by Audi, thas is VW.

Lamborghini Cheetah

Under contract from Mobility Technology International, the company developed a design of a 4WD vehicle. The American army commissioned the MTI to find a replacement for the Jeep. The model was designed and built in California and sent to Italy for trials and fine-tuning. The whole thing ended up in a courtroom because the MTI apparently stole ideas from Ford. In spite of this, the Lambo was born. A massive steel chassis bore a laminated hard-top body, supported by a tubular frame. It could be easily replaced with an armored body. Its cross-country tires were said by the factory to be bulletproof. The vehicle was powered by a V8 5.9L engine (183hp @ 4000, 104 mph, or, in the desert, over 87 mph, from 0 to 62 mph in 9.0 s) mounted in front of the rear axle. The Cheetah featured permanent AWD, a 3-speed auto transmission and two differentials. When empty, it weighed 4,502 lbs. It had a 118-in-long wheelbase,

The Lamborghini Cheetah, 1977

The Lamborghini Cheetah, 1977

a length of 170 in, it was 74 in wide and 62 in high. The Americans took the only specimen to California for trials, where an accident broke the car to pieces.

Lamborghini LM 001

In Geneva 1981, the new owners presented a prototype of the LM 001 featuring an AMC V8 5896cc engine (180hp @ 4000, 99 mph, and 75 mph in the desert) and Chrysler automatic transmission. A V 12 Lambo 4754cc version was scheduled. It differed only in small details from its predecessor. They tried to impose the LM 001 on the American army and fished also among petrodollar sheiks. But only a single specimen of the LM 001 was destined to be built.

Lamborghini LMA and LM 002

During trials in Arabia, the LM 001 was overheating, its brakes weren't working well, and its stability in jumping over dunes was not great. The only solution was to put the engine in the front, and that's how the LMA was born (the letters stand for "Lamborghini Military Anteriore," meaning with an anterior engine, or perhaps "Lamborghini Mimran Anteriore," after the owner Mimrano, who believed in and supported the project). A 5-speed transmission from the Countach model contributed to the 50:50 division of weight between the two axles. A tubular space chassis was reinforced by a steel plate, but torsion bars remained. This

The military Lamborghini LM 002

The Lamborghini LM 002

One of the last units of the Lamborghini LM 002

4-d model was 1,102 lbs heavier than the LM 001 and carried more than 6 persons. The LMA made its debut in Geneva in 1982, fitted with a V12 Lambo 4754cc engine (332hp @ 6000, 117 mph, from 0 to 62 mph in 12s), and a 5-speed ZF transmission, which gave the option of disengaging the FWD. Satellite navigation was indispensable for driving in the desert. Further specifications: wheelbase—116 in, length—188.7 in, width—79 in, height—73 in, ground clearance—11.6 in. When empty, it weighed 5,732 lbs and had a capacity of 76 gallons of gasoline. For continuity's sake, it got the name LM 002. Preparations for a military version—the LM 003—distinguished by a TD VM 3590cc (150hp @ 4200) with a 5-speed ZF transmission were under way, when it turned out that the engine was too weak for such a heavy vehicle. Only a single prototype was made. A series-produced LM 002 was announced for 1984 but in the end it did not appear until Brussels 1986. The base for this showcased model—as well as the whole series production—was a prototype of the LM 004 from 1984. The model underwent improvements in the form of body parts made of aluminum and laminate. The heart of the car was originally a Lambo 7257cc ship engine (420hp @ 5400), which turned out to be too heavy. The vehicle negotiated a 70% slope. Dimensions: wheelbase—118 in, length—193 in, width—79 in, height—73 in, curb weight—5,952 lbs. The choice of engines settled on "4- valve" V12

Lambo 5167cc engines (450hp @ 6800, over 130 mph, from 0 to 62 mph in 8.5s), sometimes also a 7.0L ship engine. The LMs had specially-developed Pirelli Scorpion tires. Their bodies were made in Spain and sent to Italy. The receiving technicians complained about their bad quality. A 4-d cab enclosed 5 comfortable seats and the model could seat another 6 persons in the open back part. The first owner of the series-produced LM 002 was the King of Morocco. Several armies expressed their interest, but the model was mainly bought by sheiks. The Saudi army ordered 300 units with more spartan equipment. The first 40 units featured a machine gun and a Countach engine, while the last 157 units had a Lambo Diablo engine. In 1993, they also built a station wagon version with an elevated roof, but large-scale production did not occur. For export to the U.S., they prepared 60 vehicles with a modified specification. It was nicknamed "Rambo-Lambo." The LM 002 was in the lead in the 1987 Pharao's Rally, and in the same year the Munari / Mannucci crew did a great job in the off-roaders' rally in Greece, although it did not finish the race. A year later, Munari was supposed to drive the LM 002 factory special in Dakar, but participation by the already-prepared model was prevented by lack of finances. The vehicle was produced from 1992, and about 328 units were made altogether. There are rumors of there having been a 6x6 version built for a certain sheik, and drafts are known to exist of the successors to this most expensive off-roader of the world from the late 80s and 90s, but their actual construction isn't likely to have taken place.

The Lamborghini LM 004

The Lamborghini LM 004

Land Rover (Australia)

Land Rover   ❾ ❷

The Moorebank quarter of Sydney, Australia, was the place where the LR Series IIA and III 88" and 109" were assembled. They corresponded to their British counterparts, with some exceptions. In 1978 they sold the LR 88" Game. In the late 1970s, the Jaguar Rover Australia company (JRA) knew that it couldn't compete with the Land Cruisers fitted with 6V diesel engines that controlled a very profitable sector of the market. Its Solihull headquarters agreed that as of mid-1981 they were to be getting the CKD LR Stage I V8 and mounting a big Japanese 4V Isuzu 4BD1 3856cc direct injection engine (D, 97hp @ 3200), originally designed for a 7-ton truck. It was noisy and uncultivated but it did the job well and, until production ended in 1984, it was featured in three out of four LR Series II with long wheelbases. The Isuzu remained on offer even for the LR One Ten generation as an optional engine at a premium; they carried "3.9D" name-plates. The Land Rover One Ten appeared on the fifth continent in late 1984, only as a 10-seat "County Station Wagon." The most expensive trims of this model, featuring V8 engines, were exported to Italy as complete cars, while all the others were assembled by JRA from CKD. The Australians extended the One Ten's chassis (with a cab supplied from England) to 120 in and equipped it with an Australian-made aluminum superstructure. The result launched in 1985 was a little platform truck, with a platform undisturbed by wheel cutouts, with a capacity to carry 2,866 lbs—the One Ten Heavy Duty. It was usually nicknamed "the 120." It roughly corresponded to the English One Ten HCPU. It was available exclusively with an Isuzu diesel engine. Since the end of 1985, the One Ten V8 model got a 5-speed Santana LT85 transmission, which appeared under the cowl of the diesel versions as well, at the beginning of the following

The Australian Land Rover 88 Game, 1976

year. One outlandish phenomenon was the local-produced Dual Cab, aka "110 County Pick-up." A shortened rear part of the pick-up was added to the station wagon. They were powered by V8 or diesel Isuzu engines. The short Ninetas were not imported to Australia. Another unique Australian bird was the One Ten Heavy-Duty 6x6 made in 1986, with 3 powered axles and a 4,409-lb payload capacity. It was a civilian derivative of the Project Perentie program. In the early 1980s, the Australian military needed a vehicle that Solihull was not able to offer them. In 1982, long before similar activities in England, work began on a three-axle 6x4 vehicle with an option to engage the 3rd axle. Under normal circumstances, the wheels of the front and 2nd axles were powered. Power was distributed via the LT95A—the latest version of a 4-speed transmission of the Range Rover Generation I. The 3rd axle was automatically engaged when the inter-axle differential lock was locked and reduction gear was put in. It was propelled by the third articulated shaft obtaining torque directly from the transmission. The clutch was vacuum operated. The wheelbase between the 1st and 2nd axle was a "normal" 120 in. The rear double axle was equipped with longitudinal half-elliptic springs connected with a rock shaft distributing the axle load. This design gave excellent performance both on the road and in the off-road. Civilian versions, available since 1986, were powered by gasoline V8 3.5L engines, while military specials had a TD Isuzu (115hp).

LR is responsible for a number of interesting vehicles designed according to the requirements of the army. For tenders that the army invited for floating vehicles, the company came up with a vehicle with a front breakwater and a canopy roof. Long before that, the 6V LR Series II could be spotted on the Vietnam battlefield. In 1982, the Australian army announced the Perentie Project (a perentie being a species of lizard characterized by camouflage and an ability to survive in extreme conditions), whose objective was to renew the motor pool, numbering 3,000 vehicles. Candidates had to satisfy the conditions of an offset program which was intended to ensure that most development and production operations be carried out in Australia. The preliminary conditions for a contract for a 1-ton were fulfilled by Jeep, Land Rover, Mercedes and Toyota. JRA mandated Ray Hapgood as head of the program, and he scored. As many as 2,600 units of the 1-ton Perentie One Ten replaced the LR Series III 109." Before the contract was signed in 1987, the vehicles were subject to a severe trial program. The soldiers in-

The Australian Land Rover 88 Series III, 1978

sisted that the vehicles be equipped with diesel engines (Isuzu 3.9L) and other features, such as placing the spare wheel externally in the rear. For the sake of unification, 4-speed transmissions were installed in both the 6-wheelers and the 4-wheelers. The vehicles, featuring a dozen versions with an open or enclosed body, more or less of the 110" standard, were supplied in contingents stipulated by the contract until 1994.

Land Rover Perentie 6x6   ❷ ❾

Another requirement from the army—a vehicle with a carrying capacity of 1.5–2.0 tons of cargo—was met by JRA's 6-wheeler featuring a TD Isuzu engine (see above). In this weight category, the LR 6x6 had no competitors except the Mercedes Unimog. The military vehicles had stronger axles, a reinforced frontal 4-pinion differential, frontal springs, all shock absorbers, new wheels. A ladder chassis, treated with an anti-corrosive, bore a steel space frame of a cab with aluminum body parts fastened to it. The vehicle bore a number of purpose superstructures such as a field workshop, a transporter for 12 persons, an ambulance, and a Rapier artillery tractor. The panels of the bodies were in some cases (ambulance) made of heat-insulated laminate. The Solihulls were air-conditioned. All modules featured a unified attachment system so they could be easily replaced on another chassis. The SAS patrol and surveillance vehicles for tough guys made a good impression. One of the versions was the Perentie Desert Patrol Vehicle, which carried a Suzuki off-road motorcycle suspended in the rear. Its 96 gal. fuel capacity enabled it to cover 1,000 miles in the desert without refueling. The SAS had a soft spot for free

space. Not even the ambulance had a hard-top roof. In the course of time, the 6x6 Perenties were equipped with bodies 8 inches wider, 2.6 inches longer and 2 inches higher. This modification lent the vehicle extra space for 3 soldiers in the front. After the spring of 1989, JRA offered the 6x6 Perentie also to non-Australians. Precise numbers are not yet available, but at least 3,000 units of the Perentie 110" 4x4 are known to exist, in addition to at least 700 6x6 military vehicles. More than 70 % of their parts are "born" in Australia.

The Land Rover 6x6 Perentie 6x6—an ambulance

Land Rover (Great Britain)

Rover is one of the oldest British car manufacturers. In 1877, John Kemp Starley and William Sutton founded a bicycle factory in Coventry. In 1884, Rover introduced a revolutionary safe bicycle (in Poland, "rover" is a term for bicycle); the first motorcycle—the Imperial—appeared in 1903, followed a year later by an automobile with 8hp. The factory produced bicycles, motorcycles and cars simultaneously. In the 1920s, during one of the crises the company went through, Spencer Wilks was appointed director. His brother Maurice became the head engineer. Spencer slimmed the company down and unified its production program. The pre-war Rovers had a reputation as quality cars with a high degree of standardization. But the company was never financially healthy and suffered from insufficient capital.

Rover passed through the hands of many owners: in 1973–75, it became part of the Leyland corporation (Rover British Leyland UK Ltd.); in 1975–78, it was renamed Leyland Cars, British Leyland UK Ltd. and in 1978–80 Jaguar Rover Triumph Ltd.; in 1980–86, it went under Light Medium Cars Division, BL Ltd.; in 1986, the Rover Group Ltd. emerged, which was further divided by its manager Graham Day into the Austin-Rover passenger-car division, and the Land Rover Division. In 1988, the Rover Group was nationalized and sold by Her Majesty's government to the British Aerospace armaments and aircraft company for 150 million GBP. In the second half of the 1980s, the British

public started calling out "Keep Land Rover British," which led to the establishment of a financially weak company called Rover Cars. In 1994, BA sold it to BMW for 800 million GBP. In 2000, fed up with the low earnings coming from this black hole swallowing hundreds of millions, the Munichers sold the Rover and MG makes to the Alchemy Partners company, which sold it in May of the same year for 20 million pounds to Phoenix Consultation, a company led by a former manager of Rover. In 1992, LR showed a profit of 120 million GBP, followed by 88 million in 1996, and in 1999 a loss of 100 million. After making the fateful decision, BMW needed cash in order to complete the business with Phoenix. Therefore it decided (in 2000) to sell LR to Ford for 1.84 billion GBP, while keeping the Mini.

Over 1.5 million Land Rovers were made by 1993. At the turn of the century, their number exceeded 1.7 million, over 70% of which are still roadworthy! Land Rover, the icon of 4WD vehicles, celebrated its 50th birthday in 1998. What was originally a clapped-out project was to become an indestructible toiler and one of the most famous British vehicles. It saved Rover from bankruptcy and literally caused a small company to become a major car manufacturer. It was the only British vehicle to make good sales at any time, regardless of the state of the economy. It was exported to many countries. Land Rovers have been believed to be employed by all the armies of the world except Albania and North Vietnam. A whole 80% of the production went for export, every fifth car had a diesel engine, and 2 out of 3 featured a 109" wheelbase. Part of the production was exported as CKDs. They were assembled all over the world. In the 1980s and 1990s, owing to the company's higher quality re-

Winston Churchil and a Land Rover

quirements, changes in global politics and a different approach on the part of other governments, the number of assembly plants was limited to Australia, Kenya, Malaysia, Morocco, South Africa, Turkey, Brazil and Zimbabwe; in 2001, production was launched in Thailand. The process of legalization of the franchise for the Iraqi company Morattab is not looking good. In the first years of the millennium, sales have been as high as ever.

Land Rover ❷

Maurice Wilks owned a large homestead in Anglesey. For work on the farm, he'd use Jeeps. In 1947, Spencer Wilks—full of worries about the firm—paid him a visit, and when he saw the run-down cars, he asked his brother what he was going to do when the Jeep wore out. "I'll buy myself a new Jeep. It's the only car of its kind out there." After a long ride around the homestead, including sand dunes, moors, woods and mountains, Spencer got fixated on the project of "Land Rover." The vehicle was approved for production on September 4th, 1947. It was designed as a farming vehicle, temporarily serving as lifeboat for the firm. The designer Gordon Bashford did not try to hide the fact that its main dimensions and chassis were "borrowed" from the Jeep. The body was supposed to be made of light alloys because Rover did not have quotas for steel plates or money to build presses. The prototypes had a steering wheel positioned in the middle, and there were no doors, roof or other equipment. They were powered by a 1.4-L engine from a 10hp model from the 1930s, which soon gave way to a 1.6L from the Rover P3. There were prototypes "learning" to plow, harrow, power threshers, lumber mills and other farming and forestry equipment, transport cattle and pull platform trailers, "believing" they were doing jobs that their future owners—farmers—would require.

The first generation— Land Rover Series (I)—was produced in 1948-57. A 25-unit pilot series from September 1947 had been launched after 18 months of development. The company got 50 orders. An international premiere took place in Amsterdam in 1948; in the same year, 3,048 Land Rovers were made, followed by 8,000 and later 20,000. The first series-produced vehicles did not differ much from the prototypes. At the 1st motor show held after the war—

The Land Rover on the cover of a pamphlet

The Land Rover (Series I) in Mexico, 1957

London 1948—the company showcased a station wagon version, later a van. This model met with such indifference that it disappeared in 1951. A drastic tax rate imposed on this "passenger car" made its price uninteresting. The situation was saved by a successful lawsuit filed by the owner of the vehicle with the police, and it was definitively resolved by the introduction of VAT in 1973. The vehicles had rigid axles and leaf spring suspensions. The first series was fitted with a gasoline 4V IOE (=OHV aspiration, SV exhaust) 1595cc engine (50hp @ 4000), enhanced in 1952–54 to 1997cc (52hp @ 4000), from the P4 sedan. The wheelbases of the first Land Rovers were 80 in long, later also 86 in and 107 in. In the fall of 1954, the 100,000th specimen rolled off the Solihull assembly line. In 1956, the wheelbase was extended to 88 in and 109 in, and since then all LR models began to bear this name. The respective lengths were as follows: 80 in / 86 in / 107 in / 88 in / 109 in; the width was 63 in, the height was 80 in, and the weight was +4,255 lbs. Eight months later, a diesel OHV 2052cc (51hp @ 3500) started to be fitted, at a premium. The Land Rover (including the next generations) had permanent 4x4 drive. At the beginning, and also later, there were models (usually with 4V engines) with an option to disengage the FWD. The main transmission had 4 speeds at first, and later 5 speeds (with a growing number of synchronized gears). When the Austin Gipsy appeared, Maurice Wilks had the vehicle's shape retouched. The 1st generation is known as Land Rover Series I. Their payload was 1,001 lbs (80") and they negotiated a 45° side tilt. Payload ratings of other models were: 999 lbs (the 86"), 1,499 lbs (the 107"), 1,347 lbs (the 88"), 1,499 lbs—or, with bigger wheels—1,997 lbs (109"). Ground clearance: 8 in (the SWB), 9.8 in (the LWB). The numbers of units produced differ from source to source. Historian James Taylor in his "The Land Rover Story – Part I" maintains: 39,879 units in 1948–1951, 38,747 units in 1952–1953 (80," 2.0L) in 1954–1958, 49,342 units (86") and 27,346 units (107"), 42,076 units in 1956–1958 (88" and 109").

The Land Rover Series II from 1958–61 had a frame chassis with similar body-types. The most eagerly-awaited feature was the 2.0L OHV engine, which was supposed to replace the previous IOE type. But the innovation was not approved by the board of directors and the Series II had to keep its original power unit. Payload ratings: 1,550 lbs (for the 88"), 2,412 lbs (for the 109"). Production couldn't keep up

The Land Rover IIA 88 and 109, 1971

with demand. Eight factories participated in production in the Birmingham area. Numbers of units of Series II produced: 110,067 units (88" and 109") in 1958–61.

In 1961, the Series II became known as the Series IIA (1961–71). The vehicle got a 4V OHV 2286cc engine (77hp @ 3 500), and the diesel OHV engine was also modified to this capacity 5 years later. Between 1967 and 1980, the 109" model was available with an optional 6V IOE 2625cc engine (83hp @ 4500), and after Geneva 1979 also a V8 OHV 3528cc (91hp @ 3500). By that time, the Land Rover had got a chassis with permanent 4x4 from the Range Rover. In 1958–71, a total of 549,311 units of the LR Series II and IIA were made. Mr. Taylor lists numbers which don't include the units made in Spain, the 88" and 109" military specials, or the CKD kit cars after 1965: 1961–1971 (88" and 109")— 343,298 vehicles, including the 109" one-tons.

The Land Rover Series III was produced between October 1971 and 1974. It came a year after the Range Rover. The model got a fully-synchronized transmission. In 1968, the main headlights were moved from the grille onto the fenders. This is where the history of the LR with leaf springs ends. From the start of its existence until 1961, a total of 310,475 units were made; from 1962 until the end of the IIA series in 1971 (including the FC), as many as 351,813 units were manufactured. A book covering the 50 years of this model's history mentions 538,862 units of the Series III made in 1971–83.

The Land Rover III 109, 1975

Land Rover Model 110 a 90, Defender ❷

The Geneva 1983 motor show saw the debut of the dramatically modernized Land Rover Model 110 ("One Ten"), followed 15 months later by the Model 90 ("Ninety"). The original 4V 2.3L engine, rebuilt to a 2495cc (83hp @ 4000), was available in addition to the existing V8. The Italian VM diesel engines from the 1980s sometimes need high maintenance. After 1985, a diesel 2495cc engine (67hp @ 4000) was available, and a TD 2 495cc (107hp @ 3800) in the fall of the same year at the NEC, which replaced the VM. The vehicles featured a one-piece front glass, a new grille pushed forward and a coil spring suspension. In April 1982, the better-equipped LR Series III County with a different body color was presented. (In March 1983 the original LWB were replaced by the new One Ten County vehicles, and in June 1984, the SWBs were superseded by the Ninety County model). In December 1987 the vehicle was retouched. The short models (SWB) featured a 7.5-in-high ground clearance, the stretched LWBs had an 8.5-in-high ground clearance. The longest version was represented by the One Ten Crew Cab double-cab (December 83-June 85), followed by the One Ten Seven (July 85-August 90). Dimensions of the 90 / 110 / Crew Cab were as follows: wheelbase—93 in / 110 in / 127 in; length—147 in / 175–184 in / 198 in; width—70.5 in; height—80 in.

In the fall of 1989, the LR underwent slight revisions (the dimensions remained the same) and was renamed "Defender," including the 90, 110 and 130 models. Vehicles with a traditional all-canvas roof were supplied to the military and to customers in the tropics. The Defender 130 Crew Cab is not a hit of the latest fashion. The photo shows a model from 1983, featuring a 127-in wheelbase, which was marketed as "Defender 130." The Defender became the best-selling 4x4 in Britain in 1990. In 1998, its simple Tdi engines could no longer meet the demands for emission and noise limits. A reaction was a modern TD BMW Td5 pump-jet engine, which has since 1999 been fitted in several models. Mainly for expedition purposes and third world countries, the Tdi continues to be produced in Brazil and Argentina, because, even in 2003, a village blacksmith in a South American pampa will have trouble fixing a broken down electronic system. The ladder chassis frame, rigid axles, a pair of longitudinal control arms, the Panhard rod in the front, the trailing wishbone in the back and coil springs

The Land Rover 90, 1991

everywhere have been retained. The Defender is not endowed even with the most basic comforts, and a radio is useless with all the noise. On the road, it tilts when turning, and soon is barely able to keep up. Speed must be kept down. A vehicle of a different make, with only a part of the Defender's negative qualities, would be entirely unsalable. Still, its sales are rising, along with the desire of the well-to-do to escape for at least a while from the over-technologized world. For the Defender is a king in the off-road, with an optimal chassis, a cross-country reduction and a ground clearance of 8.5 in (or 9 in for the Defender 90). The helpful ABS combined with the ETC (anti-slip system) and a man-

ual lock of an inter-axle differential are available (at a premium). The vehicle has a fording depth of 25.6 in. The overhang angles of the Defender 90 SW, the 110 SW, and the 130 are: 48°/50°/50° and 49°/34.5°/34°. The Defender has a 45° slope, and a 45° (30°) side tilt. The vehicle has a curb weight of +4,365 lbs, and a payload of 1,720 lbs. The model 2002 featuring minor modifications was shown at the IAA 2001. The hard-top trim was equipped with rustproof back doors and it had undergone slight revisions of interior and chassis, and Panhard rods. The model even came with only a single key (before, there were 3: an ignition key, a door key, and a gas tank key), a central locking system, electrically operated windows, ABS and ETC. Available models include: the S, the SE, the E, and the County to top it all.

On July 29th, 1993, the 1.5-millionth LR–Defender 90SV in the U.S. specification was produced. Land Rovers began to be dispatched to the U.S.A. in 1949. The different environment required specifications, known as the NADA (North American Dollar Area), or as the NAS (North American Specification). The American branch gave rise to the Golden Rod prototype featuring a V8 engine, which was sent for approval to the factory in Britain. Production did not occur, because the Range Rover was about to be launched. The Defender One Ten (NAS) V8 was tuned as the Range Rover. In addition to that, a 500-unit series of the Defender 110 was produced. Not even the Defender itself managed to avoid a limited series. The 1998 Turin show was where the Defender No Limits based on the 90 was dis-

The Land Rover Defender limited-series Tomb Raider, 2001

played, to celebrate the 50th "birthday" of the make. The—similarly rusticised—Defender Heritage 90 was launched in London 1999, followed by the Defender X Tech shown at the NEC 2000. In 2001, the French LR offered the Defender Technium based on the 90—a station wagon hard-top Td5 vehicle. The IAA 2001 saw the Defender 110 Tomb Raider crew cab (limited series), and the Defender XS was marketed in England in 2002. The Defender Project SVX (Special Vehicle X, based on the 90 Td5) first appeared at the IAA in 1999. The popularity of the pick-up trucks was enhanced by the lightweight Defender, which was used by the charming, intrepid archeologist Lara Croft, the Tomb

Raider, for her aerial descent into the jungle. This vehicle was showcased in Geneva 2001. In 1983–97, a total of 327,400 units of the LR 90/110/Defender were manufactured. Geoff Upex, the head designer, is preparing a new generation of the Defender—the L317—for launch in 2005.

Land Rover special-purpose trims ❷ ❾

The military had their own idea of a Land Rover. The first examples were built in 1943 under the code name of FV1800. Lack of time made them go for a completed vehicle. In March 1948, two specimens of the 48 pre-production series of LR test cars were handed over to the army for tests. The vehicles passed the tests and Rover received a contract for 48 vehicles (to replace the Jeeps) that same year, soon followed by a contingent of 1,878 units. The army had one more thing in mind. A modified chassis of the LR 81" was fitted with a 4V Rolls-Royce B40 engine, with a capacity lowered from 2.8 to 1.6L. The engine, which was considered for the FV 1800 was worth a whole LR. The power unit had a 50% higher performance and weight than a standard Rover engine. In May 1949, the army signed a contract with Hudson Motors to fit thirty-three LR chassis with Rolls-Royce engines. The name of "Land Rover 81" (80 mph) caught on. Since the early 1960s, a whole range of mili-

The Land Rover 110—the armored Shortland

The Land Rover Centaur, 1979

tary prototypes have been made. The army was looking for a $^1/_4$ ton multi-purpose vehicle for paratrooper operations. As helicopters weren't able to transport vehicles weighing more than $^1/_4$ ton, hopes were being pinned on vehicles (on pallets) designed to be thrown off airplanes with parachutes. Frequent damage to the cars, off-the-mark descents and progress in the construction of planes soon put an end to this episode. In July 1966, the first test specimens of a $^1/_2$ ton vehicle appeared. Later, some of them were modified and named Lightweight. The series-produced $^1/_2$-ton 88" vehicle from 1968–84 already corresponded to the simultaneously manufactured civilian versions. Its wheelbase was 101 in long. The Series IIA gave rise to 2,989 military $^1/_2$-ton vehicles. The company also produced special half-track, three-axle, armored and amphibious vehicles. For desert operations, the SAS squads used special vehicles with a pink finish (the Pink Panthers). Two major finalists in the competitions were Short Brothers and Harland from Belfast (e.g., the armored Shorland or the Armored Personnel Carrier), and Alan Milstead (the half-track Centaur). In addition to the British army, the LR "conquered" the armies of the Commonwealth, then NATO, and eventually it was used by armies in 140 countries of the world. A political decision of the government not to sell advanced technology to a potential enemy was circumvented by third world dictators by buying Land Rovers in Spain or even Iran. The British Ministry of Defense decided to replace the specials based on the LR Series III with the new Defender XD. However, the novice failed the tests and the company got a cold shower. In the end, the contract went to Puch for 394 Pinzgauers. However, a revised Defender XD proved useful too, and before the fall of 1996, the army had ordered 7,925 units. The Desert Patrol Vehicle (known as "Dinkies"—a little brother of the bigger, pink "Pinkies") was used in the deserts of the Gulf War and in Bosnia. The SVO developed and, as of 1993, also supplied, specials based on the One Ten model, fitted with a V8 engine according to the US Rangers specification. Well known too are the military Defender 130 and vehicles with a 127"-long wheelbase, the Rapier weapon tractors, the Marshalls' and Locomotors ambulances, the Shorland Series 5 and Hornet armored vehicles finalized by external contractors including Short Brothers and Glover Webb.

It was mainly at the army's bidding that 5 prototypes were produced featuring a platform truck body with a carrying capacity of 1.5 ton and a wheelbase length of 129 in, which gave rise to military utility vehicles, later known as the Forward-Control. Another prototype was the Forward-Control 120". In 1962–66, a trambus version appeared named the Forward Control 109", which was presented in September 1961. A total of 3,193 units of the FC 109" were produced. It was followed by the Forward Control Series IIA—a 1-ton on the basis of the Series IIA 109" a 110," used mainly by the military. A total of 308 units were made in 1968–71. In 1966, the Forward Control 110" Series IIB was presented for the first time. A total of 2,305 units were made in 1967–72. Only the British army had the special right to take the Forward-Control 101 1-ton vehicle (2,669 units in 1975–78), aka 1-Tonne, featuring a vertical front end face on an LR Series III chassis and a V8 engine. This expensive chassis with coil springs (the older design with leaf springs was featured on all the other LRs until 1984) was normally complemented by a one-axle trailer (FC 110). The fantastic abilities of the 6x6 version in driving through bottomless pits of mud or overcoming obstacles are legendary. The wheelbase of the car was 109 in long, its total length was 193 in, it was 75.7 in wide, 102 in high and weighed 4,504 lbs. The role of the successor of the 101 in the mid-1970s was planned for a platform truck known as the Llama, built on a One Ten chassis, featuring a V8 engine, many components known from other LRs from the current generations, and a payload capacity of 2 tons. In 1986, the army received two prototypes, but the vehicles did not make it.

The Land Rover 101—the military Forward Control in a pamphlet

Land Rover – SVO ❷

There was a growing number of customers with special requirements. It was a good business. In June 1985, the company established a Special Vehicle Operations (SVO) department. It participated in preparing and supplying special vehicles. In the mid-1980s, the role of the SVO became so important that it was fair to consider it a "fourth marque," just as the author of the idea, Geroge Mackie, would have wished. SVO was the first supplier of the Crew Cab pick-up truck. Some specimens were equipped with double rear axles, purpose-built superstructures, armory and similar features. Since the end of the 1990s, SVO has been coming up with action models of civilian vehicles. One of the first Land Rovers with disc brakes was the 90SV (Defender) pick-up truck. In 1987, it was followed by the Land Rover Cariba (Defender 90SV). The convertible won many admirers in the U.S., where it was pronounced the "Four-Wheeler of the Year" in 1994. The NEC 2000 saw the debut of the Freelander, the Discovery, and the Range Rover Autobiography limited-series models.

Land Rover Discovery a Discovery II ❷

The Discovery made its first appearance at the IAA 1989. It was a successor to three prototypes, one of which was displayed at the NEC 1986 as the Range Rover Olympic (at the time, Birmingham was bidding to organize the Olympics). The vehicle had a Range Rover body. The company wanted to respond to the growing popularity of Japanese off-road station wagons. The sales of the 3-d Discovery (also a 5-d after the NEC 1990) were painfully slow to pick up steam. It featured a Defender chassis but its body was derived from the Range Rover. The first version available was fitted with a V8i engine (3532cc, 145hp @ 5000) and a 200 Tdi engine (2494cc, 113hp @ 4450). It had a 100-in-long wheelbase, it was 178 in long, 70.5 in wide, and 75.6 in high. Its overhang angles were 39°/21°. Its curb weight was 4,303 lbs (V8) or 4,266 lbs (2.5 Tdi), and its payload was 1,753 lbs or 1,731 lbs respectively. Models available in Great Britain included: the ES (after 1994, with a high level of equipment), the Mpi (with a 2.0L gasoline engine), the Tdi (200 Tdi and 300 Tdi), the V8 (V8), the V8i (V8 3.5 and 3.9L, injection). In Germany in 1991/92, the

The Land Rover Discovery III, fall 2002

The Land Rover Discovery modified for transporting the disabled; NEC 2002

Emotion action vehicle appeared, followed by the Sunseeker in 1992; in 1995 came limited-series models of the Hunter, the Sailor, the Parcours and the Sunset. A little later came the Esquire and the Trophy. A total of 353,843 vehicles of the 1st generation were made between 1989 and 1997.

Following a facelift in the spring of 1994, the 2nd generation of the vehicle was prepared. The new Discovery (II) made its debut in Paris 1998 (with a sneak preview a year before), also featuring 4x4 drive, an inter-axle differential and a hard suspension—with only slight stylistic touch-ups but only 5 doors, with a new interior, filled with electronic systems known from the Freelander and complemented with ACE, SLS, EBD and HDC. Its active, adjustable chassis has air suspension. Electronics are so abundant that the microprocessors don't communicate with each other via standard cables but the Multiplex—a digital interconnection. The vehicle is 7.5 in longer and 2.8 in wider. Power comes either from a gasoline V8 4L engine or a new cultivated 5V 2496cc Td5 BMW engine (132hp @ 4200) with direct injection. It negotiates a 100 % slope, a 42° side tilt, and features 40° / 19° overhang angles, an 8.2-in ground clearance and a 19.7-in fording depth. When empty, the vehicle weighs 4,652 lbs and carries up to 1,697 lbs of load.

The Discovery won the "Best Compact Sport-Utility" prize in 1999. In 2001 came the time for the Adventure action vehicle, followed a year later by the Adventurer in Great Britain, and the Metropolis—a dark-painted model with high-tech equipment. A facelift was presented in the fall of 2002 as "the model 2003 (code L318)" of a generation characterized mainly by concentrated main headlights, grille and details making it look more "civilized" and more like the RR III, as well as minor engine modifications. For European distribution, the Td5 now features a special steering unit with a 2-degree reaction to the gas pedal engagement (quick reaction for the road, linear reaction for the off-road). For the U.S. market, the 4.0L engine was replaced with a more powerful 4.6L power unit. All specimens come with a 4-speed auto transmission with two gear modes—"Normal" and "Sport." The Td5 engine is only available with a 5-speed manual transmission. Just like its predecessor, the model is equipped with an inter-axle differential with a lock. The forthcoming Discovery L319 with a Defender body is scheduled to appear in 2005.

The Camel Trophy used to be considered something like the Olympics for four wheel drive vehicles. The teams representing their nations were asked to cover almost 1,000 miles in identical vehicles in a terrain without roads, while fulfilling a large number of tasks. Only the vehicles for the first year—1980 featuring a crossing of Amazonia—were all supplied by Jeep. Ever since then, Land Rover has run the show, using the Discovery between 1990 and 1998. Since 2003, the company has participated in the 4 Challenge—a similar tournament, but without a cigarette background.

Range Rover ❷

In 1951, production of the unmarketable LR station wagon was terminated. In April 1952, Maurice Wilks launched the development of the 2-d Road Rover station wagon based on the already-prepared P4 sedan. In 1954, Graham Bannock,

the manager, researched the U.S. market. He noticed a growing demand for 4x4 leisure time vehicles. The Rover 2000 was the basis for the next Road Rover station wagon. Further development was influenced by the Ford Bronco, and the model was originally fitted with a 6V from the P5. The prototype bore a Road Rover name-plate, but the name Range Rover was introduced in 1968. On June 17th, 1970, the curtain went up for the press. The unique concept of a car that can take you hunting on muddy tracks in the morning, and to see the opening night of a show in a theater in the evening, was ahead of its time by decades. The Range Rover started a worldwide interest (outside of America) in off-road station wagons with an other than purely working character. Its bodywork was created by a team of designers—Gordon Bashford, Spencer King and David Bach. The RR is a 3-d (later also 5-d) station wagon—see Monteverdi), with a luxurious and comfortable interior, permanent AWS and

The Land Rover Range Rover 5-d, 1972

The Land Rover Range Rover first generation, 1968

an option to disengage the FWD. It was mounted on a ladder frame, and fitted with a gasoline V8 3528cc engine (135hp @ 4750), a gear-reduction transmission with a manual differential lock, rigid axles, where the rear axle featured a Boge Hydromat automatic level compensation, and disc brakes. Two of these vehicles covered the distance between Alaska and Chirogodo—the southernmost point of South America—in 99 days. (The accompanying LR 88," bought second-hand in Panama, managed the journey without a problem. An identical adventure was undertaken in 134 days by two English eccentrics with an LR 88.) The 1986 Turin motor show saw the debut of a TD version with a 4V VM OHV 2494cc engine (113hp @ 4000). One of the lucky owners of the rare short version is the British royal family. All of its members, including Queen Elizabeth herself, often drive their personal RRs and LRs around their es-

tates. The RR is the only vehicle so far to have been displayed in the Louvre. In July 1978, the Jaguar, Rover and Triumph marques split off from the British Leyland holding. 400 million GBP had originally been allotted for the modernization of off-roaders; however, Sir Michael Edwards, Chairman of the BL Board of Directors, shrank from such high expense at the last minute, and authorized only a "small" expansion. An independent division—Land Rover Ltd.—was established in August that year. In November 1979, they used the lowered sum to expand the production of the RR by 50% (450 units per week), and in June 1984 came up with a 5-d variant. The original automatic 3-speed Chrysler transmission (which turned out to be unsuitable in extreme conditions) was replaced with a German-made manual 4-speed ZF transmission in 1985, or with a manual 5-speed one in 1983. The sales, especially of the vehicles featuring auto-

The Land Rover Range Rover 4.6 Vogue, 2000

The Land Rover Range Rover Vogue LSE, 1994

matic transmissions, were roaring. In October 1985, the more powerful Vogue models were introduced, featuring an injection (165 hp @ 4000)—with the exception of vehicles with V8 engines. The RR became a truly luxurious model. December 1986 brought about an electronic injection system for the V8, as well as a massive campaign in the U.S. The vehicles were equipped with horizontally-ribbed grilles, in contrast to the original—vertical—arrangement. Specifications: wheelbase—100 in, length—176 in, width—1,780, height—70 in, weight—(+)3,902 lbs. After October 1989, the model was shortened by 0.8 in and broadened by 1.6 in.

In 1992, this 20-year-old model received the EAS—electronically adjustable gas suspension with five-positions (3 for movement selected by the driver, an automatic one for parking, and one for getting in/out). The stretched model (wheelbase—108 in, length—183 in, width—71.5 in, height—72 in, weight—4,575 lbs), was marked "LSE." The vehicle has a 7.5-in ground clearance and carries 1,025-15,013 lbs. In 1991/92, the Westminster and Ascot action models were sold in Germany. Production of 3-d models was terminated in 1994. The original generation did not leave the scene in the fall of 1994. It proceeded to be sold as "Range Rover Classic." Its time to go did not come until 1996. There follows a summary of models in Great Britain: the Tdi, the Turbo D, the Vogue, the Vogue SE and the Vogue LSE, and the following limited models: the Schuler Automatic (1980, 25 units), the In Vogue (1981, 1,000 units), the Automatic (1982), the Limited Edition (1983, 325 units), the CSK (initials of Charles Spencer King—the "father" of the Range Rover, 200 units). European models included mainly the following limited ones: the Trophy (D, 1981), the 20th Anniversary (CH, 1990, 60 units), the Ascot (D, 1982, based on the Vogue SEi), corresponding with the Brooklands Green (also NL and CH, 1993, like Brooklands, 150 units), the Balmoral (E, F; 1983), the Countryman (E, 1993), the Silver Fox and the Silver Spring (F, 1992), the Vogue S (I; 1993), the 3,9Ei (P; 1993). Models that appeared in the U.S. included: the GDE (Great Divide Edition—after a trans-American expedition, 1990, 400 units), the Hunter, the County, the County SE, and the County LWB. During 26 years of production, a total of 317,615 RR 1st generation were "born." The vehicle also went down well with crude-oil sheiks. They took to the special versions, such as the open

RR, modified by specialized workshops, including FLM Panelcraft, Wood and Picket, Rapport International, Panther, Monteverdi, Arden, Robert Jankel Design, Carbodies and many others. Ogle Design prepared a short elevated armored RR with glass windows for the Pope. This model has also been used by armed forces. In 1980–84, the factory launched a modest model called the Fleet Line, designed mainly for traffic police. The Special Project Department and specialists such as Lomas and Pilcher-Greene built civilian and military ambulances (some on a 135-in wheelbase), fire-engines (some with 3 axles—e.g., the Carmichael), and specials for rescue squads and bodyguards.

BL intended to send these vehicles to the 1970 London-Mexico Rally but did not manage to get them ready in time. They did not appear until January 1976, in a 6,250-mi long-distance race from Abidjan to Nice. They finished first and second, with three other Range Rovers among the first ten. The Range Rovers appearing in raid rallies were mostly made in France and Australia (the 1978 London-Sydney marathon). In 1979, they took part in world cup rallies (Bandama Rally, Safari). The models for the Paris-Dakar Rally were fine-tuned mainly by BL France. In 1980 Christine Beckers won the Ladies' Cup in a lightweight RR; and in 1981, the Metge / Giroux crew won the historically first gold in the World Cup—in a special made by Tom Walkinshaw Motorsport under BL's baton. In the following years, the RR fleet was managed by Austin Rover France—a renamed importer of these vehicles. A vehicle of its team (called Halt Up!) finished second overall in 1984; the Halt Up! team repeated the same ranking in 1987, in a model built in Solihull. In 1987, the Toleman team in the Enduro T89 (4.2L V8, a Kevlar body) failed. Engines tuned by JE Motors (124 mph in the desert) brought P. Tambay in 3rd position in 1988, and M. Smith in 4th position in 1988. In January 1989, the factory started work on Group T featuring a torsen differential and a JE Motors 3.9L engine (215hp, 140 mph), but the project was dropped after the Discovery appeared and the factory focused on the Camel Trophy. A French team—ETT (Eggenspiller Tout Terrain)—continued to participate in raid rallies. Eggenspiller equipped the lightweight vehicles with Kevlar bodies, and V8 4.8L engines (250hp).

The Land Rover Range Rover, 1994

Range Rover – generation II ❷

In October 1994, Generation II was launched, called "the King of Off-Roaders." It did not differ much from its forerunner. The grille ribs were now horizontal. A modification of the rear made loading of luggage more difficult. The ladder frame became more solid and safer. The rigid axles were lightened and reinforced. Most body parts were made of aluminum. The model was 1.2 in longer and 2.4 in higher than its forerunner, and it featured an improved air-suspension of wheels. It was equipped with 7 computers controlling the BECM (Body Electronic Control Module). Thanks to its top-quality high-tech equipment, it was immediately years ahead of its competitors. The most expensive model of engine was a V8 4552cc (226hp @ 4750, 140 mph), but a V8 4273cc (202hp @ 4850) was also available. The price of 46,550 GBP included an anti-slip mechanism, automatic transmission, electric seat and roof adjustment. The RR II had a 4V TD engine with an intercooler 2497cc (136hp @ 4400), from the 5th and 7[th.] BMW series. It negotiated a slope of 90 %, a side tilt of 29°, a ford as deep as 19.7 in, it had a 8.4-in ground clearance and 30°/23° overhang angles. Models featuring the EAS (electronic air suspensions) differed in terms of their overhang angles (34° and 26°), side tilt (26°) and fording depth (23.6 in). Basic engine models included: a DT (TD), a DSE (TD, more expensive equipment), a HSE (4.6L), a SE (4.0L). A limited model named the "30th Anniversary Limited Edition" was showcased in Geneva 2000; and a 400-unit edition of the Range Rover Westminster was shown in Geneva 2001.

Range Rover – generation III ❸

After entering the company, BMW made its first big investment: 300 million GBP for a reconstruction of the RR (code L322). The concept of the New Range Rover with permanent AWD did not change. The vehicle is all brand new, built with the assistance of Bavarian engineers and with a unification of some of their designs (engines, chassis tuning) with the BMW X5. Ford became the owner of the division, but it was too late for changes and the RR had to keep its original equipment. The BMW engines are expensive. The company is considering a "re-armament" of the RR III to a 4.2 V8 Jaguar engine, and/or even a 6.0L V12 Aston Martin power unit. They are manufactured at a new assembly line in Solihull. The vehicle made its debut in London 2001. It came exclusively as a station wagon, and it gained a more

The Land Rover Range Rover III, 2002

The Land Rover Range Rover III, 2002

elegant body mounted on a steel skeleton of a self-supporting steel floor platform with three supporting frames. Compared to the RR II, the RR III features a 5.3-in-longer wheelbase, it is 9.3 in longer and 1.9 in higher. All its wheels are suspended independently, on McPherson struts with coil springs in the front, and double longitudinal and transverse control arms with an air-suspension in the rear. The front and the back both feature transversal stabilizers. The vehicles are fitted with aluminum gasoline BMW V8 32v 4398cc engines (286hp @ 5400, 129 mph) with the VANOS variable valve timing technology (unleaded gasoline with 91–95 octane rating), or a cultivated economical in-line Td6 Common-Rail engine—6V 2926cc (177hp @ 4000, 140 mph) with a compressed-air cooler. The model weighs +5,379 lbs and carries 1,168 lbs or 1,345 lbs of load. The RR III is loaded with electronics, thanks to which it degrades its

competitors in the off-road. The Steptronic automatic 5-speed transmission has an option of a manual gear change. It is complemented by an electronically-controlled cross-country reduction. An inter-axle torsen II differential variably distributes torque between the front and rear wheels with the ratio raging between 25:75 and 75:25. The ETC II system regulates the slip by applying the brake (which mostly eliminates the absence of axle differential locks), and there is also the HDC system for ascending steep slopes. A computer automatically chooses between the harder road mode and the softer off-road mode of the air-suspension. The DSC (dynamic stability control) optimizes the adjustment of the chassis depending on the state of the road and driving style; the type used in the RR III is exceptional in that it (or, more precisely, the part influencing the engine and not the brakes) can be de-activated in the off-road, and the driver thus maintains control over the vehicle. Electronic control of tire pressure, ABS + EBD, ESP and 8 airbags all contribute to the safety of the crew. Interconnected air suspension (the RR III has adjustable ground clearance—up to 11 in) will ensure that a wheel that would otherwise remain suspended in mid-air, receives the highest air pressure, which enables it to remain in contact with the road. The vehicle's overhang angles are 35° / 27°, its fording depth is 19.7 in. Models include: the SE, the HSE and the Vogue. The "king" has once again confirmed his dominance in the realm of luxury SUVs. It has topped the chart of the "Top Gear" BBC magazine/TV show, and was named as "Best 4x4 Off-Roader of the Year 2002" in the Auto Express Magazine new car honors. A 5-seat Baby Range Rover (L320) is scheduled to appear, featuring a Discovery platform and Jaguar V8 and diesel V6 engines.

Land Rover Freelander   ❷

The IAA 1997 saw the debut of a 5-seat off-road / road vehicle (code CB40), known to the public as the Freelander, represented by i, XEi, di and Xedi models. It was designed by Nick Fell, who had also designed the MGF. This revolutionary vehicle was designed as member of a (newly established by the manufacturer) segment of vehicles for leisure time with equipment such as heated front seats and a tempomat. It is the first LR featuring a self-supporting body, a long 5-d station wagon and a short 3-d station wagon or softback—a rather conservative version of a pick-up truck. All

The Land Rover Freelander, 1998

its wheels are suspended independently on McPherson struts with torsion bars. They are powered by in-line 4V engines— a gasoline 1725cc engine (120hp @ 5550, 140 mph), and an economical, but less cultivated and a little "smoky" TD Rover V6 2497cc (177hp @ 6250, 102 mph) with direct injection. It carries up to 882 lbs of load. It is what Americans call a "4x4 passenger car," with a variable distribution of torque between the front and rear wheels (80% of it goes to the rear on rough terrains). Other features include a viscous coupling and a manual 5-speed differential, without a rear differential lock, whose function is fulfilled by the ETC (electronic anti-slip control), and it has no reduction. It has ABS (the first 4x4 in the world to feature ABS was the RR)

The Land Rover Freelander 3-d V8 Softback, 2002

but, most importantly, ETC and HDC (Hill Descent Control), which improve its ability to manage rough terrains and make hill descent safer. The IAA 1999 was where the Freelander Commercial first appeared. As soon as the Freelander V6 featuring a KV6 engine from the Rover 75 appeared, sales rocketed in the U.S., Japan and Middle East, just as expected. As many as 70% of the vehicles were fitted with V6 2497cc engines (177hp @ 6250). On demand, the Freelander V6 can be equipped with a JATCO-Steptronic, automatic 5-speed transmission, inspired by F1, with "Normal" and "Sport" gear modes, giving the option of a manual or automatic gear change. Further characteristics: wheelbase—101 in, length—172.5 in, and later (since 2000) 175 in, width—71 in, height—69 in, ground clearance— 7.3 in, overhang angles—30°/34°, slope—70 %, side tilt— 26°, and fording depth—15.8 in. The vehicle's curb weight is 3,483 lbs and it carries 1,102 lbs of load. In Europe, it is available with S, GS and ES equipment. In 2000, it was fitted with a refined, economical BMW Td4 1950cc engine (112hp @ 4000, 103 mph). In the U.S.A., the S, SE and HSE are available. The British limited series from 2002 includes: the Serengeti and the Kalahari, the French includes the Freelander 360°. A facelift—the L314 model—was announced for 2003. NB: The Freelander Generation II was introduced at the IAA 2003. Plans have been made for a better-quality interior and a new transmission and, most importantly, 4V and 6V Ford engines should replace the current Rover engines and push the vehicle to the top of its class. A brand new Freelander (L315) is scheduled for 2004. The hopefully best-selling 4x4 in Europe should be a triplet of the Ford Maverick and the Mazda Tribute; it should feature Ford engines, a self-supporting body and independent wheel suspension.

Land Rover South Africa

Land Rover ❷

One of the firms that assembled Land Rovers in South Africa was Leyland South Africa. The history of Land Rover assembly there goes back to the 1950s. In 1984, Leyland sold its share to AAD—a local company, which proceeded to produce LRs with coil springs in 1985–95. It was necessary that some components be supplied by local companies, in order to avoid a 100% import duty rate. Of some interest was a conversion of the LR One Ten featuring a 127"-long wheelbase, 6x6 drive and usually a V8 engine. About 40 "dachshunds" were sold in 1986–1992. Besides the army (which had an itch for armored vehicles), these 16-seat station wagons appealed to safari services in South Africa and Zimbabwe. In 1994, BMW bought Rover. The Germans terminated the contract with AAD and moved the LR to their assembly plant in Rosslyn near Pretoria, where they had operated since 1977. The opening ceremony for the new LR assembly plant on March 24th, 1995, was attended by Queen Elizabeth, who had also launched the Midrand headquarters in 1993. The factory had a capacity of 2,500 Defenders and 620 Discoveries. The first version to roll off the assembly lines were the Defender 110 pick-up trucks and station wagons fitted with V8 and 300Tdi engines, followed in the fall by Defenders 90 and later still by the 130 featuring a TD 2.5L engine (113hp) or a gasoline BMW 2.8L engine (193hp). The vehicles, differing in small details from their British counterparts, were exported to sub-Saharan coun-

tries and Australia. After Ford took over the LR marque, the company's South African activities became part of the Ford Motor Company of South Africa (FMCSA), and the production of "Africa's most popular vehicle" was moved to Silverton near Pretoria. The transfer lasted 6 weeks, owing to Ford's philosophy expressed by the slogan "100% manual," or the maximum manual input, with minimal investments. The same "line" had in the past been used by Mitsubishi. The new workplace was opened in August 2001. The daily output was 6 cars with a roughly British specification, followed by 12 the following year, although the line's capacity is 20 cars. A prototype of the Defender 147 High Capacity Station Wagon was the last to be "born" in Rosslyn. This station wagon, seating up to 11 persons, is derived from the Defender 110 chassis with a 176.5-in-long wheelbase. It has an extra pair of side doors and the passengers sitting in the 2nd and 3rd rows enjoy 40% extra space. The front and rear overhang remained the same, while the wheelbase was extended by 37 in. The C-pillars were added and the Heavy Duty wheel suspension had to be reinforced. The rear axle got an extra pair of coil springs and steel wheels, and it was reinforced. Power was provided by a Td5 engine, which superseded the simple Tdi in South Africa in 2002. Unless a spare wheel is suspended on the tailgate, this 5.3-m-long vehicle should fit into a standard garage. The first 10 units are supposed to have been made in 2001. This model is aimed at safari services. In 2000, a total of 1,440 Defenders were manufactured. Assembly of the Freelander started in South Africa in 2002. In the same year, the company sold 1,008 Defenders to Angola and in 2003 they are supposed to have sent the rest of the 216 Defenders 110 CSW and 130, along with the 3000 Freelanders (TD4 and KV6) to Australia.

The South African Land Rover Defender 147, 2002

Lexus
(Japan)

In 1988, Toyota established a subsidiary named Lexus. Not by coincidence does its name evoke luxury. In contrast to the Acura (Honda) and the Infiniti (Nissan) marques, which also included off-road vehicles, Lexus found its home both in North America and Europe. The vehicles are mechanically almost identical with models made by their parent car manufacturers.

Lexus LX 450, LX 470 ❷

A luxurious station wagon with permanent 4WD appeared at the end of 1985. It was in fact the Land Cruiser 80 and was powered by a 6V "1FZ-FE" 4477cc engine (215 hp @ 4600, JIS, 109 mph). The LX 450 model featured an inter-axle differential with a manual lock, a viscous coupling, and a gear-reduction transmission. The transmission had 4 speeds and was automatic. There was a ladder chassis, rigid axles with coil springs and a Panhard rod; upon request, a stabilizer could be mounted in the rear. The Lexus had a 112-in-long wheelbase, a length of 190 in, was 72 in wide and 73 in high,

The Lexus LX 470

and its ground clearance was 8.7 in. An empty car weighed +4,982 lbs, and its payload was 948 lbs. Generation II made in 1998—the Lexus LX 470—has a lot in common with the Land Cruiser 100. In addition to an altered appearance, it features a V8 "2UZ-FE" 4664cc engine (234hp @ 4800, SAE, 109 mph). In this case, the vehicle has a 5-speed auto transmission. This 8-seat, 5-d station wagon is packed with the latest mechanical and technological devices. Its front wheels are suspended independently with torsion bars and a stabilizer, while the rear axle remains rigid, identical with the LX 450. Length has increased by 2.8 in, width by 4.3 in, and curb weight by 419 lbs.

Lexus GX 470 ❷

A downsized Lexus GX 470 made its debut in Detroit in 2002. It's distinguished by a 5-speed transmission and air suspension with an adjustable ground clearance. Other characteristics: wheelbase—110 in, length—188 in, width—73 in, height—74 in, ground clearance—8.7 in; the curb weight of this 5-d station wagon with 5–8 seats is +4,674 lbs, and its carrying capacity is 1,422 lbs. This model can reach a maximum speed of 112 mph.

Lexus RX 300 ❸

The Lexus RX 300 was launched in March 1998 and a retouched version of it in Detroit in 2003. It uses the mechanics of the Toyota Harrier. A gasoline V6 "1MZ-FE VVT-i" 24v 2995cc engine (201hp @ 5600 1/min, 112 mph) powers the front or (in another version) all wheels. So does a more powerful "3MZ-FE VVTi" 3302cc engine (233hp @ 5600,

112 mph) except that the automatic transmission has 5 speeds instead of the original 4. The 4WD model has an inter-axle differential and a viscous coupling. This 5-seat, 5-d station wagon is self-supporting, with McPherson independent wheel suspension and torsion stabilizers. It has disc brakes with ABS. Other features: wheelbase—103 in, length—180 in, width—71.5 in, height—63 in, ground clearance—7.5 in, curb weight—(+)3,968 lbs, and payload—1,036 lbs.

The Lexus RX 300

The ZAZ-969, 1966

The LuAZ 13021, 2000

LuAZ (USSR and the Ukraine)

In the 1950s and early 1960s, LuMZ produced spare parts and special bodies for trucks (GAZ) and buses. In 1961, they showcased the Celina—a 4 WD prototype based on the Zaporogets (a Ukrainian car similar to the Fiat 600D). In 1967, the company was renamed LuAZ (Lutzk Auto Works). The communist planning machinery forced upon it the role of a producer of "Jeeps with a small engine." Their quality was miserable, so their Russian nickname "pansam sclepan"

(do-it-yourself) won't come as a surprise. In spite of that, waiting lists were endless. It often happened that the rejects that were returned to the factory to be fixed, went missing after they'd been repaired. 4 WD vehicles were highly sought after and unavailable, except in the Soviet Ukraine. Specimens for export (to Italy) were from 1988 fitted with Ford Fiesta 1117cc engines (48hp), as opposed to the original ZAZ 1200cc power units (34hp). Apart from the number code name, the vehicles were sometimes available as "Volin" (after the historic name of the Volyne district, where the town of Lutzk was situated). After political changes in 1989, the vehicle was offered to foresters and people living in the country. Production dropped dramatically in the 1990s—from about 2,500 cars made in 1994 to only 4 cars made in 1998; after that, things got slowly better again. The

The LuAZ 969M, 1986

The LuAZ 969M, 1986

The ZAZ-969

company tries to survive by offering an extended choice of modernized models and promises of innovations. The LuAZ-2301 delivery vehicle made its debut in Kiev in 2001. Between 1997 and 2000, the LuAZ's were assembled in Russia. The company's economic situation has been helped by the assembly of the VAZ vehicles (including the 2121 Niva), and the UAZ 31512, the 31514 and the 3160. In 2000, the company assembled a total of 2,245 VAZs and 295 UAZs, on condition that 15% of the components had to be Ukrainian-made. A year later, 3,962 units were produced. LuAZ, whose 81% stocks went to UkrPromInvest in 2002, has made investments, and hopes for an output of 150,000 units in 2007.

ZAZ-969

ZAZ, based in Zaporogie, Ukraine, developed and started to produce 2 models featuring an air-cooled engine (30hp): the ZAZ-969 V—the first Soviet vehicle with FWD—and the ZAZ-969 4x4. In 1966 or 1967, their production was stopped and transferred to a new factory in Lutzk. The engine—an air-cooled V4 OHV MeMZ-996A—was, in contrast to the Tudor ZAZ-965, mounted frontally and powered the front wheels. After a 2x4 van (1965/66), a 4x4 version was introduced in 1970, featuring 110 lbs of extra weight. It came with optional RWD (that could be engaged manually). A reduction ratio of 1.2 and a differential lock along with a ground clearance increased to 11.2 in (thanks to a 1.785 re-

The LuAZ 969M, 1986

duction in the wheelhubs) made sure that the vehicle would do a great job driving through mud and snow. The brakes had independent circuits for the front and rear wheels. On the road, it was able to carry 4 passengers and 220 lbs of luggage, or 2 passengers and 551 lbs of luggage at a speed of 47 mph. It was also known as "Volin."

LuAZ-969A

The LuAZ-969A from 1975 was a transitory model. It was marked by a 1197cc engine (40hp), a 1,294 reduction in wheels, a wheelbase of 71 in, a length of 133 in, width of 62 in and a modified front face. The metal grille remained, as in the case of its predecessor. The number of the first-generation LuAZs exceeded 54,000.

LuAZ-969M

The LuAZ-969M appeared in 1979. It was curvier, with a plastic grille. Its wheelbase was 71 in long; the total length of the model was 133 in. It was 63 in wide and 70 in high. Its horsepower had increased by 4hp (53 mph). A steel body was welded onto a ladder frame. The driver and front seat passenger were protected by a removable plastic roof. The rear seats could be removed, providing the car with a luggage area. The vehicle carried 2 passengers and 573 lbs of cargo, or 4 people and 265 lbs of baggage, plus a trailer weighing 661 lbs, including the load. The vehicle's ground clearance was 11 in, its overhang angles were 30° and it had a 17.7-in fording depth. This model was produced until 1989, with a total of almost 127,000 units made.

LuAZ-967

The military version looked like a motorized skateboard. It featured a simple design and an ability to parachute from Antonov planes. It had an 11-in-high ground clearance. Power was distributed from a centrally-positioned transmission. It had FWD for the road, and RWD was added for the off road. The wheels were suspended independently, with torsion bars. Its flat bottom and top allowed for mounting superstructures, transporting the wounded, an installment of weapons as well as comfortable sleep. Thanks to a 7.2:1 compression ratio, its engine burned even lower-quality gasoline. The army used the LuAZs with trailers in tow. The

The LuAZ 967 military ambulance

launch assembly in Poland was not realized. A prototype of the LuAZ 1901-Geolog floating vehicle with 6 wheels and the D Lombardini appeared. Since 2000, the vehicles have been marketed with gasoline ZAZ 1.2L engines (57hp) and HZIM 1.5L D (51hp) engines, complemented since 2001 by a gasoline VAZ (23021 version) 1.5L (72hp) power unit.

LuAZ-1301   ❷

In 2001, an off-road 3-d station wagon 4x4 was derived from a prototype of the LuAZ "Proto" — a 4x4 pick-up truck with a plastic body and a 4V (53hp) Volin-1302 engine. The model can hardly be compared to a product of any other make. It was designed by a development office in St. Petersburg. In the end, the company decided against producing the new vehicles and instead resumed the production of a more conservative prototype — the LuAZ-1301 — 8 years after its introduction. The obsolete welded skeleton of its body with plastic external panels designed by the LuAZ designers and the original chassis are borne by an old Tavria engine. This model features a 135-in wheelbase, permanent 4x4 drive and an inter-axle differential. A total of 30 test units were built in 1992.

vehicle with a driver carried 882 lbs of load, while its weight was 1,980 lbs and it had a top speed of 56 mph. The front window could be reclined onto the hood. The driver was seated on a seat in the longitudinal axis of the car. The vehicle was buoyant.

LuAZ-1302   ❷

The rejuvenation process went hand in hand with the availability of the new ZAZ and MeMZ-245 liquid-cooled OHV engines from Melitopoli. The liquid-cooled 4V OHC ZAZ 1091cc power unit (53hp, 94 octane, and 56 mph) comes from the Tavria model. By virtue of its length (135 in) and a steel van body, the curb weight of the vehicle reached 2,138 lbs. The model has 4x4 drive and an inter-axle differential. It negotiates a 90% slope, has a ground clearance of 11.8 in (13" wheels), or 13.4 in (14"). It will get through places that the Niva and other models can only dream of. Its body is welded from pressed panels and features plastic accessories. Some of the cars were fitted with a 3V TDi 1206cc engine (60hp). The vehicles with undercharged 4V Lombardini 1.4-L engines (36hp) were given the name "Foros." In 2000, the range of body types was significantly extended to include: a soft-top convertible (LuAZ-13024), a convertible (1302), a camping car (13021-07), a pick-up truck (13021), a 4-d double-cab (13021-04) and, since 1999, also a doorless beach vehicle (1302-5 Foros), and an ambulance (13021-08) based on the 13021-07 minivan. The intention to

The LuAZ 1301, 2001

Mahindra & Mahindra (India)

M&M consists of twenty divisions. The car-making branch of Mahindra & Mahindra has a long history behind it. In 1947, the first kit cars of Utility Vehicles, Jeeps FC (= Forward Control), and Willys Overland were assembled here. By 1962, the percentage of India-made components was 70 %, and 97 % by 1967. Export was launched at the same time. In 1974, the company signed a cooperation agreement with Jeep, and 5 years later the government passed a plan of cooperation with Peugeot concerning Diesel XDP 4.90 engines. An engine manufacture was opened in Ghatkopar in 1981. Another engine shop—of franchised gasoline and Diesel Peugeot engines—was established in Igatpuri in 1983. In 1988, M&M signed a memorandum of affiliation with the Indian branch of the Nissan trucks, and since 1989 they assembled the Peugeot 504 Pick-up. In 1991, a total of 10,000 vehicles were manufactured in the CKD form. M&M was the only Indian car manufacturer that managed to increase production during the crisis year of 1993. The scattered choice of models starts with the Champion / Champion DX three-wheelers. An endless collection based on the Jeep includes specimens with old appearance (the military Rakshak and Striker, the civilian Classic, the MM, the Commander, the Marshal, the Quadro, the NC, the Pick-up and the Utility); more modern versions (the Bolero, the MaXX, the Pick-Up CBC and the MM ISZ—related to the Single Cab and Double Cab pick-up trucks); the most modern versions include the Scorpio station

wagon, the MPV Voyager SL—after 1997 (= the old Mitsubishi L 300), the FJ 470–DS4, Tourister and FJ Minibus lightweight buses, and platform trucks—the CabKing 576 and 576 DI, the DI 3200 and the LoadKing. Most versions are made for distribution within India; only a few of the versions made for export feature a steering wheel on the left-hand side.

Mahindra UV

The first packing cases containing 75 kits of a CKD truck with a trambus cab—the Jeep FC-150—were opened and assembled in October 1947. In 1965, gasoline engines were available in addition to the original diesel ones. By 1967, all cars were equipped with a 4x4 drive, and the same year also brought about a 4x2 variant, a 101" wheelbase and an enclosed all-steel body. Export was launched in 1969. The 1200 UV was bought by Yugoslavia, others were exported to Ceylon, the Philippines, Singapore and Indonesia. In the following year, the 3304 UV was exported, mainly to Yugoslavia and Indonesia. In 1975, the FC 260 truck with a diesel engine was introduced.

The Mahindra MM Serie

Mahindra Jeep ❻ ❾ ❷

Given this book's spatial constraints, it is impossible to provide a comprehensive account of the tangled web of types and models of this make. The design of the vehicle has not changed in the 55 years of its existence. A ladder frame carries a steel welded body. An open body type was followed by a soft- and hard-top, a station wagon, a van, a pick-up truck, a double-cab, a chassis with a cab, and specials including an ambulance and military vehicles. Some series, such as the Bolero, the Bolero Camper double-cab, the Savari, the Single Cab, the Double Cab, the Armada Grand and the Quadro featured a curvier appearance. Both rigid axles had half-elliptic longitudinal springs. Most models are available in both 4x2 and 4x4 variants. Originally, the vehicles were equipped with transmission with the 2nd and 3rd gears synchronized; later, they featured 4-speed and eventually 5-speed transmissions, and an auxiliary reduction for the 4x4 versions. With some exceptions among the latest vehicles, all wheels are fitted with drum brakes. The first engine type used was a 2199cc gasoline Jeep "Hurricane" with an F-head (72 and 75hp @ 4000, SAE), followed later by a D Peugeot XDP 2112cc

engine (62hp @ 4500, DIN), a gasoline 2112cc (94hp @ 4500, DIN), a gasoline 2555cc (103hp @ 4500, DIN), a 2112cc natural-gas-engine (68hp @ 4500, DIN), a D 2498cc (73 and 76hp @ 4000 and 4500), and a 2523cc (50, 55 and 58hp @ 3000, 3000 and 3200) engines. The wheelbases are between 80 and 106 in long, and the ground clearance is 7.9 in.

In 1949, the Mazagon assembly plant assembled their first Jeep CJ3 (or still called "CJ2," according to some sources), the Willys Overland, and in 1954, a proper CJ3B franchise was launched in partnership with Kaiser Jeep and AMC. In 1974 more economical International Harvester diesel engines were introduced. At the same time, the CJ 4A appeared, fitted with a new transmission and an optimized rear axle drive. A year later, the CJ 500 D was launched, featuring an MD 2350 diesel engine. In 1983, the CJ4 and the CJ 500 with a franchised D Peugeot engine appeared. The CJ 640 DP was introduced in 1986, followed by the CJ 340 DP in 1989. Evolution continued with the CJ 500 DI fitted with an MDI 2500 direct injection engine. In Bombay 1985, the Mahindra MM 540a, with few differences from the previous model, made its debut. Later that year, the MM 440 appeared. In 1987, the MM series was extended to include the MM 540 DP—a "wagonette" station wagon. The MM 550 series was complemented in 1997 by a Hard Top and a Soft Top, and later by the MM 540 and the 550 XDB. In 1991, the Commander series was launched, with models including the 650 DI and the 750 DP / HT, which did very well on the market. It resembled the Jeep CJ3B. Since 1995, the Commander series has also been known as "CL." In 1996, the 5-d Commander Hard Top appeared. Twelve months later, the Commander 650 DI featuring an extended wheelbase was presented, as well as the CL Hard Top and Soft Top. The year 1993 stands out for the appearance of the Armada series. An 8-seat vehicle was added in 1997. The Armada Grand is also currently available. Since 2001, other coolers à la Alfa Romeo

have been used, distinguishable by their grille and fitted in the Mahindra MaXX station wagon and the stretched version of "MaXX Lx," 2WD and 4WD. As far as military versions are concerned, the 2000 New Delhi motor show witnessed the debut of the Rashak—an armored 3-d, 6-to-8-seat station wagon with a XD3 PC 2498cc engine (76hp @ 4500), a 5-speed transmission and 4x4 or 4x2 drive. The 4-seat Striker was an open variant thereof. Since the late 1960s, Mahindras have been exported in a completed form or as CKD car kits. The kits were assembled in Greece, mostly with Peugeot 2112cc indirect injection engines (60hp @ 4200), or direct-injection 2498cc power units (76hp @ 4500), a 4-speed transmission with an overdrive (available at a premium), optional FWD and a manual freewheel lock on the front wheel hubs. The wheelbase was 80 / 91 / 130 in long. The Brave and Chief limited models were developed (1990), as well as the General Patton Special, the De Luxe and the Marksman (1991), which could,

although rarely, still be found in England. They suffered from very poor construction quality, poor driving properties, a lack of luxury and a chaotic, unsupported distribution network. An assembly project was also considered in Slovakia.

Mahindra Scorpio ❷

A prototype of the Scorpio was showcased in 1998, followed by series production in 2001. This 5-d station wagon seats 7–9 passengers. In addition to a 4x2 version, a 4x4 is also produced, featuring electrically controlled FWD, available as an extra. There is a 5-speed transmission, and a 4V SZ 2600 Turbo DI 2609cc engine (109hp @ 3800). The 2WD version has the front wheels suspended independently, with coil springs and a torsion stabilizer; the 4WD version features a torsion bar suspension. The rear axles are rigid, with leaf springs. When empty, the 2WD version weighs 5,534 lbs. In 2002, negotiations took place with Auto Lada about assembling the vehicles in Russia.

The Mahindra Bolero, 2003

The Mahindra Scorpio Silver, 2003

Maruti
(India)

Maruti Gypsy ❷

Maruti Ltd., named after a sacred Indian monkey, appeared in 1973. The son of the Indian Prime Minister Indira Gandhi was behind an ambitious project for a general-population car for 2 with a 0.7L air-cooled engine. In 1982, the Maruti Udyong Ltd. company was established as a joint venture of the Indian government and Suzuki. The Japanese share grew steadily to 40% in 1987 and 50% in 1992. Having obtained a franchise in 1982, Maruti first assembled and later produced the small "800" (=Suzuki Alto). Other ex-Suzuki models followed suit, including the Zen, the Esteem, the Baleno, the Wagon R, and the Omni microbus. Preparations for the Vitara and the Grand Vitara are underway.

Since 1985, Maruti has been franchise-producing the Suzuki Jimny / Samurai SJ 410, generation 1981. Power is supplied by a 4V OHC 970cc engine (45hp @ 5500, SAE, 65 mph). A driver of the 4x2 version has a 5-speed transmission at hand, as opposed to the 4 speeds for going forward for an owner of a 4x4. Both feature a 2-speed reduction. The Gypsy axles are rigid with leaf springs. The wheelbase is 93.5 in long, the length is 158 in, the width is 58 in, the height is 75 in, the ground clearance is 8.7 in, the curb weight is 2,017 lbs, and the payload is 1,102 lbs. The model carries up to 6 persons or 772 lbs of load. In 1996, the pick-up truck convertible version and the 3-d station wagon Gypsy King with a 1.3L engine (60hp to 80hp), and in 1998 a 5-d station wagon, were launched.

The Matra Rancho

Matra-Simca (France)

TALBOT

A company whose name changed several times (but always contained the words "Matra-Sports") existed between 1965 and 1979, and later operated—until 1984—as the Matra-Simca Division Automobile of the Chrysler concern. Matra produced aircraft and armaments systems. This small car-manufacturing division gained renown for its sports cars: it was involved in the F1 and was thrice victorious at Le Mans. In 1983, the factory was bought by Renault. The assembly plant has built non-mainstream vehicles, such as the MPV Espace, since 1984.

Matra-Simca Rancho ❹

In 1977–84, the unrivalled Matra Rancho (2x4) recreational vehicle was produced, based on the Simca 1100 with an elevated glassed-in station wagon part and plastic protection strips. The wheels were suspended independently with stabilizers and torsion bars. A de-tuned 1442cc engine of the Matra Bagheera sports car (80hp @ 5600, 90 mph) worked with a 4-speed transmission. Other features: wheelbase—99.3 in, length—170 in, width—65 in, height—68 in, weight—2,489 lbs. A total of 20,938 units have been made.

The Matra Rancho

The Matra Rancho AS

The Matra Rancho

The Matra Rancho X

Mazda
(Japan)

In 1920, the Toyo Cork Kogyo company was founded in Hiroshima. At first, it produced bottle corks, later (since 1930) motorcycles, and a year later the DA 482cc three-wheeler. It was sold with the marque of "Mazda," derived from the name of the company's founder Jujiro Matsuda, and of Ahura Mazda—the god of light. Sixty-six vehicles were sold in the first year. After the war (1958), they went back to trucks, and in 1960 they returned to passenger cars. Mazda made a name by using Wankel rotary engines on a massive scale. In 1979, 24.5% of stocks were obtained by Ford, which has owned 33.4% since 1996. Mazdas are produced in Japan and other countries; in some countries, Mazdas are made under the name of Ford. There haven't been many 4x4 specimens. In the early 1980s, AWD was featured on the Mazda 323F road model. Since October 1998, the company has been making the Suzuki Jimny with a 3V "turbo" 0.7L engine as the Mazda AZ-Offroad. The Mazda Premacy MPV based on the 323 (from March 1999) has 2x4 drive. A big MPV from the fall of 1988 (4x2) has since the spring 1989 been available as a 4x4, but it's only a road vehicle.

Mazda Pick-up—B-Series ❻

The first Mazda-made pick-up trucks (4x2) were the B 360 and the B 1500 in 1961. They were modified in 1965 and again in 1977. In the 1970s, the B series pick-up trucks, featuring 1.6-, 1.8-, 2.0- and 2.2L gasoline engines, and a D 2.2L engine, were exported to America, South Africa and Europe. By 1985, nearly 1.8 million pick-up trucks were made, after which they were replaced by the new generation—the B Series. The choice of lightweight utility vehicles includes the Scrum (the smallest pick-up truck), the Bongo / E 2000 and other platform trucks, vans, minivans and minibuses.

Mazda Fighter / Bravo / B Series (Thailand) ❷ ❻

In 1999, the first vehicles left the gates of AutoAlliance, founded in 1998 by Ford (45%), Mazda (45%), and a couple of Thai companies (10%). (Mazdas have been produced in Thailand since 1950.) AutoAlliance-made vehicles contain 70% of local components. In the first year, a total of 24,009 Mazda pick-up trucks and 29,593 Ford pick-up trucks are made. In June 1999, Mazda began selling the vehicles in Europe under the name "Mazda B Series / Fighter," while Ford distributes them as "Rangers." These 2-d pick-up trucks with an extended cab or 4-d double-cabs carry 5 people. The vehicles feature a ladder chassis and independently suspended wheels with torsion bars and a stabilizer. The rear axle is rigid with leaf springs. An economical 4V OHC 12v 2499cc engine (109hp @ 3500, 97 mph) powers the rear wheels. If necessary, FWD can be engaged with a jaw clutch in the left drive shaft, and disengaged again by a Remote Free Wheel button.

The Mazda Tribute, 2001

The rear differential has a limited slip system (75%), and a 5-speed transmission has cross-country reduction. The B Fighter has a 118-in-long wheelbase; it is 198 in long, 67 in wide, 69 in high. It features an 8.1-in ground clearance, a curb weight of 3,770 lbs and a payload of 2,458 lbs. Its fording depth is 17.7 in, and its overhang angles are 35°/28°.

Mazda Tribute ❸

The 2000 Los Angeles saw the debut of a 5-d SUV. It was developed in cooperation with Ford technicians. It has a 5-seat self-supporting body made of steel. Power is provided by a 4V 1988cc engine (124hp @ 5300, 103 mph), or a V6 2OHC 24v 2967cc engine (197hp @ 6000, 112 mph). The Tribute has permanent AWD with a variable distribution of torque between the front and rear axles. The 3.0L engine works with a 4-speed automatic transmission, while the 2.0L engine is connected to a 5-speed manual transmission. The wheels are suspended independently, on McPherson struts with a stabilizer in the front, and on longitudinal and transversal arms with coil springs and a stabilizer in the back. Dimensions: wheelbase—103 in, length—173 in, width—72 in, height—69.5 in, ground clearance—7.9 in. The curb weight is 3,435 lbs for the 2.0L version, and 3,671 lbs for the 3.0L version. Payload ratings are 1,246 lbs / 1,235 lbs, respectively. Fording depth is 17.7 in and overhang angles are 30°/31°.

The Mazda B 2500 4x4, 2003

Mebea
(Greece)

In the late 1950s, Reliant began practicing the policy of "exporting automobile industry" to underdeveloped countries. In 1958, they prepared a project of a vehicle not made in Britain. It was produced by Autocars, an Israeli company, as "Sussita" station wagon; as "Anadol" sedan by Otosan, a Turkish company, as "Dolphin" by Sipani in India, and as a lightweight "Fox" by Mebea in Athens. Mebea existed in the 1970s and 1980s. It began with the Reliant passenger and delivery three-wheelers.

Mebea Fox   ❹

The Mebea Fox was a pick-up truck designed for beach use and minor commercial purposes. It was a Reliant Fox franchise. Its 2-d fiberglass body could take 2 or 4 passengers and cargo for a ride. The rear wheels were powered by a 4V Ford 848cc engine (40hp @ 5500) via a 4-speed transmission. The Fox featured an 85-in-long wheelbase; it was 133 in long, 61 in wide, 59 in high and had a 12.6-in ground clearance. It weighed 1,151 lbs and carried up to 705 lbs of crew and cargo. It was available with a hard-top cab and a canvas tilt in the back, or as a convertible with a canvas tilt for the crew and luggage.

The Chrysler Hellas Farmobil

Specials form Greece   ❷ ❽ ❹

The land of mountains and beaches was the place where many other interesting vehicles, such as the Mahindra & Mahindra and the Puch G, were produced and assembled. In the 1980s, Automeccanica s.a. based in Athens assembled the Lada Niva Soviet off-roader—including the 2121, the 2121V Van, the 2121P Pick-up, the 2121A Cabrio with a 4V 1570cc engine (76hp @ 5400) and originally with a 4-speed, and later 5-speed transmission and reduction. In the 1970s, Chrysler Hellas distributed the Farmobil, a lightweight work pick-up truck with a flat, air-cooled 2V 697cc engine (38hp @ 5000, SAE) powering the rear wheels. Its doorless body was borne by a ladder chassis. All its wheels were suspended independently with coil springs. An empty Farmobil weighed at least 1,252 lbs and carried 1,358 lbs—2 or 4 people plus cargo. Its wheelbase was 69 in long; it was 132 in long, 63 in wide, 67 in high and had a 9-in ground clearance. In the late 1970s and early 1980s, the Samba company produced the Amico—a beach pick-up vehicle based on the Fiat 127, in a franchise of the Italian company Fissore.

The Mebea Fox

Mercedes-Benz (Germany)

In 1883 Karl Benz founded the Benz & Cie company. Two years later he tested a three-wheeler—the world's first vehicle with a combustion engine. Production started in 1887. Gottlieb Daimler established his firm in 1882. In 1885, he built his first motorcycle, followed by his first automobile a year later. The two companies merged in 1885. Benz used the Mercedes marque for its cars. (In the late 19th century, Mr. Jelinek, an Austro-Hungarian consul in Nice, originally from Bohemia, ordered a Daimler, improved it considerably and named it Mercedes after his daughter.) The company took over both the improvements, and—after 1901—the name. Over the next 110 years, the Mercedes-Benz marque of the Daimler Benz AG concern became a world-famous producer of top-quality, safe and costly vehicles. In 1998, it signed a contract with Chrysler. The Germans put in 57%, the Americans 43%, and together they created DaimlerChrysler, which contains MCC, AMG, McLaren, Mitsubishi, Hyundai (former Mercedes marques) and Dodge, Plymouth, Chrysler and Jeep (former Chrysler marques). During the war, the company produced the Mercedes-Benz 170VK with 5 seats. A gasoline 4V SV 1697cc engine (38hp) powered the rear wheels via a 4-speed transmission. In the front, the model had an independent wheel suspension with a transversal leaf spring, and with coil springs in the rear. The same concept was applied to the 320WK, except for a 6V SV 3208cc engine (78hp). The W152, known as the G5, was a 2- or 4-d soft-top. It was distinguished by its permanent AWD, a 4V SV 2006cc (45hp), a 5-speed transmission and 2W or 4W steering. The heavy off-road Mercedes-Benz 1500A weighed 5,897 lbs. Its rear or all wheels were powered by a 6V OHV 2594cc engine (60hp) via a 4-speed transmission and an auxiliary 2-speed gear-reduction transmission. Leaf springs suspension was featured. Its complete opposite was the elegant 6-wheel convertible (for Hitler and his generals)—the Mercedes-Benz G4 (6x4)—with an 8V OHV 5401cc engine (110hp), a 4-speed transmission and a reduction and leaf springs.

Boehringer / Mercedes-Benz Unimog ❷ ❽ ❾

In the summer of 1945, the Boehringer company began work on a 4x4 work vehicle. It was introduced in August 1948 in Frankfurt as "Unimog." In May 1951, this promising project was passed over to Daimler-Benz. Boehringer managed to manufacture about 600 units. Since that time, half a million Unimogs of several generations have been produced, all with a legendary ability to work in extreme conditions. The Unimog charmed the Japanese, who used it as an expedition vehicle. They built the Urban Unimog, a concept car, which the Germans followed up in the late 80s with a concept of the Fun Mog—a "sports" vehicle for leisure time. The Unimog has participated in many raid rallies. In 1985 it won the "Dakar."

The Unimog Fun Mog based on the U90, 1991

Mercedes-Benz G (Austria, Germany) ❾ ❷

The Mercedes G (G stands for "Geländewagen"=off-road vehicle) is the result of efforts to prepare a military "Euro-Jeep" in the mid-1970s. The plans fell through but the company decided to implement the intention anyway, because it had several military orders up its sleeve. Steyr Puch, which now completes the cars, contributed to its development. It equips ladder frames and bodies made in Graz with German devices, mostly derived from Mercedes passenger cars. In Austria and some other countries, they are sold under the name "Puch"; small numbers are assembled in Greece. Generation G 460 / 461 was made in the period between 1979 and 98. It had RWD and optional FWD, a 100% lock—a standard feature after 1985, except the G 461, where extra cost was charged. The 1st generation featured a 4-speed manual transmission or, at a premium, a 4-speed automatic transmission with a reduction. A 5th gear has been available since 1983. Rigid axles had stabilizers and coil springs. The wheelbase of a 3- and 5-d station wagon was 95 / 112 in; the vehicle was 163 / 181 in long, 67 in wide, and 76 / 36 in high. Since 1987, handfuls of cars with a long wheelbase—123 in—have been made. The curb weight is +3,913 lbs, the minimum payload is 1,213 lbs. Models include: the 230 G (1979–82, a gasoline 4V 2298cc engine, 102hp @ 5250); the 230 GE (1982–96, ditto, 122hp @ 5100); the 280 GE (1980–90, a 6V 2746cc engine, 150hp @ 5250); the 240 GD (1979–87, a 4V TD 2399cc engine, 72hp @ 4400); the 250 GD (1987–91, a 5V D 2497cc engine, 84hp @ 4600); the

300 GD (1980–91, a 5V D 2998cc engine, 88hp @ 4400); the 290 GD (1993–98, a 5V D 2874cc engine, 95hp @ 4000); and the 290 GD Turbo (1998, 5V TD 2874cc engine, 120hp @ 3800).

The 2nd generation from 1990–96—the G 463—is characterized by permanent 4x4 drive, a manually lockable inter-axle differential, and 100% locks on the front and rear differentials. The vehicles feature either 5-speed transmissions (which disappeared in the mid-1990s) or 4-speed ones; after 1998, 5-speed automatic transmissions with a reduction have also been available. The ladder frame and rigid axles have remained. Other features of the 3- and 5-d station wagon: wheelbase—95 / 112 in, length—169 / 184 in, width—67 / 69 in, height—76.4 / 76.2 in. Its curb weight is +4,519 lbs and its minimum payload is 1,146 lbs. Models: the 230 GE (1990–94, a gasoline 4V 2 298cc engine, 126hp @ 5000); the 300 GE (1990–94, 6V 2960cc engine, 170hp @ 5550); the G 320 (1994–98, a 6V 3199cc engine, 210hp @ 5500); the G 320 (since 1998, a 6V 3199cc engine, 215hp @ 5500); the G 500 V8 (since 1998, a V8 4966cc engine, 296hp @ 5750); the 250 GD (1990–92, a 5V D 2497cc engine, 94hp @ 4600); the 300 GD (1990–94, a 6V D 2996cc engine, 113hp @ 4600); the 350 GD Turbo (1994–96, a 6V TD 3449cc engine, 136hp @ 4000); the G 300 TD (1996–2000, a 6V TD 2996cc engine, 177hp @ 4400).

The 290 D—the most retouched version so far—appeared in the summer of 2000; it was fitted with a 5V D 2874cc engine (120hp @ 3800), but production was terminated in the fall of 2001, including the TD Common Rail engine: a V8 32v 400 CDI with two turbochargers and an intercooler (since 2000,

3996cc, 250hp @ 4000), and a 5V 270 CDI (since the fall of 2002, 2688cc, 156hp @ 3800). This generation came with greater improvements than any of the other G models before, involving the dashboard and GPS-supported Merian navigation.

Mercedes ML (U.S.A., Austria) ❸

In May 1997, a luxurious SUV was introduced in the U.S., made in Tuscaloosa. Europeans could first admire it at the IAA in 1997. A 5-d station wagon body for 5 (or up to 7, on request) passengers is bolted onto a ladder frame. The ML has permanent AWD with 48:52 power ratio, an inter-axle differential and, since the beginning of 2001, a disengageable ESP. The transmission has 5 speeds and a reduction. The disc brakes possess ABS and EBD. All wheels are suspended independently with coil springs and a stabilizer. At the IAA 2001, the company introduced a slightly facelifted version with common-rail engines, known from the G. Models: the ML 230 (fall 1997–2000, a gasoline 4V 16v, 2295cc engine, 150hp @ 5400); the ML 320 (1997–2000, a gasoline V6, 18v, 3199cc engine, 180hp @ 5800); the ML 320 (since 2001, ditto 218hp @ 5600); the ML 430 (2000–01, a gasoline V8, 4260cc engine, 272hp @ 5500); the ML 55 AMG (since IAA 1999, a gasoline V8, 24v, 5439cc engine, 347hp @ 5500); the ML 270 CDI (since IAA 1999, TD common-rail, 5V, 20v, 2688cc engine, 163hp @ 4200); the ML 500 (IAA since 2001, a gasoline V8, 24v,

4966cc engine, 292hp @ 5600); the ML 400 CDI (IAA since 2001, TD common-rail, V8, 32v, 3999cc engine, 250hp @ 4000); and the ML 350 (since fall 2002, a gasoline V6, 18v, 3724cc engine, 234hp @ 5600).

The Mercedes-Benz ML, 2001

The Mercedes-Benz Lorinser M, 2001

The Mercedes-Benz Sprinter 4x4, Brno 2002

Mercedes—off-road—modifications ❷ ❸

The clientele has different wishes. They are fulfilled by accessories or kit packages of the AMG make (owned now by Mercedes) or of a colorful choice of specialists including Brabus, Carlsson, Hamann, Lorinser and many small ones such as A.R.T. Tuned engines, transmissions, chassis including springs and shock absorbers with different characteristics are available in addition to luxurious and inessential accessories. In Geneva in 2002, the Baur car body works (now a part of the IVM Group) introduced an attractively modified study of the G-Cabrio XL semi-convertible.

Mercedes – MPV and light utility vehicles ❶ ❻ ❼

For better traction of the permanent wheel drive, these limousines/ station wagons use a 4WD "4matic" system with an inter-axle differential and other electronically controlled tricks. The Sprinter, lightweight van, minivan, chassis and chassis with a dual cab usually feature 4x2 drive, but they also come with a 4x4 (50:50) option. Road vans and A-class MPVs, the Vaneo and V- classes do not have this option. In 2003, the Sprinter had the following wheel drive versions: engageable AWD (261), permanent 4x4 drive (262), or a 261 version with an auxiliary gear-reduction transmission (263).

A study of the Baur G-Cabrio XL, 2002

Minerva (Belgium)

The Minerva Commando

Minerva

The Minerva company founded in 1903 was based in Mortsel, a suburb of Antverp, Belgium. Before the war, it became famous for its luxurious vehicles. After the war, it fell into a deep depression. For the army, the company designed a 4x4 based on the Fiat, but the soldiers did not take the bait. Minerva (along with Willys) did not give up and, in 1951, became one of the bidders in a tender invited by the army for a contract for 2,500 lightweight off-road vehicles. That is why in 1952 Mr. van Roggen, its boss, bought a Land Rover franchise. The Belgian armed forces had used the LR since 1948. They made an order for 10,000 vehicles and from 1953 the model was also available to civilians. The Minervas were faithful servants for decades. The Minerva Land Rover had an 80" chassis. At first, complete disassembled cars were imported from Solihull as CKDs. But it did not take long before 63% of the components including the chassis, steel body and other parts, began to be manufactured manually in Belgium; only the drivetrains with 1997cc engines and transmissions continued to be imported. Minervas can easily be distinguished from Land Rovers by their slanted front fenders and different headlights. Production was terminated in 1956. The army bought 8,440 cars, while 1,456 were taken up by the police force, border patrols and some civilians. In 1951-56, a total of 9,905 CKDs were dispatched

from Britain. Other sources mention about 18,000 units of the Minerva with chassis made in Belgium, out of which about 1,100 featured an 86" wheelbase and were introduced in 1954, as in England. Part of the contingent is said to have had 4x2 drive. The army mothballed some of the new vehicles by putting them in emergency mobilization storage. It is rumored that in the 1990s it was possible to buy an almost unused Minerva very cheaply in Belgium. In 1953-56, the factory produced SV Continental engines. These engines were used in several prototypes of off-roaders which were introduced a few days after the contract for Land Rovers ran out. They featured a self-supporting steel body with an engine on an auxiliary frame, a short or a long wheelbase and were able to negotiate a 70% slope. The Minerva C20 was a civilian version and the Minerva M20 was a military version. In 1956, the company went bankrupt. The street where the factory used to stand still bears the name Minervastraat.

Mitsubishi (Japan)

MITSUBISHI MOTORS

The Mitsubishi in the Dakar—a replica of the PX-33

Yataro Iwasaki worked his way up to being a rich businessman through his own efforts. In 1870, he bought 3 steamboats and founded Tsukumo Shokai; five years later, he renamed this promising steamship company Mitsubishi Steamship Company with three diamonds in its logo (mitsu=3, bishi=diamonds), which was a copy of the coat of arms of the family of Iwasaki's parents. The diamonds symbolized the three most important principles for Shokai: responsibility to the company, honesty and straightforward conduct, and patriotism. In 1901, Ryukichi Kawada, manager of the shipyard, imported a steam car from the U.S.A. and became the first driver on the territory of the Japanese empire. In 1917, he assembled his first car, and in 1920 he made the T-1, his first truck. In 1931, the company came up with the first Japanese-made Diesel engine, and in 1934 the PX 33, a passenger convertible with (among others) a diesel engine and 4x4 drive—the first four-wheeler/4x4 in Japan. In 1970, an independent division of Mitsubishi Motors Corporation (MMC) was established, specializing in the production, assembly and distribution of cars. In 1970, Chrysler acquired a 15% share of MMC. At that time, the cars began to be sold in the U.S., and soon after that in Europe. In 1999, MMC came up with a revolutionary design of a direct-injection gasoline engine—GDI. Since 1999, it has supplied GDI engines to the PSA group and it reached an agreement with Fiat on the joint development and pro-

duction of the sports LUV 4x4. Since 1982, Mitsubishi has held an 8.8% share of Hyundai, and, since 1983, an 8% share of the Malayan-based Proton. By virtue of its connection with Chrysler, 34% of Mitsubishi was taken over by DaimlerChrysler in 2000. Mitsubishi produces or assembles motor vehicles in 18 countries: Hyundai in South Korea, Mahindra in India, Liebao in China, Morattab in Iran, Proton in Malaysia and Colt in South Africa. Besides off-road vehicles, there were several generations of tourers with 4WD, including the Lancer EVO—a first-class race car; the Galant / the Legnum / the Aspire—middle-class sedans and station wagons with 2x4 or 4x4 drive, and a compact "Colt."

Mitsubishi Jeep

In 1953, Mitsubishi began importing CKDs and assembling Kaiser-Frazer Jeeps, but the Americans voided the contract. In the same year, the Japanese obtained a franchise to manufacture the Jeep CJ3B of the Willys Overland Corp com-

The Mitsubishi Jeep Turbo, early 1970s

pany. They produced Jeeps until 1999. The vehicles were almost exclusively purchased by armed forces, and later armies of the U.S. in the Pacific, Southern Vietnam, South Korea and other countries in the Far East. The vehicle was slowly and gradually modernized. The first specimens were fitted with a 3-speed transmission, a 2-speed auxiliary transmission with an option to disengage the FWD, and rigid axles with longitudinal leaf half-elliptic springs. Other features: wheelbase—80 in, length—131 in, width—63 in, height—73 in, ground clearance—8.3 in and weight—2,734 lbs. They were powered by Japanese engines: at first, a gasoline 4V F-head 2199cc engine (70hp); later a 2384cc engine (110hp JIS), or a D 2659cc (80hp, JIS), preceded by a 2199cc (gasoline—76hp SAE / diesel—61hp SAE); later gasoline 1995cc and 2555cc engines. The vehicles had a seating capacity of 4–9 persons, their wheelbase was 80, 88 or 104 in long, and they came with the following body types: soft-top, hard-top, and station wagon.

Mitsubishi Pajero ❷

The PX 33 (made in 1934) can be considered the forefather of Japanese off-roaders. Four other variants were derived from it in a short time. One of them was powered by a D Mitsubishi 4454D 6V OHC 4390cc engine (70hp). A number of specimens served in WWII as 7-seat commander vehicles. They featured a 4-speed transmission and a 1-speed auxiliary transmission, which—along with 4 drive shafts—helped to power all wheels. The model had a 112—in long wheelbase; it was 165 in long, 63 in wide, and 65 in high. The 4x4 convertibles with a high ground clearance became famous for their long lifespan and were used in mountainous areas and places where roads were only beginning to be built. Mass production did not occur.

In 1969, the factory prepared a concept of the Minica Jeep (an off-roader based on the Mitsubishi minicar), a study of the Pajero II in 1973, the Jeep Concept in 1977, followed in 1978 by a study of the Pajero, ready for production. A pajero

The Mitsubishi—a new model series, England, 2001

The Mitsubishi Shogun Sport, 2000

is a Patagonian felid famous for its strength, perseverance and adroitness. The model was introduced in Tokyo 1979. Distribution began in 1981: as the "Montero" in North America and Spanish-speaking countries, and as the "Shogun" in Great Britain and Japan. The first generation was codenamed L 040. Versions: 3- and 5-d station wagon with a normal and (since 1985) elevated roof, a hard-top and a soft-top. They carried 4 to 7 passengers. Engines: a gasoline 4V 2555cc engine (103hp @ 4500, 89 mph); a V6 2972cc engine (141hp @ 5000, 102 mph, automatic—96 mph); a TD 2346cc engine (84hp @ 4200, 87 mph); a 2477cc (84hp @ 4200, 88 mph), a TD intercooler since 1988—95hp @ 4200, 89 mph).

The Pajero 2.3 TD was the first off-roader to feature a turbo-diesel engine. It had a 5-speed transmission or, from 1987, a 4-speed transmission with a 2-speed reduction, along with a 2.6L engine. The rear wheels were powered, with an option to engage the "front'. The front wheel hubs had automatic freewheels. The rear featured a limited slip differential. The model had a ladder frame, independently suspended front wheels with a stabilizer and torsion bars. The rear axle was rigid with leaf springs. Since 1989, the 2.6L model had coil springs in the back and a year later the same was true about specimens with a TD engine. Dimensions: wheelbase—93 / 106 in, length—155 / 181 in, width—66 in, height—73 / 78 in, ground clearance—8.1 in / 7.7 in (2.5 TD) / 7.3 in (3.0 V6). Curb weight is +3,219 lbs, a maximum payload is 1,444 lbs. Overhang angles are 36°/26°. The Pajero will conquer a 25°–30° slope. After production was terminated in Japan, a franchise was bought by Hyundai. The model continued to be made in Korea as the "Galloper" (first generation).

In 1991, the 2nd generation V 20 was born, with curvier contours and a bigger, short body version. A convertible with electrically-controlled two-piece roof appeared. Engines: a 3.0L V6 engine (150hp @ 5000, 102 mph); a V6 24v 3497cc engine (208hp @ 5000, 111 mph); 4V engines—a TD intercooler 2477cc (99 hp @ 4200, 88 mph),

and a TD 2835cc (125 hp @ 4000, 97 mph). A new version of AWD—Super Select—worked with a Multi-Mode system. The Pajero had an inter-axle differential with a viscous coupling; power was distributed between the two axles in a 50:50 ratio. The shock absorbers were adjustable to 3 modes. The brakes on more powerful models—all with discs—had ABS. Other features: wheelbase—95 / 107 in, length—163 / 186 in, width—70 in, height—71.5/ 73.5 in, ground clearance—7.9 / 8.1 in (3.5 V6 and 2.8 TD). The curb weight is +4,101 lbs, maximum payload is 1,411 lbs,

The Mitsubishi Pajero 4x4, 1983

H. Auriol at the wheel of the Pajero during the 1992 Dakar

167

The Mitsubishi Pajero Sport, 1999

overhang angles are 36°/27°. The model negotiates a 27.5° slope. In July 1996, the Pajero underwent a minor facelift, but it retained its mechanics. It was soon followed by the Pajero Sport 5-door station wagon.

The 3ʳᵈ generation 3- and 5-d station wagon V60 arrived in the fall of 1999 as "Pajero 2000." (The previous generation continued to be produced as the Pajero Classic.) They were characterized by a revolutionary rigid self-supporting body with a lowered floor but the same ground clearance. The Pajero excels with its impressive choice of engines: a gasoline GDI V6 24v 3497cc engine (220hp @ 5500, 118 mph); a V6 24v 3800cc engine (218hp @ 5500, SAE); a V6 24v 2972cc engine (170hp @ 5000, 109 mph); a new 4V TD 16v direct-ignition 3200cc engine (160hp @ 3800, 106 mph) and a TD 2477cc engine (115hp @ 4000, 93 mph); and a 2835cc engine (125hp @ 4000). Permanent 4x4 drive (Super Select) distributes power in a 33:47 ratio; it has an inter-axle differential with a manual lock and a viscous cou-

pling, disengageable FWD, a rear limited slip differential and a manual lock of the rear differential. In addition to a 5-speed manual transmission or a 5- or 4-speed automatic one also features a 2-speed reduction. The Pajero was the first off-roader fit with an alternative regime of semi-automatic transmission (automatic transmission) with a direct manual transmission but without stepping on the clutch. All wheels are suspended independently, with a stabilizer and coil springs in the front. The wheelbase is 100 in long (3-d) or 107 in long (5-d); the model is 166 / 181 in long, 75 / 70 in wide, 68 / 75 in high, and has a 9-in-high ground clearance. Curb weight is +3,968 lbs / 4,597 lbs, payload is +1,565 / +1,510 lbs. Overhang angles are 42°/24°, and fording depth is 23.6 in. By the end of 2001, over 2.1 million Pajeros were made in Japan, out of which 1.5 million units were exported. Mitsubishi sends the Pajero to many raid-type of sports events. The model won the FIA Long-distance Rally World Cup five times. Mitsubishi and Ralliart, its sports team, has

The Mitsubishi Pajero 5-d, 1999

participated in the Rally Paris-Dakar from the very first year; it won gold 8 times. Besides carefully prepared "series" vehicles, the company sent a number of "specials" to Dakar: in the 1980s, it deployed cars whose bodies were replicas of the historical PX-33 on a Pajero chassis. In Paris 2002, the Pajero EVO station wagon-coupe made its debut; a few months later, it was placed on a sharp start.

Mitsubishi Pajero Sport / Montero Sport / Challenger ❷

The Pajero Sport appeared in July 1996, followed by a facelifted version in the fall of 1999. An elegant body was bolted onto a ladder frame of the L 200 Pick-up truck with a shortened wheelbase. Its chassis is equivalent to that of the stretched V 20 and includes a complete aggregate, front, side doors, and an L200 dashboard. Power is provided by a TD 2477cc engine (99hp @ 4000, 93 mph) or, outside of Europe, also 2.8 TD and 3.5 V6 GDI (with an auto transmission) engines. The model has permanent RWD (Easy Select 4WD), and the front wheels can be engaged before reaching

The Mitsubishi Pajero EVO, the Dakar Rallye 2003

a speed of 62 mph; there are semi-automatic freewheels in the front wheel hubs and a rear limited slip differential. There is a 5-speed or a 4-speed automatic transmission with a cross-country reduction. The front wheel suspension is equivalent to that of the Pajero, the rear axle is rigid with a Panhard rod, coil springs and a stabilizer. The Pajero Sport has a 107-in-long wheelbase, it is 179 in long, 70 in wide, 68 in high and has an 8.1-in-high ground clearance. Its curb weight is 4,178 lbs, and it has a payload of 1,279 lbs. Its fording depth is 19.7 in and it has 37°/26° overhang angles.

Mitsubishi Pajero Pinin / iO (Italy / Japan) ❷

The Pajero Pinin was showcased in Japan in June 1998, and subsequently in Europe, where Mitsubishi has it produced by Pininfarina in Italy ("io"= Italian for "I"). The Italian company contributed to both its styling and name. Mechanically, it is a smaller and simpler Pajero. This short 3-d station wagon offers little luggage room, in contrast to a longer and more mature 5-d version—the Pinin Wagon. The MMC classifies them as SUVs (as opposed to the Pajero, which is an off-roader). Power is supplied by a gasoline 4V 1.8 MPI 1834cc engine (114hp @ 5500, 100 mph); alternatively, a gasoline GDI 16v 1999cc direct injection engine (129hp @ 5000). The latter is equipped with a Super Select 4Wdi system with optional FWD. The model features a 5-speed transmission without a reduction. It has an interaxle differential and 4x4 drive with a 50:50 ratio. Another variant has RWD, optional FWD, an inter-axle differential with a viscous coupling and a reduction. The front wheels are suspended independently on McPherson struts with a stabilizer; the rear axle is rigid with a Panhard rod, a stabilizer and coil springs. Further characteristics: wheelbase—90 / 96.5 in, length—147 / 159 in, width—67 in, height—67

/ 68.5 in, ground clearance—7.9 / 6.9 in. Curb weight is +2,668 lbs / 3,120 lbs, payload is 1,058 / 937 lbs, overhang angles are 33°/38°, fording depth is 19.7 in.

Mitsubishi Outlander / Airtrek ❷

The SUV Airtrek, designed for active pastimes, made its debut in the summer of 2001. Its European launch (Outlander) took place at Geneva 2003. This newcomer borrowed its 4WD mechanics from the Space Wagon. It was fitted with 4V engines—1,997 / 2,378cc, 16v (an MPI, from the Galant and the Space Wagon models with 136 hp / a MIVEC with variable timing of the valves from the Eclipse coupé with 165hp). The top-quality Sport will get, in addition to its current power 2.4L unit, a gasoline turbo 2.0L (240hp @ 5500)— combined only with permanent 4x4 drive and a manual transmission. The Outlander is available with front wheel drive (2WD) or AWD with the power distributed between the axles in a 50:50 ratio. The 4WD has an inter-axle differ-

The Mitsubishi Outlander, 2003

ential with a viscous coupling. Transmissions: a 5-speed manual or a 4-speed automatic (only for the 2.4 L MIVEC). Other features include: a self-supporting 5-d body, independent wheel suspension—of the McPherson type with a stabilizer in the front and with trailing arms, stabilizer, and coil springs in the back. Wheelbase—103 in, length—179 in (174 in for the Airtrek), width—69 in, height—66 in, ground clearance—7.5 in. Curb weight—(+)2,976 lbs / (+)3,197 lbs (4WD); payload—606 / 827 lbs.

Mitsubishi L 200 / Pajero Pick-up / Strada (Japan / Thailand) ❷ ❻

The late 1960s saw the debut of the 2nd generation of the L200 pick-up trucks. In time, they made their way to Europe. The 2nd generation of the L200 was showcased at the IAA in 1993 (or in 1991 in Japan); it had a lot in common with the Pajero L 040. The L 200 generation V20 was powered by a TD 2.5L with or without an inter-cooler (87hp @ 4200/99hp @ 4200, 89 mph), with an option to engage the FWD at standstill. A 68% limited slip differential was fitted in the rear, while the front wheel hubs featured automatic freewheels. The front axle was independent with a torsion bar suspension; the rear axle was rigid with longitudinal leaf springs. The car had a 116.6-in-long wheelbase, it was 194 in long, 69 in wide, 69 in high, and it had an 8.5-in-high ground clearance. When empty, the model weighed 3,616 lbs, and its payload rating was 1,951 lbs. What were originally work machines became a social affair. The model grew and was presented with increasingly better equipment. After October 2001, for marketing reasons, it became known as "Pajero Pick-up" (in some European countries). The L200 became the basis for the Pajero Sport, which inherited most of its predecessor's mechanics and also to a certain degree its facelifted appearance. Pick-up trucks of a new "lifestyle"

are produced in Thailand: a 2-seat version (EK GL), a 2-d 4-seat version (KK GL) and a luxurious 4-d, 5-seat version (DK GLS). They are powered by a TD 2477cc engine (115hp @ 4000, 94 mph). The transmission has 5 speeds with a reduction. The Easy Select 4WD has optional FWD (before reaching a speed of 62 mph) and a 100% lock of a rear differential.

The L 200 has a 116-in-long wheelbase, it is 197 / 202 in long, 67 in / 70 in wide, 69 / 71 in high, and has a ground clearance of 8.3 in (the luxurious, two-colored, 5-seat DK 4WD GLS has a 9.3-in ground clearance). The model's curb weight is +3,693 lbs and its maximum payload is 2,546 lbs.

The Mitsubishi L200 Pick Up, Dakar 2002

Mitsubishi Space Gear / Delica

The Delica—a minivan based on the Pajero—was launched in May 1994. Since 1995, it has also been available with 4x4 drive. This LUV was awarded the title of "The Four-Wheel Drive of the Year" by an Australian magazine named Overland. Power is supplied by: gasoline engines— a 16v 2351cc (132hp @ 5500 1/min), a 1997cc (116hp @ 6000), a 24v V6 2972cc (185hp @ 5500)—and turbo-diesel engines—a 2477cc (99hp @ 4200) and a 2835cc (125hp @ 4000). Starting with the models of 2000, the choice of units changed to gasoline 16v 2351cc (128hp @ 5500), while the 2.0L (113 hp), 3.0L V6 and both D have been retained. A 5-speed manual transmission was available besides a 4-speed automatic one. Power is transmitted to the rear wheels, or (with some models) to all wheels, with an inter-axle differential, a viscous coupling and a 2-speed reduction. The 4WD 2000 models featured RWD with optional FWD, while the rest of the mechanics remained the same. The LUV has a ladder frame and an independent McPherson suspension with a stabilizer in the front. The rear axle is rigid with a Panhard rod, coil springs and a stabilizer. A 5-d body seats up to 9 persons. Other features: wheelbase—110 / 118 in, length—181 / 197 in, width—67 in, height—76.8 / 77.2–81.5 in, ground clearance 7.5 in. Curb weight is +3,660 lbs/ (4WD) 3,825 lbs, payload is 1,598 / 1,863 lbs.

Mitsubishi – MPV 4WD

A vehicle known as the Space Wagon, the Chariot (Japan) and the Colt Vista / Eagle Summit Wagon (U.S.A.) is an MPV from 1983 with 2x4 drive or, since 1984, 4x4 drive. In May 1991, the 2nd generation appeared, including the Space Wagon Van. The 3rd generation made its debut in Tokyo

1997; it was purely a road vehicle. The 4-d MPV Space Runner is a shortened variant of the Space Wagon. In 1997, Generation II of this model was launched. Also available was the Space Runner Van delivery vehicle. The Mitsubishi Space Star (2x4) minivan from the fall of 1998, made in Europe exclusively for the European market, has the same purpose. In February 2003, production of the Grandis was launched in Japan; its European launch was planned for April 2004.

Mitsubishi Delica / L 300 / L 400

In 1968, the company launched the Delica LUV, a Pick-up / Truck with a 1,323-lb carrying capacity. It was followed a year later by a van, station wagon, minibus and chassis. Later they became known as the L 300. Versions with 4x2 drive were complemented by 4x4. In the early 1980s, the L 300 Generation II poured into Europe. Generation III appeared in 1986; the 4th generation from 1999 is also available as "Mazda Bongo." In 2000, an updated version was introduced (but not in Europe): the L 300 / Delica Export (4x2 and 4x4). Since 1994, bigger versions including the Delica Cargo / L 400 (4x2 or 4x4) have been marketed.

The Mitsubishi L300 4x4, Andorra 2001

The Monteverdi Range Rover 5-d, 1981

Monteverdi (Switzerland)

Peter Monteverdi started his career as the owner of a car maintenance shop and a gas station; later, he was involved in rebuilding, producing and restoring luxury cars. He owns a car museum in Basel. He has modified models such as the Monteverdi Subaru Integral (4x4) and the Toyota Super-Ace (4x2).

Range Rover 4-door Monteverdi Design

Unwittingly, the Swiss played the role of guinea pig. The Range Rover was originally sold with 3 doors. Rover agreed that FLM Panelcraft would rebuild it as a 5-d vehicle, but was not happy with the result. Then in Geneva in 1980, Monteverdi introduced his 5-d RR. The truth of the matter is hazy. A LR communiqué says that somebody remembered afterward that the special projects department had approved the remodeling "sometime in 1979." It is not known if

Monteverdi knew that the factory was preparing its own 5-d RR, which was subsequently introduced 16 months after Geneva 1980. The Swiss left work on the body to Fissore—an Italian company, which was supplied from England with new 3-d vehicles with a basic white finish. Monteverdi modified and sold a total of 50–350 Range Rovers; he had planned on 300 units per year (Fissore mentions 250 bodies). The vehicles with a more luxurious interior found buyers in Europe and the Middle East. In Geneva in 1982, Monteverdi introduced a supercharged engine, but within a month he terminated these activities. A supercharged (3-d) RR was also showcased in Geneva in 1983 by another Swiss company—Nova Swiss.

Monteverdi Safari

In Geneva 1976, the Monteverdi visionary uncovered a luxurious 3-d 5-seat car—the Monteverdi Safari. The International Scout off-roader served as the basis. This prototype was designed and manufactured by Fissore. An American V8 5653cc engine (165hp @ 3600, SAE, 106 mph) purred under the cowling. At an extra charge, a 7206cc engine (305hp/4200) was available. A 3-speed automatic transmission transmitted torque to the rear wheels. By means of an auxiliary 2-speed gear-reduction transmission it was possible to engage the FWD. The Safari also featured an automatic lock on the rear differential, a manual lock on the front differential and automatic freewheels in the hubs of the front wheels. At extra cost, the station wagon version was equipped with a manual 4-speed transmission. The vehicle had a ladder chassis with rigid axles featuring half-elliptic springs and torsion stabilizers. Other features: wheelbase—100 in, length—180 in, width—70.5 in, height—68.5 in, ground clearance—7.5 in, curb weight—4,189 lbs and payload—2,866 lbs.

The Monteverdi Sahara, 1981

The Monteverdi Sahara, 1981

The Monteverdi 260F

Monteverdi Sahara ❷

In May 1978, the Safari got a more modern and sporty sibling—the Monteverdi Sahara—based on a newer version of the International Scout II. It was a 3-d station wagon for 5 persons, with a matt black vinyl roof. The Sahara featured the same engine (a 5.7L), drivetrain, chassis and wheelbase as the Safari. It differed in that it gave a choice between a 4-speed transmission with a differential lock and an option to disengage the FWD on the one hand, or a 3-speed Chrysler automatic transmission on the other hand. Its curb weight

was 110 lbs higher, its ground clearance was 0.2 in higher; the car was 171 in long and 68 in high. Apart from all that, it also featured a D V6 3253cc engine (82hp @ 3800 SAE, 90 mph).

Monteverdi Military ❷ ❾

Rayton Fissore came up with a large number of off-roaders with a plain-and-simple shape and equipment, which the Swiss meant to sell through the Saurer company to the Helvetian army. In Geneva in 1979, he showcased the basic Monteverdi 230 M (=Military), without doors and with mica side windows in a canvas roof. It served as a basis for the civilian Monteverdi 250 Z and the Monteverdi 260 F—a trambus with a canvas tilt for transporting personnel. These vehicles were presented in Basil 1979. All were powered by 4V Chrysler 3203cc engines (87hp). Monteverdi sold the prototypes and a franchise to Saurer, who planned to mass-produce them. However, Saurer then bought Daimler-Benz and put this promising project on ice.

The Monteverdi Toyota Super-Ace, 1983

The Morattab Pazhan Double Cab, 2000

The Morattab New Pazhan V6, 2000

Morattab
(Iran)

Morattab
Land Rover / Pazhan,
Morattab Pajero ❷

The Morattab Industries, established in 1958 and based in Teheran, started assembling Land Rovers in 1962. In the second half of the 1980s, it began taking CKD car kits from the Santana LR, Series IIIA. The Iranians gradually took over the production and developed their variants. As much as 75 % of components were Iran-made. That is how they came by military $^1/_2$-tons. They differed in appearance from the original because the $^1/_2$-ton combined components of Series IIA. The factory in Farsi dispatched the 88" and 109" military models. The Irani lightweight has much in common with the Spanish Militar / Ligero. Some are exported, to countries such as Algeria. The political orientation of the country after the 1973 Israeli-Arab War, as well as the complex relations in the region complicate the official and authorized cooperation between Land Rover and Morattab. The vehicles, now called the Pazhan 2400 GS / GSV / GL / GD / GLD / Single Cab, Pazhan 3000 GLV / GLD Double Cab, and since 2002 also the New Pazhan V6-3.0, introduced in Teheran 2001, are a spitting image of Defenders. According to a law, 80 % of the components must be Irani-made. The company produces 3- and 5-d station wagons and pick-up trucks with one or two rows of seats. The engines recruit from a choice of a 2.4L 4V engine (105hp) and a new model—a 3.0L V6 (160hp). There were plans for 2002 to assemble the Pajero GL / GLS (franchise, a short Mitsubishi Pajero, 1991–99) presented in Teheran in 2001, with the following V6 engines: a 3,0L (161hp) and a 3.5L.

In 2002, a total of 653 vehicles were produced, although the factory's capacity is 1,000 units. The company was supposed to become part of IDRO (Industrial Development and Renovation Organisation) but, in 2002, property relations were divided between IDRO (32%), private investors (14%) and the Azadeghan foundation (54%).

The Morattab Pazhan V6 3000 GLV, 2000

175

Moretti
(Italy)

The Moretti Midimaxi 127

In 1926, Giovanni Moretti established an engineering plant, which turned out to be a company involved in rebuilding automobiles. In the early 1970s, it had a yearly output of 5,000 vehicles. The 1977 Turin motor show saw the debut of Moretti's "Van Paguro," a model with limited cross-country ambitions.

Moretti Minimaxi 500, Minimaxi 126 ❹

This 4-seat beach vehicle (4x2) was based on the Fiat 500 F. It first appeared in Turin in 1970. It had a rear, air-cooled 2V 499.5cc engine (18hp @ 4600, 59 mph) and independently suspended wheels. Its successor based on the same concept—the Minimaxi 126—was presented in Turin in 1973, featuring a 594cc engine (23hp @ 4800, 65 mph).

The Moretti Minimaxi 500

Moretti Midimaxi Fiat 127, Panda Rock ❹

The 1971 Turin motor show saw the debut of the Midimaxi Fiat 127 (2x4) with a 4V 903cc engine (47hp @ 6200, 87 mph). In the second half of the 1970s, a hard-top version was also available. The Midimaxi II was followed in Turin in 1982 by the Midimaxi III with features of the younger-growing Fiats 127, with a "1050" engine (50hp @ 5600, 87 mph) and a 5-speed transmission. In April 1982, they showcased the Panda Rock 30—a recreational convertible with a 2V 652cc engine (30hp @ 5500, 71 mph), and the Panda Rock 45—with a 4V 903cc engine (45hp @ 5600, 87 mph). Later, they came up with similar models—the Moretti Uno Folk and the Moretti Regata Skipper.

Moretti Sporting ❷

Moretti also took up the Campagnola model, and dressed it into a 3-d glassed-in station wagon body. Only a negligible number of units were made.

The Moretti Midimaxi 127

MTX
(Czech Republic)

MTX Buggy ❹

In the late 1960s, talented people began actualizing their dreams. A thirst for race cars was quenched by MTX workshops integrated into the Metalex company—a specialist in metallic paint. The profits of Metallex helped finance the cars. The workshops professionalized, and became unrivalled east of Germany. Since 1970, they have produced small numbers of the 2-seat MTX Škoda Buggy (4x2)—the first Czech-made autocross special—with parts from the Škoda 100/110. In 1973, the buggy MTX 2-02 (the same mechanics) was launched, followed in 1988 by the MTX 2-04 with an engine from the Lada 1600 (Metalex 150hp @ 7000). The designer, Mr. Král, designed the MTX Beach Buggy. It was supposed to be produced by a Prague-based Verold company and it was showcased in Prague and Brno.

Large-scale production was called off. In 1992, MTX completed a prototype of the Verold Bagheera (Brno 1992) with components of the Škoda Favorit. Verold backed out of the project, and MTX rebuilt the car to feature the mechanics of the Ford Fiesta (1.1–1.8-L, with a viscous self-locking differential on request, 2x4) and produces them in small series. In 1980, MTX supplied the army with the UAZ 469 BI— a remodeled parade vehicle.

The MTX Škoda Buggy

The MTX—a UAZ parade vehicle

The MTX 2-04 Buggy

177

MX Cooperation (Lichtenstein)

Xavier Jehle of Schaan, Lichtenstein, bubbled with ideas. In 1978, he founded the AR-Studio Xavier Jehle. One of its first projects was the Mathies-Buggy. The MX Cooperation make came up with a novelty—Méhari-style cars with components of the Citroën 2CV / Dyane / Ami, inspired by the Namco Pony. This open vehicle carried 4-5 passengers. The MX Safari weighed 1,290 lbs.

The company also produced the Diavolino—a small jeep-style car. This 2-seat polyester vehicle was powered by a 2-stroke air-cooled 250cc motorcycle engine (12hp) or a Lawile 125cc engine (6hp), later also a 4-stroke 1V Honda 340cc power unit (11hp) with a 4-speed transmission with Fiat components. The Diavolino weighed 750 lbs and it was 81.5 in long and 52 in wide. Specifications of the innovated

version: length—91 in, width—58 in and curb weight—1,014 lbs. The company was shut down sometime in 1992.

The idea of a small Jeep-like car was taken up by IMC. The Piccolino was built in Switzerland and was supposed to be mass-produced in Italy. A 2V D Ruggerini 650cc engine (50 mph) powered the front wheels over a Variomatic centrifugal transmission. This car, featuring a length of 83 in, a width of 50 in and a curb weight of 838 lbs carried 2 persons. The absence of a trunk was counterbalanced by a trailer with a maximum total weight of 1,323 lbs.

In the mid-1980s, a Swiss vehicle named "Strega" made by the ZRB Automobile company was introduced. This 2+2-seat car was 105 in long and 52 in wide, it weighed 807 lbs, and was powered by a 4-stroke air-cooled D 750cc engine (18hp). It featured a 4-speed transmission and a polyester body for 2 adults and 2 children. All "Jeeps" could usually be driven by people from 16 years of age.

The MX Cooperation line-up

Namco
(Greece)

Namco Pony   ❹

This importer of Citroëns from Thessaloniki was active in
1976–85. From the moment the company was established
until 1983, it produced "Pony" recreational and work vehicles that shared the design of the Méhari and the Dalat. They
featured a Citroën 2 CV platform with independent wheel
suspension and 2x4 drive. Their 2- or 5-seat body could fea-

The Namco Pony

The Namco Pony

The Namco Pony

The Namco Pony

ture a laminated hard-top. The company also ventured
a recreational vehicle called "Pony Camper." Power was
provided by a 2V 602cc engine (32hp @ 5400, 73 mph) or
a 597cc engine (32hp). The Pony was exported to many
countries. An amazing 4,000 units were made every year
(17,000 overall).

Nissan
(Japan)

The Nissan Patrol Carrier 4W66, 1956–1958

In 1911, Masujiro Hashimoto founded 1911 the Kwaishinsha Co in Tokyo. The name of its first vehicle—DAT—was also an abbreviation of the names of the people who helped him establish the company: Kenjiro Den, Rokuro Aoyama and Meitaro Takeuchi. In 1925, they merged with the Osaka-based Jitsuyo Jidosha Co., a producer of the Lila 1.3-L vehicle. They continued to manufacture both models, changing their names a few times, which now included the word DAT. In 1931, the firm swallowed the Tobata Imono Co., and named their new product "Datson" to mean "the son of DAT;" unfortunately, in Japanese the word "son" sounds a lot like destruction, devastation, ruin. And as the new factory had just been hit by a hurricane, the name evoked undesirable associations. They modified it to "Datsun," hoping that the "sun" will protect them from future calamities. In 1936, they signed a contract with Graham-Paige to buy a franchise for the Crusader from it. Since 1937, they have produced the model under the marque of Nissan (Nissan Motor Co. emerged in June 1934), which became associated with more luxurious models, until, in 1983, it became the only one to be used by the company. After 1938, Nissan focused on utility vehicles, army supplies (the legendary Nissan 180 truck, 4x2) and the production of aircraft engines. After the war, it produced the 4W72 (all but a copy of the Dodge WC52); this was a $3/_4$ -ton 4x4 vehicle with a 6V SV 3670cc engine (105hp), a 4-and 1-speed transmission, RWD with optional FWD, rigid axles with leaf springs, featuring a 110-in-long wheelbase, a length of 187.5 in, a width of 80.5 in, a height of 93 in and a curb weight of 6,063 lbs. In the early 1960s, this model was followed by the Nissan 4W73—a 4x4 $3/_4$ -ton car with a 6V OHV 3956cc engine (125hp), but a 4-speed transmission and roughly the dimensions and appearance of the Dodge M37. For civilian distribution, it was named "Nissan Carrier"; later it was produced in India. A significant European acqui-

sition was the purchase of 35 % of Motor Ibérica in 1980 from the Massey Ferguson company. In the late 1980s, the share of Nissan in the company was 84.4 %. In the mid-1980s, this coalition of companies included also Nissan Diesel and Fuji Heavy Industries with ties to Subaru. In the late 1990s, the company got into a crisis. It was saved by Renault, which swallowed up 36.8 % of its stocks in March 1999. The French managers took draconian measures (they unified the models and harmonized them with Renault), paid for by the company. Production is carried out in 16 countries. Alternative AWD has been featured on touring Nissans—e.g., since March 1982, the compact Sunny / Pulsar, since 1980 their bigger brother—the Bluebird, and the Primera since the fall of 2001. Studies with an off-road character included the Nissan Crossbow 4x4 introduced at the IAA 2001, or the Yanya in Geneva in 2002. Attractiveness was a feature of the powerful off-road Trailrunner 4x4 Coupé introduced at the IAA 1997.

Nissan Patrol 60 ❷

In 2001, the Patrol celebrated 50 years of existence. Not even Nissan succeeded with its 4W-60 in a 1950 competition for a Japanese army 4WD. The year 1951 saw the launch of the 4W-70—a Nissan reminiscent of a Jeep. This off-roader had a canvas roof, a few hard benches, a gasoline 6V SV

The Nissan Patrol 160 Safari, 1980–1983

3670cc engine (85hp), rigid axles with half-elliptic leaf springs and optional FWD engageable at a standstill. It was later renamed to "4W-60." In 1953, mass production commenced in an Oppama factory. The vehicles were bought by the police force, firefighters and the first six were exported to Argentina. The L4W-60 made in 1955 was fitted with a "92" (92hp) engine and simultaneously the 4W-61 appeared, featuring an SV 3956cc engine (105hp). In 1958, the 4W-65 was born, for the first time also as an 8-seat station wagon and a year later the 4W-66 got a rebuilt OHV 3956cc engine (125hp @ 3400). The FWD on the 1960 model could be activated in motion. A 3-speed transmission and rigid axles with leaf springs were retained. In the late 1950s, these vehicles were exported to numerous countries, including the U.S. after 1961. In1960 the car got a new appearance, interior and—for the first time—the name "Patrol." It featured a 3-speed transmission with an auxiliary 2-speed reduction. Thanks to a stabilizer of the front axle, applied to an off-roader for the first time, the model had fantastic driving properties and adaptability of the chassis to terrain. It gained a reputation as a reliable and tireless toiler. The Nissan forded through a depth of 28 in, increased to 40 in after installing special equipment. In addition to the L-60 soft-top, a KL-60 hard-top appeared in the U.S.A. in 1963. In 1968 its engine got an additional 5 horsepower; simultaneously, a very long pick-up truck 62Z(L)G60H appeared, featuring a 3-speed transmission, but an engine with 145hp. In 1974, the Patrol 60 series finally got a 4-speed transmission and a 4.0L engine (145hp). Apart from a pick-up truck, Nissan offered a short and long soft-top (L)60, a 3-d stretched and short station wagon W(L)G60, a 3-d hard-top K(L)60 and superstructures including a mobile movie projector. Dimensions: wheelbase—87 / 98.5 in and 110 in (pick-up truck), length—148.5 / 177 in and 160 in, width—68 / 67 in (station wagon), height—78 / 75 in and 77 in (hard-top) and 74 in (pick-up truck), ground clearance—8.7 in, or 8.4 in (long versions). When empty, it weighed +3,483 lbs and carried 6 or 8 persons or 2 people and 1,763 lbs of cargo, or 2 people and 2,205 lbs of cargo (pick-up truck). In 1974, output first exceeded 10,000 units. The 1st generation of Nissan 60 ceased to be produced in 1982 with a total output of 170,000 units.

Nissan Patrol 160 / Safari (Japan, Spain) ❷

In November 1979 the 2nd generation—Patrol 160 (sometimes with an MQ code)—made its debut, featuring AWD. This vehicle with a new body was fitted with 6V engines—a gasoline OHC 2734cc (120hp) and a D OHV 3224cc (95hp, since 1983 a TD, 110hp). The MC-4 military variant had a 4V D 2.8L engine. It featured a 4-speed transmission, and also a 5-speed transmission with a reduction since 1983 for the D version. The axles remained rigid with longitudinal leaf springs. In 1984, the model underwent a facelift, obvious from the transition from round to rectangular main headlights. In 1985, a 5-speed transmission appeared and after 1988 only one engine type was available: a TD 3.3L. Simultaneously, production was launched of the (cheaper) K260 and W260 in Spain, which were a follow-up to the franchise-made Patrols TH and TB from 1983 with Iberian-made Perkins engines. They were bought both by civilians and armed forces. The engines of the late 1980s included: 6V a 2753cc (120hp @ 4800, 134hp @ 5200, JIS) and a 3956cc (150hp @ 3800, SAE) 6V engines; a 6V D 3246cc engine (95hp @ 3600), a TD 3246cc engine (120hp @ 4000). For the Spanish market, they provided also 4V 2702cc engines (70hp @ 3600). Optional FWD was maintained, but an extra fee was charged for a rear limited slip differential. The transmissions have 4 or 5 speeds with a reduction, or there is a 3-speed automatic transmission. Some models featured drum brakes in the front. Other features: wheelbase—93 / 117 in (station wagon), length—160

The Nissan Patrol 160, 1983–1987

and 167 in / 185 in (station wagon), width—67 in, height—72 / 73 in and 71 / 72 in (both a station wagon), ground clearance—8.3 in. A 3-d soft/hard top seats up to 5 people and (when empty) it weighs +3,605 lbs; a 5-d 5 to 10-seat station wagon weighs +3,880 lbs (when empty). Available versions included a station wagon and a hard top with a "normal" and elevated roof, a convertible, and a short and stretched pick-up truck. There are conflicting data about termination of production of the model (in Spain). Some sources mention the year 1990, but the 260 series was sold in Spain until the beginning of the new millennium. The truth is that production did not finish until June 2001. The Patrol was successfully used as an expedition vehicle and won laurels in motor sport events. In Dakar, it came first overall in 1989; in the previous year it finished second. It won 5 times in its class. In 1992, it won the Rally Paris–Moscow–Bejing, 4 times the Rally of Pharaos, 5 times the Rally Atlas. More golden wreaths were awarded to Nissan pilots from the United Arab Emirates, Portugal, Spain, Tunisia, Italy, Australia and other countries. In 1993, it won gold in raid rallies in the category of designers.

Nissan Patrol GR / New Safari ❷

In 1988, the company introduced the Patrol GR (GR = Grand Raid)—a more expensive 3-d (4-5 people) or 5-d (4–7 people) station wagon with a "Y60" code, manufactured exclusively in Japan. This model is considered the 3rd generation of the Patrol. It was geared toward new customers, who weren't looking for a work vehicle but a vehicle for active pastimes and driving around the city. The GR has more comfortable equipment and adjustment of the chassis with a ladder frame, and geometrically more precise rigid axles with coil springs. In the front there is a Panhard rod, with

The Nissan Patrol 5-d, 1981

a stabilizer on request, and the rear axle has both features. The car has RWD with optional FWD. Freewheels in the hubs of the front wheels are deactivated manually or automatically, there was a two-speed reduction and, in the rear, a differential with a lock. The manual transmission has 5 speeds, the automatic one has 4 speeds and double torque increased by a torque converter. Engines: a 6V TD 2826cc engine (115hp @ 4400, 93 mph) and a 4169cc engine (125hp @ 4000, JIS, 93 mph). The 1990s brought new power units: the 6V TD 2826cc engine (116hp @ 4400) was joined by 6V TD 4169 cc engines (145hp @ 4000) and a gasoline engine of the same capacity (175hp @ 4200, JIS and 160hp @ 4000 ECE). The transmissions and the 2-speed reduction remained the same. The rear differential had a manual lock and a different gear ratio spacing of the 5-speed manual transmission or an auto transmission. Disc brakes were installed. Other features: wheelbase—95 / 117 in, length—

The Nissan Patrol Safari, 1985

The Nissan Patrol GR Y61, presented in 1998

167 / 190 in, width—71 / 76 in, height—71 / 78 in, ground clearance—8.1 in, curb weight—(+)4,048 / 4,156 lbs and payload—1,356 / 1,819 lbs.

The 6th generation of the Patrol made its debut at the IAA 1997. The Nissan Y61 was the first off-roader in the world to feature an electrically-controlled, disengageable rear axle differential. The dimensions remained the same. In addition to the familiar TD 2.8L (now 129hp @ 4000, 96 mph—it ended in 2002), there was a gasoline 6V 4479cc engine (200hp @ 4400, JIS, +106 mph), a 4V TD 16v direct-injection 2953cc engine (170hp @ 3600, JIS, +103 mph, 158 @ 3600, since the end of the last decade), and a 6V TD 4169cc engine (160hp @ 3600, JIS, +93 mph). This generation of the GR doesn't feature an inter-axle differential, but its differential is equipped with a 100% lock. The FWD can be engaged before reaching a speed of 25 mph. Other characteristics: wheelbase— 95 in, length—175 in, width—76 in, height—72 in, ground clearance—8.7 in, fording depth—27.6 in, overhang angles—37° /30°. When empty, the vehicle weighs +4,894 /

5,148 lbs and has a payload of 1,433 / 1,642 lbs. A station wagon version, retouched at the end of 1999, had 3 or 5 doors and even more luxurious equipment.

Nissan Terrano / Pathfinder ❷

The development of the Nissan Terrano followed the same recipe used in the mid-1980s by Opel, Toyota or Mitsubishi. An attractive and well-equipped body was bolted onto a shortened chassis. For comfort's sake, leaf springs were replaced with torsion bars or, even better, coil springs. Besides a diesel engine, a gasoline 6V power unit could be found under the hood. Nissan chose the same path. It used the "Light Duty" Pick-up as a base. The newcomer from August 1986 was known as "Terrano" at home, and as "Pathfinder" in the U.S. This 3-d 5-seat comfortable leisure-time station wagon perched on a ladder frame. For export, the company installed a gasoline 4V 2388cc engine (101hp @ 4800, or, for the local market, 103hp @ 4800, JIS, 93 mph), a gasoline V6 2960cc engine with central fuel in-

The Nissan Patrol GR Y60 SWB 1st generation (1988–1997)

The Nissan Terrano Pick Up, 1985

The Nissan Terrano, 1982

The Nissan Pathfinder Luxury Edition, 2001

jection (136hp @ 4800; or 147hp, SAE for the U.S.; or 140hp, JIS for Japan) and a TD 4V 2663cc engine (100hp @ 4000, 85hp @ 4300, atmospheric). The rear wheels were powered, and there was optional FWD. The freewheels in the front wheel hubs were automatic. A cross-country reduction and a limited slip differential were also available. There was either a 5-speed manual transmission or a 3-speed planetary automatic one, plus a converter with a double increase of torque. Other features: wheelbase—104 in, length—172 in, width—67 in, height—66 in, ground clearance—8.3 in, curb weight—(+)3,682 lbs. In 1997, a TD 3.2L engine was introduced.

The child of the 1999 modernization wave has only one name: Pathfinder. In 2001, a gasoline V6 3498cc engine (220hp @ 6000, 109 mph) finally appeared. This luxurious

5-d, 5-seat station wagon features AWD with a variable distribution of driving power between the wheels of both axles, including a case in which 100% of power is transmitted to the rear wheels. The model has an electronically-controlled viscous coupling cooperating with a 4-speed auto transmission and a 2-speed reduction. The rear axle is equipped with a limited slip differential. The body is now self-supporting, with an independent McPherson suspension in the front and a rigid rear axle with coil springs, Panhard rod, and a stabilizer. The wheelbase is 106 in long. The model is 183 in long, 72 in wide, 69 in high, and has an 8.3-in-high ground clearance. When empty, it weighs 4,299 lbs, and its payload is 992 lbs. This model appears rather sporadically in Europe, as it is geared mainly toward North-American customers.

Nissan Terrano II (Spain)

Since 1993, the Nissan Ibérica assembly plant in Barcelona released the Nissan Terrano II and the Ford Maverick "Siamese twins." They were constructed by Nissan's "technological center" in Cranfield, GB. The Terrano II is a 5-seat 3-/5-d station wagon. Power is provided to the rear wheels with optional FWD engageable before reaching a speed of 25 mph; the front features automatic freewheels, while the rear axle has a limited slip differential. Power units: 4V - engines—a gasoline 12v 2389cc engine (124hp @ 5200, 99 mph), or a TD 2664cc engine (99hp @ 4000, 90 mph). Transmissions: 5-speeds with a 2-speed reduction. The Terrano II has a ladder frame, double wishbones in the front and torsion bars; in the rear is a rigid axle with longitudinal arms, a Panhard rod, and stabilizers everywhere. Other features: wheelbase—96.5 / 104 in, length—161 / 180 in, width—68 in, height—71 / 71.5 in, ground clearance—8.3 in, curb weight—(+)3,571 / 3,858 lbs, payload—1,499 / 1,830 lbs.

In July 1996, the Terrano II was remodeled, with some additional touch-ups in 1999. In the spring 2002, the façade was improved, characterized by a new grille, plastic parts, and rectangular headlights that incorporated fog lights. Its name is simply "Terrano." Power is supplied by a TD 2664cc engine (125hp @ 3600, 96 mph), and a 2953cc engine (154hp @ 3600, 106 mph) from the Patrol. In some specimens, a gasoline 4V 2.4L engine (118hp) survives. The

The Nissan Terrano II Fun Beach and Outdoor Top Style, 2001

length has changed to 167 / 186 in while keeping the same wheelbase; the model is 69 in wide and 71.5 in high. When empty, it weighs +3,748 / 4,001 lbs, and its payload is 1,786 / 1,687 lbs. Its fording depth is 17.7, and its overhang angles are 35° / 26°.

Nissan X-Trail   ❸

Nissan did not introduce an SUV in Europe until the IAA 2001. The vehicle in question—a 5-d 5-seat station wagon with a self-supporting body—offers plenty of space and equipment. The X-Trail has AWD, with an option to disengage the RWD manually or automatically; in the latter case, the driving power is divided in a 57:43 ratio. The SUV has a limited slip differential in the back and ESP. It is fitted with 4V gasoline engines—a 16v 1998cc (140hp @ 6000, 110 mph), a 16v 2488cc (165hp @ 6000, 116 mph), and a TD Common-Rail 16v 2184cc (114hp @ 4000, 103 mph). If it features a D engine, it has a 6-speed transmission without

a reduction (for gasoline engines a 5-speed or a 4-speed automatic one). Its chassis, derived from a passenger car, works with an independent suspension of the front and rear wheels. The front features a McPherson strut and a stabilizer, while the back has control arms, coil springs and a stabilizer. The model has disc brakes with ABS and EBD. The Nissan has a 103-in-long wheelbase, it is 177 in long, 69.5 in wide, 66 in high, and has a 7.9-in-high ground clearance, a curb weight of +3,197 lbs and a payload of 1,213 lbs. The X-Trail negotiates a 11.8-in fording depth and its overhang angles are 28°/25°.

The Nissan X-Trail, 2001

The Nissan Terrano II police car; Alcocebre, Spain, 2002

Nissan Pick-up ❷ ❻

In 1934, Nissan started producing pick-up trucks (4x2, and since 1980 also 4x4) related to passenger cars. Their engines use both diesel and gasoline for fuel. The pick-up trucks had 2-d 2-seat cabs (Long Body) or 4-to-5-seat 2-d cabs (Double Cab). In 1997, the 16th generation was presented. Recently, the pick-up trucks have appeared as an independent type for suburban driving and active pastimes. The latest retouched versions were made in 2001. The model got more chrome-plated parts, a unifying front panel and a better interior (Navara equipment). This pick-up truck features RWD, an option to engage the FWD before reaching 31 mph, automatic freewheels of the front wheels and a limited slip differential in the back. There is a 5-speed transmission with a 2-speed reduction. One of the engines is a TD 4V 2488cc (133hp @ 4000, 101 mph). A steel Pick-up / King Cab /

Double Cab body is bolted onto a ladder frame. The front wheel McPherson suspension has torsion bars and a stabilizer, the rear axle is rigid with leaf springs. Other features: wheelbase—116 in, length—197 in, width—72 in, height—67.5 in, ground clearance—8.7 in, fording depth—17.7 in and overhang angles—31° / 31°. Curb weight is 4,145 lbs, payload is 2,161 lbs.

Nissan Prairie ❶ ❼

This compact MPV, derived from the Sunny, with a front transversal engine and RWD, was launched in August 1982. After September 1985, a version was available that featured optional RWD and a gasoline 1974cc engine (91hp @ 5200, JIS, 99hp @ 5600, with a catalytic converter—98hp @ 5200). In the fall of 1988, the 3rd generation named Prairie / Prairie Joy appeared, now with permanent 4x4, with

The Nissan Pick Up, 2002

power distributed in a 50:50 ratio between the axles, and with McPherson struts. The 4WD was equipped with an inter-axle viscous coupling differential, and a rear limited slip differential (for an extra charge). The Prairie / Liberty from the fall of 1998 has more of a road character.

Nissan Vanette / Serena (Japan, Spain)   ❼ ❽

The Vanette has been made in Japan since 1986. The Vanette / Serena 2nd generation—a 4-d 7- to 8-seat station wagon or van—was premiered in Japan in July 1991. Since 1992, it has been made with 4x2 drive in Spain. A bigger 16v 4V 1998cc engine (126hp and 130hp @ 6000, JIS, 106 mph) was also mounted into the 4WD version (50:50), in combination with a 5-speed manual transmission or a 4-speed automatic one; the same goes for the other engine—a 4V D 2283cc (75hp @ 4300, 91hp, JIS, 84 mph).

There was a limited slip differential in the rear. The front featured a McPherson axle with a stabilizer, in the rear there was a double wishbone, a transversal arm, transversal leaf springs and, at a premium, a stabilizer. Some models with a D engine featured a rigid front axle. The 3rd Japanese generation from 1999, also known as the Mazda Bongo, has 4x2 and 4x4 drive. Body-wise, these are minibuses, station wagons, vans, minivans and platform trucks with a payload of 1,102–2,205 lbs and one of the following engines: a 1.8L (90hp) or a D 2.2L (79hp).

The Ford Maverick in the foreground, the Nissan Terrano II in the background; Alcocebre, Spain, 2002

OMAI
(Italy)

Omai Sheveró ❷

OMAI based in Ortona left its mark in 1988, and disappeared four years later. The 4-seat off-road Sheveró had a soft-top (Cabrio), or a metal hard-top (Metal Top). A ladder chassis was borne by rigid axles with longitudinal leaf springs, complemented by bar stabilizers. Mechanical parts were shared with the Fiat. A 4V D SOFIM 2445cc engine (72hp @ 4200, 84 mph) was connected with a 5-speed transmission, 2-speed reduction and locks on the freewheels. It was also equipped with an inter-axle torsen differential and axle limited slip differentials (25 % in the front, 50 % in the rear). The wheelbase was 91 in long, the length of the model was 156 in; it was 67 in wide, 76 in high, its ground clearance was 10.6 in, its curb weight was +3,814 lbs, its fording depth was 23.6 in. It negotiated a 90 % slope and a 43° side tilt. Its overhang angles were 47° / 45°.

The OMAI Cabrio, 1989

Opel a Vauxhall (Europe)

In 1868, Adam Opel founded a firm, which 18 years later made the first ordinary velocipede. In 1893, his sons completed their first car—the Lutzmann, which was mass-produced after 1902. General Motors bought 80% of its stocks in 1929. GM assembled cars in Germany from 1927. The Vauxhall company was established in Britain in 1857, and in 1903 it prepared its first car—the 5 HP. GM took control in 1925. The makes grew stronger under the American flag. Since the 1970s, lower expenses and growing investments have led to a unification of components and later also models—not only among the makes which include Bedford in the LUV category in Britain, but in the worldwide activities of GM. Opel occurs in continental Europe and gradually also in overseas; both British makes are active across the English Channel. One assembly line releases identical vehicles with different labels. Opels / Vauxhalls are made in 10 countries, as Chevrolets in 6 countries, and as Holdens in Australia. Formerly also in Japan as Isuzus and in South Korea as Daewoos. The European GM patterned some sedans, station wagons and coupes—Vectra and Calibra—also as 4WD.

Opel / Vauxhall Frontera / Frontera Sport (Great Britain) ❷

The Frontera made its debut in Geneva in 1991. Opel (and Vauxhall) entered among off-roaders. In the same year, a 5-d 7-seat station wagon was followed by a 3-d 4-/5-seat Frontera Sport, for weekend road trips taken by young people. The models made in Luton—a Vauxhall factory—are in fact Isuzus. More precisely, they were clones of the short Isuzu MU / Amigo from January 1989 and the stretched Isuzu MU Wizard (from January 1991 as a derivative of the Isuzu Rodeo with features of the Isuzu Campo pick-up truck. Fronteras had RWD with optional FWD. The lockable freewheels in the front wheel hubs were automatic, with a manual lock at a premium. An extra fee was charged for a rear limited slip differential. There was a 5-speed transmission plus a 2-speed reduction. The vehicle featured disc brakes in the front, and after 1995 also in the rear. The front trapezoid axle had a torsion bar suspension and a stabilizer. The rear axle was rigid, with half-elliptic springs (until April 1995), later with coil springs. The body was attached to a ladder chassis. For the first 4 years, the model's European engines lacked spark. They were gasoline 4V engines—an Opel 1998cc (115hp @ 5200, 98 mph), a 2410cc (125hp @ 4800, only Frontera)—and an indirect-injection TD intercooler 2260cc power unit (100hp @ 4200). The situation

changed after a facelift in the spring of 1995, when a 2198cc engine (136 hp @ 5200, 100 mph) was introduced and, above all, a Japanese TD 2772cc engine (113hp @ 3600, 93 mph). In addition to a station wagon version, the year 1994 brought the Sport soft-top, which did not make a great impression, though. Its wheelbase was 92 / 108 in long. The model was 166 / 185 in long, 70 / 68 in wide, 67 / 67.5 in high. After the spring of 1995, its ground clearance was 7.3 in, and 8.1 in after that date. When empty, it weighed +3,500 / 5,258 lbs (gasoline) and 5,600 lbs (Diesel). A van was also available.

In late 1998, generation II of short and long versions appeared. A rear limited slip differential is series-supplied, the FWD can be engaged before reaching 62 mph. A 4-speed auto transmission is available in a combination with a 2.2L engine (136hp). Besides the above-mentioned engine only 2 new power units have been left: a gasoline V6

24v 3165cc engine (205hp @ 5400), and a TD—an in-line 4V 2172cc direct-ignition engine (116hp @ 3800). Dimensions: wheelbase—96.5 / 106 in, length—169 / 184 in, width—70 in, height—67 / 69 in, ground clearance—9 in. When empty, the model weighs +3,660 / 3,792 lbs, and its payload is 1,411 lbs.

Opel / Vauxhall Monterey (Great Britain) ❷

The Monterey is the 2nd generation of the Isuzu Trooper. It appeared in April 1992 and was available almost until the end of the 1990s. For a few years, it was rivaled on some markets by original Japanese Troopers, which sold well through other business channels. The European models were better equipped and more expensive. This short and stretched station wagon had 3 or 5 doors (and 5-seats), RWD and optional FWD with automatic freewheels and a limited slip differential at an extra charge. It had a 5-speed manual or a 4-speed automatic transmission (only in combination with a gasoline engine). Its chassis was equivalent to that of the Frontera, with the exception of coil springs and Panhard rods in the rear. Engines: a gasoline V6 24v 3165cc engine (177hp @ 5200, 106 mph) and a TD in-line 4V 3059cc direct-ignition engine (114hp @ 3600, 93 mph). Dimensions: wheelbase—92 / 108 in, length—169 / 185 in, width—69 in, height—72 in, ground clearance—8.3 in. The Monterey had a curb weight of +3,957 / 4,145 lbs.

The Opel Monterey, 1998

The Opel Monterey, 1998

Opel Campo
(Japan, Thailand)

The Campo pick-up trucks from the Far East appeared in the 2nd half of the 1990s in the Opel network. They included the 1st generation produced since 1997, the 2nd generation pro-

duced since 1998 — with a 4x2 and 4x4 drive and bodies including a pick-up truck, the Sport and the Crew, and featuring 2.5 DI and 3.1 TDS engines. Their wheelbase was 119 in long and their payload rating was 2,127–2,205 lbs. The Opel Campo is nothing other than the Japanese (Thai) Isuzu Pick-Up / TFR / Campo.

The Opel Campo, 1998

Oto Melara
(Italy)

Oto Melara Gorgona Combat ❾ ❷

In 1984, Engineer A. Costa founded the Oto Melara SpA armory in La Spezia, Italy. He tried to break through with the Gorgona—an armored vehicle. The Command—a gargantuan sedan (1984)—or the military Combat (August 1985) resemble the Lambo LM 002. The models had an aluminum 4-d 4-seat body. Power was supplied by a rear longitudinal gasoline 4V Fiat 2445cc engine (95hp @ 4200, 75 mph)—

the Gorgona R 2.5, or a TD VM 2393cc engine (100hp @ 4200 1/min, 75 mph). The vehicle was equipped with permanent 4x4 drive, a 5-speed transmission, a 2-speed reduction, an inter-axle differential and both axle differentials with an automatic lock and bulletproof tires. Its frame was made of steel and aluminum. The wheels were suspended independently on McPherson struts. The wheelbase was 98.5 in long, the vehicle itself was 184 in long, 67 in wide, 64 in high, and its ground clearance was 15.2 in. When empty, the Combat weighed 6,019 lbs and the Command weighed 5,754 lbs; their payload was 661 lbs. The vehicle managed a slope of 75 % and a 40° side tilt and had the same overhang angles—40°. Production was terminated in the early 1990s.

A column of 110 Otokar Land Rovers

Otokar (Turkey)

 **KOÇ**

In 1963, Izzet Unver founded a bus company called the Otobüs Karoseri Sanayi A. S. In a suburb of Istanbul, he manufactured the "Apollo" public transport buses and trucks in a Magirus-Deutz franchise. In the early 1970s, a majority of the firm went to the KOC financial group. Otokar is one of the most important suppliers of buses and minibuses (with Deutz engines) for Turkish public transportation. In addition to the Sultan buses, the company produces the 80 P10 / 80 P15 trucks, semi-trailers and trailers and bodies of trucks. It took up their production after taking over the Istanbul-based Fruehauf Tasit Araclari Company.

Otokar has been assembling British Land Rovers since 1986. The ambitious Turks soon introduced some new parts of their own and extended the program with variants unknown in England. The capacity of 2,000 units of the Jandarma plant was insufficient. The firm has also been trying to make it abroad. The vehicles were taken up by the Pakistani army. Sometimes Otokar sells vehicles at places to which the originals couldn't be exported for political reasons. Turkish state institutions buy $^1/_4$ of the production. The remaining $^3/_4$ are specials for the army, police and paramilitary forces and these have been produced since the mid-1980s. Some vehicles are also bought by rescue squads, miners and telecommunications. In January 1996, the company moved from Istanbul-Bahcelievler to modern assembly halls in Adapazari-Arifiye. In 2000, a total of 2,398 LRs were made there. In 1987, they assembled 400 paramilitary One Tens, mostly for the ministry of defense and interior. They resembled the English Defenders. The name "Defender" did not come into use in Turkey until 2001. The vehicles are powered by the following engines: V8 3.5L (134hp), or 4V TD 2.5L (111hp). The models supplied by the factory include: the 90, the 100 and the 130 for 2–11 persons and a cargo. The 110" and 127" chassis are purpose-built for ambulances, fire engines, rescue squads, breakdown vans and laboratory cars. Focus is also put on armored and military specials. The Zirhli Personel Tasiyici armored troop carrier resembles a LR. (In 1987, the Turks bought a franchise of the tactic LR). The Cobra and the Akrep (=scorpion) do not have any civilian use, and neither does the 111 E.5 Z—transporter of valuables.

The Otokar Land Rover 130

Peugeot (France)

PEUGEOT

In 1890, the Peugeot brothers founded one of the biggest and oldest car manufacturers. Armand Peugeot first started with bicycles, followed by a three-wheeler in 1888, and a car in 1891. In 1974, this strong company obtained 38.2 % of stocks of Citroën, and in 1978 the European branches of Chrysler. The foundations of the PSA group were thus laid, as we know it today—after a "slimming and rejuvenating diet." Both Peugeot and Citroën operate seemingly independently, but their technological and production cooperation is all the closer. Neither one left a significant trace in the 4WD domain. Peugeot was also one of the car manufacturers to make a half-track "passenger" open vehicle: the 201 A model. All 5 units made in 1933 were powered by a 1.5L engine but, in contrast to Renaults and Citroëns, they did not cause any public or commercial sensation. The 4x4 drive has for years been provided by a Dangel engine for the 504 robust pick-up trucks, the practical Partner, rejuvenated in Paris 2002, the Expert van and the J5 / Boxer delivery vehicles. Proof that the company pulled off the 4x4 technology is brought by the phenomenal winner of many rallies—the 205 Turbo 16 (1981), recast as the 205 Turbo 16 Grand Raid (1987, it won—along with its successor—11 out of 11 races including the "Dakar" in 1987 and 1988), replaced with the 405 Turbo 16 (1988, winner of the "Dakar" in 1989 and 1990) all the way to today's Peugeot 206 WRC, the king of the World Cup in 2000–02. The 205 Turbo 16 Grand Raid and the mechanically-identical 405 Turbo 16 finished first in the Pikes Peak 1988 and 1989. In Paris 2002, the company introduced a study of the Sésame—a small "urban 4x4 vehicle," only 146 inches long, a successor to the Escapade project from 1999.

Peugeot 203 R / RA / RB / VLTT / VPS ❷

Many Jeeps were left over after the war, but the government wished to have its own lightweight off-roader. In 1947, after much confusion, the authority in charge finally specified the technological parameters of the sought-after vehicle and invited tenders from big French producers. Neither Citroën, nor Renault, nor Peugeot were interested, and the contract went to Delahaye. In 1951-55, it supplied the army with vehicles. However, the army did not get used to their relatively complex design. Before the problems could be eliminated, Delahaye lost the contract, which meant the death of the company. The baton was taken over in 1955 by Hotchkiss. In 1957–66, it produced franchised Jeeps.

Peugeot woke up from lethargy and in August 1950 applied for a homologation of its own creation—the 203R—as a farming vehicle. One of the few vehicles similar to the Jeep was presented to army representatives. The model was mechanically identical to the Peugeot 203 sedan (powered by a 4V OHV 1290cc engine, 45hp) presented in 1948, and featured rigid axles with leaf springs. As the army found the

The Peugeot 203 VPS, 1950

The Peugeot 203 VPS

The Peugeot P4, 1986

engine too weak for its purposes, the company came up with two specimens of the 203RA the following year, with a 1468cc engine from the 403 sedan (the vehicle was also known as the 403RA or the VLTT (Voiture Légère Tout-Terrain=a lightweight off-road vehicle). Not even then was the army content. As many as 10 or 12 Peugeots were built. As the military Delahayes suffered from serious problems, Peugeot gave it a third try in 1954 with the 203RB—a modification with a modified front panel. The army ordered 12 units and tested them in 1955-56, but Hotchkiss was faster and won the army contract. Peugeot did not stop trying and in 1957 it seemed that the VSP (Vèhicule Spéciale Peugeot) was cured of its teething problems. Nevertheless, a buyer was not found, and thus the project was terminated.

Peugeot P4

The Hotchkiss Jeeps eventually reached retirement age in the late 1970s. In 1977, Stemat of Aveyron prepared an off-road prototype of the Veltt, based on the Peugeot 504, including gasoline and diesel engines. In February 1981, the Ministry of Defense signed a contract with Daimler-Benz to

produce 15,000 units of the G-Type in France. A hundred workers in the factory in Sochaux assembled the Peugeot P4's from German components and with French aggregates. A vehicle weighing 3,858 lbs could reach a top speed of 68 mph. A delivery version was launched in 1982, followed by 3 civilian versions in 1986, presented at the 1986 Val-d'Isère off-road motor show. They, too, had emergency canvas doors and a roof tilt. These vehicles, exported also to French dependencies, did not achieve good sales owing to high purchase and maintenance costs. They were relatively popular with firefighters. A Peugeot XD 3 2498cc engine (70.5hp @ 4500 1/min), known from the 504 sedans, was complemented by a gasoline 4V 1971cc power unit (87hp). It powered all wheels via a 4-speed transmission. A 2-speed reduction was available. Both rigid axles featured coil springs, and there was a stabilizer in the front. The model had a 95-and-112-in-long wheelbase, it was 165 / 183 in long, 67 in wide and 75 in high. It had a curb weight of 4,178/ 4,553 lbs and carried 1,653 / 2,205 lbs of cargo. The Peugeot-Talbot-Sport factory team sent a tuned P4 with 3.0L V6 engines (196hp) and 5-speed transmissions to the 1987 Rally Pharao and 1987 Dakar, with good results. In 1982–92, a total of 13,647 units were made.

The Peugeot 307 Caméléo, 2002

Phooltas (India)

The Phooltas Transmotives company based in Patna arose in 1991 from the Trishul Autocrafts Private company. For a while, Phooltas produced the Trishul Tourer, which evidently could not satisfy changing demands.

The Phooltas Champion, 1993

Phooltas Champion   ❶ ❷

From 1991 till the mid-1990s, when it suspended its activities, Phooltas focused on building a vehicle with the appearance and proportions of a Jeep. The Champion was designed in a similar way to the Tourer. Its 6-seat body was open and doorless. A 4V Simpsons (Perkins) P-4 3150cc engine (55hp @ 2400) was chosen as a power-provider. There was a 3-speed transmission. Customers who paid extra for permanent AWD version got an auxiliary 2-speed gear-reduction transmission on top. The vehicles featured rigid axles with longitudinal half-elliptic springs. Specifications: wheelbase—101," length—163.5 in, width—67 in, height—78 in and curb weight—4,652 lbs (4x2) or 4,795 lbs (4x4).

The Poncin VP 2000

The Poncin VP 2000

Poncin
(France)

Véhicules Poncin SA from Tournes, a company founded by Gilles Poncin, existed in 1981–93. The planned annual output was approximately 250 vehicles. The Ardennes Equipement company began participating in improving the 4x4 and 6x6 versions, as well as the development of an advanced 4x4 model. Poncin was supposed to move to new premises with a test bed in Sedan, France. The company exported its products to neighboring countries, and was gearing up for Egypt and the Near East. It has announced the sale of a franchise for its 4x4 and 6x6 vehicles to a Dubai-based company.

Poncin VP 2000 ❽

The company's specialty was vehicles designed for nearly untraversable terrains with an optional trailer of similar qualities. Rim bands were put on for driving through mud and snow. The floating VP was used for work on the beach, fishing or as a snowmobile. The standard VP 2000 and the VP 2025 were followed by the bigger VP 2500 and the VP 4000. All models featured 6x6 drive (the VP 2800 had 8x8).

A steel space frame bore a polyester laminate body. That guaranteed low weight, rust and water resistance. The VP was a 2-seat vehicle with a targa arch and a luggage space behind a flat 2V Citroën 2CV 602cc mid-engine (30hp). There was a 4-speed transmission. Tests results were full of praises for the acrobatic abilities of the vehicle in open country. The VP negotiated a 45° slope and side tilt. Its ground clearance was 8.7 in long. Length x width x height: 104 x 67 x 39 in. When empty, the vehicle weighed 1,367 lbs and carried up to 948 lbs of load.

Poncin 4x4 ❷

In the late 1980s, Poncin came up with an open 2-seat vehicle without side doors resembling the Jeep. Seats for 2 more persons could be mounted in the cargo area. The model had an optional canvas roof. A gasoline Renault 2165cc engine (106hp, 78 mph) powered the rear or all wheels. Alternatively, a Renault TD 2068cc power unit (88hp @ 4500) was available. A 4-speed transmission contained also 1 "long and slow gear" for driving off-road. The front and the rear differentials were, for an extra fee, equipped with a lock. The wheels were suspended independently with coil springs and disc brakes. The length with a spare wheel on the tail panel x height x width: 137 x 63 x 67 in; wheelbase—84 in, ground clearance—12.6 in. When empty, it weighed 2,535 lbs, and it carried a maximum load of 1,102 lbs. The Poncin 4x4 managed a 45° slope, and a 54° downhill grade. A new model—the De Luxe—was prepared for launch in 1991, and further plans included production of a new 4x4 off-roader with a 4V Ford 2.3L engine.

Poncin 6x6 ❷

A bigger and more rectangular "Poncin 6x6" with a targa arch was born in 1990. Poncin advertised it as a vehicle carrying up to 10 people or 2,205 lbs of cargo. It is mechanically identical with the 4x4 version. The only engine used is a gasoline 2.2L power unit (106hp, 75 mph). The Poncin 6x6 manages a maximum downhill grade of 45°. It is 177 in long, 69 in wide, 72 in high. The wheelbase length is 84 in between the 1st and 2nd axle, and 38 in between the 2nd and 3rd axle. The Poncin 6x6 has a 12.6-in-high ground clearance, and a 3,527-lb curb weight.

The Poncin 4x4

The Poncin 6x6

Porsche
(Germany)

The name of Ferdinand Porsche is mentioned in the Audi, Steyr and VW subsections. In 1930, he established a design office in Stuttgart, which prepared a large number of models. After the war, he started business in Gmünd, Austria, but soon moved the company to Stuttgart in Germany, whose economy seemed more promising. Some sports and race specials featured AWD, e.g., the incredibly expensive Porsche 959, based on the rather unexceptional 911, but with a rear 6V boxer engine (450hp) and computer-controlled differentials. The model made its debut in 1983. Its prototype won the 1984 Dakar and a series-made unit won the 1986 Dakar.

Porsche 597 ❷

Porsche built several 4WD vehicles, but did not mass-produce any of them. This state of affairs was to be changed by the 597 "Jagdwagen" model from 1954. In the course of 5 years, the company built 71 prototypes. They had a canvas tilt with one wide and later two shallow cutouts, and a heightened door sill instead of doors. These features lent the vehicle a 20-in fording depth. A spare wheel was mounted on the front panel, and a 1.5L (later 1.6L) boxer engine in the rear, and there was AWD. An empty 597 weighed at least 2,183 lbs. The first version had an 81-in-long wheelbase; the vehicles with a reinforced platform

from the final developmental phase had a wheelbase of 95 in. The army gave priority to the DKW Munga, which put an end to the Project 597.

Porsche Cayenne ❸

The SUV Porsche, the fastest series-produced 4WD, kept us waiting until the 2002 Paris motor show. The 5-seat 5-d Cayenne is mechanically related to the VW Touareg, which had a world premiere several hundred yards away. This Porsche combines high-quality equipment, the latest technologies and qualities of a sports car and a four wheel drive. The Cayenne S is powered by a gasoline V8 32v 4511cc VarioCam engine (340hp @ 6000, 150 mph, acceleration from 0 to 62 mph in 7.2s) in combination with 6-speed manual or automatic transmission. The Cayenne Turbo has the same engine, but with supercharging (450hp @ 6000, 103 mph, from 0 to 62 mph in 5.5s) and a Tiptronic 6-speed auto transmission.

By pressing a button on the steering wheel, the driver can "change gears" as he or she wishes. The drivetrain is represented by a sophisticated PTM (Porsche Traction Management), which under normal circumstances transmits torque via an inter-axle differential and a manual lockable multi-disc clutch in an optimum division between the axles— 38:62. It has a cross-country reduction. As soon as one of the axles begins to slip, the system automatically transmits up to 100% power on the non-problematic axle. Additionally, the mechanics includes PSM (Porsche Stability Management), ABD and ASR. The Cayenne has air suspension and 6 ground clearance levels adjustable by electrically-con-

The Porsche 597

The Porsche 959, 1986

trolled shocks. The standard level of ground clearance is 8.5 in. It can be lowered to 2.4 in on the highway, or heightened by 2.2 inches in the off-road. An active chassis adjustment (PASM) works only in one of three regimes—"Komfort," "Normal" and "Sport." A rear differential lock and disengageable stabilizers are charged extra. Other features: wheelbase—112 in, length—188 in, width—76 in, height—67 in, curb weight—(+)4,949 lbs, payload—1,797 lbs, overhang

angles—29° / 26°. The Porsche will drive through a 20-in-deep ford, with a 22-in air suspension.

The Porsche Cayenne S, 2003

Portaro
(Portugal)

The Portaro 260 DCM

The Lisabon-based Sociedade Electro-Mecánica de Auto-móveis company has been assembling the Romanian Aro 24 under the "Portaro" marque since the mid-1970s.

Portaro Celta ❷

The ambitious Portuguese have showcased models in Geneva since 1978. To the Celta 250 from 1976, the company added (in 1978) the Celta 260 Turbo and the Celta 260—the first Portuguese car to be equipped with a TD 4V Daihatsu 2530cc engine (D 75hp @ 3600, TD 95 @ 4300, 70 mph, TD 81 mph). The Portaro featured disc brakes. Two wheelbase lengths were available: 93 and 126 in (the Celta 320), with a 156.5 / 196-in length, a 70-in width and a 76 / 73-in height. A soft-top version had canvas sides either with or without a plastic "window." Its data were identical with those of the ARO. The vehicles had a 4-speed transmission and a reduction. Toward the end of the era. a 5-speed transmission was introduced. Later, the choice was extended by gasoline 4V Volvo engines: a supercharged Celta 210 PT Turbo 2127cc engine (155hp @ 5500, 99 mph), and a 230 PV 2320cc atmospheric engine (112hp @ 5000, 87 mph).

The Portaro 260 Celta

The Portaro 240

200

A column of Renaults in the Sahara desert, 1923

Renault (France)

In 1898, brothers Louis and Marcel Renault built the Voiturette 3/4 CV; subsequently, Louis had it patented and set about producing it. Marcel got killed in the 1903 Paris–Madrid car race. Louis ran the factory until the end of the war, when he was accused of collaborating with the Germans. The company was nationalized. After 1955, its trucks bore the marque of "Saviem," later reorganized to "RVI." Renault experienced both expansions and downfalls. It was privatized in the 1990s. In 1983–87, it owned the American AMC company, which also incorporated Jeep. In 1999, they bought 51% of the Romanian Dacia and 36.8% of the Japanese Nissan. The models presented after 2000 began to be unified with Nissan.

In 1923–25, Renault became entangled in competition with Citroën. It organized trans-Saharan and trans-African races of open Renaults 10 CV with 6x4 drive. After the war, it produced the Goélette R2086 4x2 trambuses and vans, which were taken up by the army with 6x6 and 4x2 chassis, or as the Galion R2167 4x4 Sinpar 1 $\frac{1}{2}$-ton vehicles. That is when Renault closely cooperated with its exclusive modifier of the R 4 / 6 / 12 road vehicles from 2x4 to 4x4 versions. In Geneva 1983, a "tougher" Renault 18 Break 4x4 was introduced, featuring a 1647cc engine (73hp), since 1985 produced in a 18 TX Break 4x4 version (with a turbo 2165cc engine, 103hp), and a 18 Break GTD 4x4 version introduced in March 1983 and featuring a TD 2068cc engine (67hp). The R 18 ended in 1986. It was replaced by the R 21, whose R Nevada station wagon version continued the 4x4 tradition, but it did not make a great impression. The Espace, the father of MPVs, was launched in February 1984. After February 1988, there was also the Espace Quadra 4x4.

Renault Colorale ❷

In 1950, the robust Colorale station wagon / minivan (a compound of Coloniale and Rurale) was introduced. Its body was taken from the Prairie taxi vehicle and a related Savane pick-up. In Paris 1951, the company showcased a 4x4 model, followed in 1952 by a series-model with a payload of 1,102 lbs in the off-road and 1,653 lbs on the road. It had permanent AWD, a 4-speed transmission and a 2-speed reduction. Power was provided by a gasoline 4V 2383cc engine (48hp @ 2800, 56 mph, in 1953-56 and then 60hp @ 4000). The axles were rigid with longitudinal leaf springs. An empty vehicle weighed 4,167 lbs. It had a 105-in-long wheelbase, it was 173 in long, 58 in wide, 71.5 in high, and had a 22.2-in-high ground clearance. The 4x4 models included: the Prairie, the Savane and the Pick-up. The Colorale went down best with farmers, the police force and, in 1954-56, the Norwegian army. One participant in the 1983 Dakar Rally followed the steps of adventurers with a truck featuring a Colorale body and a R 2087 4x4 chassis. In 1952-55, a total of 1,151 4x4 units were made.

The Renault Prairie R 2092, 1953

Renault 4 / 6 Rodéo, 5 Rodéo ❹

The Renault 4 Rodéo was introduced in 1970. It served well in the country and for "beach rides." It was derived from the R4—a popular vehicle with a front engine and 2x4 drive. It was produced for Renault by an A.C.L. company, later by a reorganized Teilhol. The Rodéo had a plastic body with a 4V OHV 845cc engine (34hp @ 5000). Its wheelbase was 95 in long and it had a curb weight of 1,444 lbs. This model was produced until 1981. In 1973 it was followed by a more rectangular and robust R6 Rodéo with a 1108cc engine (47hp @ 5300 68 mph) from the R6. A more modern power unit—a 1289cc engine (45hp @ 5000, 71 mph)—appeared in 1980. The various body modifications were covered with a canvas tilt. The last units were assembled in 1986–88 without much fuss. The 1981 Geneva motor show saw the debut of the rectangular Rodéo 5 with distinctive bumper guards,

side skirts and robust B-pillars. The first specimens were shiny orange combined with matt black. Its wheelbase was 96 in long, and its curb weight was 1,587 lbs. It featured the mechanics of the R5 and the well-known 1,108ccv engine. Teilhol made the model until 1982. The last time it appeared was in a pamphlet for 1985.

Renault Jeep (USA, France) ❷

In 1983–87, the company made use of its ownership of the make of Jeep. The Renault network distributed the Jeep CJ7 soft- and hard-tops (May 1982–87 with a D Renault 2068cc engine, May 1983–87 also with a gasoline Renault 1992cc engine), later replaced with the Jeep Wrangler Texan / Laredo / Sahara (1990, 2464cc engine). Another model was the Jeep Cherokee / Cherokee Chief—a 3-/5-d off-roader (1984–87 with a D 2068cc engine, since 1990 with a D 2068cc, and a year later with a TD). Another model—

The Renault 6 Rodéo

available after 1992—was the Cherokee Limited with a gasoline engine or a TD. Production of the Jeeps ended in 1993.

Renault Scenic RX4 ❸

In 1996, the company was the first to introduce a compact MPV—the Scenic based on the Mégane, 2x4—a lower middle class car. It was facelifted in the spring of 1999 and a year later, it was followed by the first Renault-made "SUV"—the Scenic RX4. The company established a category of small 2-liter SUVs. The model has been developed and produced in co-operation with Steyr. Its 5–d 5-seat body assumed a tougher appearance thanks to a higher placement, a side protection strip all around and a spare wheel in the rear. It has permanent AWD with a variable distribution of power between the axles. The front wheels, with a brake slip control, are engaged permanently, and the rear ones are engaged automatically once the viscous coupling is activated.

The Renault Rodéo 6

The RX4 has a 5-speed transmission and is powered by a 4V engine—either a gasoline 1998cc engine (140hp @ 5500, 112 mph), or a TD Common Rail 1870cc engine (140hp @ 4000, 103 mph). The body is self-supporting,

The Renault Rodéo 6 (left) and 4 (right)

An X-ray of the Renault Scenic RX4, 2000

with McPherson struts and a stabilizer in the front, and an independent suspension with coil springs and a stabilizer in the rear. Disc brakes are installed. In the off-road, the vehicle is much tamer than it might seem. Overhang angles—30°/36°, fording depth—9.8 in, slope—38°, wheelbase—103 in (the standard Scenic: 101 in), length—174 (164) in, width—70 (67) in, height—68 (66) in, ground clearance—7 (4.7) in, curb weight—(+)3,228 (2,726) lbs, payload—1,157 (1,235) lbs. A new Scenic was presented in Geneva in 2003 without an RX4 counterpart.

Renault Kangoo 4x4   ❷ ❽ ❹

The Kangoo from December 1997 again was in a class of its own. This practical elevated 5-d 5-seat van/station wagon has RWD. In April 1998, the Pampa model featuring a higher ground clearance appeared, followed finally in 2001 by the Kangoo 4x4. It differs by plastic fender flares. Its permanent 4x4 drive comes from the Nissan. At first, the front axle is engaged; once a front wheel slips, an electro-magnetically- and pressure-oil-controlled multi-plate clutch is activated and the rear wheels are engaged in a ratio of up to 57:43. The Kangoo 4x4 has an automatic anti-spin regu-

The Renault Scenic RX4, 2000

lation system which slackens the slipping wheels. There is 5-speed transmission. The Kangoo 4x4 uses gasoline engines—a 1870cc (80hp @ 4000, 99 mph), and a 1870cc dCi (80hp @ 4000, 88 mph). The body is self-supporting. The front wheels feature McPherson suspension, while the rear wheels have double-control arm suspension with coil springs. It is a practical vehicle, able to fend for itself even in extreme terrains. Its wheelbase is 103 in long. The vehicle itself is 157 in long, 66 in wide, 75 in high, and has an 8.1-in ground clearance, an 11.8-in fording depth, and its overhang angles are 29°/36°. When empty, it weighs 2,866 lbs and its payload is 1,213 lbs. In Paris 2002, Renault tested public opinion with a concept car of the Kangoo Break Up pick-up truck, with a "4x4 soul," an open tail panel and a rear roof part and high body side panels for transporting out-door sports equipment.

Renault –
lightweight utility vehicles and concept cars

Minibuses, minivans, pick-up trucks and platforms bearing the marque of Estafette featured a classic arrangement, while the 4 F 4 / F 6 compact vans had 4x2 drive. A successor to the Estafette—the Trafic—was available with 4x2, 2x4 and 4x4, as well as with a wide choice of body types and gasoline and diesel power units. The Master, its big brother, came with 4x2 and 2x4.

At the 1997 Geneva car show, the company showcased a 3-axle concept of the Pangea—an articulated expedition vehicle (which turned out to be a predecessor of the Kangoo), followed in 1998 by the Zo—a compact aluminum 3-seat off-road roadster; a vision of the future is suggested by the

The Renault Kangoo 4x4 on the track of the Dakar Rallye – 2000

A study of the Renault Kaleos, 2000

A study of the Renault Pangea; Geneva, 1997

Kaleos model, which combined the comfort and driving properties of a luxurious sedan with off-road characteristics including 4x4 drive. It has an adjustable chassis with a 4-inch range with a combination of a pneumatic and hydraulic suspension, a hybrid 2-L engine (170hp) and an electric motor, a Proactive auto transmission, ESP, an emergency brake booster and ASR. Other features: wheelbase—108 in, length—178 in, width—75 in, maximum height—67 in, approximate weight—4,410 lbs. The best teams in the world in Dakar go in fear of Jean-Louis Schlesser (a 1988 and 1989 raid rally world champion), who in connection with the Renault Sport team prepares the Renault Elf Buggy / Mégane with 2WD and a V6 3.5L engine; by 2000 he had won twice, and a third victory was snatched from him by his former partner Kleinschmidt on Mitsubishi Pajero, who committed a quite indecent foul on him.

A study of the Renault Zo; Geneva, 1998

The Renault Buggy Mégane during the 2000 Dakar Rallye

206

Repetti & Monteglio (Italy)

The Repetti & Monteglio car body works was established in 1960 and specialized in armored and iron-bound vehicles, designed for armed transport, and for post offices and other customers seeking to transport their money safely in a bulletproof limousine.

Repetti & Monteglio Panda 4x4   ❷ ❾

The company built patrol wagons based on the Fiat Panda 4x4 with armor-plating and downsized bulletproof windows. In the late 1980s and early 1990s, it came up with 4x4 prototypes including an open 2-seat off-roader and a sleeker soft-top for active relaxation.

The Repetti & Monteglio—the armored Panda 4x4

RMA a Amphicar (Germany)

The Rheinauer Maschinen & Armaturenbau GmbH company based in Rhineland, Germany, whose daily bread was producing pipes and fixtures for water, gas and petroleum products distribution, embarked in 1987 on developing an amphibious vehicle.

RMA Amphi-Ranger

This robust 3-d station wagon with a self-supporting aluminum waterproof body carried 4+2 persons. Its predecessor was the Amphi-Ranger 2800 SR (Seewasser-Resistent), which the company developed and produced for its own use in laying, inspecting and repairing pipes. The vehicle aroused interest, and the company decided to sell a modernized version of the RMA to other firms and private businessmen. (In Germany, it was against the law for a private individual to use a floating vehicle.) The sturdy RMA was mechanically identical with the Ford Scorpio 2,9i V6. At first, it was powered by a 2792cc engine (135hp @ 5200, 87

mph), replaced in 1986 by a 2933cc engine (145 hp @ 5500). For everyday driving, the rear wheels were engaged, but there was an option to activate RWD and use 100% differential locks on both axles. Movement in water was achieved by means of a pressure screw (9 mph). The wheels were suspended independently, with coil springs. Dimensions of the RMA: wheelbase—98.5 in, length—185 in, width—76 in, height—75 in, ground clearance—9.8 in. Other features: curb weight—4,277 lbs, payload—1,896 lbs. The vehicle managed to climb an 84% slope, and did not capsize in a 40° side tilt. Overhang angles—40°/35°.

In 1961–68, another German corporation produced the Amphicar—a recreational amphibious convertible. Out of 3,000 units, many were sold in the U.S. A self-supporting steel body offered a ride to a couple of adventurers. The Amphicar was powered by a British-made 4V Triumph Herald 1147cc engine (38.3hp @ 4750, 65 mph on the road and 7 mph in the water). The engine was mounted in the rear and powered the rear wheels via a 4-speed transmission. Movement in water was ensured by two screws. The vehicle had an 83-in long wheelbase, it was 171 in long, 62 in wide, 60 in high. It featured a ground clearance of 9.3 in, a curb weight of 2,315 lbs and a payload of 661 lbs.

The RMA Amphi-Ranger

The Amphicar, 1962

Samas
(Italy)

SAMAS

The Samas Yetti

Samas Yetti ❷

In 1968, the Societá Albese Meccanica Autoveicoli Speciali (SAMAS) company prepared the Yetti—an off-roader with a Fiat 850 engine. In 1971, the vehicle was equipped with a 4V Fiat 127 power unit (903cc, 47hp @ 6200, 62 mph), and the Samas Yetti 903 was born. The Yetti had RWD powered via a 4-speed transmission, but the rear wheels could also be engaged. Maneuvering was improved by steerable rear wheels. Additionally, a cross-country reduction and a rear differential lock were installed. The wheels were mounted on an independent control-arm suspension with Yetti coil springs. The body was either a soft-top or a hard-top. The Yetti had a 69-in-long wheelbase, a length of 122 in, a width of 58 in, a height of 71 in and a ground clearance of 12.2 in. When empty, it weighed 1,984 lbs and had a payload of 882 lbs, which according to the producer represented 5 persons and 110 lbs of luggage, or 2 persons and 728 lbs of cargo. The Yetti negotiated a slope of 100 %, and the maximum side tilt was 39°.

Santa Ana, Santana (Spain)

In the spring of 1954, the ministry of industrial affairs launched an industrialization program in the Jaén province, Northern Andalusia. Admittedly, the government officials did not have a specific idea of what they were doing, but that couldn't stop them from inviting tenders and seeking investors. Among the participants was Alfredo Jiménez Cassina, a young industrialist, with a plan to build a factory producing farming machinery among the world's biggest olive plantations. Surprisingly, he received support from the government. He and his friends bought land near Linares, Spain, and named it "Santa Ana." That is the origin of the company's name—Metalurgica de Santa Ana SA (MSA). The first assembly hall went up in 1955, but nobody knew what was going to be produced in it. A universal multi-purpose vehicle was agreed upon. As the only vehicles made in the country were Jeeps produced according to a franchise, Cassina showed interest in a franchise for Land Rover. Rover knew that mountainous, underdeveloped Spain held good prospects. It had looked into the possibility of assembling CKDs in 1953, but to no avail. Dictator Franco demanded that at least 70 % of components be made in Spain. Rover agreed and the contract was signed in 1958. Cassina's plans were supported behind the scenes by Tabanera Romagosa SA, an importer of Rovers. According to the contract, all responsibility fell on the Madrid-based importer, but soon it was clear that two can never rule the

roost. In March 1959, the contract was revised to include Rover and MSA as the two contracting parties. The first Land Rover left Linares in November 1958. The capacity of the assembly plant was 2,500 units, but no more than 800 units per year were made before 1968. Production grew steadily. The company manufactured transmissions for a local branch of Citroën in Vigo, and bought a franchise for a van. The Commer Santana was featured at the MSV Brno 1967. Farming machinery was also produced. The company expanded by adding a factory in Manzanares, a suburb of Ciudad Real, and a distribution center in La Carolina near Linares. Since 1981, the vehicles bore the marque of Land Rover Santana. The early 1980s were the heyday of Santana's fame and profits. Santanas would sometimes be seen at places where the British couldn't sell Land Rovers. Then the climate changed. However, not even the pressure of Japanese competition inclined the Spaniards to innovate the vehicles. The British soon developed an aversion to the excessively independent (competition-like) Spanish activities in Central and South America and Iran. Santanas were exported to Columbia, Afghanistan and Pakistan. The crisis climaxed in 1986, when Santana signed a franchise contract with Suzuki. Five years later, when both Land Rovers and Suzukis came from a single "stable," Rover terminated the partnership. The main reason was not competition production, but growing indebtedness. In England, Rover was trying to move on to more modern and luxurious models; Santana did not follow this trend. The Spanish thrived in Europe but they lost markets overseas. Under these circumstances, it was unthinkable in 1989 to launch the mass-production of Land Rover Santanas with leaf springs. In June 1990, Rover Group decided to sell its

23 % to the MSA company. Santana produced a total of 287,067 units with an 88" wheelbase, 143,779 units with a 109" wheelbase, and 44,355 specials and CKD car kits for export overseas. The earlier-mentioned "divorce" harmed Santana's interests a lot. In 1991, Suzuki became the key stockholder by gaining 49% of the company's stocks, and renamed it Santana Motor SA. Several hundred employees had to be laid off and, moreover, production for Citroën was discontinued. Things got so bad that in1993 Suzuki sold 83.74 % of its stocks to IFA holding, run by the regional government of

Andalusia. In 1994, the assembly line in Linares was stopped and Santana filed for bankruptcy. A year later, the government took complete control over the company. It managed to extend the contract with Suzuki by other models. Production was carefully launched and in 1996, the company showed a small profit. In 1998, the management defined a strategic plan of developing an off-road-vehicle. In 1999, the factory's total output was 34,355 units; a year later, it was 33,821. The contract with Suzuki came to an end in 2000, and a new one is currently in force until 2006. A new model was to be introduced in 1998 (there were rumors about a European off-roader with Ford or Peugeot engines), but the debut of the PS-10 concept car did not occur until the 1999 Sevilla car show.

Santana Land Rover ❷

The Santana Land Rover appeared in 1959. It was equivalent to the British LR Series II 88" and 109." It was fitted with 4V Rover gasoline 2286cc engines (57hp @ 4250, 59 mph), or with diesel 2052cc engines (52hp @ 3500). In 1962, the horsepower of the gasoline engine was enhanced to 62hp and export was launched simultaneously. Assembly of the vehicles in Britain was sometimes saved by supplies from Santana. As far back as 1961, the Spanish had received a "yes" from the British to export. The first units were headed to the Middle East, South America and Africa. In 1962, Santana moved on to the LR Series IIA. In 1968, 5-d Land Rovers were launched. They became popular among taxi-drivers in the Spanish countryside. The following year, another modernization of the vehicles took place and an improved military variant was introduced. In 1970, the Especial models were

The Santana Land Rover 88, 1989

launched, featuring "de lujo" (= de luxe) equipment. In 1972, the appearance of the headlights now situated in the fenders changed, and more. In Britain, the Series IIA were produced at that time, and this change did not show until the later Series III. A one-piece front glass was introduced in Spain in 1972; in England, it did not come until 1986. A total of about 10,000 units of the Santana Series IIA were made. In 1977, the Santana 109 made its debut. It came exclusively in a stretched version and with a gasoline (104hp) or a diesel (94hp) 6V engine, both of the same capacity—3429cc. The military Santana 88 and 109 Militar were born in the late 1970s. Version 88 is derived from the British Lightweight, with a gasoline 4V 2286cc engine. The army bought approximately 3,500 units, others were exported to Egypt, Morocco and probably also Algeria. The 4V engines made in 1981 were marked by a five-bearing crankshaft but the camshaft was propelled by sprockets—not by a belt, as was the original. The 109 models with 6V engines and Especial (= station wagon) hard-top bodies were equipped with openable side windows and a laminated roof. Santana terminated the Series III in 1982, when yearly output had reached 4,000 units. In October 1982, it was replaced by the Series IIIA. The Spanish couldn't get over a British innovation—coil springs and permanent 4x4 drive. They feared the reaction of their South American customers. The IIIA is in fact a markedly improved Series III with a couple of "parabolic" leaf springs. Drum brakes in the front were replaced with disc brakes, and a steering booster was added. In 1982, the luxurious Cazorla models were introduced. In addition to the existing 4-speed transmission, the vehicles were later equipped with a new 5-speed LT85 transmission (like the British One Ten), at an extra charge, with the following regimes: 2-wheel drive, neutral, AWD, and 4x4 with a reduction. The vehicles were fitted with the above-mentioned 4- and 6-V diesel- or, less often,

gasoline-engines. The original diesel 4-V engine remained in use, with a new addition in the form of a turbocharger (75hp). The model was civilized by means of a different grille, a one-piece front and three wipers. It was similar in appearance to the LR One Ten. Its description is equivalent to more luxurious Station Wagon models; the appearance of the rest was left in the Series III phase.

Models: the 109 4-Cil, the 109 6-Cil, the Super Turbo (an old 4V TD), and the Cazorla (109," 6V gasoline / diesel engines), the 88 / 109 Super, later the 88 / 109 Super Turbo, and lastly the most luxurious variant—the Cazorla 6-Cil. The Santana Gran Capacidad—a long 119" pick-up truck—had the appearance of the Series III, only 4V engines and a 6,945-lb curb weight. It was equivalent to the HCPU British model. The Santana Series IIIA was produced until the end of 1980s. Many units were exported as CKDs to Iran. In 1987, the firm attempted to rationalize its program by reducing the number of models, engines and transmissions. The 2.25L engines of both fuel types were written off and replaced by a British gasoline 4V 2.5-L and a turbo-diesel. The gasoline engines were soon mounted only into units for export. The only transmission to survive was the LT85. Production of the Ligero, Turbo and Cazorla models was discontinued. They were replaced by the basic 2.5 DC, 2.5 DL and 3.5 DL, the luxurious 2500 DC, 2500 DL and 3500 DL, and the 2.5 DLE (D=diesel, C=corto for "short," L=largo for "long," E=especial). Specifications were almost identical with those of their British cousins: slope—45°, side tilt—43°, overhang angles of the 109" (and the 88" in parentheses)—53° (46°) / 27° (36°), ground clearance—8.3 in (7.9 in). Dimensions: length x height x width—187 in, the Especial Station Wagon—182 (149) in x 79 (77) in x 66 in, wheelbase—109 in (88 in), curb weight—3,461 lbs, Especial Station Wagon—3,902 (3,086) lbs, payload—2,624 lbs, Especial Station Wagon—2,183 (1,676) lbs.

The Santana Land Rover Cazorla 6 Cilindros, 1982

Santana Ligero   ❷

In 1980, civilian customers finally lived to see the military lightweight Santana—a leisure time vehicle aptly named Ligero (=lightweight). The Ligero sold wonderfully. It was a genuine Spanish modification with an impractical, minimalized, aluminum open body, with rectangular headlights and a massive tubular frame; it was available in yellow, orange or white. In time, disc brakes were installed in the front and torsion bars in the rear. Basic dimensions: length x height x width—144 x 78 x 62 in, wheelbase—88 in, ground clearance—8.3 in. The Ligero weighed 3,329 lbs and carried 1,433 lbs of persons and cargo. Production was terminated in 1987.

Santana Forward-Control 1300 to 3500   ❷ ❽

In 1967, the company introduced the Santana 1300, equivalent to the British Forward-Control. The model, based on the LR Series IIA 109," was produced until 1977. In 1978, a bigger 2-ton Santana 2000 based on the LR was introduced, including a version with a trambus cab. It was inspired by the British FC with a 101" chassis. The Spanish model differed in terms of a wheel suspension and was fitted exclusively with 6-V engines, in contrast to the original with a V8. The factory produced chassis, pick-up trucks, pick-up trucks with a cab for 4, dumptrucks, 4-seat dumptrucks and 8-seat, slightly uncomfortable minibuses. The design of the front and rear panels was a Spanish rarity. This model did not bear the name of Land Rover. By 1990, a total of 920 units had been made. Even after the contract with LR had run out, the off-road trucks powered by 6V engines continued to be produced. In 1994, the year when production was discontinued, they bore the name Santana 2500 and Santana 3500. All models had permanent AWD, but after the 6V engines were introduced and the rear axle was reinforced, they got an option to disengage the FWD.

The Santana 1300, Spain, 1999

Santana 2.5 ❷

After the Brits had stepped out, MSA launched production of the LR Series IV, but without the marque of Land Rover. There were the 88" and the 109" with coil springs, bodies roughly equivalent to the Series IIIA, but in a pure utility form. The luxurious versions disappeared. Only 6V diesel engines were retained, while the gasoline 4Vs were featured only in the vehicles for export. Models: the 2.5DL, the 2.5DC and the export models — the 2.5GC and the 2.5GL (G for "gazole" = gasoline). Production of the Series IV was stopped in February 1994.

Santana M-300 ❷ ❾

M-300 is an abbreviation for a military prototype (M=military), never mass-produced, based on the Santana Gran Capacidad with a 119" wheelbase and an Italian D 6V VM engine (105hp). MSA pinned its hopes on the model. At that point, partnership was considered with Nissan Motor Ibérica, but that company had its own off-roader — the Patrol. In early 1994, this intention died the same death because of MSA's deep financial problems.

Santana Suzuki SJ 410 ❷

The contract required the Spanish to manufacture up to 10,000 small Suzuki off-roaders per year. The Suzuki considered it a way of circumventing customs regulations. Assembly of the SJ 410 started in 1985, followed by the SJ

413 in 1986. The original 1L vehicles were made only in Japan. After transferring production to Santana, the original engine was replaced with a 4V 1324cc power unit (63hp), since 1992 with 68hp and a 4-speed transmission (SJ410), and after March 1987 (for all SJ410 and SJ413 models) a 5-speed manual transmission. The driver chooses between 4x2 and 4x4 drive. The SJ410 / SJ413 has an 80-in wheelbase and the following dimensions: length x height x width — 135.5 x 66 x 60, later 63 in. The model weighs +2,028 lbs and has a ground clearance of 8.3 in. The available body versions include a hard-top, a soft-top, a stretched pick-up truck, the Sport, Style models and the limited-series

The Santana Suzuki SJ 410 Courréges

Rhino and Tobago. In 1989, the SJ 413 was renamed "Samurai."

Santana Suzuki Samurai ❷

The Samurai, including a pick-up version, was launched in 1989. A special model on the home market in 1990 was the Samurai MIL. The Samurai Long Body, another interesting model, stretched by 21 in, made its debut in Barcelona 1997.

The model underwent modernization in 1999. It is powered by a gasoline 1.3L engine (69hp) and carries 694–882 lbs of cargo. A diesel 1.9L power unit (64hp) is also available. The offer consists of a 3-d station wagon, a 3-d convertible and a 3-d hard-top. In the early 1990s, the Courréges special model was distributed in France. Production of the Samurai in Japan was terminated at the end of 1997.

The Santana Samurai Pick Up, around 1997

The Santana Suzuki Samurai Long Body, around 1997

Santana Suzuki Vitara ❷

The Santana Suzuki Vitara, 1991

The Vitara is another model that was not produced in Japan after 1997. In 1990, a 2-d beach convertible was born, and a 5-d station wagon was also available, featuring a longer wheelbase. In addition to the original Japanese gasoline 4V 1.6L (80hp) and 1.6L16v (96hp) engines, a modern diesel Peugeot HDI 1.9L power unit (90 hp) came into play in 2001. According to the information given by the producer, the ground clearance is 8.3 in. Special models include: the Mustique (1992), the Rossini (1994), the SE Executive (1990), the Sport—a foundation for further improvements, the Verdi (1994) and the X-EC (1993).

Santana Suzuki Jimny ❷

In Barcelona 1999, the company presented the Santana Suzuki Jimny Canvas Top Cabrio—a beach vehicle with a gasoline 1.3L engine (80 or 82hp). The newcomer of the year 2002 was a special model—the Suzuki Jimny Pepe Jeana.

Santana PS-10 ❷

After the premiere of its concept car in Sevilla 1999, the series-made orthodox PS-10 was modestly launched in Paris 2002. The resurrected company claims that producers of off-roaders have abandoned the original formula and launched into the fashionable SUV sector. Santana offers a genuine off-roader for the most extreme work conditions of professionals. Even civilian vehicles must meet army criteria. In terms of shape, it is more than inspired by the Santana 2500 (ex-LR Series IV); it is differentiated through its front and rear masks. Its body is made of aluminum with a sandwich plastic-laminate roof. An optimalized ladder frame bears a 4V D Common Rail IVECO/PS10 2.8L engine (125hp

@ 3600, 87 mph). The engine is connected with a 5-speed LT-85 transmission with a reduction. The Santana has permanent 4x4 drive, with an option to disengage the front wheels. It features rigid axles with longitudinal elliptic springs, and disc brakes. It negotiates a 20-in-deep ford, a 45° slope, a 40° side tilt, and has an 8.3-in-high ground clearance. Its overhang angles are 50°/30°, or 60°/38° for the military version. It has a payload rating of 2,205 lbs. The PS-10 has the following basic dimensions: length x height x width—184 x 69 x 79 in, wheelbase—110 in, curb weight—6,724 lbs. The Paris motor show received information about these models: a 5-d station wagon with an elevated roof with or without a non-glass rear panel; an ambulance, a fire engine, an emergency repair vehicle. Military versions: a pick-up truck with up to 10 seats, a soft-top and a paratrooper vehicle.

The Santana PS-10 military paratrooper vehicle, 2002

Savio
(Italy)

The Stabilimenti Savio G. company was founded by Giuseppe Savio in 1919 in a suburb of Turin, Italy. It went bankrupt in 1989 and was subsequently remolded into the Savio SpA Holding. In Turin in 1976, it showed the potential of the Fiat Campagnola. The Savio Albarella from Turin 1968 was another beach-off-roader creation (4x2) inspired by the Fiat 500 F. The Savio 127 Albarella (2x4) was introduced in Turin 1971. Similar to it were the Panda 30 / 45 and the Uno. Nowadays, Savio builds ambulances, mail delivery vehicles and a transporters of valuables, and lightweight armored vehicles for the police and armed forces. They are sold in Italy, Greece and Tunisia.

Savio Jungla

The Jungla made its debut in Turin in 1965, but large-scale production was not launched until a year later. The vehicle was designed by Fiat, but produced by Savio. A rear 4V Fiat 600D 767cc engine (32hp, SAE, 59 mph) powered the rear

The Savio Savana, 1966

wheels. All wheels had independent suspension. The Jungla with a 54-in-long wheelbase was 126 in long, 79 in wide, 56 in high, and had an 8.5-in ground clearance. It weighed 1,322 lbs and had a curb weight of 838 lbs. The vehicle managed a 30% slope and a 35° side tilt. In time, the "600" was replaced by the Spanish Seat 600E. The output of the first six-year period was about 2,000 units, with a total output of ca 3,200 units by 1974. The same assembly line produced negligible numbers of the bulkier Savio Savana (Turin 1966) with Fiat 124 mechanics. The 1974 Turin car show saw the debut of the Jungla 126 (594cc, 23hp, 65 mph). Production was discontinued a year later. The model was on offer in the second half of the 1970s.

The Savio Jungla 600, 1992

The Savio Albarella

Sbarro
(Switzerland)

Franco Sbarro was a car-racer, designer, manufacturer and distributor of cars. In the 1990s, he founded and now runs a school of car design in the hills above Geneva. At the 1986 Geneva motor show, he presented a study of an overgrown buggy featuring Boeing wheels and based on the Mercedes G, the Monster "G" (4x4). In 1990, he launched the Evasion BX 4x4—a 4-seat beach study with a plastic mono-cockpit and a curb weight of 1,984 lbs. He used a Citroën BX chassis platform, while keeping the 1.9L engine (109hp @ 6000). The model had 5-speed transmission, an inter-axle differential, a torsen differential in the rear, and disc brakes. To the 2003 Geneva car show, he brought the unique Citroën 4x4, which enthralled many potential customers.

The Sbarro Evasion BX 4x4, 1990

Sbarro Windhound ❷

In Paris in 1978, he surprised everybody with his large 3-d off-road station wagon de luxe. It's designed to carry any power units ranging between V6-V12, according to each customer's wish. The showcased specimen was fit with a BMW 3.0 CSI engine, but in 1978–85, when Sbarro built customized vehicles, the clients opted for Mercedes and Jeep engines. A 4-d variant was available after 1979. The choice of transmissions included 4- or 5-speed manual or automatic transmissions. Standard features included cross-country reductions and 4x2 or 4x4 drive. The wheels were suspended independently with coil springs and transversal torsion stabilizers. Hydraulics lent the model a ground clearance of between 9.8 and 16.5 inches. The top speed oscillated between 112 and 124 mph. The wheelbase was 106 in long, and the model was 67 in wide and 71 in high.

The Sbarro Windhawk 6x4 hydraulic

The Sbarro Windhound 4x4

Interior of the Sbarro Windhound 4x4

Sbarro Windhawk ❷

Geneva 1980 witnessed another stage of the Wind-hound's development. A third powered axle had been added. (A year later, the company brought to Geneva an alternative version with RWD.) This model was mounted on a Mercedes G chassis. The engine was taken from the 450 sedan, but Windhawk could again feature any engine. It had a 5-speed manual transmission + 2 reductions and all three differentials with locks. This 5-d station wagon weighed 4,409–5,512 lbs and had a 112-in-long wheelbase (28 in between the rear wheels); it was 67 in wide, 71 in high, its ground clearance was 10.6 in high and it had a top speed of about 112 mph. The total number of Sbarro Windhawks could virtually be counted on the fingers of one hand.

The Sbarro Windhound 4x4

The SCAM at the Baja Italia, 2002

The SCAM, 2002

SCAM
(Italy)

In 1995, development work began on a lightweight off-road extreme truck in Gavirate near Varese, Italy. The SCAM prototype was introduced at the 1998 SAIE exhibition in Bologna. In 1998, the company was joined by a producer of the Gasolone lightweight universal trucks. Since 2000, the company has been producing the SM series (for lighter terrains) and the SMT series (for more extreme terrains); in total, about 200 units are produced per year, mainly as carriers of

special superstructures. Some were bought by the armies of Spain and Poland. It is fair to say that the SCAM is functionally identical with but more advanced than Bremach (the same designer, Mr. Brenna). The SCAM is differentiated mainly by its frame and AWD—the Bremach has disengageable FWD. The SCAM features permanent wheel drive on both of its rigid axles with leaf springs and a stabilizer, a rear differential lock and an inter-axle differential lock, and a dual 6-speed gear-reduction transmission. Reduction is engaged at a standstill and a front differential lock is available on request. The cab is a modified Fiat. The vehicles with a 112-or-126-in-long wheelbase are powered by TD Iveco 2.8L engines (125hp).

The SCAM in Africa, 2002

Scoiattolo
(Italy)

The AP Scoiattolo, 1971

The La Nuova Carrozzeria company based in Arco, Italy, was a specialist in off-roaders and leisure-time vehicles. In 1971, it was part of the Carrozzeria Arrigo Perini (AP) corporation. Later, its vehicles were distributed with the marque of Scoiattolo.

Scoiattolo ❹

A prototype of the Scoiattolo (=squirrel), 4x2, emerged in 1966, but series-production was not launched until 1969. The model's doorless body must have been too constricted for 4 people. A 2V 499.5cc engine (22hp @ 4600, SAE, 50 mph) from the Fiat 500 purred in the rear, connected with 4-speed transmission. All wheels were suspended independently. Specifications: wheelbase—51 in, length—112 in, width—72 in, ground clearance—9 in, curb weight—1,146 lbs, and payload—728 lbs. It existed until 1973. In 1975, it was replaced by the Scoiattolo II with Fiat 126 mechanics (594cc, 23hp @ 4700, 50 mph). The wheelbase was now 73 in long, and the model itself was 117 in long, 54 in wide, 61 in high, and had a 5.5-in ground clearance and a curb weight of 1,455 lbs.

Super Scoiattolo ❷ ❹

The Super Scoiattolo (4x4) was mechanically identical to the Seat 600. It featured a 4-seat body with a couple of emergency doors and a roof borne by steel tubular frames. A 4V Fiat 600 D 767cc engine (32hp @ 4800, SAE, 56 mph) powered all—independently suspended—wheels, via a 4-speed transmission. Specifications: wheelbase—51 in, length—116 in, width—179 in, ground clearance—8.7 in, curb weight—1,367 lbs, payload—661 lbs. This model managed a 100 % slope, a 40° side tilt and a 12-in-deep ford.

The Scoiattolo, 1981

The Sinpar R4 military vehicle

The Sinpar R4 Plein Air

Sinpar
(France)

The Sinpar represented the 4x4 mechanics of Renault and Saviem in France since the 1960s. Conversions were carried out with the official approval of Renault. The vehicles were sold by selected distributors of the makes. The Appareils Sinpar company is located in Colombes, France. In addition to 4x4 drive, it also offered its own 4x4 body variants, mostly of convertibles or beach vehicles. Besides cars, the company also sounded out lighter utility vehicles. In 1968, the firm prepared the Torpedo S—an off-roader with a body supplied by the Brisonneau & Lotz company—but series-production in France did not occur; the vehicles were brought to life by a Renault representative in the Philippines.

Renault 4 4x4 and 6 4x4   ❶ ❹

The Renault 4 4x4 Sinpar (1964–83) featured a standard road body; alternatively, it came as a glassed-in van. In contrast to the run-of-the-mill 2x4 "population," these vehicles featured a "4x4" sign on the grille. Sinpar added RWD. In order to engage the RWD, it was necessary to stop the vehicle, or drive at a maximum speed of 0.6 mph. Space requirements called for a modification of the fuel tank and other chassis components. All wheels remained on independent suspensions. Besides attractive factory bodies, including the open Plain Air with trapezoid side door cutouts, the best-known models were the Plain-Air, the Pick Up, the Torpedo, the Ambulance and a lightweight vehicle for the armed forces. In the early 1960s, the R4 4x4 Sinpars successfully participated in a number of races held in France and North Africa. A similar principle was used in building and distributing variations of the bigger Renault 6 4x4 Sinpar fastback "Berline," or the Fourgonnette delivery vehicle.

The Sinpar R4 4x4 Fourgonnette

Renault Sinpar NBS 12   ❹

In the early 1970s, Sinpar and Renault sold the Renault NBS 12 together. "NBS" are the first letters of the French words neige-boue-sable (=snow-mud-sand). The Renault got a new rigid rear axle, and the original FWD had been changed to permanent 4x4 drive. Features available at a premium included a clutch of bigger diameter and a "super first gear" for especially slow motion, which replaced the cross-country reduction. Power was provided by a standard gasoline 4V 1289cc engine (60hp @ 5250, SAE). On request, a fuel tank with a 24 gal. capacity was installed instead of the standard 13 gal. tank. The available body versions were equivalent to those of the R12—a 5-seat station wagon and a 2-seat delivery vehicle. Specifications: curb weight—2,194 lbs, payload (including crew and cargo)—2,601 lbs, length—173 in, wheelbase—70.5 in.

Utility vehicles
Sinpar Renault / Saviem   ❽   ❾

A useful helper in the communal domain was the compact Sinpar Castor, featuring a 75-or-87-in-long wheelbase. The vehicle was 141 (164 in) long, 67 in wide and 90 in high. It was powered by a diesel engine (75hp), mounted longitudinally in a trambus cab under the driver's bench. The transmission was installed under the rear part of the engine and distributed power to all wheels. The cab came either as a soft-top or a hard-top (Torpedo). The Castor served as

a carrier of all kinds of equipment. Other types included the Super Goelette with a capacity to carry 1,764 lbs of cargo, and the Super Galion with a 3,307 lbs payload. They featured a trambus cab, permanent AWD, and managed to climb up a 40% slope. They came either with gasoline or diesel engines, a cab with either 1 or 2 rows of seats, or alternatively a Torpedo cab. Sinpar distributed a chassis (4x4), with a Mini Camion cab—the MC 2 and MC 4 with a load capacity of 2t and 4t respectively. A large number of units were taken up by the armed forces.

The Sinpar Super Goelette

Sovamag
(France)   SOVAMAG

Sovamag is practically a synonym for heavyweight military vehicles of the marque of Auverland, which is now part of the Groupe Servanin. The company focused on off-roaders and special vehicles with a payload rating between 1,102 lbs and 5,516 lbs. The company offers 3 model series of vehicles to the armed forces, rescue squads or firefighters.

Auverland "Militaire"

This lightest series managed to keep the marque of Auverland. It contains a range of vehicles including semi-civilian models and sheer specials featuring components and chassis of the Auverland A3, A3 SL and A4.

Sovamag TC 8 / 10

The TC 10 series is the centerpiece of the offer. It succeeded the TC 8 A from September 1988 and was modernized in January 1991. It was equipped with a diesel Peugeot 2498cc engine (71hp @ 4500, 81 mph), and had the following specifications: wheelbase—109 in, length—163.5 in, curb weight—3,726 lbs. Its body was made of steel and featured 3 doors, 8 seats and a canvas roof. The TC 8 / 10 is closely related to the A3. A ladder frame is reinforced with tubular cross members. Both axles are rigid with longitudinal leaf half-elliptic springs. The body was welded from a steel plate. A rectangular hood covers a 4v TD SOFIM 2800cc engine with 92hp at most, and @ 3600. There is a 5-speed SOFIM transmission, connected with a 2-speed Auverland transfer transmission, which makes it possible to disengage the FWD. The rear differential is equipped with a manual

The Sovamag TC 24 Pompier fire engine, 2000

The Cellule Ambulance, 2000

lock. The twelve series versions include: a chassis with a 2-d cab; a 2-d Pick Up truck and platform truck with a Baché tilt; several variants of a minibus, including the armored Blindé SL; the Pompier fire engine and other tank containers; and the Ambulance for 2 or 4 injured persons. The vehicles are able to get through a 24-in ford, climb up a 45° slope, or negotiate a 40° side tilt; its overhang angles are 53°/44°. The factory produces 2 wheelbase lengths: a short—109 in (the Court), and long—121 in (the SL=Super Long). Length (for the TC 10 DT/TC 10 DT SL models)—175 / 193 in, height—83 in, width—65 in, ground clearance—9.4 / 10.6 in, curb weight—the same versions (chassis with a cab)—4,123 / 4,277 lbs, payload—2,491 / 3,439 lbs.

Sovamag TC 24

Broadly speaking, what has been said about the design of the TC 10 is also true about the TFC 24. Its engine is tuned to 122hp @ 3600, 68 mph. It features an auxiliary transmission but not the Auverland type. The half-elliptic springs are assisted by a pressure pneumatic system, and there is a limited slip differential in the rear. The vehicles negotiate a 35-in ford, a 45° slope, and a 35° side tilt. Their overhang angles

The Sovamag TC 10 Ambulance

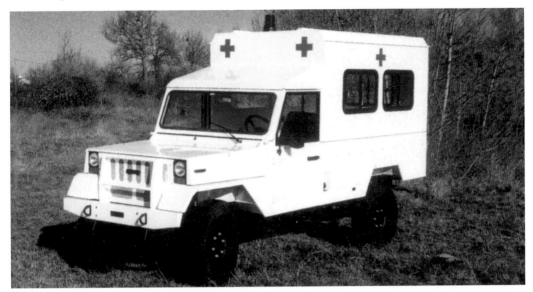

are 65°/45°. Two wheelbase lengths are series-made: short—142 in (the Court), and long—173 in (SL–Super Long). The length of the chassis (for the TC 24/TC 24 SL models) is 203 / 242 in respectively. The vehicles are 90 / 93 in high, 78 in wide and feature an 11-in ground clearance. The curb weight of the same version (chassis with a cab) is 5,357 /5,512 lbs, payload is 5,666 / 5,512 lbs. There are more than 12 body types. Trucks for 3 passengers in the cab and 14/24 men in the well are used for transporting army personnel; these trucks are also available in an armored form, and/or with a trailer. Other models include chassis with cabs, various platform trucks, armored minivans, armored vehicles, and tank containers.

The Sovamag TC 24 Baché Canvas Top platform truck

The SsangYong Istana, 1995

SsangYong
(South Korea)

The origins of this corporation go back to 1939, when a number of independent textile producers and other commodities were consolidated. The SsangYong Corp. was established in 1954. One of its divisions—the SsangYong Motor Company (SYMC)—claims to have been founded in 1954. But that is not the case: it was the Ha Dong-Hwan—a producer of off-roaders and trucks and buses—that was founded at that time. In 1977, it was renamed the Dong A Motor Company, to be swallowed up by the SsangYong Business Group in 1986, which changed it to "SYMC" in 1988 and incorporated the British Panther into it. In 1991, they bought a franchise to produce light utility and passenger Mercedes vehicles including engines and transmissions. In return, Mercedes obtained 5 % of the SYMC. (Utility

Mercedes vehicles have been made since 1994, passenger cars since 1996.) The factories are situated in Songtan and Pupyong, suburbs of Seoul, South Korea. In the mid-1990s, the Istana (="palace" in Malayan)—a 4x2 minibus and van were introduced in Europe, following 4 years of preparations; however, sales were not satisfactory. In 1998, SsangYong became part of Daewoo. SsangYong produces its models under the original name as well as with a Daewoo marque. The SsangYong off-road vehicles are assembled in Indonesia, Malaysia and, in 1998–2000, also in Poland. In 2001, the company took a high number of draconian money-saving measures, but the objective of selling 120,000 units was reached, and sales are rising.

SsangYong Korando 4x4 ❷

SsangYong took over the producer of Jeeps—the Dong A, or, more precisely, Keohwa. In August 1988, the company revamped the vehicles. This explains the origin of the name

The SsangYong Korando 4x4, 1994

The SsangYong Korando, 1998

"Korando 4x4" as a one-word linguistic corruption of "Koreans can do." The models were exported to over 30 countries, including Europe since the early 1990s. A 3-d station wagon did not achieve as much popularity as a 2-d convertible (or a soft-top). The vehicles seated 4, 6 or 9 persons. In 1996, the Korando Adventures model was available in Italy, featuring numerous camping accessories. The axles were rigid with leaf springs and telescopic shocks. A 4V D Daewoo 2238cc engine (68hp @ 4000, 78 mph) with whirl chambers was mounted in front of a ladder frame. Other features included a 5-speed transmission, freewheels in the wheel hubs, a reduction and an option to disengage the FWD. The Korando negotiated a 45° slope and a 38° side tilt, its overhang angles were 45°/30°. The wheelbase was 95 in long (the K-4 and the K-6), or 114 in long (the K-9). Other specifications included: length—152 / 184 in, width—67 in, height—73 in, curb weight—3,505/ 3,417 lbs, payload—1,014 lbs. Production was terminated sometime in 1998.

SsangYong KJ – MJ ❷

After 1995, the program was rejuvenated by Mercedes-Benz franchised components. In the late 1990s, the exported units were marked as "SsangYong KJ" (for a 3-d later known as "Korando"), and "MJ" (for a 5-d Musso with a longer wheelbase). The later-used model names have been complemented by the KJ / MJ code names since 1998.

SsangYong Korando / KJ – second generation ❷

The 1995 London motor show experienced the debut of a prototype of a more richly equipped generation of the Korando, followed by a series-produced model a year later. It has also been sold as Daewoo since 1998. The original concept of a 3-d hard-/soft-top did not change, while the body

curves drifted apart from the Jeep. Their offer included an austere military version. The prototype featured a 4V E 602 Mercedes D 2874cc engine (95hp @ 4000); the series model was also equipped with an E 20 gasoline 1998cc power unit (150hp @ 4000, 16v, 106 mph), an E 661 / 601 D 2299-L (80hp @ 4000, 16v, 93 mph), an E 662 L / EL D 2874cc engine (100hp @ 4100, 99 mph), an E 23 gasoline 2295cc engine (160hp @ 3800, 112 mph), and an E 32 gasoline 3198cc power unit (210hp @ 4000, 24v, 130 mph). The Korando has AWD or RWD. It has either a 5-speed manual transmission, or a 4-speed automatic Daimler-Benz transmission; a 2-speed gear-reduction transmission, a rear limited slip differential and ABD are available on request. The front axle has independent torsion bar suspension with a stabilizer, while the rear axle is rigid with leaf springs and Panhard rod. There are disc brakes, and ABS and ABD on request. The wheelbase is 97 in long. Other features include: length—168 in, width—73 in, height—72.5 in, ground clearance—7.7 in, slope—40.3°, side tilt—44°, fording depth—20 in, overhang angles—28.5° / 35°. In 1999, the

The SsangYong Korando Family, 16th place, Dakar 1994

model won the Panpas Rally in Argentina and the Baja Rally in Mexico. In 2000, a version with an uncovered rear roof part was introduced.

SsangYong Korando Family ❷

The Korando Family model represented a comfortable 5-d station wagon with rich equipment. In the early 1990s, a small number of units were exported to Europe, for example France. The Family is a retouched version of the older generation of the Isuzu Trooper. It was introduced in March 1990. This 7-seat model had the following versions: the R and the RS. This ladder frame vehicle had the front wheels suspended independently with torsion bars and a stabilizer, and a rigid axle with leaf springs and a Panhard rod in the rear. The engine—a 2,2L Diesel was equivalent to that of the Korando 4x4 (70hp @ 4000). Some units were fitted with an alternative—a D Peugeot XD 2498cc engine (79hp @ 4500). It featured a five-speed transmission, a reduction and optional 4x4 or 4x2 drive. Its wheelbase was 104 in long. The vehicle was 178 in long, 66 in wide, 70 in high, and had a 7.9-in-high ground clearance. It weighed 3,704 lbs and had a payload of 1,235 lbs. The Family tackled a 38° slope, a 38° side tilt and had 38°/28° overhang angles. It finished eighth in the 1994 Dakar race. In addition to the R (basic) and the RS (sports) models, the lineup later included the RV (luxury, D), the RX 2.6i (sports-luxury, gasoline engine) and a utility VAN. Besides the original 2.2L engine (R, RS, now 68hp @ 4300), the RX 2.6i was also fit with a gasoline 4-V Isuzu 2559cc power unit, (120hp @ 5000), and a D 4-V (RV) Peugeot XD3P 2498cc engine (79hp @ 4500). The rear wheel suspension now consisted of five elements, including a stabilizer and coil springs. The vehicle

The SsangYong Korando Family, 1994

negotiated a 42.5.o slope and a 38.9° side tilt. Since 1995, the Family II "generation" (New Family) was available, differing from the previous version only in details, except for the engine—a franchised 4-V Mercedes 2299cc power unit (154hp @ 4000). Keeping the same wheelbase length, the vehicle was 178 in long, 69 in wide, 74 in high, featured a 7.9-in ground clearance and a curb weight of 3,979 lbs. It seated 7/9 passengers. Production was ended around 1998.

SsangYong Musso ❷

The luxury Musso, with ambitions to compete with the Range Rover, has replaced the Family, from which it was derived. It shares its mechanics with the Korando. "Musso" is Korean for "rhinoceros." It was launched in Korea in August 1993, and a year later in Europe at the NEC, where it won a prize for design. Since 1998 it has also borne the mark of Daewoo. Designer Ken Greenley had worked for Aston Martin and Rolls-Royce. The following outfits were available: the basic, the SE and the GSE. Engines are also identical with

The SsangYong Musso, 1998

those of the Korando: an E 32 / EX 32—3.2L (220hp), an E 23 / EX 23—2.3L (140hp), a 602 EL—TD 2874cc (120hp @ 4000, 97 mph), a 602 EL—D 2.9L (98hp) and a 601—D 2.3L (77hp @ 3800, 84 mph). The model has a five-speed transmission and its gasoline engines can be coupled to a four-speed Daimler-Benz auto transmission. The Musso has permanent AWD and a reduction. In 2001, it underwent a facelift. Variants appeared of a gasoline 2.0L engine (129hp @ 5500, 16 v, 96 mph), a TD 602 TD 2874cc engine (120hp @ 4000), a 5-V TD 601 TD 2299cc engine (101hp @ 4000); new transmissions were introduced—a 5-speed Borg Warner or TREMEC transmission, and a 4-speed automatic BTRA transmission—and an optional 4x2 mode. The chassis is the same as that of the Korando, but with electronically-adjustable ECS shock absorbers. The STICS chassis optimization cooperates with ABS. The wheelbase is 103 in long. The vehicle is 183 in long, 73 in wide, 73 in high, and it has a 7.5-in ground clearance. The curb weight is +4,255 lbs, payload is 1,290 lbs. The vehicle negotiates a 90 % slope, a 44° side tilt, a 20-in-deep ford and has 34°/27° over-

The SsangYong Musso, 1998

hang angles. The Musso finished second in the 1994 Pharaos Rally in the 4x4 category; in 1995 and 1996 was one of the first ten vehicles in the finish of the Dakar race.

SsangYong Rexton ❸

"Rexton" is an artificial name—a compound of "rex" (=Latin for king) and the English word "ton." This luxury SUV, the first made in Korea, appeared in January1998 (Y200—a concept car), followed by a series model in the spring of 2002. Half of the 20,000 units produced in 2001 and 70,000 units in 2002 have found their home in Europe. Its 5-d station wagon body is welded from steel plates. Insulation, powerful heating and air conditioning guarantee a comfortable drive, even when the outside temperature reaches -40°F or +122°F. A reinforced and braced chassis comes from the Musso. A better digital communication between the drivetrain and chassis is taken care of by a CAN-BUS system. In Europe, the following 4x4 models have been introduced: E32—gasoline 3199cc engine (220hp @ 6500), 602TD—TD 2874cc engine (120hp @ 4000) and E23—gasoline 2295cc engine (150hp @ 6200). There is either a 5-speed manual transmission or a 4-speed BTRA automatic transmission, with optional drive modes including "Power" (off-roader), "Normal" and "Winter." The wheelbase is 111 in long; the car is 186 in long, 74 in wide, 69 in high, the ground clearance is 7.7 in high, and the curb weight is +4,105 lbs.

The Queen of England on board the Steyr Haflinger

Steyr-Daimler-Puch (Austria)

In 1899 Johann Puch launched production of bicycles in Graz, Austria. He proceeded to manufacture motorcycles and subsequently also cars. Before the war, the company sustained cooperation with Hans Ledwinka, a deviser of the wonderful off-road concept of a central tube frame of Tatra—a car manufacturer based in Moravia. Steyr-Puch became known as a concern producing trucks, weapons and franchised Fiats. Nowadays, Steyr-Daimler-Puch along with Magna Steyr and Eurostar are part of the DaimlerChrysler empire. Each of the companies serves a different role: Eurostar produces European versions of the MPV Chrysler Voyager and the PT Cruiser. Magna Steyr supplies mainly 4x4 vehicles. It develops them for its own, as well as foreign, makes: the Alfa Romeo 164Q4 / 33 S 16 Permanent 4 / 155 Q4, the Audi A3 / S3 / TT quattro / TTS / V8L, the Fiat Panda 4x4 / Ducato 4x4 / Citroën C25 4x4 / Tempra 4x4, the Ford Galaxie 4x4, the Lancia Y10 4WD / Dedra and Delta Integrale, the Renault Scenic RX4, the Jeep Grand Cherokee, the Mercedes—type G / M / ML / E 4Matic, the Opel Vectra and Calibra 4x4, the Seat Leon 4x4, the Škoda Octavia 4x4, the VW Golf Country / Golf / Bora 4motion, the Sharan 4x4 / Van T3 / T4. Experience in assembling off-roaders helped the company design its own off-roader vehicles, including the Steyr 270 1500/A, built by Porsche. In 1941–44 a total of 12,500 units thereof were taken up by the

The Steyr Pinzgauer with a TD engine

Wehrmacht; others were consigned to Auto Union. Both the 8-seat convertible and the 1 $^1/_2$-ton featured 4x4 drive and a gasoline V8 OHV air-cooled 3517 cc engine (85hp @ 3000), a 4-speed transmission and an auxiliary 2-speed transmission with disengageable FWD, and a rear differential lock. The front axle had an independent torsion bar suspension; the rear axle was rigid, with leaf springs. The Wehrmacht accepted 1,200 units of the 5-seat open Steyr 250 (4x2) with a boxer 1158cc engine (25hp), a 4-speed and gear-reduction transmissions.

Steyr Haflinger

The year 1959 saw the launch of the Haflinger 700 AP off-roader, named after a strong Alpine horse species. It was derived from Ledwinka's original design. This open 4x4 vehicle served as a transporter of 4 soldiers, an ambulance, a weapon carrier, or a civilian pick-up truck with a laminated cab. Power came from an air-cooled 2-V OHV 643cc boxer engine (24hp @ 4500, or 27hp since 1967). It featured a 4-speed transmission (a 5-speed one since 1966), with an overdrive. The FWD was disengageable. The wheelhubs acted as a reduction. The wheels were suspended independently on hinged half-axles with coil springs. Specifications: wheelbase—59 in (after 1962 also 71 in), length—111 in, width—54 in, height—54–69 in, ground clearance—9.4 in, curb weight—1,433 lbs, payload—1,102 lbs. The Haflinger negotiated a 100 % slope. A 16-year production run ended in 1974, with a total of 16,647 units made.

Steyr Pinzgauer

The series-made Pinzgauer, a successor to the Haflinger, appeared in 1971, following 10 prototypes built since 1967. It was endowed with bigger dimensions, towing capacity and engines. This vehicle designed purely for work purposes, was tailor-made for the requirements of the military. It received its name from an Alpine breed of hardy, strong horse. It is built around a Ledwinka central tube with hinged half-axles featuring coil springs. The 6x6 models are fit with leaf

The Steyr Pinzgauer, 1997

The Steyr Pinzgauer 4x4 and 6x6, 1997

springs in the back. Both the 4x4 and 6x6 vehicles are AWD, with an option to disengage the FWD. All axles feature differentials with 100% locks. The 1985 IAA saw the debut of a TD version, produced since 1986. The original gasoline 4-V had a capacity of 2.5L. The 6-V TD 2383cc engine (105 hp @ 4250, 76 mph) came from VW. There is a 5-speed manual or a 4-speed auto transmission. In addition to that, the vehicle has a reduction, and the 4x4 versions are equipped with a system designed to maintain the same ground clearance. Besides the chassis for specified superstructures, the company produced soft-tops, platform trucks, 3-/5-d station wagons, ambulances, fire engines and rescue-squad specials. The vehicles carry 2–14 persons. Other features: wheelbase—95 in (4x4) / 87 +37 in (6x6), length—176.5 / 207 in,

width—71 in, height—80.5 in, ground clearance—13.2 in. When empty, the vehicle weighs +4,409 / +5,511 lbs, and it has a payload of 3,307 / 4,409. The capacity of its fuel tank is 38 gal. Its fording depth is 27.5 in. It has a 100% slope capacity, a 36° side tilt and 40°/45° overhang angles. In 1991, the manufacturer won a tender from the British military, and subsequently supplied nearly 400 vehicles, which were assembled in Great Britain. The Austrians supplied the armed forces in 24 countries with their Pinzgauers. The soldiers can use models with a 1.5-m fording depth or the Protector armored version.

The Steyr-Puch G chassis, 1993

The Steyr-Puch G fire engine—a long 3-d station wagon, 1993

Puch G / Mercedes-Benz G ❾ ❷

According to a 1973 contract, the Austrians helped develop and now produce Mercedes off-roaders. These series-made vehicles appeared at the end of 1978. The civilian versions include a short convertible with a hard-top over the driver, a 3-d and a stretched 5-d station wagon, a short / long van, a glassed-in van, a chassis, a pick-up truck with a stretched cab, an ambulance, and a fire engine. In 1992, the hundred-thousandth vehicle was driven off the assembly line; some were exported as CKDs. In 7 countries around the world, they are known as Mercedes, in 5 countries as Puchs, and the

French assembled them (with Peugeot engines and transmissions) as the Peugeot P4. By 1996, the Swiss army had taken up 5,300 units, the German army purchased 12,000 units by 1992, and, over the same time period, the Dutch military bought 3,200 units. The G 460 / G 461 series was followed by the 463 updated generations. This model will tackle an 80% slope, a 54% side tilt and 34° / 29° overhang angles.

The company has also developed and produced, in partnership with VW, the (mainly military) Steyr Noriker off-roader, with a payload of 3,307–4,409 lbs, based on the VW LT with a wheelbase length of 102 or 114 in.

The Steyr-Puch G pick-up truck

Subaru (Japan)

Fuji Heavy Industries Ltd. is active in many industrial domains. Its vehicle products bear the mark of "Subaru." The company's origins go back to 1917, to the establishment of the Nakajima aircraft research laboratories. The Fuji Sangyo Ltd. company emerged from reorganization in 1945. Six out of its twelve divisions joined in 1953 to establish Fuji Heavy Industries; Subaru was founded in July of the same year. It was named after a Japanese word for a star constellation of Pleiades (in Greek mythology, the seven daughters of Atlas who were transformed into a group of stars). The company's first car—the 360 (4x2) model—was made in 1958. It was fit with a rear 2-V 360cc engine. The FF-1 (977cc) from 1966 was the first 2x4 vehicle. The main "trump" of the company later on was passenger cars with boxer engines and 4x4 drive. The company got to 4WD thanks to a tender held by the Tohoku Electric Supply Company, which supplied power to the island of Honshu. The TESC needed a vehicle capable of transporting staff even in severe winter conditions. This is how the Leone Station Wagon AWD was born in September 1972. The All Wheel Drive (AWD) system rests on the following principle: if the wheels of one axle begin to slip a little, the ratio of power transmitted by each axle changes automatically: the power transmitted onto the slipping axle is decreased; on the other hand, the non-slipping wheels acquire a higher torque.

Subaru 4x4 sedans   ❶

Subaru focused exclusively on 4WD road vehicles with ambitions to drive on barely accessible mountain roads. Its models included: the smallest Rex (1972), the Rex 700 (1986), the Vivio (May 1992 till fall 1999, manual transmission or a CVT centrifugal auto transmission and 2WD or 4WD), and the Justy (a prototype presented in Tokyo in 1983, at the 1995 IAA in Europe; 2WD, 4WD). Since 1971, the company has been making the Leone sedans, station wagons and coupes, in 1974 equipped with AWD for ordinary customers. Being the first Subaru model, it went down very well as an export vehicle. The 2nd generation was launched in 1979, followed by the 3rd, with new bodies, in 1984. Not all the vehicles, especially the ones for export, featured optional RWD by means of an auxiliary transmission, as opposed to the "normal" 2x4. Permanent 4x4 drive was again featured on some 1987 models. They were called

The Subaru SVX, 1993

the 4WD (5-d station wagons). In the spring of 1985, the Leone / 4WD gave rise to the sharp-featured Subaru XT Coupé / Alcyone (4x4) and 1.8L turbo engines (120hp, 124 mph), with a 6-V 2.7L engine (150hp JIS, 137 mph). A prototype of the new SVX coupe (Tokyo 1989) with permanent AWD and a 6-V 3319cc boxer engine (220hp, 233hp, JIS, 143 mph) was also presented. The model featured an inter-axle planetary differential with a viscous coupling, and another viscous coupling in the rear axle, with a smooth division of torque between the front and rear wheels. There was a 4-speed automatic transmission. In October 1992, the Leone was replaced by the Impreza with FWD or AWD (a central differential, a viscous coupling). The Impreza was built on a shortened Legacy platform. Its self-supporting

bodies come either as sedans, or sports station wagons, or coupes. Hand in hand with a very successful rally performance on the part of this make, the attractive Impreza WRX3 appeared, with fantastic road-going abilities,; the Impreza WRX STi from 2002 had a maximum horsepower of 265hp.

Subaru Legacy / Outback / Lancaster ❶

The Legacy was launched in 1989. In 1997, the Outback / Lancaster 5-d station wagon appeared. The original 4-V 1.8L engine was replaced in the fall of 1991 in Europe with a 2.0L (125hp @ 5600, 117 mph or 155hp JIS), or a turbo engine (280hp @ 6500, JIS, coupled to a 4-speed

The Subaru Legacy—an ambulance version, 1993

auto transmission, 260hp). Besides the automatic, a 5-speed manual transmission was available. The front or all wheels were powered. The model featured an inter-axle differential with a viscous coupling, and a rear viscous coupling on request. The torque was distributed in a 1:1 ratio. Another possibility, if desired, was a Dual Range gear mode with normal and slow off-road regimes. The biggest engine featured is a 4-V 2457cc boxer engine (156hp @ 5600, 129 mph) with both transmission options and a Dual Range reduction with a different range of gears, depending on the driving dynamics. The Legacy is a 5-seat sedan or station wagon. Its wheels are suspended independently on McPherson struts, with a rear stabilizer. Air-vented disc brakes have ABS. Specifications: wheelbase—104 in, length—186 in (the Outback), width—69 in, height—62 in, ground clearance—7.9 in, curb weight—(+)3,197 lbs, payload—981 lbs, fording depth—11.8 in, overhang angles—22°/17°. In 2000, a 6-V 16v 2999cc boxer engine (209hp @ 6000, 130 mph, 220hp JIS) was introduced (the Outback H6: 3.0), which is mounted along with a 4-speed auto transmission and a Dual Range. The Outback station wagon is regarded as an independent model.

Subaru Forester   ❶ ❸

At the 1995 IAA, the manufacturer showcased a concept car of the Subaru Streega—a new version of an off-road station wagon with a 2L boxer engine (250hp), permanent 4x4 drive and ABS. The end of the summer 1997 brought the SUV Forester to Japan. As of the following year, Japanese customers could enjoy a 2.0L engine with two turbochargers (250hp @ 6 500, JIS). A 5-d heightened station wagon was fit with the well-known 16v 2.0L boxer engine (125hp

@ 5600), a turbo version thereof (170hp @ 5600), or a 16v 2.5L boxer engine (150hp @ 5600). A drivetrain with a Dual Range, a self-supporting steel body and wheel suspension resemble those of the Outback. In this case, the wheelbase is 99 in long, the vehicle is 176 in long, 68 in wide, 63 in high, and it has a 7.5-in-high ground clearance. Its curb weight is +3,197 lbs, and its payload is 937 lbs. The Forester will manage a 12-in-deep ford and its overhang angles are 23°/19°. In March 2000, the Forester was facelifted and its 2nd generation was showcased at the 2002 NEC. Its engines got more powerful—1994cc (125hp @ 5600, 112 mph, turbo 177hp @ 5600, 78 mph or 250hp @ 6500 JIS). A 5-speed manual or a 4-speed automatic transmission and the McPherson axles were maintained. The new model is 1 in longer and 0.8 in lower.

The Subaru Forester 20XT world premiere at the NEC 2002

Subaru Baja

Subaru recalled the 1970s to mind—a time when it produced the Leone and the Brat "baroque" pick-up trucks based on the Leone 1st generation. In Los Angeles in 2001, it showcased an elegant concept of the Baja free double-cab for leisure time. The model's youthful appearance and smooth driving properties were captivating. In contrast to its American competitors, it isn't based on a work vehicle, but on a passenger car with independent wheel suspension. It was fit with a 4-V DOHC 2457cc flat opposed-piston engine (162hp @ 5600). There is either a 5-speed manual or a 4-speed auto transmission. Permanent AWD has an inter-axle differential with a viscous brake (with a manual transmission) or an electronically-controlled multi-disc clutch (with an auto transmission). Stabilizers and coil springs are everywhere. The Baja is 187 in long, 69 in wide, and 62 in high. Its curb weight is 3,503 lbs and its payload is 1,052 lbs. This

model, with shiny yellow paint and a pronounced plastic protection strips all around, was presented at the 2002 Paris motor show; preparations are under way for its European campaign.

Subaru Rex Combi, E 10 / 12

Since the 1960s, Subaru has also been making small vans which appeared in Europe in the late 1970s. Some of them were derived from the Rex, the Justy or the Leone. These vans were alternatively available as 4x4. The first models included the Rex Combi and a bigger series of the E 10 / E 12, followed later by the Sambar Truck, the Pleo Van and the Leone Van. Their bodies were mainly small, narrow vans, microbuses, station wagons, and pick-up trucks.

The Subaru Baja; Brno, Czech Republic, 2003

The Suzuki Wagon R+, 1997

The Suzuki LJ 20, 1972

Suzuki
(Japan)

The Suzuki LJ 20—the first station wagon, 1973

Suzuki has been known as a producer of motorcycles since 1956. The origins of the company go back to 1909, when Mr. Michio Suzuki founded the Suzuki Loom Works in Hamamatsu, Japan. The first four-wheel vehicle made in October 1955 was the Suzulight, carrying a two-stroke 2-V 360cc engine. Many models of small cars ensued and production of motorcycles was increased in the Iwata, Toyama, Osuka and Kosai assembly plants. In August 1981, Suzuki signed a strategic contract with General Motors on the distribution of the economical Japanese vehicles in the U.S. GM obtained 5% of Suzuki shares and another 3.5% was acquired by Isuzu—another Japanese acquisition of GM. Suzuki is perhaps the world's most successful producer of lightweight off-road vehicles. Since the 1990s, the Suzuki lineup has also included the Alto compact road vehicles with

4x4 drive and, most importantly, minivans—the Wagon R+ (since 1999, 4x2, 4x4), the Ignis / Swift (since 2000, 2x4, 4x4) and the Liana (since 2001, 2x4, 4x4).

The Suzuki Ignis Rallye, 2001

The Suzuki Jimny, 1998

Suzuki Jimny / LJ
(Japan, Spain) ❷

Work on this small Jeep-inspired off-road vehicle began in 1968, when Suzuki bought the rights to the HopeStar ON 360 primitive off-roader from the Hope Motor Company, then on the verge of bankruptcy. A series bearing the model name of LJ and trim names "Jimny" or "Brute IV" first appeared on the (home) market in 1970. The "LJ" stands for "Light Jeep," and the name "Jimny" is a result of a misun-

derstanding: when the Japanese representatives of Suzuki first visited Scotland, they decided to coin the new model "Jimmy"; however, somewhere on the way between Scotland and Japan, the term got distorted to "Jimny"... This comfort-free vehicle was open, with 3 seats and a spare wheel placed behind the front passenger seat and next to the rear odd seat. The door openings equipped with zippers were designed to hold canvas "doors." A motorcycle two-stroke 360cc engine (25hp, SAE) was cooled by air. The LJ10 existed only as a convertible. Its "trademark" feature is the horizontal ribs of the grille. The first units were taken up by a power-distribution company for technicians checking the electric wiring and waterways in mountainous wooded terrains. The LJ20 is an improved LJ10 with a liquid-cooled engine (28hp SAE), and a hard-top or soft-top body. The LJ20A and the LJ20E differed in terms of rear lights, and all the LJ20 units featured vertical grille ribs. They were the first LJ vehicles to be exported. A motorcycle engine seemed sufficient for the home market, but it wouldn't do for export. Therefore, a more powerful air-cooled 0.55L engine was introduced. The LJ20 with a 3V 539cc engine (horsepower decreased to 26hp) was imported into the U.S. by the IEC company, but in 1973 a strict new emissions law forced termination of the import. The LJ50 (from 1976) went down extremely well in Australia (since 1974 it was imported as

The Suzuki SJ410, 1982

The Suzuki LJ10, 1970

the LJ20) as a leisure-time vehicle. The model was sold as an LJ50 / 55 (or Jimny 550 / SJ10) hard-top, soft-top or convertible. The Australians' interest continued with the bigger LJ80 (since 1977, a year later in Australia; 2nd generation since 1979), equipped with a liquid-cooled 4-V 797cc engine (41hp @ 5500, SAE). It came with a slightly retouched grille. Available were hard-top and soft-top versions, the LJ80V station wagon and the LJ81K pick-up-truck—the first Suzuki truck exported to the U.S. The 2nd generation of soft-tops featured exclusively all-metal doors. The year 1978 brought the first Suzuki off-roaders to Europe, namely the Netherlands. They were also known as the Eljot. The 4x4 Suzuki vehicles soon (and for long) overshadowed the rest of the vehicles manufactured by the make. Until 1982, the wheelbase was 76 in long (or 77 in for the Hope), the vehicle was 125 in (118 in) long, 55 in (51 in) wide, 67 in (69.5 in) high, and its curb weight ranged between 1,323 and 1,642 lbs (1,378 lbs).

The fall of 1981 saw the debut of a markedly facelifted enlarged version with a new interior and a softer chassis. Power came from 2-stroke 3-V engines: the SJ30 —539cc (28hp @ 5000, SAE), the Jimny 550—547cc (34hp @ 6500, JIS), and a 4-stroke 4-V engine (the SJ410): 970cc (45hp @ 5500). Specifications: wheelbase—80 in (or also 94 in for the SJ410), length—126 in (135 and 158 in for the SJ410), width—55 in (58 in for the SJ410), height—67 in. Between the spring of 1990 and the year 1999, the Jimny 660 was available—a replacement for the Jimny 550. It was fit with a 657cc engine (55hp @ 5500, JIS). After the fall of 1992, its horsepower was 58hp and. A year later it was distributed under the simple name "Jimny," and since 1999 as the Samurai; at the same time, the front wheels could be equipped with freewheels, if desired. The SJ410 found its way into new markets. The LJ series was present on the British market in 1979–81, and was replaced by the SJ series after June 1982. Action models were also available, including the Rhino (with a rhinoceros motif), the Sport, the Style and the Tobago in England. The 1st generation models were made until 1990.

The 2nd generation of the Jimny was launched in Japan in the fall of 1998, under the slogan "Smart In the City, Tough In Nature." It replaced the older and a-notch-classier Samurai series. Its development followed the usual principles used for the Jimny since 1988—an extended wheelbase and

thus also the length, a higher degree of comfort and space, more powerful engines, RWD and optional FWD.

In late 2000, a diminished version named the Jimny J2 appeared in Japan, only with RWD and fit with a 3-V 12v 658cc turbo engine (64hp @ 6500, JIS). Specifications: wheelbase—89 in, length—134 in, width—58.5 in, height—66 in, curb weight—2,050 lbs.

As far as mechanics is concerned, the model featured a robust ladder frame and a body made from pressed steel plates. Its axles were rigid with half-elliptic springs in the front and transversal leaf springs in the rear. In 1972, a manual 4-speed transmission and reduction were mounted. Starting with the Jimny 550 and continuing until today, a 5-speed, direct transmission with reduction is always featured, with some exceptions: the Jimny SJ 410 (1981–98, 4-speed transmission and a reduction), the Japanese Jimny (2WD since 1998), and the Jimny 2nd generation (Wide) with a choice between a 5-speed manual transmission with a reduction and a 4-speed auto transmission. The total weight is 2,513 lbs (the LJ 80) or 2,866–3,075 lbs (the SJ 410). The top speed is 66–70 mph. Ground clearance of the 4x2 vehicles from the fall of 1998 was 7.5 in, and 7.3 in for the 4x4 version. Other features include a 90% slope, a 45° side tilt, and about 20 in of fording depth. The Jimny is manufactured in Venezuela (Chevrolet, since 2000), Spain (the Santana Canvas Top Cabrio; since 1999 Spain has been the sole producer of the Jimny and Jimny Cabrio models), India (the Maruti Gypsy based on the 1981 generation and made since 1985). The Jimny plays the role of a cheap small leisure-time vehicle for young people's city rides and weekend road trips.

Work on the Jimny 3rd generation has been under way since 1998 in Japan only in an assembly plant of Mazda, whose "Mazda A-Z–Offroad" is a Jimny look-alike. The name Jimny Wide has been around since the 1997 Tokyo motor show and only in Japan; in Europe it is known simply as the Jimny series. The 2002 Paris car show saw the debut of a study of the Jimny Oxbow—a colorful beach version; at the same time, the company announced the launch of a limited-series Jimny Maori 4x4 both with a closed-in and an open body.

The Suzuki LJ80, 1980

239

Suzuki Samurai / SJ (Japan, Spain, India)

The series of Samurai (=Japanese warrior) on a chassis with the same (or extended) wheelbase as the Jimny was a bull's-eye. The Samurai SJ 413 has a wheelbase of 80 or 94 in, a length of 135 and 158 in, a width of 58 in, a height of 67 in, a curb weight of + 2,028 lbs. Its ground clearance is 8.8 in (sometimes 8.3 in). It has a 90% slope, a 45° side tilt, and a 20-in fording depth. Power comes from 4-V engines—a 1325cc (64 hp @ 6000) and a 1298cc (69hp @ 6000). Other models have been fit with a 657cc engine (58hp, JIS), a 970cc engine (45hp @ 5500), or a TD Peugeot 1905cc engine (63hp @ 4300, ECE). This model made its debut in the fall of 1984 and its production ended in 1998. After the Jimny got a facelift in 1981, the Samurai differed from it in appearance and in terms of a greater degree of comfort. The Jimny's rigid axles and leaf springs were naturally retained. There was a 5-speed transmission with reduction. In the course of 1984, disc brakes appeared in the front. The factory improved the vehicle's stability by widening it. The first Samurai bore the name SJ 413. To this day, the company has used either the name Samurai or the code name SJ for the model, depending on the specific markets and time periods. In some cases, the Jimny and Samurai series intermingle. Just like the Jimny, the Samurai's number code usually gives away the engine capacity; e.g., the SJ 413 is fit with a 1.3L engine. The total weight as stated by the producer is +2,932 lbs (the SJ 413), and the top speed is 78–87 mph. This successful model is sold in over 100 countries around the world. Besides Japan, it was produced in India (the Maruti Gypsy). European demand was since 1985 mostly covered by the production of the Santana—a Spanish branch of Suzuki, which over the year became the sole supplier of the car. The Spanish version (the Jimny 1300 4x4) is made in Malaysia by the local Suzuki branch; in Pakistan, Suzuki-

The Suzuki Grand Vitara, 1998

PAK produces it as the Potohar station wagon; in the Philippines, the model is made as the open Suzuki Jimny, while in Indonesia, the station wagon is known as the Suzuki Katana. The model won great acclaim in the U.S., where it was claimed to be "a tough 4x4 for minimum money" or, in another magazine, "a city toy." Scamp, a British small-scale producer, uses its chassis, often even refurbished ones, to build vehicles or car kits, resembling an open off-road vehicle from the 1930s (the Rowfant Roadster) and the Mk3 GT 4x4 a small two-seat off-road convertible or station wagon.

Suzuki Vitara / Escudo, X-90 (Japan, Spain)

The summer of 1988 brought the Vitara—a more powerful and "civilized" off-roader. Known in Japan as the Escudo (its 1st generation existed in 1988–97, followed by the equally-successful 2nd generation), and as the Geo Tracker in the U.S. (short version). It went down in history as the first off-roader in Europe and the U.S., the possession of which became trendy. The Vitara was fit with a modern aluminum

The Suzuki Samurai, 1996

4-V 1590cc engine (95hp @ 5600, ECE), and, since 1996, with a 1995cc engine (136hp @ 6500, ECE). Since December 1994, the Vitara V6 has been around, with a V6 1998cc engine (136hp @ 6500, ECE) and, since 1996, also with a V6 2495cc engine (160hp @ 6500, ECE) and diesel engines—a 1905cc (68hp @ 4600) and a TD 1998cc (87hp @ 4000, ECE). Initially (1988–99), 3-speed transmissions were featured in vehicles with 4V 1.6 and 2.0L engines but, since 1994, the models with V6-engines, and later the whole production, began featuring a 4-speed French GM auto transmission, alternating with a 5-speed manual transmission with a reduction. A higher degree of luxury was achieved by an independent front wheel suspension with a stabilizer, by replacing leaf springs with coil springs in both axles and by installing a standard steering booster. The vehicles had a ground clearance of 7.7 or 7.9 in, an 80% slope, a 40° side-tilt and a 17.7-in fording depth. The Vitara has a wheelbase of 87 or 97 in, it is 140 or 143 in long, 66.5 in wide and 65 in high. Besides a station wagon, a short convertible version is the real "fun factory." The vehicle's attractive appearance with a protective targa arch invites a ride along the beach. The X-90 model was presented at the 1995 IAA and series-produced in 1995–99; after that, this version became part of the Vitara / Grand Vitara "palette." Action models included: the Mustique (1992), the Rossini (1994), the SE Executive (1990), the Sport, the Verdi (1994) and the X-EC (1993). By the beginning of 1998, a total of 1.4 million Vitaras had been sold around the world, becoming the most popular off-road vehicles on the European market and winning 13 world prizes, including countries as diverse as Germany, Greece and Chile. The vehicles were imported from Japan (1988–97) or Spain (after 1990). The production run was ended in 1999. Other models originated in Ecuador, Egypt (the Chevrolet Vitara), Malaysia (the Vitara 4x4 station wagon), the Philippines (convertible), Taiwan (the Escudo 5-d and 3-d station wagon), Indonesia (the Sidekick, 4x2) and China (the Tonggong—TG 2020H JA type, which is in fact a 3-d Vitara with a 1.6L engine, produced since 2000).

The Suzuki Vitara 4u², London, 1999

Suzuki Grand Vitara, XL-7, (Grand Escudo)

 ❸

The Grand Vitara was introduced in the fall of 1997 as a follow-up to and the 2nd generation of the Vitara. In some markets, the two series intermingle. Mechanically, the two vehicles are very close. As with the Vitara, the Grand Vitara is available (in some countries at least) with 4x4 or 4x2 drive. Noteworthy is its engine—a modern D 4-V HDi Peugeot / Citroën common-rail 1997cc (109hp @ 4000, ECE); other engines include: a 1590cc (94hp @ 5200, ECE), a 1995cc (128hp @ 6000, ECE), a 2494cc (144hp @ 6200, ECE), and a TD 1998cc (87hp @ 4000, ECE). The Grand Vitara has an 87-in-long wheelbase; it is 151 in long, 67 in wide, 67 in high, and weighs +2,646 lbs. An interesting model was celebrated in London in 1999—the Grand Vitara GV2000 4x4, fit with a 2.0L 16v gasoline engine, a short wheelbase and either with a 3-d station wagon body or with an attractive targa-roadster body. In addition to an older 3- and 5-d station wagon version, both the 2000 Tokyo and the subsequent 2001 Detroit motor shows featured the SUV Suzuki XL-7—a 7-seat station wagon version of the Grand Vitara with the following specifications: wheelbase—110 in, length—184 in, width—70 in, height—64 in, and a V6 2xDOHC 24v 2737cc engine (173hp @ 5500, SAE). Also the Suzuki XL-7 comes with RWD or permanent AWD, and an inter-axle viscous coupling. It is with either with a 5-speed manual transmission, or a 4-speed auto transmission with a reduction. Ground clearance is 7.7 in for the SWB and 7.9 in for the LWB; the model will tackle a 70% slope, a 40° side tilt and a 20-in fording depth. The visitors to the 2002 Paris

motor show could admire the Grand Vitara XL-7 Edition Limitée—a special model with numerous improvements. The models are manufactured in Japan for the home market as the Escudo / Grand Vitara (station wagon and convertible) and the Grand Escudo / Grand Vitara XL-7. Worth mentioning is the Grand Vitara Van and the Grand Vitara Pick-up which was introduced in Tokyo in 2000. Since 1998, various versions of the Grand Vitara and the Chevrolet Tracker twins have been rolling off the assembly lines (4x2 and 4x4) in the GM/Suzuki-CAMI joint venture factory in Canada. Other places of origin include Ecuador, Argentina (4x2, 4x4) and Taiwan.

The Suzuki Vitara GV 2000, 2000

Škoda
(Czech Republic)

The Škoda Popular 1100

On September 30, 1895, Václav Laurin & Václav Klement established a workshop in the Czech town of Mladá Boleslav, then part of the Austro-Hungarian Empire. They began with bicycles, and went on to manufacture motorcycles after 1899. At the 1905 Prague motor show, they presented the Voituretta—at first only an engine and by the end of the year a vehicle. The L&K automobiles became famous for their innovative design and reliable construction. Since 1919, the Pilsen-based Škoda factory—a European industrial giant—made farming, industrial and weapon transporters, locomotives, aircraft engines, airplanes, weapons and, since November 1924, also the franchised luxury Hispano-Suiza. In 1925, the Škoda factory merged with L&K, from which point the Laurin vehicles became known as Škodas and bore a feathered arrow logo. After WWII, Škoda became independent, and in 1991 it became part of the VW concern. In 1938–41, the company supplied as many as 54 "Populars"—lightweight off-road vehicles based on sedans—to the armies of Hungary, Germany and other countries. The SV engine was converted to the war-time OHV 1089cc (32hp). The Popular (4x2) featured a 4-speed transmission. Its wheelbase was 98 in long. In 1941–43, Škoda produced 1,631 vehicles based on the civilian Superb 3000. This middle-class model (4x2) featured a 6-V OHV 3140cc engine (80hp), a differential lock, an independent suspension with transversal leaf springs, and a 135-in-long wheelbase. The open heavyweight 903 type (6x4) based on the Superb 3000 and used mainly for SS weapons, as a military staff convert-

ible and an ambulance, had 3 axles, a 4-speed transmission and a reduction. It featured a 133+36-in wheelbase, and it was 203 in long, 71 in wide, 75 in high, and weighed +4,850 lbs when empty. A 6x6 variant was tested. A total of 45 units were made of it. Similar 6-seat open bodies were featured on other Czech heavyweight 6-wheel commander vehicles as well, namely the Tatra and the Praga AV from 1936–39 (nearly 400 units, 6x4, 6-V Praga 3468cc engine, 70hp, wheelbase—116 (+) 36 in, length—201 in, width—69 in, height—73 in, weight—4,806 lbs).

Škoda—4WD vehicles of the 1950s (Czechoslovakia) ❷ ❽ ❾

In 1946-50, the company supplied the army with the open Škoda 1101 VO / P with a canvas tilt and RWD coupled to a 4-speed transmission. A 4x4 version had a reduction. Its

The Škoda 1101 P; Brno, Czech Republic, 2001

The Škoda 973 Radio vehicle, Brno, Czech Republic, 2003   *The Škoda Trekka*

wheelbase was 98 in long. The vehicle was 155 in long, 59 in wide, 62 in high and weighed 2,116 lbs when empty. In 1951, the Škoda 1200 sedan served as a base for several updated prototypes with aluminum 4-V 1.5L engines: a 159-in-long 4x2 emergency vehicle and a 141-in-long 4x4 with a cross-country reduction. In 1953, the Warsaw Pact armies held a tender for a lightweight off-road army vehicle. The Škoda 973 (4x4), nicknamed Babeta (after a musical movie in which it was featured), passed with flying colors the army tests in climbing up gulches, and in driving through Czech mud and DDR sands. The company began preparing large-scale production, but the Moscow headquarters decided that GAZs/UAZs be made instead, in spite of their worse driving properties in rugged terrains, where they'd proven to be heavier and slower. In 1952-56, over 30 units of canvas-covered staff and connecting vehicles were produced, featuring permanent RWD and optional FWD. They were fit with 4-V 1491cc engines (52hp @ 4200, 56 mph), 4-speed transmissions with a synchronization of the 3rd and 4th gears, en bloc with a reduction and transfer case. The differential with a mechanic ball lock is a Czech patent. The rear differential has a cardan brake. The wheels were mounted inde-

pendently on a trapezoid torsion bar suspension. The vehicle was 138 in long, 66 in wide, 70 in high, it weighed +2,624 lbs, its payload was 1,102 lbs; it had a 15-in ground clearance, a 23.6-in fording depth, a 100% slope and 55° / 55° overhang angles. Unique were the five floating vehicles (the 972 type) with a 1221cc engine (45hp @ 4200, 53 mph), a screw propeller and an exhaust pump, propelled by a gear-reduction transmission shaft. This 4x4 amphibian had an 87-in-long wheelbase (the former versions were shorter), it was 178 in long, 68 in wide and 70 in high. It weighed 2,975 lbs and its payload was 992 lbs.

In the late 1950s, they prepared 23 open trambus prototypes of the Škoda Agromobil under the name Puch Haflinger. Series-production did not occur. They used components of the Škoda 1203 (4x2) van.

In New Zealand, the Motor Industries LTD (MI LTD) importer assembled a number of small series of the Škoda-Trekka vehicle mainly from Czech components from 1966. The annual output of the workshops was 1,200 cars. A shortened chassis of the Octavia Combi (4x2) was used and the resulting vehicle was a "grandchild" of the Škoda 973. The Trekka (4x2, 4-V OHC 1221cc engine, 47hp @ 4500, 71 mph,

The Škoda Superb 3000 4x2

4-speed transmission, synchronization of the 2nd through 4th gears) was on request equipped with a New-Zealand-made Balanced Traction differential with a lock. All wheels were suspended independently. The six body types available, including a pick-up truck, a station wagon and a beach vehicle, were welded from steel plates and featured laminated superstructures. Dimensions: wheelbase—85 in, length—133 in, width—63 in, height—75 in, ground clearance—7.5 in, curb weight—(+)1,583 lbs and payload—1,102 lbs. After 1971, the Trekkas were exported as CKDs to Indonesia. In 1968–71, the Skopak—a Škoda-Pakistani cooperation project—was carried out concerning a lightweight van, a pick-up, a station wagon, based on the Octavia Combi with a 1,102-lb payload. Similar activities took place in Turkey, but on the basis of the Škoda 1202 (4x2) minivan / pick-up truck. The Škoda 1202 Kamyonetleri pick-up truck featured a Turkish steel body and a 1,565-lb towing capacity. An end was put to these promising activities by the political events in Czechoslovakia and in the world in 1968, as well as by the fact that Škoda switched over to rear engine vehicles. In the early 1970s, the company built five 4-seat "736 buggies" with aggregates of the Škoda 100/110.

Škoda Octavia 4x4 Kombi ❶

The Škoda Octavia 4x4 Kombi will manage a barely passable road, dirt road or a reasonably hard, wet meadow. It made its debut in the fall of 1999, with a TD 4-V 1896cc engine (100hp @ 4000, 114 mph). This station wagon / sedan with permanent AWD features an electrically-controlled Haldex clutch in an oil bath. At first, power is transmitted onto the front wheels, and as soon as these begin to slip, the Haldex is activated and gradually transfers part of the power onto the rear wheels to reach a final 50:50 ratio. There is a 6-speed transmission. Other 4x4 Octavias are fit with TD 1896cc engines (90hp / 110hp @ 4000 / 4150) or gasoline 4-V 1984cc engines (116hp @ 5200, 123 mph) and turbo

1781cc engines (150hp @ 5700, 136 mph). All the power units are coupled to a 5-speed manual or a 4-speed auto transmission. The vehicle has ASR. The body is self-supporting with McPherson struts and a torsion stabilizer in the front, and a likewise independent rear suspension with a stabilizer and coil springs. There are disc brakes with ABS, ESP and EDS. The Škoda Octavia 4x4 has a 99-in wheelbase, a 178-in length, a 68-in width, a 58-in height, a 6-in ground clearance. Its curb weight is 3,329 lbs, and its payload is 970 lbs. First-class 4WD technology is featured on the Škoda Octavia WRC, a successful participant in World Cup rallies. Its successor—the Škoda Fabia WRC—was introduced in Geneva in 2003. Young people could enjoy their free time in a 2-seat pick-up truck or a 2+2-seat convertible (the cargo area of the pick-up truck carries a bench for 2, protected by a canvas tilt). The Škoda Felicia Fun (2x4) with an attractive color design appeared in the late 1990s.

The Škoda Felicia Fun, 1999

Tarpan, Honker (Poland)

The FSC Lublin company produced the GAZ fire-engines after the war until the 1960s, and the Zhuk 4x2 vans in 1958–98. Since 1993, the vehicles have borne the Lublin trademark. In May 1995, Daewoo Motor Polska (DMP) obtained 61% of the stock of the FSC Lublin company, and by the end of the 1990s, the Koreans' share had risen to 90%. In 1998–2000, the firm assembled the SsangYong Musso off-roader and the Korando. In late 2001, Andoria s.a.—a diesel engine producer from Andrychów—expressed interest in buying the bankrupt Lublin and Honker makes of the insolvent DMP. The transaction came off and on February 1st, 2003, Andoria Mot took control of the Lublin assembly plant. The Lublin 3 delivery vehicles (there is also a 4x2 version, featuring a rear differential lock available at a premium; the new 8-seat Combi station wagon, and the Brigade double-cab), with a planned monthly output of 300 units, and the Honker off-roaders are mounted with Andoria diesel engines. The latest reports say that the make was bought by the Russian Kamaz company, but that production in Poland should be maintained.

The Poles were looking for a vehicle suitable for driving over broken paths in the country. Prototypes of the Tarpan and Warta minivans based on the Syrena sedan were presented in late 1971. The Tarpan weighed 2,579 lbs and carried 1,102 lbs of cargo; the Warta's curb weight was 2,756 lbs and it had a 1,323 lbs towing capacity. Both vehicles featured components of the Fiat 125p and the Nysa delivery van. A later prototype—the Warta-2—had the capacity to carry either 1,653 lbs of cargo and 3 persons, or 6 persons. This model was showcased in 1972. It was powered by a 2.1L engine (50hp @ 3600). Its ladder chassis and body parts came from the Zhuk, while the drivetrain and independent wheel

suspension were taken from the Warszawa sedan. The rear axle, taken from the Warszawa pick-up truck, was rigid with half-elliptic springs. The length of the model was 202 in, with a 106-in wheelbase. Production was entrusted to the Wielkopolskie Zaklady Naprawy Samochodów company in Poznań-Antoninek. In late 1972, the first 25-unit series was driven off the WZNS assembly line. In May 1973, production was transferred to the Lublin-based Fabryki Samochodów Ciezarowych assembly plant, which in November 1975 was renamed Zaklad Samochodów Rolniczych (FSR), based in Poznań. Gradually, the vehicle acquired more parts from the Fiat 125p. In 1973–1976, a total of 8,533 units of the Tarpan 233 pick-up truck / minivan / station wagon were made, fit with 4-V M20 2417cc engines (70hp @ 4200) or OHV S-21 1481cc engines (70hp @ 5400), coupled with a 4-speed FSO transmission and, since 1978, a differential lock. The 1978 Poznań car show saw the debut of the Tarpan 235 with a 2,205-lb towing capacity, a remodeled chassis, front wheel suspensions and body modifications. Output exceeded 5 thousand units in 1977, and 6 thousand a year later. The engine came from the Fiat 125p. At the turn of the 1970s and 1980s, prototypes of an off-road station wagon were built by FSR with a contribution from the FSO—the

The Tarpan Honker, 1993

Italian Fiat ("Tarpaniello"). This model was a pre-image of the Honker. The Tarpan 237 was discontinued in 1991, in favor of the Honker.

Tarpan Honker

A single series-made off-roader has been made in Poland. It was named Tarpan after a hardy Tatras breed of horse. Prototypes of this off-roader were designed by the Warsaw Technical Institute and a similar military institution in Sulejowka. The FSR was chosen as a producer. The PW1 (Pojazd Wielozadaniowy) prototype of a rectangular off-

road station wagon made its debut in 1980, with a 1.5L Polonez engine (75hp); an Andoria power unit made by the Andrychow factory was also tested. The 2nd prototype—the PW2—with permanent AWD was built in 1983, and series-production started five years later in the Warsaw-based PW factory. Since 1994, the vehicle became known to the public as the Tarpan Honker (model 4011). Its mission was to replace the obsolete UAZ car pool of the police and the military. In 1988, production was transferred to the FSR Poznań factory, where units of the Tarpan 233 were rolling off the assembly line. From the turn of the 1980s and 1990s, the factory produced Honkers with three different engines: an AA

The Tarpan 233, 1977

(1.5L, 75hp), an AB (1.6L, 82hp), and a CB (1.6L, FSO Polonez, 86hp). Later, a different engine lineup was introduced. All were coupled to a 5-speed transmission. Diesel engines were tested. Later a 2.5L diesel engine (75hp) appeared, followed by a TD (100hp). The model shared some parts with the Lublin delivery vans. Its tasteless body, welded onto a chassis frame made from U-side members, was modified. Passengers were protected by a polyester laminate roof or a polyamide tilt. The PW2 / 4011 had a 110-in-long wheelbase, it was 180 in long, 75 in wide, and 85 in high. When empty, it weighed 3,682 lbs, and it had a payload of 2,205 lbs on the road, and 1,874 lbs in the off-road. Most common were vehicles tailor-made for the military and the police; the 4012—a rarely produced civilian model—resembled the police model. There was also the rare 4022 version, designed for use by various professions. The vehicles carried 8+2 or

6+2 passengers, or 2,205 lbs of cargo. They negotiated a 68% slope, and a 42 % side tilt. They featured 44°/42° overhang angles and a 31.5-in fording depth. The 4032 prototype had a shorter wheelbase—87 in—and series production did not occur. In the early 1990s, FSR along with the Czech ROSS company participated in a Czech Army tender. In January 1996, production was terminated, but in March of the same year it was resumed, after a franchise was bought by one of the DMP factories—the Lublin company.

Honker ❷

In June 1997, the Tarpan Honker was introduced, featuring a modernized drivetrain including a transmission and a TD 4CT 90-1 2417cc engine (90–100hp @ 4100). It was produced by the Daewoo WSW factory in Andrychów. Modifi-

The military Tarpan Honker—a Czech army vehicle tender; IDET Brno, Czech Republic, 1994

cations involved the seating arrangement, and the vehicle was fit with a sunroof. Since 1999, the Honker 2324 has been sold under the Daewoo trademark.

Honker II ❷

The Honker II emerged in 1999, boasting a new wheel suspension, a refined drivetrain, wiring and interior from the Lublin 3. It features an inter-axle differential with a lock and permanent AWD. Both axles are rigid, with air suspension. The model features either a standard 2+2 seat arrangement, or a "service" arrangement with benches with 2 and 2 people seated in the rear, facing each other. An 8-seat version is also available, able to carry an extra 507 lbs of luggage. The wheelbase is 112 in long. The vehicle is 184 in long, 77 in wide, and 87 in high. Its curb weight is 4,564 lbs, and its gross weight is 6,393 lbs. The top speed is 75 mph. The producer markets the Honker II as a cheap version of a real off-roader. Unfortunately, the fate of this promising project is sealed, owing to the financial difficulties faced by Daewoo and the dismal state of the Polish market. A total of 206 units were made in 2000.

Honker 2000 ❷

The year 1999 saw the debut of a refined Honker II — the Honker 2000 — with independent front wheel suspension. (The Honker 2000 specification features both the original and the new version.) It is powered by an Italian TD VM 2499cc engine (100hp @ 4000), or a Polish-made TD 2.4L (95hp). A new feature is a 5-speed transmission and the Borg-Warner clutch. In addition to permanent 4x4 version, RWD version with optional FWD is also available. The wheelbase is 112 in long. The model is 183 in long, 69 in wide, 78 in high, and weighs 5,864 lbs. It negotiates a 68% slope, a 20° side tilt, and 44°/42° overhang angles. It has an 8.7-in ground clearance and a 31.5-in fording depth. The 2003 Poznań car show

The Tarpan Honker, 1993

saw the debut of the Honker 2000 pick-up trucks and the 2000 Platform Truck. In the first half of 2003, a total of 320 Honkers were produced, out of which 220 were taken up by the army, 50 went to the military and some went for export.

The Honker 2000, Poznań, 2001

The Honker—the 2003 model; IDET Brno, Czech Republic, 2003

Tata
(India)

In 1868, Jamsetji Nusserwanji Tata founded a business organization with a vision of industrializing the Indian subcontinent. A representative of the 6th generation in the 150-year history of the family currently runs the firm, which has by now become an industrial group with 250,000 employees. On October 15th, 1932, TATA Airlines—a predecessor of Air India—was established; Sir Dorab Tata piloted the first airmail flight from India to Pakistan. In 1954, the holding was renamed TELCO. In 1945, production was launched of franchised Mercedes. By 1971, their buses and trucks bore the Tata-Mercedes Benz mark, and later Tata. In the early 1980s, pick-up trucks appeared and Land Rovers with both short and long wheelbases began to be assembled there. The partnership with Mercedes ended in 1969, when it was transferred under the Tata Engineering and Locomotive Company (TELCO), in which Mercedes has a 10% share. More factories have been established around India—in Pune, Jamshedpur and most recently Lucknow. The Pune factory specializes in assembling units of the E-class Mercedes for the Indian and Asian markets. Original Tata vehicles date back to 1991. Since about 1993, the Estate 5-d station wagon has been available mainly in India, inspired by the T-Class Mercedes with D 2L engines (68hp). Seven out of ten middle-class and heavyweight trucks cruising the Indian roads bear the Tata mark. Since 2001, the pick-up trucks have been assembled in Malaysia and Egypt. For the 4x4 version, Tata produces a Borg Warner "Super select 4 Wheel Drive" transmission with "Shift on the Fly"—an electronic engagement of FWD before reaching 37 mph.

Tata Tatamobile 207, Telcoline, Pick-up

The year 1988 brought the 2-d Tatamobile 207 Pick-up (Single Cab—SC), followed 8 years later by the Tatamobile 207 Crew Cab (CC) with 4 doors and two rows of seats for 5 persons. It is distributed in Europe as the Pick-up or the Telcoline and, since October 1994, it has been known in England as the Loadbeta Pick-Up. The Mercedes technicians have their fingerprints on the model. Other body versions include a chassis, a dump truck, or a version with an elevated laminate cover for the cargo area. There is a ladder

The Tata Telcosport, Spain, 2002

The Tata Telcosport, 1996

chassis. A 4x4 drive version comes with an option of electrical engagement of FWD. The model features a 5-speed transmission, and some models are equipped with a reduction. The front wheel suspension is independent, while the rear Salisbury axle is rigid. The SC version has two 2 wheelbase options and 3 length options; while the CC version is only available with 1 wheelbase length and 2 options of total length. The slope is 32% (4x2) or 75% (4x4), and the ground clearance is 6.7 / 6.3 in.

Tata Sierra / TelcoSport ❷ ❸

This 3-d SUV has been rolling off the assembly line in Puna since 1991. A model with a couple of D engines and a gasoline engine is exported as "TelcoSport" to Asia and Africa, and in Europe mainly to Spain, Benelux and Greece. In England, it is known as the Ghurkha (after a Himalayan tribe of outstanding warriors), in Italy as the Tata Sport. In 2000, the more powerful Sierra Rage and Sierra Sport (4x2 or 4x4) appeared. The model features a steel body, a ladder frame with reinforcements, a classic drive layout and a 5-speed transmission. The 4x4 version has electrically-engageable FWD and a reduction. It negotiates a slope of 71% (the original version) or 76% (the later variants). Its ground clearance is 6.3 in high. The front wheels are suspended independently and equipped with an automatic lock in the wheel hub; the rear axle remains rigid. The payload of this model is 3,968 lbs.

The Tata Telcoline, the 2001 Geneva Motor Show

Tata Sumo ❷

The Sumo is a "broad-shouldered" station wagon designed for work in the off-road terrain. It is closely-related to the Mercedes G. In Europe, it can be encountered in Spain and other countries. In 2000 a modernization program brought along the Tourin (D 1.9L, 68hp) and the Spacio (D 3.0L, 90hp) models. A year later, these were followed by models with a modified nose—the Sumo SA (10 persons), the Sumo SE and the Sumo DS (8 persons). The following year brought the re-styled Sumo Premia (D 2.0L, 68hp). In addition to the classic 4x2 drive, there is optional RWD, plus a gear-reduction transmission. The Sumo is fitted with an independent wheel suspension in the front (with an automatic lock in the wheel hub), and a rigid rear axle. It has

The Tata Sumo, 2001

a 4,145-lb payload, a 6.3-in-high ground clearance, and a 72% slope. With 6–9 passengers, a driver and reasonably heavy luggage on board, it can reach a maximum speed of 71 mph.

Tata Safari ❸

The Safari compact SUV was available since the end of 1997. It was predestined mainly for the more demanding foreign customers. The assembly line was supplied to Pune by Nissan Australia. The design of the model was developed in the IAD studio in Britain. In Europe, the Safari was showcased at the 1998 NEC, where the public were invited to choose a name for the vehicle; they chose the name "Leisure."

The Safari Blazer was scheduled for launch in 2002. A ladder frame bore a modern steel body. Gear options (the fifth works as overdrive) mirror those of the previous type, except for a new feature—a limited slip differential. The model carries up to 6 persons plus a driver. Its payload is 4,497 lbs (4x4) or 4,233 lbs (4x2). It has an 8.1-in ground clearance and a slope of 30% (4x2) or 80% (4x4). Thanks to a TD 2.0L engine, it reaches a top speed of 96 mph. Alternatively, a gasoline version has been available since 1999. Work on a 3-d model is under way.

The Tata Safari, 1999

Tatra
(Czech Republic)

air-cooled 8V 3981cc engine (74hp). Its wheelbase was 129 + 37 in long. The total length of the vehicle was 234 in. It was 79 in wide and 103 in high and weighed 6,173 lbs.

The first functional automobile in Central Europe was built in a factory owned by Ignác Schustala—a horse-drawn carriage producer— in 1897. It got the name Präsident. In 1898, it undertook a trip from Kopřivnice (or Nesselsdorf in German), Moravia, to Vienna. In that same year, the firm, renamed to Nesselsdorfer Wagenbau–Fabriks Gesellschaft, built the first truck. After 1919, it assumed the name Tatra, in memory of a trip to the Tatras—the highest mountain range in Czechoslovakia. Its vehicles bear the original handwriting of designer Hans Ledwinka, namely the concept of a central tube frame, hinged half-axles and air-cooled engines. To this day, the world-famous Tatra trucks are almost unbeatable in the off-road. In 1940–43, the company supplied the German army with the V809—a middle-class off-road passenger vehicle with an air-cooled OHV 2470cc engine (50hp), a 4-speed transmission and a 2-speed reduction. There was an option to engage FWD on rough tracks. The wheels featured a transversal leaf spring independent suspension. The wheelbase was 110 in long. In 1946, the factory built closed-in V8 vehicles for army officers. A higher class of vehicles was the heavy-weight 6x4 Tatra 82 with flat, air-cooled 4-V 2490cc engines (55hp) and the same mechanics. The wheelbase was 133 + 36 in long. The vehicle was 221 in long, 79 in wide and 77 in high. It weighed 5,512 lbs. In 1935–36, a total of 325 units of the Tatra 82 6x4 vehicles were made. Even more robust was the Tatra 93 with an

The Tatra 82, 1935

The Tatra 93, 1941

The Tatra 805 fire engine, made in 1955, waiting to be restored.

Tatra 805 and 803 ❷ ❾

In 1953, the company launched the Tatra 805 — a lightweight truck, nicknamed "Duck." For an interim period, the vehicles were produced by Škoda. This trambus 1 ½-ton bearing different body-types proved useful both in the military and the civilian domain. It was also a successful expedition vehicle. The Czech explorers Zikmund and Hanzelka toured the whole world in various silver Tatras. Thanks to a central tube with a driveshaft hidden inside, they were unrivalled in the off-road terrain. Power came from an air-cooled gasoline 8-V OHV 2545cc engine (75hp). FWD could be disengaged. The wheels were suspended independently on axles with torsion bars. Specifications: wheelbase — 106 in, length — 186 in, width — 87 in, height — 102 in, ground clearance — 15.7 in, curb weight — 6,063 lbs, and payload — 3,748 lbs. In 1955–60, a total of 7,214 units were produced.

A prototype of the Tatra 803 — a small commander off-roader — was "born" simultaneously with the Duck. It was intended for use as a lightweight paratrooper vehicle, ambulance, box van and towing vehicle with an air-cooled 8-V engine and a 79 / 102-in-high wheelbase. The factory made two prototypes, which, however, remained under a cloak of secrecy for decades. Enthusiasts from Brno,

Czech Republic, converted one 805 model into an 803 with a Tatra V6 OHC 2622cc engine (125hp) taken from the 613 sedan. This successful replica was showcased in Brno in 2000. The car, named Červený drak (the Red Dragon) after a strong 18° Brno beer, was originally designed as a special for off-road races.

The Tatra 803 "Red Dragon;" Brno, Czech Republic, 2002

A prototype of the Tempo Land Rover 86

The Tempo Land Rover 86

Tempo
(Germany–FRG)

Tempo ❷

Tempo, owned by Oscar Vidal from a Hamburg suburb (1933-56), made its living by producing three-wheelers and vans. In 1955, Vidal sold 50% of its shares to the Rheinstahl-Hanomag company, which obtained 100% in 1965, and in 1970 became part of Daimler-Benz. The original Tempo vans survived until 1977 under the make of Mercedes. The German border police needed 6-seat 4WD vehicles. It chose the Land Rover but did not accept its long delivery times. A franchise contract for production of 250 units was signed in 1952. British chassis were imported to the factory in Harburg, where the vehicles were assembled and equipped with all-steel bodies produced by Herbert Vidal & Co— a firm owned by the brother of the Tempo owner. The Tempos differed from the Land Rovers by a higher structure and storage boxes in the front fenders. Part of the first batch of the 80" model was made by the Minerva company, Belgium. The border police took up the first specimens in April 1953. In August 1953, after supplying 190 vehicles, the producers switched over to the 86" version (58 units). This model, unlike its predecessor, featured an aluminum body. The last units were dispatched in 1955, but Tempo guaranteed servicing and sold new Land Rovers for another 10 years.

One of the first units of the Tempo 88

The Tempo 88

The Tempo Land Rover

The Tempo Land Rover

Toyota (Japan)

In 1918, Sakichi Toyoda built a spinning factory from scratch. Kiichiro Toyoda, his older son, invented numerous improvements of the looms and, being a capable businessman, he sold his patents to a British company. Using his royalties in 1926, he restructured the firm producing modern textile looms to Toyoda Automatic Loom Works Ltd. In 1933, Kiichiro founded an off-shoot of his father's firm—the Toyota Motor Co.—specializing in automobiles. In 1935, he built the first G1 Toyota Truck and the A1 passenger car. After 65 years of its existence, the company became on of the world's biggest car manufacturers. In 1967, it acquired Daihatsu—its competitor—and a year later Hino—a utility vehicle producer. In 1988, it founded Lexus. Besides Japan, it has been making vehicles in 21 other countries.

During WWII, the firm produced a 5-seat vehicle for the army—the AB (4x2) model fit with a 6-V OHV 3389cc engine (65hp). After the war, it came up with a replica of the Dodge WCD52—a $^3/_4$-ton (4x4) FQ10 with a 6-V OHC 3878cc engine (125hp) coupled to a 4-speed transmission, an auxiliary transmission, RWD and optional FWD. The model had rigid axles with leaf springs. Specifications: wheelbase—118 in, length—201 in, width—81 in, height—92 in,

weight—6,195 lbs. In the early 1960s came the Toyota 2FQ15L featuring almost identical mechanics and parameters. Large numbers of them served in the armed forces of Japan, the U.S.A., Southern Vietnam and South Korea. The KCY 4x4 truck is a war child, as is its derivation—the KCY/SUKI floating transport vehicle. In 1942, the Toyota technicians acquired a few trophy Jeeps and used them as models to build 5 units of the AK-10—a $^1/_4$-ton vehicle with 4x4 drive. This unsightly vehicle featured a short ladder frame, axles from the truck and it weighed 2 tons. However, after the world war had reached the islands of the Japanese Empire, plans for further development were dropped.

The only wartime small Japanese 4x4 off-roader was the Kurogane (where "Kuro" means "metal" and "gane" means "black"; hence: steel), built in 1936–37 by the Rikuo company. This 2-d soft-top or pick-up truck was powered by an air-cooled V-2 1399cc engine (33hp @ 3400), it had a 3-speed transmission and permanent 4x4. A one-speed transmission served for disengaging FWD. The front axle was independent with coil springs and the rear one was rigid with leaf springs. Specifications: wheelbase—79 in, length—140 in, width—61 in, height—66 in, ground clearance—9 in, curb weight—2,337 lbs, and payload—419 lbs. A total of 4,775 units of this model were made. Modern AWD Toyotas represent a wide and confusing choice of vehicles with some models overlapping.

The Toyota BJ, 1951

The Toyota Land Cruiser J4 Hard Top

Toyota Land Cruiser ❷

The over-fifty-year-long Land Cruiser series is one of the pinnacles of the world's "four-wheelers." It deserves special attention. In August 1950, Toyota began work on an off-road vehicle, hoping for a lucrative contract from both the occupying American army and the nascent Japanese army, which had since 1951 been in the market for a new $1/_4$-ton 4x4 vehicle. A prototype was finished five months later, featuring an SB truck frame, rigid axles and a gasoline 6-V OHV 3386cc engine (85hp @ 2400). The engine came from 1938 and had been used in the GB 1 $1/_2$-ton vehicle with "code B" and a 4-speed transmission with an extremely short first gear. This Jeep-like model got the name "J," and a combination of both codes gave rise to a definitive name—BJ—of the first series-made Toyota off-road vehicle for both civilian

and military use. Unfortunately for Toyota, the Japanese army preferred the franchise-made Jeep-Willys vehicles supplied by Mitsubishi, which caused Toyota to sell only 298 units by 1953, including some to the police. Not even a promo presentation on the slopes of the holy Mt. Fujiyama helped boost sales. The wheelbase was 95 in long. The model came exclusively as a soft-top, with a "B" 3.4-L engine (86hp). An exhaustive genealogy of the model series would be long enough to cover a whole book; let us therefore focus only on the main models. NB: Unless otherwise specified, the vehicles described are 2-d models.

The 2nd generation—BJ J2 / J3—appeared in 1954. Its new, curvier body determined the appearance of off-road Toyotas until the mid-1980s. The wheelbase was altered to 90 in. Steel doors replaced the original canvas, and the longitudinal leaf spring suspension was derived from the Crown

The first Toyota BJ in Paris, 2000

257

sedan. Since 1958, two wheelbase-length options were available. The BJ 25 model (a soft- or hard-top, or a pick-up) had by that time been exported and won international acclaim. It got a second name—the Land Cruiser. Later models included: the FJ 25 (1955), fit with a gasoline 6-V 3.9L "F" engine (105hp); the FJ 28 (1958–60)—a soft- and hard-top with a 96-in wheelbase; and the FJ 35 (1956–60), with a 104-in wheelbase and a hard-top body, which was the first 4-d vehicle. New "F" engines were manufactured until 1983. Models fit with the F engines bore the name "J3."

In 1964 came the 3rd generation—the J4, later re-coded to J40—a replacement of the previous J2/J3. The J4 became a legendary brutal, invincible toiler and is produced to this day almost unaltered in Brazil as the Toyota Bandeirante. This model already featured a cross-country reduction, but coupled to only a 3-speed transmission. An F engine had, thanks to a bigger compression, 125 horsepower. A choice of multiple wheelbase lengths was reflected in the naming system. Complete vehicles of this generation were made until 1985, chassis until 1986. The models included: the FJ 40 with a 90-in wheelbase, a soft- or hard-top or station wagon

body, and an in-line gasoline 6-V "1F" engine (25hp); the BJ 40 featuring a diesel 4-V "1B" 3.0L engine (75hp), where the confusing "B" code, now used for diesel models, was purely coincidental; the FJ 40 (1975) with a gasoline in-line 6-V "2F" 4.2L engine (136hp); the BJ 41 (1979) with a D 4-V "2B" 3.2L engine (84hp); the BJ 42 (1982) with a D 4-V "3B" 3.4L engine (90hp); the FJ 43 with a 96-in wheelbase, a soft-top or station wagon body, and a "1F" engine (125hp); the BJ 43 with a "1B" engine (75hp); the FJ 43 (1975) with a "2F" engine (136hp); the BJ 44 (1979) with a "2B" engine (84hp); the BJ 46 with a "3B" engine (90hp); the FJ 45 with a 116-in wheelbase, a soft- or hard-top or a pick-up body and a "1F" engine (125hp); the FJ 45 (1975) with a "2F" engine (136hp); the HJ 45 (1972–80) with a diesel 6-V "H" 3.6L engine (90hp); the HJ 47 (1981) with a D 6-V "2H" 4.0L engine (103hp); and the BJ 45 (1982) with a "3B" engine (90 hp). In 1968, the 100,000th Land Cruiser rolled off the assembly line. The year 1972 brought a new 4-speed transmission, which gave way to a 5-speed one in most markets in 1982. In 1980, round headlight rims replaced rectangular rims and the triangular front door quarter vent windows disappeared.

The Toyota Land Cruiser Wagon G, 1986

The year 1965 brought, along with the J4 series, the Station J5 station wagon. The Land Cruiser was no longer a coarse work tool; growing numbers of mainly American customers were looking for a fancier off-road 5-seat station wagon for private use, offering the highest-possible degree of comfort. Safety levels had been increased. The FJ 55 was mounted on the same chassis as the J4 series, but it had a far more elegant station wagon body — mostly in two-color finish — which set it apart from the coarse-featured J4. It held on until 1979. A swan song of this generation was the BJ 55 (1979–80) fit with a D 4-V "2B" engine. The models included: the FJ 55 — a 4-d station wagon with a 106-in wheelbase and a gasoline in-line 6-V "1F" 3.9L engine (125hp); the FJ 55 (1975) with a "2F" engine (135hp); and the BJ 55 (1979) with a "2B" engine (84hp).

In 1980, a 14-year production run of the J5 was terminated by the launch of the 6th generation — a 4-d station wagon. This novelty was marked by a higher degree of luxury, a modern design and a choice of two engines. Early in 1985, the obsolescent "F2" was replaced by the more powerful "F3" rejuvenated version (model FJ 60). In 1986, Toyota as the first producer in the world introduced an off-roader with an overcharged diesel engine. The technicians took the time-tested "H" engine block and mounted on it a new cylinder head including a turbocharger; the "12H-T" engine was endowed with 136 horsepower and a much higher torque. The Land Cruiser HJ 61 became the fastest 4x4 vehicle with a TD engine on the market. In 1987, the HJ 61 got a facelift, characterized by two pairs of rectangular lights instead of one round pair. This body was featured on the vast majority

The Toyota Land Cruiser J6

of representatives of this generation. In 1988, the "3F" was equipped (on request) with a Lambda probe and a controlled catalytic converter (155hp), but this innovation did not receive any ovation in Europe. The models included: the FJ 60—a 4-d station wagon with a 107.5-in wheelbase and a "2F" engine (135hp) and since 1985 a 4.0L "3F" engine (137hp); the FJ 62 (1988) with an in-line gasoline 6-V 4.0L "3F-E" engine (155hp); the HJ 60 with a "2H" engine (103hp), the HJ 61 (1986) with a "12H-T" engine (136 hp); and the BJ 60 (1981) with a "3B" engine (90hp).

A successor to the J4 "aging workhorse" was launched in 1984 as the J7 series. An ingenious car kit design of the body made it possible over time to create an unusually high number of variants, divided into two categories of different characters. A ladder frame, the same for both categories with small exceptions, was in the first case borne by rigid axles with leaf springs. The robust vehicle had little comfort to offer, but it made up for it by a great adaptability to low-quality roads. In contrast to it stood a version with rigid axles and coil springs (known as Prado in Japan), longitudinal bars and a Panhard rod for the bituminous roads prevailing in Europe and the U.S.

The Toyota Land Cruiser J7

The former became known as "Heavy Duty," while the latter was nicknamed "Light Duty." They differ in appearance by their "noses"—the LD has a broader mask, integrated blinkers, and its fenders are enclosed in the front and reach up to the bumper; in contrast, the HD features a hood markedly narrow in the front, with the parking lights and blinkers protruding from the side, and open fenders in the front. The LD was fit with two different 4-V 2.4L engines—a "22R" gasoline engine (105hp, later 110hp), and a "2L" atmospheric diesel engine (71hp), since 1986 a "2L-T" engine with a turbo (86hp, and 90hp since 1990). Hand-in-hand with the above-mentioned increase in horsepower, the LD was equipped with a wider engine hood and rectangular lights. In 1993, the lazy "2L-T" engine (90hp) gave way to new dynamic TD 3.0L "1KZ-T" and "1KZ-TE" engines. The year 1988 brought the LJ/RJ 73 variants with a longer wheelbase. In Europe, the GFK 2-d soft or hard-top models were available; elsewhere also 4-d versions with a 104-in-long wheelbase and named J77, J78 and J79 depending on the mounted engine, which did not make it to the old continent until 1993. The Light Duty J7 models included: the RJ 70—a soft- or hard-top with a 91-in wheelbase and a "22 R" engine (105hp, or 110hp since 1985) or (since 1985) a 2.4L "22 R-E" engine (113hp); the LJ 70 with a 2.45L "2L" engine (72hp), (since 1986) a "2L-T" turbo engine (97hp); the KZJ 70 or the KJ 70 (1993) with a "1KZ-T" engine (125hp); the KZJ 71 (1993) with a "1KZ-TE" engine (129hp). In 1985–96, the "2L" engine was not supplied; the other engines were the same as those mounted in the 91-in-wheelbase models. A new code name—"73"—replaced the "70"; similarly, the "74" replaced the "71" and the "76" replaced the "72," a hard- or a soft-top vehicle with a 102-in wheelbase. The RJ 77 4-d station wagon (1990–96) had a 107-in wheelbase and a "22R" (110hp) or a "22R-E" (114hp) engine; the LJ 77 (until 1993) featured a "2L-TII" TD 2.45L engine (90hp); the LJ 79 was fit with a "3L" engine (87hp), while the LJ 78 (1991–93) carried a "2L-TE" power unit (95hp); the KZJ 77 (1993) featured a "1KZ-T" engine (125hp), and the KZJ 78 (1993) was powered by a "1KZ-TE" engine (129hp). The two-millionth vehicle was sold in 1990.

The J7 Heavy Duty series from 1984 lived to see the new millennium. In time, it became ever more heavyweight and featured an increasing number of variants. The original FJ 70/73 models started with the 4th generation power units; in 1985, the stretched FJ / HJ 75 appeared, the latter with an "H" engine from the HJ 60. In 1990, the "B" and "H" engines were replaced with a 6-V diesel nicknamed "Lasre" and marked "1HZ" (4.2L, 129hp) and a 5-V "1PZ" diesel engine (3.5L, 116hp). In 1993, gasoline power units were added to the choice, when the obsolescent "F" series gave way to a modern in-line gasoline 6-V 4.5L "1FZ-F" engine (DOHC, 24 v, 190hp) and a "1FZ-FE" (injection, 213hp), respectively. In 2000, many HDs underwent major reconstruction. The front rigid axle, partly derived from the J8, already featured coil springs, longitudinal arms and Panhard rods. The wheelbase of the pick-up truck was extended to 125 in and the rear marking of each model's name was altered as follows: the HZJ 70 to the HZJ 71, the HZJ 73 to the HZJ 74, and the HZJ 75 expedition station wagon to the HZJ 78 and the HZJ 79 pick-up truck. The Heavy Duty J7 models included: the FJ 70 soft-top and station wagon with a 91-in wheelbase and a "3F" engine (137hp); the BJ 70 (until 1990) with a "3B" engine (90hp); the BJ 71 (1987–90) fit with a "13B-T" TD 3.4L power unit (124hp); the PZJ 70 (1990) powered by a "1PZ" engine (114hp); the HZJ 70 (1990) and the HZJ 71 (since 1999) with a "1HZ" engine

(132hp); the FZJ 70 (1993) with a "1FZ-F" engine (190hp) or a "1FZ-FE" power unit (215hp). After 1984, the same engines were used as those mounted on the 91-in-wheelbase models, but a change in naming occurred: the "70" became the "73," the "71" was changed to the "74" (a soft- or hardtop with a 102-in wheelbase); there were also the "PZJ 77" (1990) 4-d station wagon with a 107-in wheelbase and a "1PZ" engine (116hp), and the HZJ 77 with a "1HZ" engine (132hp). A pick-up version was available only in 1985–1999. The same engines were featured as those in the 91-in-wheelbase models, but a change in naming occurred: the "70" became the "75" and the "71" turned into the "78." The wheelbase of this soft-top station wagon or pick-up truck was 116 in long. The HZJ 70, or the HZJ 79 after 1999

featured a 125-in wheelbase, a pick-up body and a "1HZ" engine (132hp); the FZJ 79 was fit with a "1FZ-F" (190hp) or a "1FZ-FE" (215hp) power unit.

In 1990, after only nine years of existence, the J6 series was replaced by the J8 generation. Everything was brand new—the bodies including the front and rear face, the chassis with coil springs, and the drivetrain including the engine. The J8 became the first Toyota with permanent AWD with a manual lock on an inter-axle differential, later complemented by a viscous coupling. A new, economical 6-V turbo-diesel direct injection engine—a "1HD-T"—had at first a maximum of 166hp; it had also been successfully used from the start in the HD J7 series. In contrast to the HZJ 80 with a D "1HZ" engine, the HDJ 80 model was charac-

The Toyota 4-Runner Sporty

terized by good engine output / consumption ratio. A third unit was the aging "F" gasoline engine, finally replaced in 1993 by the "1FZ-F" engines and an injection "1FZ-FE" (FZJ 80). In 1995, the turbo diesel got a new cylinder head with a 4-valve head, which enabled it to meet the strict new emission requirements. The engine got the name "1HD-FT" and the model was coined the HDJ-FT. The J8 models included: the FJ 80 (until 1993)—a 4-d station wagon with a 112-in wheelbase and a "3F" 4.0L engine (137hp) or a "3F-E" engine (155hp); the FZJ 80 (after 1993) fit with a "1FZ-F" 4.5L (190hp) or a "1FZ-FE" (215hp) engine; the HZJ 80 (1990) powered by a "1HZ" 4.2L (132hp) engine; the HDJ 80 with a "1HD-T" 4.2L engine (170hp, or 159hp—after 1992); and the HDJ 81 (1995) carrying a "1HD-FT" power unit (170hp).

A new release of the year 1996—the Land Cruiser J9—replaced the Light Duty J7. It was the first Land Cruiser to feature independently suspended front wheels and enhanced driving comfort. Its mechanics with an inter-axle differential manual lock was derived from the J8 model. A "3RZ-F" gasoline 4-V 2.7L engine was only available on selected markets (the short RZJ 90 and the stretched RZJ 95). A TD 3.0L was, in contrast to the J7 series, equipped with an electronically-controlled fuel injection pump and the code "1KZ-TE" (the KZJ 90 / 95 and the KJ 90 / 95). 2000 was the swan-song year of this "doyen" engine and in the 2001 model year it was replaced with a common-rail diesel 16-v 4-V 3.0L direct injection engine—a "1KD-FTV" (the KDJ

90 / 95). The first V-6 engine of the Land Cruiser series was a 24-v "5VZ-FE" 3.4L power unit, coupled exclusively to a 4-speed auto transmission. The top-notch model of this series was the VZJ 90 / 95. The J9 models include: the RZJ 90 3-d station wagon with a 93-in wheelbase and a "3RZ-F" (131hp) or a "3RZ-FE" (151hp) engine; the VFJ 90 with a "5VZ-FE" engine (177hp); the LJ 90 fit with a TD 2.8L "3L" engine (87hp); the KZJ 90 and the KJ 90 carrying a TD 3.0L "1KZ-T" power unit (125hp) or a "1KZ-TE" engine (132hp); the KDJ 90 (2001) with a TD 3.0L "1KD-TE" engine (163hp). Models with a 93-in wheelbase feature the same engines, the "95" in their names is replaced with "90," and they feature a 5-d station wagon body. In 2003, the J9 model gave way to the Land Cruiser 300 / Prado generation, no longer considered an off-roader but an SUV.

In 1998, the 10th generation of the Land Cruiser was introduced. The J10 replaced the J8 vehicles. Again, we are talking two design categories with different chassis. The Heavy Duty is mounted on a J8 chassis including "1FZ-F," "1FZ-FE" and "1HZ" engines differing in small details. An even more comfortable series—the Light Duty Land Cruiser 100—is available in Europe and other countries. It is more robust than the J9 and features an independent front wheel suspension, a manually- or automatically-adjustable chassis available at a premium, an adjustable ground clearance of the body with hydro-pneumatic suspension and a "2UZ-FE"—the first 8-V 4.7L engine (235hp) in the history of the model (UZJ 100). The engine comes from the Toyota

The Toyota RAV-4 3-d, 1997

Majesta luxury sedan ("1UZ-FE"). "1HD-FTE" is the name of the latest version of a TD direct injection engine — 4.2L (204hp) with 4 valves per cylinder. The J10 models include: the FZJ 100 — a 5-d station wagon with a 112-in wheelbase and a "1FZ-F" 4.5L (190hp) or a "1F-FE" engine (245hp); the UZJ 100 fit with a "2UZ-FE" 4.5L engine (230hp or 234 k); the HZJ 100 with a "1HZ" 4.2L engine (132hp); and the HDJ 100 featuring a "1HD-FTE" 4.2L engine (204hp).

The Toyota Land Cruiser has been a popular expedition vehicle and has an exceptionally strong representation in the Mediterranean, Alpine and Pyrenean countries and elsewhere. In 1996, the Land Cruiser Colorado luxury version was introduced, followed in 1998 by the even classier Land Cruiser Amazon, and in 2000 by the Land Cruiser Amazon 50th Anniversary. The Land Cruiser has been officially distributed in more than 95 countries, and unofficially in many

others. The vehicles were assembled in countries including Pakistan, Bangladesh, Malaysia, Indonesia, New Zealand, Venezuela, Kenya, and Zimbabwe, with more or less identical parameters; models assembled in Brazil and Portugal are an exception.

Toyota Hi-Lux, Hilux, Hi-Lux Surf and 4-Runner ❷ ❻ ❽

The extensive Hi-Lux series ranks among the most successful LUVs in history. Over time, these vehicles started to make a name on the leisure car market. This model was built by the then competitor, Hino, and was sold after 1968 under the name "Briska." After Toyota acquired it, it started selling the vehicles under its own make. The Hi-Lux lineup included a station wagon and a pick-up truck. In 1972 and 1978, the vehicles were modernized, while retaining gasoline 1.6 and 2.0L engines. In 1979, a D 2.2L engine was added to the selection. In the same year, Toyota came up with a 4x4 version. Power came from the sisterly Land Cruiser. In addition to bulky models there were also the Pick-up and the Double Cab. In Japan, a 5-d station wagon version was presented in 1989 as "Hi-Lux Surf," imported to Europe in the early 1990s as "Toyota 4-Runner." In Germany, it was assembled by VW under the name "VW Taro." The 4-Runner was based on the 1987 Hi-Lux pick-up truck, but in contrast to the latter's rear leaf springs, it was equipped with coil springs, as well as more powerful engines. In 1995 the 3rd generation — 4-Runner / Hi-Lux Surf / Hilux SW4 — was launched, fit with gasoline 3.0L V6 (141hp) and 3.4L V6 (185hp) engines; direct-injection TD 2.7L engines (150hp), and 3.0L power units (145hp). This 5-seat 5-d model featured a 103-in wheelbase, a 177-in length, a 70.5-in width, a 69-in height, an 8.7-in ground clearance, and weighed +4,057 lbs. The concurrent Hilux Pick-Up had reached its 4th generation in 1997. Available were vehicles with 4x2 and 4x4 drive, manual and auto transmissions, 3-seat pick-up trucks, 5-seat

The Toyota RAV-4 5-d, 2000

2-d extra-cabs and 5-seat 4-d double-cabs. In 2003, a brand new series related to the Land Cruiser / Prado made its debut—a replacement of the Land Cruiser J9. The successor to the 4-Runner received the name Hilux Surf, a wheelbase extended to 110 in, a 4-V 2.7L engine (150hp), a 3.4L V6 engine (186hp), a 4.0L V6 engine (250hp) and a 4-v 16v TD common-rail 3.0L power unit (163hp or 170hp). The choice of transmissions includes a 4-speed automatic or, with selected models, a 5-speed manual transmission. The "4Runner," as it is spelled in the U.S., is a full-blooded SUV with many chassis and frame components of the Lexus series.

Toyota Blizzard ❷

The Toyota Blizzard from 1980 was badge-engineered from the Daihatsu Taft. It was fit with a D 2.2L engine (72hp). In 1984, a completely remolded Generation II was launched, featuring a D 2446cc engine (83hp) and a TD engine (96hp). The Blizzard had AWD and a 5-speed auto transmission with a reduction.

Toyota RAV-4 ❸

The Toyota RAV-4, presented at the 1993 Tokyo show and in Geneva in 1994, was born into a critical time of off-roader sales. "RAV-4" is short for Recreational Active Vehicle, Four-Wheel Drive, which well explains the "mission" of an otherwise rather impractical vehicle, which over time became a fashionable model for moneyed, professionally active women in urban and suburban traffic. The 1995 Geneva car show witnessed the debut of the RAV-4 with an extended wheelbase and 5 doors. This SUV was fit with a gasoline 4-V 16v 1998cc engine (129hp @ 5000 and, since the fall of 1996, 150hp @ 6000 or 165hp @ 6600), a 5-speed or 4-speed auto transmission and permanent 4x4 with an inter-axle differential featuring a locking system and a viscous coupling. A 4x2 version was made for some foreign mar-

kets. Another engine option was a 4-V 16v 1794cc (125hp @ 6000), or since 2002 a TD common-rail direct-injection 1995cc (116hp @ 4000). The RAV-4 has a self-supporting steel body. Its front wheels are suspended independently on McPherson struts, while the rear wheels have longitudinal and transverse control arms; both axles have stabilizers. Specification: wheelbase—87 in, length—151 in, width—68 and 70 in, height—64 and 70 in. The 5-d version has a 98-in wheelbase and is 167 in long. The model has a ground clearance of between 7 and 8 in. A convertible version arrived in Geneva in 1998, followed in the same place in 2000 by Generation II of this popular model.

Toyota Tercel 4x4 / Sprinter Carib ❶

The rectangular Tercel Wagon 4x4 (also known as the Sprinter Carib)—the 4th generation Corolla II / Tercel / Corsa—featuring an impressive tailgate was showcased in Paris in 1982. This 5-seat station wagon had, as did other models, FWD with optional RWD. The Wagon 4x4 was fit with a more powerful gasoline 4-V 1453cc engine (71hp @ 5600, 96 mph, 90hp JIS) coupled to a 5-speed transmission with a "slow cross-country 1st gear," or a 3-speed auto

The Toyota Blizzard, 1984

transmission. The front McPherson axle with lower transverse control arms and stabilizer had been featured in other Corollas, while the rear axle was—unlike the other Corollas—rigid with longitudinal control arms, a Panhard rod, stabilizer and coil springs. The wheelbase was 96 in long. The European versions were 164.5 in long, 64 in wide, 59.5 in high, and had a 6.7-in ground clearance. The curb weight is 2,138 lbs. This model, unrivalled in its time, found many buyers in the Alpine countries. After August 1984, Toyota fit its Corolla sedans with 4x4 as well. By that time, 212,000 4x4 station wagons had been produced. The spring of 1988 brought a new model—the Toyota Corolla RV 4WD. AWD is also featured in several masterpiece units of the Corolla and Celica Rally WRC.

Toyota MPV - Picnic / Ipsum, Model F, Previa / Estima, Ace ❼ ❽

In 1983 the 7-seat MPV Space Cruiser (2x4) was launched, fit with a 1812cc engine (78hp, later 1998cc, 87hp). It did not create a great impression. At the turn of the 1980s and 1990s, the Toyota Model F arrived, which won the heart of its Swiss customers by its 4x2 or 4x4 drive. This model's successful successor (a prototype in 1989, series-made in the spring of 1990), is known as "Estima" in Japan, and as "Previa: in Europe. A longitudinally mounted engine powered the rear axle or, in some models, all wheels via a 5-speed manual or a 4-speed auto transmission. In the spring of 2000, transversally mounted engines arrived along with the 2nd generation: a gasoline 16v 4-V 2362cc (156hp @ 5600 115 mph), a TD common-rail 1995cc (116hp

The Toyota Hi-Lux 4WD, 1986

The Toyota Picnic; Geneva, 1997

The Toyota Previa 4WD, 1994

@ 4000, 109 mph), and a V6 2995cc (220hp @ 5800, 112 mph). This road MPV has a 114-in wheelbase. The more luxurious Alphard was prepared for 2003, longer by 2 and 4 inches, and featuring 4x2 and 4x4 and exclusively a 4-speed auto transmission. The 5-d, 6-seat Ipsum minivan made its debut in May 1996; the Picnic was launched in Paris in 1996. An AWD version was available on the home market, featuring an inter-axle differential, a viscous coupling and a torsen differential in the rear axle. In 1967, the utility vehicle division came up with the "Ace" series, which proliferated into several sizes of microbuses, vans and their combo versions in 3 parallel model series. In addition to 4x2, some versions were available with 4x4. They were powered by gasoline or diesel engines. The Ace vehicles won 23% of the relevant segment of the Japanese market. Some of them would today be considered MPVs. The models in-

clude: the Lite-Ace, the Master-Ace / the Town-Ace, and the Hi-Ace.

The Toyota J7 Heavy Duty; Annecy, France, 2003

The Toyota Hi-Ace 4WD Jubilee, 1994

Toyota Caetano (Portugal)

The Portuguese company Salvador Caetano based in Vila Nova de Gaio, a suburb of Porto, produced modified Toyotas, which, nevertheless, were never featured in the Japanese catalogs.

Toyota Land Cruiser

The Land Cruiser, generation J7, model BJ 73, was designed mainly for Japanese, Italian and Mediterranean customers. This 3-d hardtop is marked by rigid axles with leaf springs and, above all, a VM 66A—an Italian 5-V TD 2494cc engine (108hp @ 4200)—coupled to a 5-speed transmission with a reduction. The model has a 102-in-long wheelbase

The Toyota Land Cruiser T Soft Top, 1990

and a 7.3-in ground clearance. It is 171 in long, 67 in wide and 77 in high. Its curb weight is 4,045 lbs, and payload is 1,488 lbs. This Toyota negotiates a fording depth of 28 in, a slope with a 45° incline and 32° / 28° overhang angles.

The Toyota Caetano Land Cruiser 250 TD; Spain, 2001

Trishul (India)

Trishul Tourer ❶

The Trishul Autocrafts company was active in 1982–91. It produced Jeep-like 2x4 vehicles. Their welded chassis bore a metal body. The marketing focus in sultry India consisted in an open doorless vehicle. The model was available with a soft-top body or, as the photograph shows, a 4-d station wagon / hard-top, taxi. The Trishul carried 6 very light Indians, or 992 lbs of cargo. Power was provided by an Italian Lombardini D 510cc engine (12hp @ 3000, 40 mph) coupled to a 4-speed transmission. Both axles were rigid with longitudinal leaf springs. Specifications: wheelbase—73 in, length—117 in, width—48 in, height—65 in, ground clearance—5.5 in, curb weight—1,323 lbs and fuel tank capacity—4 gal. In the first half of the 1900s, the Trishul company was made over to Phooltas.

The Trishul Tourer, 1990

UAZ
(USSR and Russia)

UAZ (Ulyanovskiy Avtomobilniy Zavod) used to be the biggest producer of lightweight 4WD vehicles in Eastern Europe. In 1941, a decision was made to remove strategic industry to the East, out of German reach. In August 1941, the ZIS auto works based in Moscow sent out a scout team to find a suitable location. They suggested a place in the vicinity of a railway junction on the banks of the Volga river. The first workers arrived at the Volga virgin soil from Moscow at the end of October 1941. They set to work immediately after they got off the train. Boys and girls aged 16 and 17 worked 14-hour shifts. Work went on non-stop. Despite inhuman conditions and a lack of machinery, the first five ZIS-5 platform trucks were assembled in May 1942. The city of

The UAZ (GAZ-A)

Ulyanovsk grew, as the two factories expanded. At the same time, the GAZ Molotov factory in Gorki (before 1932, and also today, known as Nizhnyi Novgorod) was unable to satisfy demand. A late-1944 order made GAZ pass on the production of the GAZ off-roaders to Ulyanovsk, and the production of the UAZ trucks to a factory in the Ural Mountains. In the spring of 1945 (until 1952), the GAZ-AA box-type vehicles began to be assembled in Ulyanovsk, at first using imported components, named the GAZ-MM. Preparations for the production of the GAZ-69 and GAZ-69A were underway in 1954-55. From the summer of 1955, by order from the secretary of the automobile industry, the UAZ factory specialized in the production of low-fuel-tank-capacity 4WD vehicles. In the mid-1950s, the company extended its model range with the UAZ-450D—its first and for a long time the only van / minibus produced in the USSR. Both were modernized over the years, but in 2002 they were still the pillar of the factory's production program. Their appearance had remained the same since the 1960s. Not even a major modernization of the UAZ-31520 off-roader from late 2001 brought a change of exterior. The first model new in every way was the UAZ-3160 made in 1997. It became the basis of a host of pick-up trucks, MPVs and other vehicles. A "Disajn-centr" (= design center) was established. In 1992, UAZ was transformed into a joint-stock company. In 2000, 68% of UAZ's shares were obtained by the Severstal concern. This co-owner invested over 100 million U.S. dollars in the reconstruction of the manufacturing halls, enabling them to manage modern components, and in preparing the launch of the UAZ-3160 and UAZ-3162. In 2001, the 60th anniversary of the company's foundation, a plan was announced for producing 100,000 units per year. By that time, a "snake" of 3.7 million vehicles had rolled off the assembly lines. The

The UAZ (GAZ)—69

The 1ˢᵗ UAZ 469 on a pedestal outside UAZ headquarters

biggest purchaser of UAZs was the army and other power centers of the USSR, the Warsaw pact members and sympathetic countries. However, the simple, electronics-free design of the vehicles backfired in more sophisticated markets in the 1990s. As a result, the vehicles had to be fit with engines made by renowned producers. Strict safety refulations have been another hard nut to crack. More significant exports have been prevented by lack of capital and homologation problems. The UAZs have been assembled in Belorussia, the Ukraine and Egypt (since 2001), in Venezuela (since 2002), and in Vietnam and North Korea. In keeping with a Soviet tradition, the company has maintained code-naming of the vehicles; nonetheless, their distribution seems to follow no logic, except possibly to confuse a potential enemy by a chaotic naming system. Within the past 25 years, 1.3

million vehicles have been produced, which the public knew as "gaziks" for years after production had been launched in Ulyanovsk.

UAZ-69 (USSR) to UAZ-31520 ❷

In 1954, GAZ launched production of the 2ⁿᵈ generation of the vehicle, passing it on to UAZ shortly afterwards. The models in question were the GAZ-69 (8 seats) and the GAZ-69A (5 seat). Both were powered by a 2.2L GAZ-M20 SV engine from the GAZ-Pobieda passenger vehicle. The UAZs featured RWD and optional FWD, a 3-speed transmission and a 2-speed reduction transmission. Their ground clearance was 8.3 in high. After 1956, they bore the name UAZ-69 (the UAZ had a flat tail panel, while the GAZ featured

The UAZ-469; IDET Brno, Czech Republic, 2003

a curved tailgate). In 1965, the company prepared an up-dated trim of the GAZ 69, but production did not occur, as the new UAZ-469 got the green light. After March 1965, the UAZ 69 vehicles were in service in the Soviet army, fol-lowed later by station wagons (the UAZ-468) and convert-ibles (the UAZ-469). By the end of 1972, a total of 634,000 units of the UAZ 69 were produced in 2 assembly plants in Ulyjanovsk. They were assembled in Romania and North Korea as well. In January 1967, the ministry for the automo-bile industry and GOSPLAN (The State Planning Office) reached a decision to implement a major modernization of the vehicle. In March 1971, P. I. Zhukov was appointed Head Designer. The code UAZ-469 stood for the 2nd generation of the UAZ, rolling off the assembly lines from December 15th, 1972. It boasted a trendy look. Its development had taken 10 years. The first series-made vehicle is perched on a pedestal outside the company headquarters. It carried 2 passengers and 1,323 lbs of cargo, or a crew of up to 7 persons. Compared to its predecessors, its more powerful gasoline engine from the GAZ-Volga sedan (2.5L, OHV, 62 mph), coupled to a 4-speed transmission from the UAZ-452, demonstrated a 30%-lower fuel consumption in the off-road. The model's ground clearance had increased by 2.8 in, and it featured larger windows, a more powerful heater and a more spacious interior. Later came TD 2.5L Peugeot-Citroën and D Citroën 2.1L engines. The UAZ 469 became the basis for the Chinese Beijing 4x4. According to the company: "In 1974, the UAZ-469B went up the Elbrus Mountain to an altitude of over 13,000 ft above sea level and managed a ride over the hillcrest between the peaks... The Land Rover only achieved a similar feat in 1997, in an attempt on the world record."

The UAZ-3907 Jaguar, 1983

The UAZ-3907 Jaguar, 1983

A prototype of the UAZ-3171 short vehicle

The model was updated after 1980. It received telescopic shocks, a new rear axle suspension, new steering and a power-ful heater. In 1982, under a contract from the army, they built the amphibious UAZ-3907 soft-top nicknamed "Jaguar" (5–6 mph). It underwent a trial a year later. It was partly based on the GAZ 3907. Production of the Jaguar, however, did not commence. In the 1980s, demand grew for this Spartan Soviet-vehicle that was heavily prone to corrosion but featured good road-going abilities. In the late 1980s and early 1990s, UAZ tried to prepare the model's 3rd generation for the Red Army. The stretched UAZ 3172 soft-top, in ad-dition to the civilian 5-d station wagon, was complemented by the short UAZ 3171. It was powered by an engine derived from the UAZ 469 but with a different capacity—2.9L (103hp). Coil springs were featured. The 1993 test drives were successful, but the collapse of the army thwarted the plans for its production. The off-roader underwent further refinements, which was reflected in the naming system: the UAZ-31512 is a civilian 4-d convertible, the UAZ-3151 is a military trim, the UAZ-31514 is a metal hard-top, the UAZ-31514-010 features coil springs, the UAZ-31519 is a 5/7-seat station wagon with a partition between the pas-senger and cargo areas. The UAZ-3159 luxury Bars (a pro-totype from late 1997 or early 1998, series-version launched in January 2001) features a ZMZ-409 engine with an elec-tronic injection. This model is a 15-in-longer, 5-d 9-seat variant of the basic UAZ-3153, produced since February 1997. In Moscow 1998, a prototype of the UAZ-2931 made

A task force in the UAZu 469 commando vehicle

A civilian version of the UAZ-3172 prototype

A military version of a rare prototype—the UAZ-3172

A prototype of the UAZ-3172 from the late 1980s

its debut, featuring a 3.9-in-longer wheelbase, a total length of 179 in, and a ZMZ 2.7L 16v engine (144hp), which was also mounted on the Bars a year later. The vehicles were equipped with ZMZ 2.5L 16v engines, or other power units of Russian or foreign provenance. Development of the UAZ-31520 5-d station wagon is under way. It's supposed to fea-

ture a gasoline ZMZ-409 injection engine and a ZMZ-410 3.0L diesel power unit. Importers to the Czech Republic and Poland fit the UAZs with D Andoria engines; in Italy, the models featuring engines made by UAZ, D Peugeot and VM are distributed as the "Explorer," "Marathon," "Marat 12V" and "Dakar." In other places, the name "Taiga" has appeared. Specifications: wheelbase—8.7 in, overhang angles—50°/40°, slope—100%. The shortened UAZ-31512 is a basis for the UAZ-3150 Shalun beach vehicle with canvas "doors" and a 2.9L engine (102hp). The Sport model is similar, with a likewise shortened wheelbase, but with no doors. Chassis taken from the UAZ-469 became the basis for a limited-series of the Jump, which looks like an off-road station wagon with buggy features—it is roofless and doorless, with a laminated body, or what's left of it. The Astero is supposed to represent a luxury off-roader. As far as engines are concerned, these vehicles are powered by just about anything mounted in other UAZs vehicles, as well as the GAZ V8 engine (200hp), which can be found under the coil of the Tchaika luxury limo. With respect to the overall datedness

The UAZ Dakar, Italy, 1994

of their design, the company decided that the last units of the UAZ 469-UAZ 3151 series would be in November 2003.

UAZ–3160 Simbir

The company is now pinning its hopes on the UAZ 3160 Simbir (= leopard) model with a new pick-up chassis. The same chassis serves as a basis for a minibus and a farmers' vehicle. A prototype was presented in 1993. It won a gold medal at the "Europe-Asia-Transit" motor show in Yekaterinburg. However, production was not launched until five years later—Feburary 13th, 1997—on new premises. The first to roll off the new assembly line was the UAZ-3153

The UAZ-3162; IDET Brno, Czech Republic, 2003

with an extended wheelbase, followed by the long-awaited novelty—the series UAZ-3160 Simbir—on August 5th, 1997. A total of 150 units were completed in 1997. The "3160" 5-d 7-seat station wagon is powered by a 2.5L engine from the UAZ-469, but with electronic injection. A 2.9L carburetor engine with 115hp (UAZ-31601) or 119hp (UAZ-31605) is mounted for the Russian market. There are other engines as well, with horsepower ranging between 90hp and 120hp (UAZ-31606). Of growing importance recently have been the ZMZ-409 2.5L 16v Russian-made electronic injection engines (Zavolzhskiy motoroviy zavod), the 4213 and 420 engine models made by the Volzhskiye Motory company, as well as the Italian TD VM engines (124hp) and some Mercedes and Peugeot engines. A diesel version of the UAZ-31604 has been produced since June 1998. In contrast to its predecessor, the Simbir features coil spring suspension. Small numbers of the 3160 soft-top model have been made since 1998. In addition to that, the UAZ-3162 has also been available since 2000—a 5-d 6- or 9-seat station wagon version with a new-fashioned appearance and a length extended by 14 in. Versions fit with ZMZ 2.7L engines (144hp) bear a "UAZ-31622" name-plate; those fit with UMZ 2.9L power units (119hp) are called "UAZ-31625," and those with Toyota 3.4L engines (205hp) under the coil are code-named "UAZ-3162T." The 2001 Moscow motor show displayed an updated Simbir 3162—the UAZ-31622 (ZMZ 2.7L, 137hp, 93 mph). On the basis of the UAZ-3162 Simbir station wagon, the company built a pick-up truck with a dual cab, naming it "UAZ-2362 Nukan." Its engines and interior are borrowed from the UAZ-3160 and the UAZ-3162, and it carries up to 1,764 lbs of cargo. Other versions of this model include the UAZ-33035 and the UAZ-33036. The pick-up is available with a laminated glassed-in hard-

The UAZ-2315

top superstructure. In addition to these models, a prototype of a pick-up truck for 2–3 passengers and 2,205 lbs of cargo was presented in the 1996/97 period: the "UAZ-2315 Pikap" has borrowed its cab and front face from the 3151 model. It should represent a counterpart to Burlak, competitor to GAZ. In Moscow in 2001, a 5-d station wagon was introduced, featuring a front face with headlights. The UAZ-2363 5-seat 4-d hard-top pick-up truck (with a ZMZ 2.7L engine, 137hp), and the UAZ-23632, were scheduled for a launch in 2003. This model series also includes the UAZ-27722 — a new ambulance for 6 people and a stretcher — and the UAZ-2760 minivan with an elevated laminated roof superstructure. Mention ought to be made of the UAZ-2772 — a 7–9-seat 5-d 4x4 van with a new-fangled appearance — as well as the UAZ-2365 4x4 pick-up truck with a canvas-covered platform. Each of the models is fit with a 5-speed transmission, a welded ladder chassis, rigid axles with coil springs or torsion bars in the front, and longitudinal half-elliptic springs in the rear. The export-oriented trims with TD 2.5L engines (110hp) are code-named UAZ-3160 and UAZ-3162. Around the year 2000, a sensational report was released of UAZ signing a contract with DeTomaso — a producer or luxury sports vehicles from Italy. Plans were laid for the Simbir to be produced in a new factory in Gioia Tauro, Southern Italy. At the 2002 Paris car show, UAZ Europa — a new European importer based in Modena, Italy — launched a business campaign; it introduced one of the 200 planned units of the Simbir from Italy, assembled in a DeTomaso plant in Modena. A total of 1,350 units were scheduled to be made by 2003 and, in 2004, the production line was supposed to be moved to a new factory in Crotone,

The UAZ-23632 hard-top, 2001

as the Gioia Tauro location had fallen through after all. The factory is reported to have swallowed up EUR 350 million of investments. The model on display was fit with an IVECO F1A TD 2.3L common-rail engine (116hp @ 3800, 93 mph). It features an 8.7-in ground clearance, a 20-in fording depth, and negotiates a 31° slope and 45° / 33° overhang angles.

UAZ-450 (USSR) to UAZ-3962 ❷ ❼

The roots of the heavily-branched UAZ-450 series reach back to the 1950s. The GAZ 69 served as the basis for a prototype of the GAZ 69 B, nicknamed "Bukhanka." This novelty was tuned in UAZ and presented as the UAZ-450A - ambulance in 1955. The factory insists that the model was unrivaled in its time, so far as its arched front face, number of seats for seated and recumbent crew, and softness of suspension were concerned. After 1957, it was complemented by the UAZ-450D platform truck. The body was mounted on a ladder frame with rigid axles and leaf springs. Power came from a 4-V OHV UAZ 2.4L engine coupled to a 3-speed transmission (later 4-speed with synchronization of the 3rd and 4th gears), RWD or AWD and a 2-speed auxiliary transmission. Disc brakes were featured. The platform truck carried 2 passengers and 1,653 lbs of cargo, while the ambulance had a capacity of 9 persons, and the minivan could take 2 people and 1,764 lbs of load "on board." The vehicless managed 30° slopes, 28-in-deep fords, with a 1,102-lb one-axle trailer in tow. Their ground clearance was 8.3 in, and they achieved a top speed of 56 mph. January 1961 brought a decision to produce updated versions of a minivan (the UAZ-451) and a truck (the UAZ-451D). Simultaneously, 4x2 models were produced. In 1965 came the modified UAZ-452. It differed slightly in appearance, ground clearance (8.7 in) and overhang angles (36°/30°). Next in line is the UAZ-452B — an 11-seat minibus. A team of young designers came up with the "Snyegokhod" — a special-purpose vehicle based on the UAZ 451D, with skis in place of the front wheels. Another curiosity was the "Snyegobolotokhod" with four caterpillar belts, designed for driving through deep snow and mud. The UAZ-452D minivan won a gold medal at the 1966 Moscow Agricultural Exhibition. Abroad-bound was the UAZ-452DM model; over a million units of it had been made, when the modernized UAZ-452A arrived in 1975. In 1974, the factory's machinery was upgraded. The UAZ-452AC

The UAZ-2360, 2001

The UAZ-3303, 2002

The UAZ-450D, 1965

well-insulated ambulance became popular in the Far North. It proved itself during desert expeditions through the Sahara (1975) and the Karakum (1979). Another renovation came in 1988, bringing with it the UAZ-3303. In 1997, models with an innovative appearance arrived at last—the UAZ-33035 (box-type) and the UAZ-33036 (canvas-covered truck), weighing 2.65–3.05 tons, with a towing capacity of 1,874–2,205 lb. They are powered by UMZ 2.4L (92hp) and 2.9L (98hp) engines. The UAZ-39094 is a double-cab. The UAZ-452 has been followed by the UAZ-3741 (in 1985), and more recently the UAZ-3741 and the UAZ-3746 4x4 minivan with a 2.7-ton curb weight, and an 1,874-lb towing capacity. The engines are the same as in the 3303. 4x4 minibuses have been produced since 1967 under the UAZ-

The UAZ-3165 Sima, 2001

The UAZ-3760, 2001

452V code name, since 1988 aș UAZ-2206, and since 1998 as UAZ-22069 with a new appearance, for 8 or 11 persons. This van / station wagon with a partly glassed-in rear end, carries 5 passengers and 1,534 lbs of luggage. The new era has called for the armored UAZ-3963 Konalu, designed for transporting money and valuables.

UAZ-39094 Fermer

The UAZ-39094 Fermer (= Farmer) pick-up truck was derived from the long-standing UAZ-450 lightweight series. It's designed for use by farmers, who have to make do with 76-octane gasoline. The late-1990s models include: the UAZ-39094 Fermer-1 with a 5-seat trambus cab and the UAZ-39095 Fermer-2 with an overnight cab. The model negotiates a 28-in-deep ford and will tackle a 30° slope.

UAZ-3165 Sima

In 1996, work began in UAZ on a 7-to-9-seat "multivan" with a 118-in-long wheelbase. The UAZ-3165 Sima was introduced in Moscow in 1999 with a 2.7L 16v engine (150hp, 99 mph). The model was scheduled for distribution as of 2003, and should be available with 4x2 and 4x4 drive.

The UAZ-3741, 2002

UMM
(Portugal)

In 1978, the Lisbon-based Unico Metalo Mecánica, LDA company bought a franchise of the 1ˢᵗ generation Cournil off-roader from the French Simi company. UMM had been established in 1977 with the objective of producing four-wheel drive vehicles. Among the founders of UMM were MOCAR, SA—an importer of Peugeot and Alfa Romeo vehicles (who later sold UMM cars)–and MOVAUTO, which owned manufacturing halls in Setúbal, 22 miles from Lisbon, where Alfa Romeo, Honda, Nissan, Peugeot and Mercedes vehicles had been assembled since the late 1950s. They embarked on UMMs as well. Portuguese army specialists contributed to the development of the military versions. The factory supplied the army with vehicles from 1979. They were up to NATO standards, adapted for paratrooper landings, as well as weapon carriers. A daily capacity of 20 units out of a total output of 95 was reserved for the UMM project in the assembly shop. UMM came at a time when the European Community market was being opened. Starting in the early 1980s, the company participated in major motor shows and took aggressive marketing steps in Europe. It took part in the Paris-Dakar type of raid rallies. It played a significant role in the off-road domain. It covered

60% of the Portuguese 4x4 market and its total output exceeded 20,000 units. It exported into most countries in Europe, Africa, Turkey, U.A.E., Sao Tomé, Haiti, New Caledonia, Taiwan and Japan. In 1995, production was discontinued and the company was closed down. The delicately refined but outdated design of its models was unable to keep up with the more sophisticated Japanese competition. The

The UMM Alter 4x4

The UMM Cournil 4x4 Randonneur, 1981

bell finally tolled for the uncomfortable, spacious utility off-road toiler. The Peugeot engines had gone down in history for their durability, but the new era dismissed them as incompetent. The minor but frequent complaints concerning its varying quality further tainted the model's reputation.

UMM 4x4 Cournil ❷

The name "UMM 4x4 Cournil" was in 1982 abbreviated to "UMM 4x4." The Portuguese took over the model without much modification. The UMM carried a diesel Indenor (Peugeot) 2112cc engine (62L @ 4500). The model either bore a name based on the code of its engine ("490"), or it featured a TD 2304cc engine of the same make (67hp @ 4500) and was distributed as "494." The vehicles were fit with 4-speed transmissions with unsychronized 1st gears and 2-speed reduction transmissions. The front and rear axle featured limited slip differentials, with a Track Lock in the rear. The front wheels had "Warner" freewheels. The axles were

rigid with half-elliptic springs, and there were disc brakes. Steel metal bodies were welded onto a ladder chassis. UMM sold 3 trims of the model, with 2 different wheelbase lengths: the Tracteur (a hard-top pick-up truck with a canvas-covered cargo area), the Randonneur (a soft-top pick-up truck), both with an 80-in-long wheelbase and a length of 133 in, and the Entrepreneur—a pick-up truck with a 99.5-in wheelbase and a 152-in length. The shorter versions were 58.5-in wide, while the longer versions featured a 62-in width. The same goes for height (78 / 80 in), curb weight (3,086 / 3,306 lb), and payload (2,646 / 2,425 lb). The ground clearance was 9 in high. The vehicles reached a top speed of 71 mph, except the "Tracteur," which was 3 mph slower. They seated up to 2+8 passengers. At a premium, a vinyl, polyester or metal hard-top roof was available, with or without different types of glass. In Switzerland, a special "Dakar" model—the Dakary—was available in 1983 (73hp); the UMM Trans Cat was distributed in Great Britain in 1986; and in 1979 the UMM 4x4 Hiker existed as well.

UMM Alter 4x4, Alter II 4x4 ❷

The Alter, known in some countries as the UMM Alfor, was a model featuring a 121-in wheelbase, a 191-in length, and a 9-in ground clearance. It was produced from the fall of 1985 until 1988. Further specifications: width—67 in, height—77 in, curb weight—3,902 lb, towing capacity—2,094 lbs of cargo, overhang angles—48°/28°, slope—over 90%, side tilt—40°, fording depth—20 in. Of great importance were its engines—a D Peugeot 2498cc (76hp @ 4500, 75 mph) and a TD (110hp @ 4150, 87 mph). The Alter had a more modern appearance than its predecessors. The most significant change consisted in the relocation of the outer "frog" headlights into the grille. Evolution came in stages and the change in appearance preceded the arrival of the

The UMM Alter Pick Up Long, 1989

name Alter. In 1987, a 2.5 L Turbo Incooler engine was mounted, coupled to a synchronized 5-speed transmission. The model kept its reduction transmission, and featured a rear limited slip differential. The front freewheels were manually lockable at standstill. FWD could be disengaged. The choice of body types hadn't changed, and the vehicle carried 2 or 3 persons in the front, and up to 6 passengers in the back. In 1998, the Alter was followed by the slightly re-touched Alter II version, which after 1990 was also available as a stretched double cab with a canvas-covered cargo area.

UMM Alter 2000 ❷

In 2000, it was rumored that production of the Alter II was to be resumed, with many minor refining touches. Power should come from a Peugeot 2088cc common-rail inter-cooler engine (110hp @ 4300, 93 mph), connected with a 5-speed transmission with optional 4x2 or 4x4. The alleged specifications include: wheelbase—101 or 121 in, total length—163 / 191 in, curb weight—3,483 / 3,682 lb. The other parameters roughly correspond to those of the Alter II. The featured soft- and hard-top bodies accommodate 2–9 passengers, and the payload is supposed to be over 2,315 lb.

The UMM Alter as a fire patrol vehicle during the 24h Le Mans race, 2002

The URO F2, 2001

URO
(Spain)

The Vehículos Especiales, S. A. (UROVESA) company, founded in Santiago de Compostela in 1981, launched production of off-road trucks only a few months after coming into existence. It has stuck to this program eversince. The F1 and F2 series vehicles with semitrambus cabs made in 1981

are in fact kit cars assembled according to the wishes of the customers. Power is supplied by a TD IVECO 5.9L engine (143–227hp). Each unit features a 9-speed Fiat (or a premium 4-speed auto) transmission, a 2-speed reduction transmission, an inter-axle differential and front and rear differentials with pneumatically-controlled locks and other transmissions in the wheel hubs. These 4x4 work vehicles used to be made by the—today likewise nonexistent—Spanish company IPV / MAFSA.

The civilian URO Vamtac VAM T4, 2001

URO Vamtac ❷ ❾

The Vamtac is an equivalent, and to a large extent even a copy, of the Hummer. It's been available since 1988. The prevailing customer is the army, and the rest of the vehicles are bought by police forces, fire departments and rescue squads. The Vamtac meets the requirements of the Spanish Ministry of Defense for full functionality at temperatures between –4° and 122° F, a payload rating of 3,307–4,409 lb; it can tow a 3,307-lb-heavy trailer, negotiates 30-in-deep fords (or fords as deep as 60 in, if fitted with a premium kit). It can be transported by Chinook helicopters and Hercules C-130 airplanes. A ladder frame carries easily detachable steel body superstructures. The wheels feature an independent suspension with coil springs and a torsion stabilizer bar in the front. The components of the axles and drivetrain in the front and rear are easily interchangeable. There are disc brakes. The company produces two series of the Vamtac. The VAM T2 is powered by a 4-V TD intercooler Fiat-IVECO 2800cc engine (122hp SAE, 73 mph), coupled to a 4-speed Fiat-IVECO manual (or a 4-speed automatic) transmission, a URO pneumatically-controlled 2-speed reduction and a lockable inter-axle differential. Both the front and the rear differentials are also pneumatically lockable from the driver's seat. Further reduction is provided by transmissions in the wheel hubs. The VAM T4 is powered by a TD intercooler in-line 6-V Steyr 3200cc engine (190hp SAE, 81 mph). The VAM T4 features an Allinson hydraulic torque converter and an automatic 4-speed transmission of the same brand. The rest is identical with the VAM T2. Both models have the same specifications: wheelbase—133 in, length—191, width—86 in, height—75 in (hard-top), curb weight—6,173–7,716 lb, payload—(+)4,630 lb, ground clearance—19.4 in, overhang

The URO Vamtac 2PH, 2001

angles—51°/52°, slope—70 %, and side tilt—60 %. The basic variants include: a chassis with a cab (the 2PH—a short 2-d cab, the 3PH—a short 4-d cab, and the 4PH—a long 4-d double cab), a pick-up truck (the 2PK, the 3PK and the 4PK, also available as a soft-top), and the Cerrados—an enclosed off-road fastback (4PC) or off-road station wagon (4PW). Another option is models with a wheelbase of 147 in and a total length of 214 in, which bear the letter "L" in their code names, e.g., "2PHL." The rest of the parameters, except the weight, remain the same. A common 2-d version seats 2, while a 4-d variant comes with 4–6 seats. On the other hand, the army uses transporters for 10–12 people, minivans with elevated roofs, such as ambulances for 2 or 4 casualties, or weapon carriers. Also available are versions with canvas "doors," with AC, or specials for firefighters and paramedics.

The URO Vamtac VAM VL, 2001

VAZ / Lada
(USSR and Russia)

LADA

In the early 1960s, Soviet cars were hopelessly out of date and few and far between. Moreover, the times were no longer favorable for unauthorized production of imitations. The country needed to master modern technologies and prompt supplies of large numbers of vehicles. On July 20th, 1966, the USSR Council of Ministers decided that a modern car manufacturing factory be built. A suitable location was found near the Kuybyshev hydro-power plant on the Volga, about 10 miles from Naberezhnyye Tchelny and about 55 miles from the Samara shopping center. All components were to be manufactured on the spot, except for a part of the ignition, headlights and windows. The annual capacity of the plant was 750,000 cars. All the infrastructure—a whole town, in fact—had to be built from scratch: endless rows of socialist prefab apartment buildings were erected on a field sloping down to the Volga River. The town was named Togliatti, after an Italian Communist Party leader, who died in Yalta. His party was the driving force of the business relations between the Russians and Fiat, which supplied the technology, as well as the vehicle itself. A contract was signed on August 15th, 1966. The Volga Car Works (VAZ) was one of the biggest factories in the USSR. Its assembly

lines were 100 miles long and it employed 180,000 people. Two years after the foundation stone was laid, a total of 100,000 vehicles had been made; production started when building operations were still in progress. It was not officially launched until August 1970, but as many as 30,000 units had already rolled off the assembly line in 1969. VAZ bought the franchise of the Fiat 124 sedan, which was reconstructed and adapted to the Russian climate, absence of quality roads, and primitive infrastructure. The models were equipped with a number code and / or the name Zhiguli (after the undulating, wooded banks of the Volga River); the 2nd generation was known as the Samara. Models for export bore the more user-friendly name Lada. Production began with the VAZ-2101 sedan, followed a year later by the VAZ-2102 station wagon. A handful of pick-up trucks with a welded tailgate was made for the USSR market. The 2nd generation—the rectangular VAZ-2108 Samara—was built in the USSR (1985). In 1995, a pilot series of the 3rd generation arrived—the curvaceous VAZ-2110. In the late 1990s, the VAZ-2345 Pikap appeared—a cross-breed made up of a VAZ 210433 front face and components of the 2108 F and 2109 F models. This pick-up truck with a wheelbase of 110 in carried 2 persons and 1,323 lbs of cargo. It featured a laminated cover over its cargo area. The VAZ-2108 F Tchelnok pick-up truck is derived from the VAZ 2108. Its relative is the VAZ-2109 F Tchelnok double cab with a 4-d 5-seat cab and a towing ca-

The Lada Niva-2131 Konsul, Germany, 1996

pacity of 661 lb. This vehicle features a nose of the VAZ 2108. All the above-mentioned models are still in production, without major alterations.

On January 15th, 1993, VAZ was transformed into the AvtoVAZ joint stock company. At the 2001 Geneva car show, the Russians held a press conference to inform journalists of a contract they had signed with GM on February 27th, 2001. GM was supposed to have arranged for the technological and financial aspect of their joint project. The Volga factory was to assemble engines, the Astra Opels, later the Niva 2123 off-road vehicle— known today as the Niva II—or the Chevrolet Niva with Opel gasoline engines and Fiat diesel engines. The GM-AvtoVAZ company is co-owned by GM (41.5 %), AvtoVAZ (41.5 %) and the European Bank for Industry and Development (17.0 %). An SUV was born on the computer screens of the Russian engineers. The production technology is brand new. The Chevrolet Niva was scheduled for launch in late 2002 in Russia, and for export after October 2003.

AvtoVAZ is an umbrella company made up of SeAZ, Bronto and VIS—a builder of pick-up trucks. The SeAZ company was founded in 1939, and after 1953 produced the S-1t vehicles for the disabled, codenamed "SMZ." In Paris in 1996, it showcased a prototype of the Lada Elf beach vehicle based on the SeAZ-1113 Oka 3-d. The Ladas used to be exported to 145 countries around the world, and now go to 60 countries; the Nivas are dispatched to 50 countries. On June 8th, 2001, the 20-millionth Lada rolled off the assembly line.

VAZ-2121 - Lada Niva ❷

In projecting the VAZ factory, the designers counted on producing an off-road vehicle. An "assembly plant within an assembly plant" was built for the Niva; it has been assembled separately. The Niva was designed as a modern, progressive vehicle. It tackled extreme conditions with its self-supporting frameless steel body, permanent AWD (a reduction transmission and a rear differential lock), and reinforced coil

The Lada Niva, 2001

The VAZ Niva-2122 Reka

The Lada Taiga, 1996

spring suspension; the only other model to boast such features was the Range Rover at that time. The leader of the Niva project was Vladimir Sergeyevich Solovtsev, and Valeriy Pavlovich Semuchkin was the head engineer. The wheelbase of the "Zhiguli" platform was shortened by 9 inches. Prototypes were made in 1971 and 1972 and featured soft-top convertible bodies and 1.3L engines. Their first series-model was assembled on April 5th, 1977 (and introduced in 1976); it had a 1.6L engine (80hp, 81 mph) connected with a 4-speed transmission, and components of the VAZ-2106. The Niva was 146 in long, had a 9.3-in ground clearance and featured 16" wheels. These vehicles were put through a series of trials in the summer of 1973 in Uzbekistan; UAZ helped with troubleshooting specific

The VAZ Niva Bora

problems. Furthermore, the factory came up with an amphibious military version of the VAZ-2122 Reka (=river) featuring an extended floor, but powered by a 1.3L engine (60hp, 71 mph on the road, 6 mph when afloat) from the VAZ-2101 sedan. The rear part of this vehicle was covered with canvas, while other prototypes featured an open off-road body with a couple of canvas doors stretched on a frame, and a protective tubular frame. Various military Nivas were designed between the late 1970s and 1988. They passed strict tests, but the Red Army never had enough money to buy them. The Niva was produced for 19 years without any modifications. In the early 1990s the Niva Bora arrived —a doorless beach prototype with aluminum body parts, similar to the "Project" in 1998.

In 1993, the Niva underwent a visual facelift, including new rear doors now reaching to the bumper, headlights, Samara seats, and a new dashboard. A refined 1.7L engine (84 mph) was equipped with single point injection. A new 5-speed transmission, again with a reduction gear, was introduced in the fall of 1985. The export models now lacked triangular front door windows. The Niva still has permanent AWD with a manually lockable inter-axle differential. Its front wheels are suspended independently on double-control arm suspension with coil springs and a stabilizer bar. The rear axle is rigid with a Panhard rod and coil springs. The model carries 4 passengers and 838 lbs of cargo. Specifications: ground clearance—8.7 in, slope—89%, side tilt—48°, fording depth—32.5 in, overhang angles—39°/36°. (Some sources quote a fording depth of 17.7 or 25.6 in, and a 58% slope.) The stretched VAZ-2130 Kedr arrived in 1992, followed two years later by the VAZ-2131 Niva (Wagoon), also known as the Niva L, with the same wheelbase but 5 doors and a UZAM 3320 2.0L engine. The company's branches in Western Europe released several convertibles. Over a million Nivas were made in 1998. In the second half of the 1990s came the VAZ-2328 Niva pick-up truck with a cab for two and a body for 661 lbs of cargo, and the VAZ-2329 Niva 2-d double cab with a cab extended by 20 in and with two rows of seats. These were followed in 2001 by the VAZ-23451 VIS Double Cab, the 2345 VIS Pickup, the 2346 VIS Niva Pickup or ambulance, and the VAZ-2121 F Niva van. Some were assembled in VIS, a satellite organization of VAZ. The Niva has been trying to break through with Wankel engines (200hp) and electric motors. Bronto produces special-purpose vehicles based on the Niva. The models for export may feature TD 1.7L Peugeot power units (75 or 82hp). Since 2000, they have been assembled in

The VAZ Niva Project

The Lada Niva California 2, 1997

Ecuador, and in the Ukraine since 2001. In Austria and France, the vehicles are known as "Taiga / Taiga SC" or "Tundra." A better-equipped model—the Niva Cossack—was available in England after May 1986 and, briefly in 1986, also the Cossack Cabrio designed in Greece. The Niva Kazbek was distributed on the Slovak market. Italian customers could enjoy the Niva Everest (made by the local Organizzazione Martorelli) fit with a Peugeot D 1905cc engine (58hp @ 4600) and the Niva Brio—a semi-convertible body with a rigid frame made up of A and B pillars interconnected at the top with the front window frame. In France, the Niva lived an independent life. It sold well in the 1980s, including the LPG engines. Models available in Germany in 1983 included: the Lada Niva UT, the Niva E, the Niva 5000 and the Niva 5000 C; and in August 1998: the Niva 21214 (1.7 i, 80hp), the Niva 21215 (with a Peugeot 1.9 D engine, 64hp) and the Niva California 2 (1.7 i, 80hp, more expensive equipment). The Niva 21214i Praktik (a van with a 1.7L single-point injection GM engine) and the Niva 21214 Praktik Special, (BOSCH multi-point injection, extended rear overhang, 948-lb towing capacity) was also produced.

Nivas heavily modified in France finished 3rd in the overall ranking of the 1981 Dakar Rally, and in 1982 and 1983 they won the 2nd place. A special with a Ferrari V8 engine (300hp) under its coil and with multiple spur-belt wheel drive won gold in the Italian Cup of the off-road speed races. Since September 16th, 1999, the Niva has been a height record holder: it managed to climb up to an altitude of 18,786 ft in Tibet, using only its own power. On April 17th, 1999, the Niva Marsh (see Bronto), or more precisely its balloon tires, touched the North Pole, after being transported a part of the way suspended from a helicopter. The Lada Niva was designed for daily use in regions with a lack of good roads, which were easily found all over the USSR at the time. This lightweight, low-cost vehicle is a noisy, plain, insufficiently equipped and not exactly top-quality model that isn't great on the road but works wonders in the off-road (especially on soft surfaces).

A Martorelli version of the the Lada Niva; Turin, 1992

The VAZ Niva-2329 pick up

VAZ-2123 Niva II

The 2nd generation of the Niva was launched in 1998. The frst series-produced VAZ-2123 Niva II appeared in March 2000. This 5-d station wagon is rounder and more wedge-shaped than its predecessors, with elongated headlights and either a 1.7L engine (80–82hp, 94 mph)—the VAZ-21233—or a 1.8L diesel engine (75hp, 87 mph)—the VAZ-21235. It has permanent 4x4 drive. The third version is fit with a 2.0L engine (16v, 115hp). According to the AvtoVAZ, the vehicle is supposed to have been produced as "AvtoVAZ-GM" until mid-2002, and as "VAZ" after that date. The Americans are planning gradually to replace both the "heart" and "coat" of the model. Further contracts between GM and AvtoVAZ were signed on July 27th, 2001, and production commenced on September 23rd, 2002. Annual output in 2003 was planned to be 35 thousand units, and 75 thousand in 2005.

VAZ / Lada 2110 to 2120 Nadyezhda

In 1989, information went around about a prototype of the 3rd generation of the VAZ-2110 passenger vehicle. The factory announced that "large-scale" production would start in 1996. Since 1999, there has been the VAZ-2111 station wagon, available also as 4x4. In 2001, a four-wheeler was showcased, fit with a 1.8L engine (110hp). The first minivan

The Lada-Chevrolet Niva, 2002

of the Russian provenance—the VAZ-2120 Nadyezhda (=hope)—made its debut in Moscow in 1997. It was derived from the VAZ 2110 and especially the Niva. The model was retouched in 1999. A year later, a Nadyeazhda model based on the Niva 2131 arrived, featuring permanent AWD, but no reduction gear as yet (it was an available option later).

The Lada Konsul VAZ-210934 Tarzan, 2002

The Lada Niva Kazbek; Bratislava, Slovakia, 2001

286

Volvo
(Sweden)

VOLVO

Assar Gabrielsson and Gustaf Larson had close ties with SKF—a producer of bearings. In the summer of 1924, they agreed to design and build cars together. Two years later, they had a design of a chassis, which they were putting together after hours with a team of young engineers. The "Jakob" ÖV 4 made a good impression at its launch in April 1927. Financial guarantees for building the assembly plant were provided by SKF. The name Volvo (Latin for "I roll") was originally used by SKF in another business operation. Volvo became famous for its good-quality, durable and safe vehicles. In 1973, it obtained 33% of the stock of the Dutch-based Daf company, and two years later it owned 75%. In 1991, the rest of Daf was swallowed up by Mitsubishi. In 1999, the automobile division of Volvo fell prey to Ford, which incorporated it, along with Aston Martin, Jaguar and Lincoln, into the exclusive Premier Automotive Group club. Some models of the S60 (AWD) and V70 tourers have AWD, the electronic Haldex system and smooth division of torque between the axles depending on the traffic situation. The S80 sedan became the basis for the speedy Volvo S80 Ambulance, a successor to the V90 Ambulance, which was supplied by Volvo (in co-operation with the Wiman car body works) in 2000 to British medical workers. The ambulance

has the safety features of sedans, including the SIPS and WHIPS side protection, 2.4L engines, both manual and auto transmissions and AWD on request. Volvo also came up with concept cars of "adventure vehicles"—the ACC (Adventure Concept Car), a forerunner of the future SUV AWD. The ACC, partly dervied from the S60, was showcased in Detroit in 2001, followed in March 2002 by the ACC 2 related to the V70XC.

After WWII, the factory produced the TPV with 4x4 drive, followed in 1953-58 by 720 units of the more modern P2104 / TP 21. This was a 4-or-5-seat military command and Signal Corps vehicle (the 9151 and the 9152) or an airport service car (the 265 TL11 and the TL12) with a body of a robust pre-war taxicab (the PV 801/802), station wagon or truck (the 953). The soldiers nicknamed it "Suggan" (= Swine) for its mighty round rear. The truck chassis bore a gasoline 6-V SV 3645cc engine (90hp @ 3600, also 105 or 115hp). It had a 4-speed transmission with an auxiliary 2-speed transmission for disengaging the FWD. The differential locks were vacuum-operated. The axles were rigid with half-elliptic springs. Specifications: wheelbase—106 in; length—185 in, width—77 in, height—85 in, ground clearance—9.8 in, curb weight—6,349 lb, towing capacity—838 lb.

The Volvo C 303

Volvo Lappländer PU / HT, C 300 / C 200 ❷ ❾

The L2304 prototype of a 0.8-ton work vehicle with a tram-bus cab appeared in the late 1950s. These vehicles, produced in the special truck division, were bought mainly by the army, unhappy with the "Swine" (as "Series 903"—a 6- and 8-seat transporter, a reconnaissance, Signal Corps and fire-fighting vehicle, weapon transporter), but they appealed to civilian customers as well (the Lappländer). In 1961–70, a total of 7,736 units were produced of the L3314 open ve-hicles (nicknamed "Valpen") and 1,116 units of the L 3315 model with a modified enclosed body. The company also made specials for paramedics and fire departments, closed-in and soft-top bodies, pick-up trucks, and chassis for spe-cial-purpose superstructures. Power came from a gasoline 4-V OHV 1990cc engine (68hp @ 4500) taken from the PV 544 sedan. In addition to a 4-speed transmission, the model featured an auxiliary 2-speed reduction gear used to disengage FWD, as well as vacuum-operated differential locks. The axles were rigid with longitudinal leaf springs. Specifications: wheelbase—83 in, length—160 in, width—65 in, height—83 in, ground clearance—11.4 in, curb weight—1,323 lbs, and payload—1,874 lbs. The Pvpjtbil 9031 (= Parisär värns pjäs terräng bil) was made on special request from the army; it was used as a a carrier of the Bofors tank destroyers, because the Lappländer, although featuring the same equipment, tended to tip over after firing. The Pvpjtbil was identical with the L3314, but had a lower and more robust build. Its spare wheel was protruding from the front face in order to dampen the impact when the vehi-cle hit the ground, because it was unbalanced and always landed "nose-down." In 1963 and '64, Volvo produced 270 of these curiosities, which were taken up by the Chilean army after serving in Sweden. Power came from a 1780cc engine (65hp @ 4500, 56 mph). Specifications: wheel-base—83 in, length—173 in, width—67 in, height—59 in, curb weight—4,123 lbs. In 1969, the Volvo models under-went modernization of both appearance and mechanics. After 1972, the heavier Cross Country C 303 4x4 / C 306 6x6 was available for civilian customers; this 5-d off-road "minibus" carried 7–8 and 14 passengers respectively. It featured 2 or 3 powered axles and an in-line 6-V 2980cc engine (125hp @ 4250, 75 / 50 mph). Speci-fications: wheelbase—91 in (4x4) / 2,720 +41 in (6x6), length—171 / 234 in, width—75 in, height—85 in, ground clearance—15 in, curb weight—(+) 4,630 / 6,834 lbs, pay-load—2,976 / 5,291 lbs, maximum slope—85%. Some in-novation occured in 1977 and along came the lighter $^3/_4$-ton Cross Country C 202 soft- or hard-top with a 4-V 2.0L en-

The Volvo C 202 station wagon

The Volvo C 202 ambulance

gine (82hp @ 4700). It had an 83-in wheelbase, a length of 158 in, a width of 65 in, and a height of 85 in. Further parameters: ground clearance—11.2 in, curb weight—3,351 lbs (the open PU) / 3,803 lbs (the enclosed HT), and maximum payload—2,216 lbs. Production continued at least the until the mid-1980s. A total of 12,000 units of the Lappländer Generation I were made in 1961–81.

Volvo XC70 Cross Country   ❶

Volvo's XC70 4WD station wagon, with a greater ability to get through rugged terrains, won a favorable response. A total of 53,857 units of the 1st generation of this 5-d vehicle—the V70XC—were made in 1997–2000. In contrast, the 2nd generation launched in February 2000—the XC 70 Cross Country—achieved this number only 12 months into its production run. The S70 / V70 (2x4) model with a 104-

The Volvo XC 70, 2003

in-long wheelbase was launched in December 1996. At the IAA in early 1997 came AWD version—the V70 XC—mounted on a platform of the 850 station wagon. The lineup was extended by the S70 AWD sedan, showcased at the 1998 Paris show. As has been shown earlier, some V70 station wagons were AWD. The V70XC model with a 5-V 1984cc turbo engine (226hp @ 5700) and a 2435cc engine (193hp @ 5100) was fitted with a 5-speed manual or a 4-speed automatic transmission. Permanent 4x4 with variable division of driving power between the front and rear axles favors the FWD and powers the rear wheels through a viscous coupling. A rear limited slip differential has been installed. The height of the AWD chassis is adjustable. The bodies are self-supporting; the wheels feature Multilink independent suspension. In February 2000, the XC 70 Cross Country was introduced—a 5-d 5-seat station wagon verging on SUV, trimmed with robust protective plastic features. It is available exclusively with 5-V gasoline 20v 2435cc turbo engines (200hp @ 5100, 130 mph) and 5-speed manual or auto transmissions with normal and sports modes, or a Geartronic auto transmission available at extra cost and featuring optional manual transmission. The chassis is equipped with the TRACS anti-slip system which functions by applying the brake, the DSTC anti-skid system and the EBD electronic brake division. Specifications: wheelbase—109 in, length—186 in, width—73 in, height—61.5 in,

ground clearance—6.7 in, fording depth—12 in, and overhang angles—23° /24°. The Cross Country Ocean Race Edition model was first displayed in August 2001, on the occasion of the World Yachting Championships, of which Volvo has been a sponsor.

Volvo XC90 ❸

The Volvo XC90—the first "pure-blooded SUV"—was showcased in the U.S. in the fall of 2001, and in Geneva in 2002. This 5-d, relatively high station wagon will accommodate 5 or 7 passengers. In contrast to the XC 70, it features a Haldex clutch. Its engine—a 2.5L, taken from an older model—now has 210hp (@ 5000), and is coupled to a 5-speed auto transmission. Another engine model—an in-line 6-V TD 24v 2922cc engine with an intercooler (272hp @ 5100, 130 mph) works with a 4-speed auto transmission, as does the TD common-rail 2401cc power unit (163hp @ 4000, 115 mph). Specifications: wheelbase—113 in, length—189 in, width—75 in, height—68.5 in, curb weight—(+) 4,189 lbs, payload—992 lbs. This model won numerous international awards, including "The Best 4x4 of the Year 2003" in the What Car Magazine competition.

The Volvo XC90—the "Best 4x4 of the Year 2003" in Britain

VW (Germany)

In 1934, Ferdinand Porsche showed Hitler a folk vehicle—the "Volkswagen" (the VW, nicknamed "Beetle" after WWII). After the war had ended, production of the VW was supervised by an occupying allied army officer. The vehicles lost their folksiness a long time ago. VW has gained control over many of its competitors: Auto Union (1965), NSU (1969), Seat (1986), Škoda (1991), Bugatti (1998) and, through Audi, also Lamborghini and Bentley (1998). VW has produced Golf, Jetta, Bora and Passat vehicles—the latter with an optional 4x4 road variant "Syncro," including the Sharan Syncro / Ford Galaxy MPV (produced in Portugal since 1986). The Touran from the 2003 Geneva show is 2x4 drive. 4x4 drive is featured on the Transporter Syncro—van, minibus or pick-up

truck, generation T3 and T4. The VW Caddy delivery truck has 2x4, the big LT has remained 4x2, although 4x4 versions were also available in the 1980s. The 5th generation of the Multivan (wheelbase—118 in) was introduced at the turn of 2002/2003 and was displayed in Geneva in 2003. The model has 2x4, but "4-Motions" are on the way.

Some concept cars, too, have featured 4x4 drive (such as the cute VW New Beetle Dune, showcased in Geneva in 2000) and some have not (a study of the Microbus or the Tarek 4x2 buggy for Dakar 2003). The VW Fun-Doka double cab for active teenagers was presented at the 1999 IAA.

Soon after the launch of the Volkswagen, Porsche came up with its lightweight combat version—the KdF / VW, Type 82, nicknamed "Kübelwagen." About 52,000 units of it were made in 1939–45. They served as command and reconnaissance vehicles, including several 4x4 versions with caterpillar wheel drive. The rear wheels were powered by a rear air-cooled 4-V OHV 1131cc boxer engine (23.5, later on 25hp

The VW Iltis; Alcocebre, Spain, 2002

The VW Iltis; Alcocebre, Spain, 2002

The VW 181, 1969

@ 3000). It had a 4-speed transmission and independent axles with torsion bar suspension. Its open body was made up of steel sheets and covered with canvas. Specifications: wheelbase—95 in, length—147 in, width—63 in, height—65 in, ground clearance—11.4 in, curb weight—1,598 lbs

The VW 181; Alcocebre, Spain, 1994

The VW Iltis Hardtop

and payload—992 lbs. The SS commanding officers and troops used the VW 87—a Beetle with an enclosed 2-d body and 4x2 or 4x4 drive. In 1942–44 came the amphibious VW 166 K2s "Schwimmwagen," based on the VW 82, with a total of 14,265 units made. It was fitted with a 5-speed transmission, RWD or AWD with two self-locking differentials and a screw propeller. Specifications: wheelbase—79 in, length—155 in, width—58 in, height—64 in and curb weight—2,006 lbs. In the 1960s, the VW Beetle platforms became the basis of beach buggies—a fashion trend that had arrived from California—and later of replicas and kit-cars.

VW 181   ❹ ❾

In 1969–79, VW produced 90,883 units of the VW 181 with an open 4-d body based on the Beetle. Power on the rear wheels came from a 4-V 1493cc rear boxer engine (44hp @ 4000), altered after August 1970 to 1584cc (44, later 48hp @ 3800 and 4000, 75 mph). The model had a 4-speed transmission and independently suspended wheels. Parameters: wheelbase—95 in, length—149 in, width—65 in, height—64 in, ground clearance—8.1 in, fording depth—27.4 in, curb weight—2,006 lbs and payload—948 lbs. Apart from civilian buyers, the vehicles were taken up by the Bundeswehr: 15,250 units for the courier service and another 1,000 units for the border patrol. The VW 181 were exported to the U.S. and other countries.

VW Iltis   ❷

Model 138—the VW Iltis from 1978–82 (9,457 units)—featured a front liquid-cooled gasoline 4-V 1695cc engine

(75hp @ 5500, 81 mph) and, in addition to a 4-speed transmission, a "sluggish" fifth reduction gear. There was optional FWD. Both differentials featured a lock. The body was open; a canvas top could be stretched on a light tubular frame and the same material was used for the "doors." A civilian version, presented at the 1979 IAA, was also available with a laminated hard-top. Plastic bumpers and protective side trims were very practical and toned down the vehicle's coarse military appearance. Specifications: wheelbase—79.5 in, length—153 in, width—60 in, height—72 in, ground clearance—9.8 in, fording depth—23.6 in, curb weight—+2,932 lbs (or +3,417 lbs for the military version) and payload—1,477 lbs. The German army, which had participated in the preliminary trials, took 8,800 units of the Iltis to replace the DKW Munga vehicles. The Iltis won 1st and 2nd place in the second year of the Dakar in 1980. VW made an agreement with Citroën and prepared a miniseries (10 units) of the Citroën C-44—which was really the Iltis with a 2.0L Citroën CX engine—for a tender for a French army off-roader. In 1983, the franchise was bought by the Bombardier company from Canada. In 1984–86, it supplied the Canadian and Belgian armies with 2,500 vehicles, and another several hundred went to Africa. Some of these were fitted with TD 1.6L engines (70hp). The last Iltises were born after 1986 in Genk, Belgium, for the Belgian army contingent, and a number were taken up by the Bundeswehr.

VW Golf Country (Germany, Austria) ❶ ❹

The lineup of the 2nd generation of the vehicles—the VW Golf (1983) and the Jetta sedan (1984)—was "joined" by the Golf Syncro in February 1986 and, after September 1987, the Jetta Syncro with 4x4 drive, a 4-V 1781cc engine (90hp @ 5200, 109 mph), a viscous coupling and freewheels in the rear wheel hubs. These vehicles were co-designed and subsequently produced by Steyr. From 1989, VW supplied the Rallye Golf, also with 4x4 drive, a viscous coupling and a 1.8L engine with a spiral G-compressor (160hp @ 5600 for the race car version, 210hp @ 6 500 for the Golf G 60 Limited tourer). In Geneva in 1990, the very different-looking VW Golf Country full of new safety features was launched, with an 8-inch ground clearance and more robust wheels than before, suggesting that this sturdy vehicle was definitely headed for the off-road. It was mechanically identical with the Syncro, including its 5-speed transmission. After 1989, the engines had the same output (98hp, @ 5400, 101 mph). The Country had the following parameters: wheelbase—98 in, length—166.5 in, width—67 in, height—61 in, curb weight—3,616 lbs. The curtain came down on the Golf Country shortly after the 1991 IAA, where the VW Golf 3rd generation was introduced.

The VW Golf Country, 1990

VW Taro (Japan / Germany) ➏ ➑

The VW Taro is one of the children of "badge engineering." In 1988, VW signed a contract with Toyota for assembling 10,000 Toyota Hi-Lux (4x2) CKD pick-up trucks per year in Germany. The vehicles, rolling out of the Hannover factory after January 1989, bore the trademark VW Taro (derived from the name of Colocasia esculenta—a potato-like herb grown throughout the South Pacific, whose rhizomes contain starch and are consumed as a vegetable). In 1995, their production was moved to Emden. According to the contract, 1/3 of the German vehicles were to bear the Toyota trademark and some of the 4x4 versions produced in the Tahara factory in Japan were to be named VW. The Germans, who did not have their own model in the lucrative, fast-develop-

ing class of one-ton pick ups, profited immensely from this marketing move, and annual output reached 15,000 units.

VW Touareg ➌

The luxury SUV VW Touareg, named after a nomadic Sahara Berber tribe and related to the Porsche Cayenne, arrived at the Paris car show in 2002. This 5-d station wagon features "4xMotion" drive with anti-slip control. (Under normal circumstances, driving power is distributed in a 50:50 ratio, but in difficult terrains 100% of the engine output can be transmitted onto either of the two axles.) Power comes either from a gasoline V6 24v 3189cc engine (220hp @ 6400, 125 mph, or 122 mph with an automatic transmission), or a V8 40v 4172cc power unit (310hp @ 6200, 135 mph), or a V10 20v 4921cc engine with two tur-

The VW Taro II 4x4, 1995

The VW Touareg—world premiere in Paris in 2002

The VW Magellan

bochargers (313hp @ 3750, 140 mph). Mechanically, the model is similar to the Porsche. The SUV Touareg gave rise to the design of the VW AAC recreational pick-up, presented in Detroit in 2002. A study of the VW Magellan from the new "crossover" class (in genetics, "crossing-over" stands for an exchange of genes or segments between associated parts of chromosomes) goes even further. In the automobile domain, this term is used for a synthesis of qualitites of various vehicle categories—in this case an SUV, a van and a road station wagon. The vehicle was named after the Portuguese seafarer and explorer Ferdinand Magellan (1480–1521). The new model was supposed to have qualities similar to those of its namesake. A special trailer could be attached to the vehicle. Power was provided by a W8 3999cc engine (275hp) and distributed onto all four wheels via a Tiptronic transmission.

The VW Transporter Syncro, December 1984

Willys-Viasa (Spain)

After 1956, a factory based in Zaragoza at the foothills of the Pyrenees produced vehicles in a franchise from the Kaiser-Jeep Corporation. In 1963, a series of lightweight off-road vehicles with a trambus cab was added. In 1974, the vehicles made in the Viasa factory began to be distributed by the Barcelona-based Motor Ibérica S.A.

Jeep Willys – Viasa, Jeep Ebro Bravo

After WWII, the sparsely-populated, mountainous and semidesert-covered Iberian Peninsula was in need of off-road vehicles. In 1960–81, the Spanish produced the Willys MB-CJ 3 series including the CJ-3B (short model) and the CJ-3B (stretched model), powered by local-made D 4-V Perkins P-4 3150cc engines (60hp @ 3600). Alternatively, a likewise-Spanish-made gasoline 4-V Barreiros 2199cc engine (51hp @ 3600, 62 mph) found its way under the coil. In 1974, these vehicles turned into the Jeep Ebro Bravo, featuring the above-mentioned engines, as well as D Perkins 1760cc (57hp @ 3600, 68 mph) or 4108cc power units. The engines were coupled to 3-speed or later 4-speed transmission. The gears were shifted manually, with the 2nd, 3rd and 4th gears synchronized. The Jeep featured a 2-speed reduction and optional FWD. Both axles were rigid, with 11 half-elliptic springs, and there were drum brakes. Viasa produced vehicles with an 80 / 101-in wheelbase. Dimensions: length

x width x height—135 / 152 in x 58 in x 72.5 in; ground clearance—23 in, curb weight—3,946 lbs / 4,464 lbs and payload—1,190 / 1,598 lbs. The Jeep Bravo was only available with an open metal body and a canvas roof. The short version accommodated 2 or 4 passengers. Models: the Bravo (standard), the Bravo S (="de luxe" with a wider range of equipment), the Bravo L (stretched, 2/8 persons). Motor Ibérica sold the Jeep Ebro Bravo under the slogan "There's nothing it can't do." Later on, it gave way to the Ebro Patrol.

The Willys-Viasa Jeep Ebro Comando

Jeep Commando, Ebro Comando   ❷

In 1968, Viasa embarked on the production of the franchised Jeepster Commando. It differed from the American model in being powered by a 4-V 2.2L Huricane F-4 engine or a D 2.0L Barreiros C-65 engine, and later by a Spanish-made diesel Perkins 1.8L (57.5hp @ 3600, SAE, and, later still, 61hp @ 4000, SAE); in the Ebro era, the Comando S had an output of 49hp @ 4000, DIN, or a bigger and more powerful Perkins 2710cc engine (65.5hp @ 3600, DIN) was mounted (the Comando HD). The vehicle tallies with the design and components of the Jeep Bravo model. Until the spring of 1976, it had been distributed by Viasa as Bella Bestia Commando; under the Ebro flag, the spelling was changed to "Comando." The model came either with an all-metal 3-d station-wagon hard-top body (the Berlina), an open body (the basic model) or a soft-top with a canvas roof (the Convertible or the Canvas top). Specifications: wheelbase—101 in, length—168.5 in, width—65 in, ground clearance—24 in, curb weight—4,464 lbs and payload—1,157 lbs (soft-top) or 1,499 lbs (hard-top).

Jeep-Viasa SV   ❷

In 1963, Viasa came up with another model, designed exclusively by Spanish engineers and using time-tested Jeep and Perkins components. Some units made in the initial phase were fitted with a 4-V 3150cc engine (63hp @ 3000), a 3-speed transmission and a reduction. Later, 4-V D 3330cc engines (71hp @ 2600, SAE) prevailed, with a 4-speed transmission, reduction and optional FWD. The trambus body was made of steel. Specifications: wheelbase—101 in, length—174 in, width—70 in, height—52 in, ground clearance—23.3 in, curb weight—6,437 lbs and payload rating—between 882 lbs (the Toledo) and 2,954 lbs (chassis with a cab). The available models included: the Furgón (3-d), the

The Willys-Viasa Jeep Ebro Bravo

Duplex (4-d, double cab, 6 passengers and 1,323 lbs of cargo, or 5 passengers and 1,653 lbs of cargo), the Campeador (a 2-d platform), a chassis with a cab, and the Toledo (4-d, minibus, 9 seats, 882 lbs of cargo). The vehicles achieved a top speed of just over 62 mph. They were also sold with a "Jeep-Avia" marque. Production was discontinued in 1980 after 17 years and an output of ca 8,000 units of the Viasa SV.

The Viasa SV

Zastava (Yugoslavia, Serbia)

The roots of the company based in Kraguyevats go back to 1851, when a workshop producing farming machinery and light weaponry was founded. Until 1939, it produced car parts; later, it assembled Chevrolet trucks, and (after 1953) units of the Jeep Willys-Overland. However, these activities were short-lived. In 1954, the Zavodi Crvena Zastava company was established—a specialist in assembling and producing Fiats, Polski Fiats, and later its own vehicles. The company achieved successful export figures—through good price, not quality. In the same period, it produced lightweight utility Fiats. In the early 1990s, Zastava was affected by the embargo on Serbia (then a part of Yugoslavia) and in the spring of 1999, it was almost completely destroyed by NATO bombers. After the war, Zastava Automobili received a $ 800,000 financial injection. In addition to passenger vehicles, it has produced the lightweight Rival and Novi Rival (an old and new IVECO Ducato) in a franchise. Besides a pick-up, double-cab, minivan, microbus and station wagon, it has also produced the Novi Rival 4x4 double-cab.

Zastava AR51 F

In the 1st half of the 1950s, components of the Fiat Campagnola AR51 off-roader were arriving by train from Turin to Kraguyevats, where they were assembled, mainly for the armed forces and export to India and other countries. Later on, some vehicles were available with alternative (and rather weak) 4-V 1.3L or 1.4L "Zastava 101" gasoline engines.

Acknowledgements

I cannot express enough thanks to my wife Zora and my son Marek for traveling thousands of miles to attend motor shows, accumulating endless piles of reference books and sorting and cataloging them, and to my son Radek for his help with the graphic design. Thanks also to Mrs. Chantal Salze for her contribution in this respect. I am grateful to Petr Stross, Jan Martof, Michal Seifert and Martin Janeček for providing their comments and study materials, and to the following Czech representatives of foreign car manufacturers for their helpful comments: Mr. Linhart of Ford, Mr. Major of Mitsubishi, Mr. Linhart and Mr. Šubrt of Opel, Mrs. Ivana Zimová of Mazda, Miss Skaličková of Renault, Mr. Jan Kuhn of DaimlerChrysler, Mrs. Zorka Mašková of VW / Audi / Škoda, Mr. Marek Vodička of Nissan, Mr. Karel Štochl of ARO / Honker, Mr. Picmaus of UAZ, Mr. Hodík of GAZ, staff of the CARTec Brno company (Land Rover), Mr. Kilián of the Dajbych company (new Santana, Bremach, SCAM), and Mrs. Petra Doležalová of Volvo. I must also express my gratitude to the staff of the PR offices at the motor shows held in Brno, Frankfurt, Paris, Turin, London, Leipzig and Birmingham, to the participants showcasing their models there and to all those who sent me materials by mail.

Photographs and reference materials

The photographs used in this book either come from the author's camera and his photo-archive, or they were provided by the individual car manufacturers represented here. Likewise, reference materials have their origin in the author's personal archive and in press releases and promotional pamphlets of the particular car makers. Some information was obtained from monographs published by major auto works, relevant encyclopedias and Automobile Revue annual catalogs.

The Land Rover Defender in the movie "Tomb Raider," 2001

Index